Past and Present Publications

English rural society 1500–1800

Past and Present Publications

General Editor: PAUL SLACK, *Exeter College, Oxford*

Past and Present Publications comprise books similar in character to the articles in the journal *Past and Present*. Whether the volumes in the series are collections of essays – some previously published, others new studies – or monographs, they encompass a wide variety of scholarly and original works primarily concerned with social, economic and cultural changes, and their causes and consequences. They will appeal to both specialists and non-specialists and will endeavour to communicate the results of historical and allied research in readable and lively form.

For a list of titles in Past and Present Publications, see end of book.

JOAN THIRSK

MA, Ph.D., FBA, FRHS, Sometime Reader in Economic History in the University of Oxford. Photo: J. W. Thirsk.

English rural society, 1500–1800

Essays in honour of Joan Thirsk

Edited by
JOHN CHARTRES
and
DAVID HEY

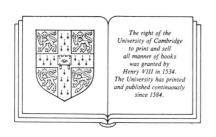

The right of the
University of Cambridge
to print and sell
all manner of books
was granted by
Henry VIII in 1534.
The University has printed
and published continuously
since 1584.

CAMBRIDGE UNIVERSITY PRESS

Cambridge
New York   Port Chester   Melbourne   Sydney

Published by the Press Syndicate of the University of Cambridge
The Pitt Building, Trumpington Street, Cambridge CB2 1RP
40 West 20th Street, New York, NY 10011, USA
10 Stamford Road, Oakleigh, Melbourne 3166, Australia

First published 1990

Printed in Great Britain at the University Press, Cambridge

British Library cataloguing in publication data
English rural society, 1500–1800: essays in honour of Joan
Thirsk. (Past and present publications).
1. England. Rural regions. Social conditions, history.
I. Chartres, John. II. Hey, David. III. Thirsk, Joan.
IV. Series.
942′.009′734

Library of Congress cataloguing in publication data
English rural society, 1500–1800: essays in honour of Joan Thirsk /
edited by John Chartres and David Hey.
    p.   cm. – (Past and present publications)
Includes bibliographical references.
ISBN 0 521 34565 0
1. England – Economic conditions. 2. England – Rural conditions.
3. Great Britain – Economic conditions – 16th century. 4. Great
Britain – Economic conditions – 17th century. 5. Great Britain –
Economic conditions – 18th century. 6. Thirsk, Joan.
I. Thirsk, Joan. II. Chartres, John. III. Hey, David.
HC254.4.E54 1990
330.942′09173′4 – dc20   89–39486 CIP

ISBN 0 521 34565 0

Contents

Contributors

John Beckett is Reader in English Regional History, University of Nottingham

John Broad is Principal Lecturer in History, Polytechnic of North London

John Chartres is Senior Lecturer in Economic History, University of Leeds

Peter Edwards is Senior Lecturer in History, Roehampton Institute of Higher Education

Alan Everitt is Emeritus Professor of English Local History, University of Leicester

David Hey is Reader in Local and Regional History, University of Sheffield

Richard Hoyle is a British Academy Research Fellow at Magdalen College, Oxford

Peter Large is a former research student and now Executive Director of Swiss Bank Corporation Investment Banking and Head of UK Mergers and Acquisitions Division

Andrew Pettegree is Lecturer in Modern History, University of St Andrews

Mary Prior is a former research student, now self-employed

Margaret Spufford is Fellow of Newnham College, Cambridge

Malcolm Thick is a former research student, now HM Inspector of Taxes

Barbara Todd is Assistant Professor of History, University of Toronto

Margery Tranter is Honorary Research Associate, Department of English Local History, University of Leicester

Donald Woodward is Senior Lecturer in Economic History, University of Hull

Acknowledgements

This volume owes a great deal to the many friends of Joan Thirsk who have provided encouragement and assistance. The late Trevor Aston was of great help in the initial stages of the project. Mrs Elsie Merrick has typed much of the manuscript. Above all, we are indebted to Jimmy Thirsk for his invaluable help with the bibliography and biographical details.

Introduction

JOHN CHARTRES and DAVID HEY

As evinced by the extensive Bibliography below, Joan Thirsk's published work has covered a wide chronological span and touched upon many different subjects. In gathering contributors for this collection of essays celebrating her distinctive academic career the editors have been forced to be selective, and to reflect only some of Joan's many interests. Indeed, these interests run far wider than her publications to date have indicated, and growing use of comparative evidence, drawn from wider European experience, is likely to characterize some of her future work. To those who have had the good fortune to have been taught or supervised by Dr Thirsk, these insights drawn from the wider European experience, from Russia to her new-found scholarly interest in Spanish economic and social history, will come as no surprise. Despite Joan's modestly self-deprecating challenge to younger scholars, 'that the work of one generation serves as an outline, awaiting improvement by the next', the present volume attempts to reflect some of her influence, rather than revise her fundamental contributions to the study of pre-modern English society.[1] The contributors are largely former research students, including her last in Oxford, Richard Hoyle, and a more limited selection from the many scholars for whom Joan has been a distinctive friend and mentor. To have reflected her interests and those who have been helped and stimulated by her work would have required several volumes.

It seems hard to believe that Joan was not committed to the study of history from the beginning of her academic career, but she went to Westfield College, London, to read German and French, and was

---

[1] Joan Thirsk, *The Rural Economy of England: Collected Essays* (London, 1984), p. xi.

1

indeed in Switzerland at the outbreak of war. This accounts in part for her linguistic facility, surely rare among native-born British historians, and for her wide international perspectives. Her undergraduate studies were interrupted by the call-up, and it was during war service as an ATS subaltern with the Intelligence Corps, in part at Bletchley, that she resolved that when her studies were resumed they would be historical rather than linguistic.[2] In London, as a postgraduate, she was a major figure in the famous Tawney seminar, and Tawney remains a major inspiration to and influence upon her work. Many of the contributors to this volume must have been advised by Joan to read Tawney for a model of crisp analytical writing without recourse to jargon. After a year at the London School of Economics, as Assistant Lecturer in Sociology, a career feature that Joan first mentioned to one of us with the wryest of smiles, she became Senior Research Fellow in the Department of English Local History at the University of Leicester in 1951. There she remained until succeeding W. G. Hoskins in the Readership at Oxford in 1965, where at least two of the contributors to this volume were among her first undergraduate students. She retired early from the Oxford Readership in 1983, disenchanted with the intensification from 1981 of cuts to a university system to which she was so strongly committed.

Many of the contributors to this volume studied with Joan at Oxford as postgraduates, or first came into contact with her when she was at St Hilda's, but she brought to Oxford an approach to social and economic history that was distinctly not that of Oxford. Though a major figure in what we have come to know as the 'Leicester School' of local history, she has reflected the 'Tawney tradition' with almost equal strength. Thus the creative force within the British Agricultural History Society and future Editor of the *Agricultural History Review* (1964–72) in her Leicester days was also an early member of the Editorial Board of *Past and Present*, which she joined in 1957. Added to the evident intellectual roots to William Hoskins and Herbert Finberg were those to Tawney, Marc Bloch, and the *Annales* school. They brought to her teaching in Oxford in both undergraduate small groups and in postgraduate supervision a breadth of vision and range of expertise that were distinct and unusual, especially so when married to the extraordi-

---

[2] Information kindly supplied by J. W. Thirsk.

nary professional commitment she exhibited towards this work. While most would think of Joan Thirsk first as a creative researcher, it is vital to recognize her major role in advanced teaching, and, as outlined below, as a proselytizing scholar, unwilling to be restrained by the walls of even Oxford's ivory tower.

Joan's early researches were on the period of the Interregnum and the Restoration, and clearly drew some inspiration from Tawney's exploration of the world of Harrington and the gentry, but also introduced her to the vital necessity of analysing the complex networks of local social and economic affairs underlying the sales of recusant lands. Close analysis of the sales of the manors of Winslow, Whaddon, and Bletchley revealed a pattern of fragmentation of these estates that represented a puzzle demanding subsequent research. This revealed links with the Leveller movement, and wider discussions of enclosure and public policy towards it.[3] Elements touching upon the distinctive character of localities, and landlordly regimes in the same county, Buckinghamshire, are found in the second chapter of this volume, by John Broad.[4] Her Ph.D. researches on the sales of royalist lands in the South-East formed the basis for some of her early publications; they clearly raised questions for the future on both the specificity of context for change and on the springs of public land policy; and the period was revisited didactically in her book *The Restoration* in 1976.

However, in the longer-term evolution of Joan Thirsk's distinctive contributions to agrarian history, it was the early work at Leicester from 1951 that laid the foundations. The two papers published in 1953, 'Fenland Farming in the Sixteenth Century' (significantly with an introduction by R. H. Tawney) and 'The Isle of Axholme before Vermuyden', outlined many of her methods, approaches, and sources for the analysis of pre-modern farming. Both were firmly revisionist without being strident: in showing the economic and social rationale of traditional fenland systems they dealt what should have been a fatal blow to the Whiggish doctrines of agricultural progress so prevalent in earlier works. The Lincolnshire fenlands were shown to have been not poor but different, with such a wealth of pastoral resources that the large population of smallholders was, even in Arthur Young's day, 'very poor respect-

---

[3] Thirsk, *Rural Economy*, pp. vi–ix.   [4] See below, pp. 27–53.

ing money, but very happy respecting their mode of existence'.[5] As so many subsequent historians have found, the traditional or established farming systems of pre-modern England possessed considerable social rationale, and many, even the open-field arable of the central Midlands, were less economically irrational than the ideologues of eighteenth-century 'improvement' ever allowed.[6] Gently debunking Vermuyden and his followers, then, Joan Thirsk's early works served as the inspiration for succeeding scholars seeking to evaluate innovation on the basis of a fuller appreciation of the status quo. These early studies were also the basis of the book *English Peasant Farming* (1957) and the shorter but parallel analysis of Leicestershire in the *Victoria County History* (1954). In the very long term, these essays set the pattern for the approach of the *Agrarian History of England and Wales*, volumes IV and V.

With this new approach to English rural history, she also carried forward a revolution in source materials begun by Hoskins and by David Chambers, which followed logically from the view that local and regional studies could advance perception of what had previously been seen as national problems. This change shifted the emphasis from the printed literary and technical sources which formed the basis of Ernle and of many of G. E. Fussell's explorations in the 1920s and 1930s towards newer Public Record Office materials, such as the records of the courts of equity, Chancery and Exchequer, and to those deposited in county and diocesan archives, above all probate inventories. Parallel with Joan Thirsk's exploitation of the former group was that by D. C. Coleman and K. H. Burley in their London Ph.D. theses on seventeenth-century Kent and Essex respectively in 1951 and 1957, and their use is extensively represented in this volume.[7] But in the longer-term development of agrarian history, it was the carrying forward of analysis of probate inventories from Hoskins's pioneering studies which was the most

---

[5] Joan Thirsk, *English Peasant Farming: The Agrarian History of Lincolnshire from Tudor to Recent Times* (London, 1957), p. 215.

[6] See, for example, the modern trend of debate over parliamentary enclosure, as summarized and reflected in M. E. Turner, *Enclosures in Britain, 1750–1830* (London, 1984), pp. 37–41.

[7] See the study by Peter Large, below, pp. 105–37; D. C. Coleman, 'The Economy of Kent under the Later Stuarts', Ph.D. thesis, London University, 1951; K. H. Burley, 'The Economic Development of Essex in the Later 17th and Early 18th Centuries', Ph.D. thesis, London University, 1957.

significant. Her extensive use of the inventory to define farm types, agricultural regions and specialisms, and the social hierarchy of the countryside in her studies of Lincolnshire demonstrated the potential of the source graphically. Thus most local and regional studies, including several of the chapters in this book, have now come to employ the probate inventory as a basic source; the regional chapters by Joan and by the late Frank Emery employed them on a large scale in the *Agrarian History*, IV, as did Alan Everitt's analysis of labourers in the same volume; inventories provided the quantitative underpinning of the regional part I of volume V of the same work; they were fundamental to major local studies such as Hey's *Myddle* and Margaret Spufford's *Contrasting Communities*; and, with the application of computer analysis, Mark Overton and others have been able dramatically to alter perceptions of regional farming patterns, crop yields, and the process of innovation.[8] The pioneering efforts of Hoskins, Thirsk, and F. W. Steer have indeed led, in E. A. Wrigley's phrase, to the gathering in of a new harvest of agricultural history.[9]

The same spirit of enquiry generated a controversial but ultimately very fruitful reassessment of the rationale of English medieval field systems. Joan Thirsk's 1964 paper on 'The Common Fields' was the product of long consideration of the apparent conflicts between observed regional and local differences in early

---

[8] Joan Thirsk (ed.), *The Agrarian History of England and Wales* (hereafter *AHEW*), IV (Cambridge, 1967), pp. 1–160, 396–465; *AHEW*, V, I (Cambridge, 1984), *passim*, and the review article by E. A. Wrigley, 'Early Modern Agriculture: A New Harvest Gathered In', *Agric. Hist. Rev.*, 35, I (1987), 65–71; D. G. Hey, *An English Rural Community: Myddle under the Tudors and Stuarts* (Leicester, 1974); Margaret Spufford, *Contrasting Communities: English Villagers in the Sixteenth and Seventeenth Centuries* (Cambridge, 1974); M. Overton, 'Estimating Crop Yields from Probate Inventories: An Example from East Anglia, 1585–1735', *Journal of Economic History*, 39 (1979), and 'The Diffusion of Innovations in Early Modern England: Turnips and Clover in Norfolk and Suffolk, 1580–1740', *Transactions of the Institute of British Geographers*, n.s., 10 (1985).

[9] W. G. Hoskins, 'The Leicestershire Farmer in the Sixteenth Century', *Transactions of the Leicestershire Archaeological Society*, 22 (1945), and 'The Leicestershire Farmer in the Seventeenth Century', *Agricultural History*, 25 (1951); Joan Thirsk, 'Fenland Farming in the Sixteenth Century', University College of Leicester, Department of English Local History, Occasional Paper, 3 (Leicester, 1953), and 'The Isle of Axholme before Vermuyden', *Agric. Hist. Rev.*, I (1953); F. W. Steer (ed.), *Farm and Cottage Inventories of Mid-Essex, 1635–1749* (Colchester, 1950).

modern open field farming, the evidence of the comparable systems of western Europe, particularly Germany, and the received orthodoxy of H. L. Gray and the Orwins. Joan's sharp perception of English regional differences in common-field practice was illuminated by analysis of comparable societies to suggest that open-field farming was not necessarily in common, and that neither cultural nor technological factors were sufficient explanations of communalism. In drawing the somewhat insular fire of many critics, this paper, and its successor, succeeded in demanding the detailed reassessment of the economic context of communal regulation of cropping and grazing in the later Middle Ages, and provoked new recognition of the great complexity, variation, and pluralism of English systems. Many of the studies gathered in Rowley's *Origins of Open-Field Agriculture*, Baker and Butlin's *Field Systems of the British Isles*, and more recent work on specific cropping and management of open fields have benefited from this rocking of the boat of orthodoxy.[10] As with her reappraisal of the fenlands, Joan's elegant and perceptive probing has helped to generate a major advance in knowledge.

Many of these questions arose from deep and original studies of the landholding, landlordism, and public policy towards the land in sixteenth- and seventeenth-century England. Here Joan's work has been to initiate the revision of her old postgraduate supervisor's favourite book, Tawney's *Agrarian Problem in the Sixteenth Century*, in the light of the modern research of Beresford, Gould, and others, in a remarkably concise Historical Association pamphlet of 1959, 'Tudor Enclosures'. Her own major research findings on the subject were presented in the chapter on 'Enclosing and Engrossing' in the *AHEW*, IV (1967), which stressed the specificity of time, place, and landlord for the full definition and characterization of agrarian problems, while pointing to some subtle and previously

---

[10] Joan Thirsk, 'The Common Fields', *Past & Present*, 29 (1964), and 'The Origin of the Common Fields', *Past & Present*, 33 (1966); J. Z. Titow, 'Medieval England and the Open-Field System', *Past & Present*, 32 (1965); George C. Homans, 'The Explanation of English Regional Differences', *Past & Present*, 42 (1969); Robert A. Dodgshon, 'The Landholding Foundations of the Open-Field System', *Past & Present*, 67 (1975); Trevor Rowley (ed.), *The Origins of Open-Field Agriculture* (London, 1981); and A. R. H. Baker and R. A. Butlin (eds.), *Studies of Field Systems of the British Isles* (Cambridge, 1973). Somewhat regrettably, it has not proved possible to reflect this rich vein of enquiry in a chapter in the present volume.

unnoticed features of Tudor legislative controls. In recognition of this enormous contribution to the analysis of rural society in the 'Tawney Century', several chapters of this tribute concentrate on the specific context of landlord, *pays*, and the structure of landholding for our understanding of social and economic change in this period. The studies by John Broad and John Beckett probe into the influence of landlords on rural change, Richard Hoyle examines the intractability of copyhold under claims of tenant right on Crown lands, and Peter Large's chapter on Ombersley assesses the vitality of communal and customary manorial structures in the challenging economic context of the seventeenth century.[11] Tawney's specification of a period of conflict between aggressive agrarian capitalism and custom has been modified by more subtle analysis stressing the importance of natural resource endowments, differential responses to population pressure, and variations in management, established practice, and public policy.[12]

These predominant themes were linked to those of the early agrarian studies as the background to perhaps her most striking field of enquiry, the linkage between agriculture and industry, appropriately set out with elegance and clarity in her contribution to the Tawney *Festschrift* of 1961.[13] The sharp awareness of the evidence of probate inventories, particularly of the radical differences they revealed between champion and pastoral regions, and of lingering differences in patterns of inheritance customs, was combined in a simple model of industrial location which, unusually for the time, stressed labour supply. Relative under-endowment of land in such pastoral regions as the Yorkshire Dales, the Midlands, and the Wiltshire dairying districts created circumstances which were fertile for the growth of textiles, and where industry joined farming as a source of family income in a dual economy. Relative plenty of land existed for such domestic regimes in some of these areas, and in others the continuing pressure of partible inheritance provided a

---

[11] R. H. Tawney, *The Agrarian Problem in the Sixteenth Century* (London, 1912); Joan Thirsk, 'Tudor Enclosures', Historical Association, general series, 41 (1959); Thirsk, *AHEW*, IV, pp. 200–55; and below, pp. 27–137.

[12] This approach contrasts with the more polemical views of E. Kerridge, *Agrarian Problems in the Sixteenth Century and After* (London, 1969), especially pp. 15, 65–111.

[13] Joan Thirsk, 'Industries in the Countryside', in F. J. Fisher (ed.), *Essays in the Economic and Social History of Tudor and Stuart England in Honour of Professor R. H. Tawney* (Cambridge, 1961), pp. 70–88.

growing incentive to the diversification of family economy. It is difficult to under-estimate the influence of this hypothesis. It formed the basis for the researches of many scholars: its influence is clearly visible in the chapters by Large and Hey in the present volume; its findings have illuminated both earlier and later studies, ranging from Dr Blanchard's analysis of Derbyshire lead mining in the Middle Ages to Mendels in the debate over 'proto-industrialization', and to Dr Kussmaul's recent association of shifting industrial location and marriage patterns; and, like all good models, it has been reassessed critically in the light of variant findings, such as Dr Spenceley's studies of Devon lace.[14] Without exaggeration, then, 'Industries in the Countryside' formed the watershed in the modern analysis of industrial location before the Industrial Revolution.

One particular industry within this broad range of rural manufacture deserves special consideration. In her analysis of the knitting industry, 'The Fantastical Folly of Fashion' of 1973, Joan Thirsk united other of her interests with her rural studies, and illuminated her analysis with the practical experience of her own recreational interest in machine-knitting. The latter surely assisted in her deft corrective to the then prevailing view of historians of fashion, that knitting was only established in England in the sixteenth century: 'This is scarcely credible. The chain mail of medieval armour is, in fact, a knitted garter stitch.'[15] This study was also the forerunner of her more general analysis of innovation in pre-modern England presented in the Ford Lectures at Oxford in 1975.[16] English knitted stockings represented a paradigm case of a broadening and deepening market for consumer goods through the process of import substitution; in a pattern of growth familiar to students of modern Korea or Taiwan, the low-grade *ersatz* products of rural copiers

[14] See below, pp. 105–37 and 343–67; Ian Blanchard, 'The Miner and the Agricultural Community in Late Medieval England', *Agric. Hist. Rev.*, 20, II (1972); F. Mendels, 'Proto-industrialization: The First Phase in the Process of Industrialization', *J. Econ. Hist.*, 32 (1972); A. Kussmaul, 'Time and Space, Hoofs and Grain: The Seasonality of Marriage in England', *Journal of Interdisciplinary History*, XV, 4 (1985); G. F. R. Spenceley, 'The Origins of the English Pillow Lace Industry', *Agric. Hist. Rev.*, 21, II (1973).

[15] N. B. Harte and K. G. Ponting (eds.), *Textile History and Economic History: Essays in Honour of Miss Julia de Lacy Mann* (Manchester, 1973), p. 53.

[16] Published subsequently as *Economic Policy and Projects: The Development of a Consumer Society in Early Modern England* (Oxford, 1978).

were in the longer term to form the basis for a major industry; and, in assessing the repatriation of William Lee's stocking frame, the study added to our understanding of the origins of the Midland worsted stocking industry. The case-study of knitting thus encapsulates the breadth of vision that has enabled Joan Thirsk to demonstrate clearly the extent to which sixteenth- and seventeenth-century industry was innovatory, and was so across a far wider field than that specified in J. U. Nef's attempt to identify an industrial revolution in the period.

The economic rationality of the unusual and the capacity for a society of small farmers to be innovatory were themes combined in several studies of specialized cropping in seventeenth-century England, beginning with the stimulating synthesis in the *Festschrift* for H. P. R. Finberg, 'Seventeenth-century Agriculture and Social Change'.[17] Consideration in that essay of the markets and locational niches for the dye crops such as woad, madder, and saffron was combined with a sharp appreciation of the economics of tobacco, liquorice, and market gardening in general, and led to more detailed analysis of the crops and their locational context in subsequent studies of tobacco and of the Vale of Tewkesbury.[18] This strikingly original work reinforced the problems faced by historians in attempting to identify periods in which the 'peasantry' of England could have disappeared, still only a partially resolved conundrum, for it made clear that small farm units, cropped with the appropriate specialized and high-value crops, provided with access to a modestly articulated market, and perhaps bolstered by landlordly support, were more than economically viable even in the apparently difficult period of the later seventeenth century. Modest tributes to this important work appear in Malcolm Thick's study of 'Root crops' below, and, on the other side of the circular flow of foodstuffs, in Donald Woodward's 'Essay on manures'.[19]

---

[17] Joan Thirsk, 'Seventeenth-Century Agriculture and Social Change', *Agric. Hist. Rev.*, 18 (1970), Supplement, 148–77.
[18] 'New Crops and their Diffusion: Tobacco-Growing in Seventeenth-Century England', in C. W. Chalklin and M. A. Havinden (eds.), *Rural Change and Urban Growth, 1500–1800: Essays in English Regional History in Honour of W. G. Hoskins* (London, 1974); and 'Projects for Gentlemen, Jobs for the Poor: Mutual Aid in the Vale of Tewkesbury, 1600–1630', in Patrick McGrath and John Cannon (eds.), *Essays in Bristol and Gloucestershire History: The Centenary Volume of the Bristol and Gloucestershire Archaeological Society* (Bristol, 1976).
[19] See below, pp. 279–96 and 251–78.

This protracted process of the evolution of Joan's thoughts on the extent, the nature, and the longer-term consequences of innovation in early modern England came to a point in the 1975 Ford Lectures. These represented a major stimulus to thought about the nature of economy and society in the period for all those who were lucky enough to attend the original lectures, or who have read the subsequent book, *Economic Policy and Projects* (1978). As Joan herself pointed out in the preface to that work, the enforced reflection resultant upon compiling the index to the volume of *Seventeenth-Century Economic Documents* (1972) demonstrated how wide a range of new industrial and other projects appeared in later sixteenth- and early seventeenth-century England, and the lectures represented the wide-ranging thoughts stimulated by this observation. In so doing, she rescued from the contemporary scorn for 'frippery' and scandalous Elizabethan or Jacobean monopoly the roots of economic change which created the systems of production characteristic of England well into the period of the Industrial Revolution. Two of the chapters in this book reflect upon this process of growth through new seventeenth-century projects: David Hey's study points to the success of the Thirsk model in respect of the Hallamshire cutlery industry; and John Chartres provides a counter in a study of the intersection of agriculture and industry, cider distilling, which remained a favoured 'project' throughout much of the seventeenth and eighteenth centuries without ever growing sufficiently strong to overcome the constraints imposed by that other seventeenth-century innovation, the Excise.[20]

Running in parallel with this broad view of innovation has been a concern to identify and evaluate the vectors of its transmission. Many of her agricultural studies have stressed the hierarchy of diffusion of new crops and systems through the gentry, the agents of the demonstration effects which led ultimately to more widespread adoption. Whereas, with some notable exceptions, studies of agricultural innovation based upon the didactic and technical literature have tended to the errors of the 'patent approach' in industry, Joan's work has stressed the need to comprehend the extent to which this literature was both read and used, and the roots of these ideas in themselves. Until very recently, few studies of the process were entirely immune from the first charge, and our understanding

[20] See below, pp. 343–67 and 313–42.

of the process is far from complete: but Joan Thirsk's work has been critical in the long-term process of linking published theory with past farming practice, a linkage for which Henry Best's (1642) usage of Tusser has long been a conspicuously isolated example.[21] Though as yet not a complete answer to the first of these critical questions, Joan's study 'Plough and Pen' (1983) is one of the few British attempts to meet these issues, being studied abroad by historians such as Beutler and Irsigler. Her arguments were refined and developed in the chapter 'Agricultural Innovations and their Diffusion' in the *Agrarian History*, volume V (1985), and reflected here in Donald Woodward's 'Essay on manures'.[22]

What has been perhaps more distinctive still has been Joan Thirsk's demonstration of the international dimension of so many of these early modern innovations. Thus the international transmission of crops, goods, and human capital recurs in her historical studies, and reveals the extent to which her unusual linguistic abilities have fed comparative insights into her work: the analysis of the process of innovation clearly looks different with insular blinkers worn! In agriculture, her studies were able to trace the intellectual currents from Heresbach into the English agronomists of the seventeenth century, and thence as discussed above to the innovative landlord. Crops introduced as a result tended to do so in part via horticulture, and this pattern, discussed in the *Agrarian History*, volume V, is reflected in Malcolm Thick's study of root crops below. Sixteenth- and seventeenth-century England was hardly so backward as to need to reinvent the wheel, but it did have to reintroduce the parsnip![23] New crops, new textiles, and new

---

[21] See *The Farming and Memorandum Books of Henry Best of Elmswell 1642*, British Academy, Records of Economic and Social History, n.s., VIII, ed. D. M. Woodward (London, 1984), esp. p. 25.

[22] Joan Thirsk, 'Plough and Pen: Agricultural Writers in the Seventeenth Century', in T. H. Aston, P. R. Cross, C. Dyer, and J. Thirsk (eds.), *Social Relations and Ideas: Essays in Honour of R. H. Hilton* (Cambridge, 1983), pp. 295–318. For reasons discussed below, p. 15, even her own chapter, 'Farming Techniques', *AHEW*, IV, was not immune from this problem, and it also characterizes E. Kerridge's *The Agricultural Revolution* (London, 1967), to an extent that is not immediately obvious. Joan Thirsk's later essay, 'Agricultural Innovations and their Diffusion', *AHEW*, V, II, pp. 533–89, the study by the late Frank Emery, 'Wales', *AHEW*, V, I, pp. 393–428, and Overton, 'The Diffusion of Innovations', have all significantly sharpened our analysis of these problems.

[23] See the chapters by Thirsk and by Thick in *AHEW*, V, II. The latter makes clear the extent to which later-sixteenth-century England was recovering arts lost during the later Middle Ages. There is therefore a striking parallel with some

methods, such as intensive horticulture, were also produced by imports of human capital. Here Joan Thirsk has long drawn attention to immigrant innovators, as indeed did her mentor, Tawney, and three of the chapters below reflect upon this contribution, indirectly in Malcolm Thick's study, explicitly in Andrew Pettegree's analysis of the process of assimilation of migrants into Elizabethan London, and, rather sadly in a study celebrating one of partly Huguenot descent, negatively in David Hey's assessment of the cutlery industry of South Yorkshire.[24]

Joan Thirsk's studies of innovation repeatedly stressed the specific social receptors of new ideas, and their roles in engendering change. Her work was very early among studies which stressed the critical nature of the conjuncture between family structure, inheritance customs, and testamentary habits in determining regional patterns of economic activity. These studies again illustrate the international dimensions of her work: ideas visible in emergent form in, for example, *English Peasant Farming* (1957), were generalized in 'Industries in the Countryside', and developed under the influence of the French school of Ariès and Duby in a series of surveys of great long-term significance. 'The Family' (1964) embodied a synthesis of these crucial elements and drew together strands of evidence from both the medieval and the early modern periods with explicit evangelical purpose, 'deploring the absence of any comparable work [to the French], or even slight signs of concern for the subject in England'.[25] To judge by the extent of historical research in the field in the succeeding twenty-four years, her preaching was an unqualified success. Elements of family and inheritance were further analysed in the essays on 'Younger Sons' (1969) and in her contribution to *Family and Inheritance* (1976).

Within this major broadening of the subject matter seen as appropriate and necessary for historical analysis she also con-

aspects of the history of the 'new draperies'. See also Ronald Webber, *The Early Horticulturalists* (Newton Abbot, 1968), which on p. 13 cites Harrison (1577) in support of the view that gardening declined to the mid or later sixteenth century and thus required reinvention.

[24] See below, pp. 279–96, 297–312, and 343–67. Joan Thirsk's Huguenot parentage came from her mother, née Frayer.

[25] Joan Thirsk, 'The Family', *Past & Present*, 27 (1964). Among the host of works picking up and developing the subject in the English-speaking world, one may cite L. Stone, *The Family, Sex, and Marriage in England, 1500–1800* (London, 1977).

tributed early to the reappraisal of women in English social history. If the largely twentieth-century advance of social and economic history had been to enhance the 'bottom-up' perception of the past in place of sterile consideration of only the top strata of society, that advance was largely insensitive to issues of gender, and the relative positions of men, women, and children in the family. Joan Thirsk was thus one of the first to refer to such issues in this country, and has continued to sponsor and assist the advance of researches in this field since. Margaret Spufford's reappraisal of the value of the probate inventory here employs probate accounts to this purpose, sources which are themselves more revealing of status and family arrangements in inheritance. But two chapters of this book explicitly acknowledge Joan Thirsk's contribution to the history of women, both significantly examining the position of women in regard to property and its transmission. Mary Prior and Barbara Todd thus reinforce earlier comments on the creative significance of Joan Thirsk's work on landholding, inheritance custom, and testamentary practice.[26]

One final area of research by Joan Thirsk to warrant mention has been her contribution to the assessment of the role of the horse in pre-modern society and the economy. In part this returns us to the early fields of her researches, in that 'Fenland Farming' had noted the distinctive association of horse keeping and rearing with fen and forest, and her analysis of farming regions in the *Agrarian History*, volume IV, had developed this theme. Long-considered thoughts on the role of the horse were distilled into the Stenton Lecture at the University of Reading in 1977. Her findings paralleled the interest in nineteenth-century horse keeping stimulated by Professor F. M. L. Thompson's essays on the subject, and thus assisted the gathering together of a series of studies of this neglected topic at the Eighth International Economic History Congress in 1982. To this research interest one of the chapters below responds, that by Peter Edwards, whose doctoral thesis on seventeenth-century Shropshire was supervised by Joan Thirsk, and whose recent book on the *Horse Trade* owes much to her inspiration.

To these many direct contributions through research to our understanding of the past have been added those through the pub-lication of collections of documentary material. The first of her two

---

[26] See below, pp. 139–74, 175–200, and 201–25.

major collections was the Redstone Memorial volume, *Suffolk Farming in the Nineteenth Century*, which in 1958 launched the Suffolk Records Society's series of publications. Edited with the assistance of Jean Imray, it still looks an exemplary sample of the materials typically of value for the analysis of nineteenth-century farming, ranging from machinery and cropping arrangements through leases and their covenants to the domestic conditions of labourers and correspondence promoting migration. Compiled at a time when the secondary literature on the period was still thin and/ or heroic in nature, it remains a useful introduction to sources and issues in research, if less typical of the pattern of publication by record societies.[27] A second documentary collection, edited in collaboration with the late J. P. Cooper, had an explicit didactic purpose. *Seventeenth-Century Economic Documents* (1972) emerged from the need to improve set documents for an Oxford undergraduate course – then still employing the collection by Bland, Brown and Tawney of 1914 for the seventeenth century – and was explicitly seen as a parallel to the three classic volumes of documents compiled by Tawney and Eileen Power for the earlier period, *Tudor Economic Documents*. Their massive collection of over 350 documentary extracts ran to over 800 printed pages, and made a vast array of materials, many from manuscript sources in public and county records, available to students at all levels. As noted above, for Joan herself the act of compilation was itself a stimulus to further research, and the collection has become a valuable aid in research on the period, as evidenced by its repeated appearance in the footnotes of scholarly articles. Raising issues and pointing to a wide range of sources otherwise not generally available, Joan Thirsk's editions of documents have achieved both a didactic and a research purpose.[28]

She has also made enormous contributions as an editor to the series of the History of Lincolnshire volumes, and, above all to the *Agricultural History Review* (1964–72) and as both General Editor and editor of two major volumes of the Cambridge *Agrarian History*

---

[27] *Suffolk Farming in the Nineteenth Century*, ed. Joan Thirsk and Jean Imray, Suffolk Records Society, I (Ipswich, 1958). J. W. Y. Higgs regarded the 'sampler' as an unusual enterprise for a record society in a review, *Agric. Hist. Rev.*, 7, II (1959).

[28] *Seventeenth-Century Economic Documents*, ed. Joan Thirsk and J. P. Cooper (Oxford, 1972), esp. pp. v–vi.

of England and Wales. To these must be added the long and thankless but valuable task of compiling, largely in association with F. M. L. Thompson, the annual lists of publications for the *Economic History Review* (1960–5), and in her own right, the annual lists of publications for the *Agricultural History Review* (1955–65) and its periodic compilations of research in progress (1958–61). Her contribution as editor to both the *Agricultural History Review* and to the History of Lincolnshire was very active and creative, one that may not easily be appreciated by those who have not encountered the same difficulties. As well as meeting impossible and unreasonable demands from some contributors and colleagues with great equanimity, she rewrote major parts of contributions to both the series and journal to speed effective publication, to the great longer-term benefit of both author and scholarship. Editorial work in the hands of Joan Thirsk has been a positive and creative contribution to the world of research.

Had she engaged in no other editorial work, her contributions in this role to the *Agrarian History* would alone have appeared outstanding. These deserve separate and more explicit recognition. She was among those gathered by Herbert Finberg at University College London in January 1956 to discuss the proposed agrarian history project, and was effectively the first designated editor of a volume in the series, with volumes I and III following soon after. The measure of her success was in part that volume IV, covering the period 1500–1640, and presenting the researches of ten different scholars, appeared some years in advance of any other, and her second volume, V, covering 1640–1750, not even commissioned in 1967 when volume IV appeared, was published in 1985, well ahead of the early-planned volumes III and VI. Her personal achievement as editor of these two volumes was immense, since in addition to the creative and positive editorial approach she brought to bear on contributors, she wrote three of the eleven chapters of volume IV, and three of twenty-one of volume V. Moreover, one of her contributions to volume IV, a very effective assessment of 'Farming Techniques', had to be written from June 1963 as a late replacement for a chapter by another author. This led to little delay in the schedule of publication, however, and to little damage to the volume. Her major achievements as volume editor were followed by her becoming Deputy General Editor of the series in 1966, and General Editor on Herbert Finberg's death in 1974. When, at some future date, the series is complete, the achievement will have been in no small measure that of Joan Thirsk.

These achievements might well add up to career enough for lesser individuals, but Joan Thirsk has been throughout a generous and proselytizing scholar, and has made a great personal contribution in the Hoskins tradition to the growth of professional skills among amateur historians. To this end she has published a number of valuable guides to sources and approaches, such as 'Sources of Information on Population' and 'Unexplored Sources in Local Records' (1959 and 1963); repeatedly taken under her wing amateur scholars in need of professional advice; and received public recognition of her contribution by being elected Chairman of the Standing Conference for Local History in 1983.[29] In addition to her commitments to Lincolnshire history, she has also been engaged in the work of the Oxfordshire Local History Association, the Edmonton Historical Society, and other national and local groups. All the contributors to the present volume can testify to her immense generosity as a scholar, constantly providing suggestions of sources and assistance with their work. Another symptom of this personal generosity perhaps may be discerned in the fact that she contributed major pieces of work to five *Festschrifts* – for Tawney, Finberg, Mann, Hoskins, and Hilton.[30] As well as celebrating the careers of senior historians, she has been a constant patron of many more younger scholars than could be represented here, and continues to be a major creative force in the social and economic history of the early modern period, a contribution recognized in her election to the British Academy in 1974. To that immensely varied and creative career, this volume is a modest tribute.

[29] For references to these items, see the Bibliography below, pp. 371, 372.
[30] Referred to above, and listed below, pp. 372, 375, 376, 380.

1. *Joan Thirsk: a personal appreciation*

ALAN EVERITT

I first saw Joan at R. H. Tawney's seminar in the Institute of Historical Research. It must have been shortly before *Fenland Farming in the Sixteenth Century* appeared in 1953, and Joan was giving a paper on that subject. The occasion remains vividly in my mind on three counts. First, and most vivid, Joan was speaking not only from her notes but from a map. A map? Yes, a *map*. Even in Tawney's seminar that was rather an extraordinary thing to do in those days. Of course there was no pin-board or anything like it in the room, and an easel had to be brought in to which the map might be affixed. Every few minutes the slight, elegant figure rose from its chair, a right-hand finger hovered momentarily, seeking a place-name, and then alighted, so to speak, on the exact spot we were to consider. Gradually, by small and patient strokes, the picture built itself up, and the second point to remain with me was the crucial distinction in the life of the Fens between the 'high marsh' and the 'low marsh'. It might be almost imperceptible to a casual eye, but Joan was never one for casual observation, and so the Holland Fen had taken on a new meaning under her hand. It was not the unintelligible agrarian landscape of historical legend; each community within it, and the area as a whole, was possessed of a complex yet coherent structure, each part of which was vitally dependent on the other. My own interest in agrarian history had hardly yet been awakened; but this way of looking at the rural economy of England was a revelation. Behind that, and this is my third impression, was the perception of a society whose customs and practices, however alien they might be to outsiders, were nevertheless the logical, intelligent response – even the only possible response – to the circumstances and conditions of its environment. Joan had refused to accept the hostile judgement of external observers; she had found

17

her way to the heart of that enigmatic world by investigating it from the inside. It was an approach that I at once found sympathetic. Reality, after all, is so much more illuminating than prejudice.

The first time I met Joan after my appointment as a research assistant to the *Agrarian History* was in the King's Library in the British Museum. Naturally we did not meet to admire the splendour of the architecture; we had a mind above such matters; at least Joan had, though I was not yet so fully regenerate myself. We did not even spare a thought for poor old Farmer George, whose books adorned the shelves around us and who, so to speak, had provided us with this rather splendid meeting place rent-free. We sat like any two tourists on one of the wooden benches, near the Reading Room end, of course, and there my first task on the *Agrarian History* was allotted to me. But *allotted* is not quite the right word. What Joan said was, 'I wondered if you would *like* to . . . ' Naturally I did like; nothing indeed could be more delightful; for what Joan suggested was that I should go down to Maidstone, select thirty probate inventories relating to the Weald of Kent and thirty relating to the Downland, and with those as a basis make a comparison between the agriculture of the two countrysides. That visit, too, was a revelation to me. I had been working on Kentish society for nearly five years and had completed my thesis; but it was on quite a different aspect of the county, and I had never looked at an inventory before.

Joan lent me her abstracts and analyses of inventories for part of Lincolnshire to follow as a model. They were systematic, as might have been expected; but they were not mechanical. As well as sheets covering crops and stock of every kind, down to the last beeskep, there was a sheet noting all manner of miscellaneous points: sheep hurdles, cheese presses, spinning wheels, and a score of other things, seemingly trivial in themselves, yet shedding a vital light on the customs of the locality. I felt that I was being taken behind the scenes of *Fenland Farming in the Sixteenth Century*. Joan was too tactful to point out that it was a very elementary lesson she had set me, and that much else had gone into that seminal paper. There were, I believe, somewhere about sixty thousand inventories at Maidstone; they were bound in volumes, unindexed, uncatalogued, and not arranged in any obvious sequence. I had to glance through hundreds to find a mere thirty for the Downs and thirty for the Weald. But it didn't matter in the least; every moment of that visit was enchantment; a wholly unsuspected world was suddenly opened up before me. It was to Joan that I owed my first glimmer of sympathy with English peasant society. I had loved the vision of reality which the thousands of Oxinden letters had revealed to me, years before, behind the façade of the Civil War. But here was something equally novel and startling, but happily recoverable in many parts of England, not only in Kent.

We had met in the King's Library because we had no room of our own to meet in. Society, I need hardly say, was still in a very primitive state in 1957, and nobody had yet thought of having an 'office', though I believe there was a rumour of such things at advanced places like Cambridge. Neither did we need a room, for we had no equipment to put in it; no telephone, no bookshelves, no filing cabinets, no files even except the most economical manilla folders we could find. On that last point Joan's husband, Jimmy, was a useful ally, and managed to find something extraordinarily cheap near his library at Acton. Our few precious thousand pounds that the Nuffield Foundation had given us were far too valuable to be wasted on meaningless status symbols. There never was a grant that was more frugally administered than that, under the auspices of Herbert Finberg and Joan. At least, with one rather revealing exception which I think, at this distance of time, it is not improper to mention.

Some time after Margaret Midgley and I had started our work for the *Agrarian History*, a great meeting of the Advisory Committee was called in London. It was a very grand meeting indeed, almost intimidating in fact, as may be seen from the list of committee members in volume IV. Now, there was nothing seriously wrong with the meeting itself, which was summoned with an important purpose, and which on the whole transacted its business successfully. But it was followed by a *very* grand lunch. I cannot quite remember where it was held, or the names of all the luminaries who were present, for I was in rather a golden haze myself, though only because I had just been asked to write one of the chapters. But I do know that at one end of the table was Herbert Finberg and at the other end William Hoskins, and the meal itself was a work of art: that I remember very clearly. Now no one is more generous in hospitality than Joan, as the contributors to this volume no doubt know. But Joan did not like that lunch; she did not like it at all. The precious Nuffield money! To think of it being poured down the drain in that way! She was really almost angry, if you can imagine such a thing. I remember it very well, because we walked to the Tube together afterwards, and just as we came out into the street there was suddenly a little cold breath of wind which quite blew away my gold haze, and enabled me to see things clearly once again. I cannot actually swear that Joan used the word 'outrageous'; but I do know that, as we descended to the train, there was a little sort of trembling emanation in the air that told you that she *thought* so. Or was it perhaps, after all, only an effect of the escalators? I have often wondered; but certainly, we never had another lunch like that one.

I must not give the impression, however, that there were serious disagreements between us as we worked on that initial volume. There weren't. We were as happy a little team as could be, with just that occasional *frisson* of debate that lends vitality to any real relationship. There could have been no more doughty champion than Herbert Finberg, whose persuasive powers had, after all, secured our money for us. Neither could there have been a better research assistant than Margaret Midgley, with her unrivalled knowledge of provincial record offices, and her lightning eye and pen. We all had perfect confidence in Joan, and if she doubted us she had too much common sense to say so until it became quite essential. So we were content with our own studies at home, our own books and book-shelves, and our own grocery boxes.

Joan, I am almost certain, had some kind of filing cabinet, for I seem to remember that the drawers would not always shut quite exactly; you know how awkward the corner of a foolscap sheet or folder can sometimes be. Now that the fourth volume has been so triumphantly succeeded by the fifth, it may seem *retardataire* to go back to the fourth and say what it meant to us, or rather what it seemed to me to mean to Joan. But because I was based in London, and of necessity we met so often, and talked so much about our researches, and those of others as they came in, I believe, looking back, that I saw the germination of some of Joan's most influential ideas.

It was one of the great advantages of working on that volume that it enabled her to extend the methods she had worked out in Lincolnshire county by county to England as a whole. I do not know how many thousands of inventories, how many scores of surveys, or indeed how many other types of record Margaret Midgley must have transcribed for us. I don't recall how many Special Commissions and Depositions in the Exchequer Joan looked at, or indeed how many I looked at myself. But the figure of eight hundred cases in the Court of Requests does stick in my mind. These were but a few of the basic sources systematically investigated. Had the rural economy and society of Tawney's England ever before been subjected to such microscopic treatment? But once again Joan's approach was not mechanical; it was adaptable to each county in succession as we came to it, beginning with Lancashire. Gradually, that approach began to point up not only the manifest contrasts that one must expect to find between, say, Lincolnshire and Lancashire, but also some of the unsuspected resemblances to be found between different parts of England apparently quite dissimilar at first sight.

Exactly when the original idea behind 'Industries in the Countryside' and 'The Common Fields', two of her most influential early papers, occurred to Joan I cannot say. Important elements in the latter at least – the evolutionary and adaptable nature of common fields – were to be found as early as 'Fenland Farming'. But I do know that as we worked on the *Agrarian History*, moving from county to county, finding one surprise after another, one variation from the accepted norm after another, Joan's thoughts and observations on both subjects were led onwards, step by step, until she reached the general arguments she was eventually able to put forward in those papers. Her instinctive feel for peasant society enabled her to bring hints and fragments of reality from many areas together, and in so doing to cast a vivid light on the origins of industry and the origins of the common fields. Few papers have given rise to more extensive research than these, few to more fruitful debate. Yet the full implications of neither, I believe, have yet been worked out. Whether we accept all the details of the argument or not, neither subject will ever look quite the same again. One finds oneself being led back to the ideas there adumbrated, as to those in others of Joan's papers, again and again.

Why is it that one finds them recurring to one's memory, often in quite a different context, years later? It is, I think, because they were not mere flashes of intuition, only slightly substantiated, like the theories or 'models' of some scholars. Whether it is those two papers, her Ford Lectures, her Stenton Lecture, her paper on 'New Crops and their Diffusion', or her work on Samuel Hartlib and his circle, they have been long pondered before Joan began to write. Behind each seemingly simple statement, there is a wealth of considered observation. Taken together her published articles, as a consequence, touch English history at many crucial places. The ability to ponder and reflect on historical evidence in this way is in fact quite rare. There are many scholars who are inclined to brush aside issues that are not central to their theme, or problems they do not understand. What is the point, after all, in wasting time on details or peculiarities you cannot explain? Nine times out of ten there isn't any point. But the tenth time it is just the puzzling circumstance, the recurring oddity or association, that opens the door to a new understanding. It has not been Joan's way, however, to brush aside baffling problems, or to shy away from those for which the sources are scattered and fragmentary, but to reflect on the evidence over a lengthy period, and keep a weather eye open for any chink of light. Sometimes that has led to papers like 'The Common Fields', revisionist but so much more than merely revisionist. Characteristically it has also meant a refusal to be drawn beyond the facts, and a willingness to confess ignorance which is both disarming and often constructive.

A year or so before she retired Joan returned to her old department at Leicester to give a seminar paper. It was a lucid, questing account of some of the conclusions thrown up by her work on the fifth volume of the *Agrarian History*. It was followed by a lengthy discussion, at the end of which there was a complex question, or rather series of questions, by Charles Phythian-Adams. I forget what they were, but Joan's response I remember very distinctly. She pondered thoughtfully for a few moments, and then she said, 'I don't know the answer to any of these questions, *but* . . . '. She had taken us a long way, raised many issues, replied to much, and then left us there, like herself, wondering, reflecting on what the real answers to the whole subject could possibly be. All of us, I believe, left that seminar thoughtful. It reminded me of an evening, years before, when I stood on the edge of the Grand Canyon in Arizona. The enormous valley below us was dark and silent. Across the Painted Desert on the further side a dramatic thunderstorm was in progress, so far away that the thunder was inaudible, and yet so brilliant that every few moments a little patch of landscape here and there was lit up with startling clarity. Hours later, when we went to bed, the lightning was still flashing over the desert; but it was not until the next morning that we could make out the real outlines of that American wilderness. Now that the fifth volume of the *Agrarian History* has appeared under Joan's editorship, it seems to me that we can piece together much that has been coming to light under her inspiration over the past thirty years.

In 1985 the University of Leicester conferred upon Joan the honorary degree of D.Litt., a rare distinction for a former member of the academic staff. I happened to ring Joan two or three days after she had received the Vice-Chancellor's letter informing her of Senate's decision. 'I just couldn't believe it', she said, 'I was completely staggered!' I was not staggered, though it was not I who put her name forward. Neither would Herbert Finberg have been staggered. She had not been appointed to the Research Fellowship in Agrarian History at Leicester by him, but by his predecessor, W. G. Hoskins; but Herbert always believed that Joan would go far. I remember the smile of utter happiness on his face when he told me that she had been appointed to the Readership in Economic History at Oxford. 'Of course, Alan', he said, as if in great confidence, 'it *is* one of the plums.' From him it was rather an engaging metaphor, for actually he thought plums a somewhat overrated fruit. But there was also a reason why the honorary degree gave her old department a pleasure beyond the acknowledgement of her scholarship, and beyond the pleasure it gave others. It was the simple fact that she had left such a deep imprint on it. I do not mean she had left imitators; that would not have pleased her, and in fact relatively few of its graduates have pursued subjects very near to her own. Perhaps it is a way of looking at the evidence that has held us close together since she left. After the seminar just referred to she kindly wrote back, and this is what she said: 'I thought the discussion went well; I found it very useful. It always does go well in your department. In some places that paper would have fallen flat. But I feel that we speak the same language.' Fortunately, as Joan's frequent visits overseas and to many parts of this country show, it is a language now quite widely spoken, though (to borrow a metaphor as inappropriate as Herbert's plums) it is not accepted as canonical by all ecclesiastical traditions.

Two essential strands in any living language are a sense of proportion and a sense of humour. There must be many individuals, many meetings, and many committees that have found their problems guided towards a happy solution by Joan's practical wisdom and her quick but never scornful laughter. 'That must be Joan', Harold Fox said to me one day as we came into the department together, and heard the gentle silvery sound coming down the corridor through an open door. It was a sound with which I had become very familiar when Joan was at Leicester herself, and we occupied adjacent rooms in the old H-Block. The walls were very thin, and the rooms poky beyond the dreams of the UGC. But if you had only three or four people for your Special Subject, you could just squeeze them into those little cubicles originally built for nurses. I had never realized before that Tudor economic documents were so humorous. Or was it perhaps the voluntary palaeography class Joan put on? Palaeography is a great opener of reluctant minds.

Since I have known them, Joan and Jimmy have lived in six different houses: three in London, two in Oxford, and one in Kent. Their first, 36A Oppidans Road, NW3, they were much attached to; but it was part of the Eton College estate, and when the lease fell in, they had to move. It was a difficult time for house-purchase, but eventually they found one that seemed suitable in Meadway, in Hampstead Garden Suburb. It was a pleasant early-twentieth-century house, and in no time, as is their way, they had made it into a comfortable, convenient home. But somehow they were not happy there; the neighbourhood simply was not their *milieu*. Joan put a brave face on it by interesting herself in the history of the suburb and in attacking the garden; for behind her work on horticultural history is a keen interest in gardening. But it was plainly hard going. There just was not enough history to the locality to awaken enthusiasm; and with the London clay only an inch or two beneath the surface, the garden proved a disappointment. Their last London home, in Strathray Gardens near Swiss Cottage, was more congenial. It consisted of the two top floors of a spacious late Victorian house, well supplied with those unappropriated nooks and box-rooms so essential to scholarship, and indeed to any rational existence, though modern builders forget them. One of these spots, perhaps once a dressing-room, had been appropriated by Joan as a sewing-room; for that was one of her favourite by-employments.

When Jimmy retired from his post as librarian at Acton Borough Library, the family was able to move to Oxford. Joan already possessed a small terraced house in one of the back streets near St Hilda's, purchased as a term-time foothold. Behind a somewhat unprepossessing exterior, she had once again quickly made a cosy home, but it was too small for the family as a whole. Finding a suitable new abode in Oxford seemed as frustrating as finding the house in Meadway; though met with the customary Thirsk composure, one sensed that it was a vexation of spirit. Eventually, however, C. S. Lewis's old house, The Kilns, on Headington Hill came into view and they bought it. It was a large early-twentieth-century bungalow, to which a wing had been added at the back; there was plenty of space, but much needed doing to it. Though it stands on a hill, looking up to the woods that crown Headington, they were almost immediately faced with a flooded garden. When that had been dealt with by an outside firm, Jimmy turned his skill as a handyman, and Martin his genius at electronics, to bringing the interior up to date. The Kilns remained their home for the rest of Joan's time in Oxford. But when she took early retirement, they decided to pluck up their roots for the last time and transfer themselves permanently to the house at Hadlow in Kent which they had purchased in the early 1950s as a holiday home. Their son Martin had qualified a few years earlier in electronics, and their daughter Jane had just graduated in medicine at Leeds; there was no further need to keep on The Kilns.

But the Hadlow house has always meant something to Joan and Jimmy, I believe, that their others have not. Is it, perhaps, that they have been happiest, freest there? It is one of six dwellings formed from the courtyard buildings of Hadlow Castle, a Gothick fantasy begun by the Barton-May family about 1790 and completed about 1852. The greater part of the castle itself was demolished in 1961. But the folly known as Hadlow Tower rising 170 feet above the astonished Weald had a preservation order on it, and together with the courtyard buildings and the parkland was bought by Bernard Hailstone, the portrait painter, who came of Hadlow stock. Jimmy and Joan undertook much of the necessary conversion themselves; they formed a charming home, with a spice of the unusual, and a pretty view over the surrounding countryside. When I visited them there once some fifteen years ago with Herbert and Josceline Finberg, Joan had already begun collecting information about the history of the castle. She showed us her folder of illustrations, of the exterior and interior of the castle, with its ornate woodwork and plasterwork. One saw at once, as she said herself, that with the destruction of that house a way of life as well as a building had departed.

Ways of life, like human lives themselves, must eventually depart; the tragedy arises when the evidence for them also is obliterated. Hadlow Castle had not been one of the great houses of England; it was not designed by any very notable architect; it certainly would not have pleased Ruskin or Pugin. Like so many buildings in Kent, it stood slightly apart from the main current of the age, in style looking back to an earlier generation, the generation of Fonthill. But it was one of the most idiosyncratic houses to be found anywhere, the last and strangest dream of a family whose origins, as Joan discovered, stemmed from the medieval yeomen of the parish. They were not among the great families of England; neither were they among the plutocratic; the realization of their dream had taken them sixty years to complete. The destruction of Hadlow Castle was a minor historic tragedy. All the more credit, therefore, to Mr Hailstone for rescuing what remained, and to those like Joan and Jimmy who restored their part with sensitivity to both past and present. In 1985 Joan's *Hadlow Castle: A Short History* was published by the village historical society. Its twenty pages, packed as one would expect with vividly observed detail, shed light not only on the history of the castle itself and the rise of the Barton-May fortunes, but on the farming and the families of the locality. As one reads it one realizes that in this neighbourhood she and Jimmy have indeed put down their roots.

2. The Verneys as enclosing landlords, 1600–1800

JOHN BROAD

Enclosure has been a recurrent theme in Joan Thirsk's contribution to early modern history. In her first book, *English Peasant Farming*, she made an adroit contribution to the debate, while her pamphlet *Tudor Enclosures* has been a key introduction for generations of history undergraduates, including many for whom it has been their only contact with the economic and social history of the period. In the sixties her views on enclosure in 'Tawney's Century' were expanded in her dominating contribution to the fourth volume of the *Agrarian History of England*. For her, enclosure has always been part of the wider agricultural and economic process – whether in stressing its relationship to engrossing in 'Tudor Enclosures' or discussing its role in the expansion of rural industry or in its relationship to changes in Fenland and Leicestershire farming and estate management.[1]

From the fifteenth century on into the age of parliamentary enclosure, great landowners were frequently the initiators of and always influential participants in enclosures. The great age of enclosure for sheep during the fifteenth and early sixteenth centuries was classically the work of engrossing landlords. During the sixteenth and seventeenth centuries enclosure by the mutual agreement of all those with property rights over an area became common. Typically it took place where there were few landowners and particularly where a socially influential family could lead and coerce 'agreement'. These influences have always been acknowledged and examples of individual instances have been frequently given. Joan Thirsk herself discussed the part played by royalist landowners in enclosures of the Commonwealth period in Leicestershire. There

---

[1] For these references see pp. 369–74 below.

have been excellent case-studies of enclosing activities over relatively short periods, such as Parker's account of the enclosures that preceded the Midland Revolt of 1607 or Thorpe's exposition of the way in which the Spencers amassed their sheep pastures during the fifteenth and sixteenth centuries and created blocks of enclosed parishes across Northamptonshire and Warwickshire. Individual parish histories have chronicled the process in all its variety. On the other hand while Batho and Clay have made some comment on enclosure as a tool of estate management in their contributions to the *Agrarian History*, there has been no study which has looked at a landed family's attitudes to enclosure over a long period. The wealth of family and estate material in the Verney papers not only reveals a rare glimpse of the thought processes that went into two major enclosures by agreement in the 1650s and 1740s, but makes it possible to analyse other enclosures in which they were involved and to see them reacting to their neighbours' attempts at enclosure at various times.[2]

Few large landowners were indifferent to the process of enclosure, but there were a number of factors which made several generations of the Verney family particularly interested in it. Enclosure was first and foremost an 'improvement'. Although in the eighteenth and nineteenth centuries improvement came to hold almost moral connotations of enhanced farming methods and increased productivity, its earlier meaning was weighted much more heavily towards the cash nexus. Improvement meant primarily increased income, and that, for different reasons at different periods, was something the Verneys very much needed. In the early seventeenth century the family's ancient estates in Buckinghamshire had been broken up to pay for Sir Francis Verney's debts when he broke free of his stepmother's bonds and turned Mediterranean pirate. His half-brother, Sir Edmund, aspired to Court advancement. This initially required the purchase of a country seat and later cash injections that severely taxed family resources. When Sir Edmund was killed holding the King's standard at the battle of Edgehill, his son Sir Ralph faced massive debts. These were augmented by the financial effects of the Civil War. Over the next

[2] L. A. Parker, 'The Agrarian Revolution at Cottesbach, 1501–1612', *Studies in Leicestershire Agrarian History*, *Leics. Arch. Soc.*, XXIV (1948); H. Thorpe, 'Lord and Landscape', in D. R. Mills (ed.), *English Rural Communities* (London, 1973), pp. 31–82.

twenty years Sir Ralph adopted a variety of strategies for recovery, including enclosure.

During the eighteenth century the Verneys had different reasons for pressing to increase their income. The first Earl Verney was a man with political and social ambitions for his sons rather than for himself. He bought land, secured enormous dowries from two daughters-in-law, and purchased a political interest. Yet he bought primarily into rural land in Buckinghamshire and adjoining counties in a period when returns on capital invested in land were poor, if not in comparison with government stocks, certainly when weighed against some of the spectacular gains in urban property, mineral-bearing land, and stock market investments. Modern historians would place the Verneys' mid-eighteenth-century income level of at best £10,000 a year precariously on the divide separating the great landowners from the gentry. To maintain the impetus obtained from windfall dowries, the second Earl engaged in a whole variety of schemes to increase income and wealth and so assert his political and social claims. At his downfall after vast speculations in East India futures, his successor was left to consolidate the Claydon estates (the central properties since 1620), which were the only remnants of the second Earl's ambitions.

These drives to increase family income were a major element in the search for 'improvements', but in two discrete periods the Verneys also used peculiar investment advantages in a number of ways. In the reign of Charles I Court office gave Sir Edmund Verney investment opportunities in Crown sales of disafforested land and fen drainage schemes, as well as monopolies, wardships, and other Court perquisites. Similarly the second Earl Verney's political life in London from 1755 to 1775 gave him contacts in even more dubious investment circles whose projects included Yorkshire common rights and urban property developments in London, as well as mining and stock market schemes.

Positive decisions to invest in unimproved land were much less common or important than the opportunities available on existing properties. Writers on enclosure since W. G. Hoskins have stressed the continuing importance of enclosure over much of the country, particularly in the Midlands during the less well-documented years from 1600 to 1750. The Verney estates were dotted from Berkshire to the Fens, but were concentrated in north-west Buckinghamshire, with substantial outliers in Oxfordshire in the seventeenth century and Northamptonshire in the mid eighteenth century. Enclosure came in a variety of guises; in the reclamation of waste, the division of intercommoned pasture, the privatization of woods, and the elimination of common fields. Enclosure almost certainly came as a result of *force majeure* as well as in piecemeal agreements, general agreements and Acts of Parliament. In many cases there appears to be no record other than the deeds, letters, and descriptions available in private papers. Certainly none of the Verney enclosures appears in the painstaking trawl through the Chancery rolls undertaken under the aegis of Professor Beresford. Overall, there were few periods when enclosure was not on the agenda in some form, somewhere on the Verney estates.[3]

I

If we look first at the period up until 1665, one of continuing inflation and rising or stable rents, we find that different policies operated on the core estate and the outlying properties. At Middle Claydon the Verneys consolidated their estates by buying up as many copyholds and small freeholds as they could. They had eliminated other freehold owners (except for the glebe) by 1625. There remained quite a number of copyholds, but every opportunity was taken to turn these into leases for 99 years or three lives during the first half of the century. A classic example of this policy at work occurred in 1636. Thomas May was a Claydon copyholder who wanted to leave. He negotiated the sale of his copyhold to another farmer, Bates, but Sir Edmund Verney intervened. He wrote:

> as for May's living, it is true that Thomas May told me he had sold it to Bates if I would give way to it; but I told May I would take it into my own hands at the rate that Bates was to give for it and so I intend still.

Bates was not deprived of his farm, because Sir Edmund promised

---

[3] For background on the Verneys see F. P. and M. M. Verney, *Verney Memoirs*, 4 vols. (London, 1892–9), and M. M. Verney, *Verney Letters of the Eighteenth Century*, 2 vols. (London, 1930). I would like to thank the Verney family for permission to use the Verney MSS at Claydon House, Bucks, and for their help over many years. Microfilm of the family correspondence is available at the British Library, Buckinghamshire County Record Office, and at various universities in the USA.

him one, perhaps even the same one, on leasehold instead of copy-hold terms. At the time of the Civil War the turnover of tenants in what was a war zone from 1643 to 1646 was very high and many copyholders gave up their tenancies. This meant that by the time of the final enclosure in 1654–6 there were many fewer copyhold rights to be compensated. There remained long leases for lives and years; the last of these fell in towards the end of the century.[4]

Throughout this period estate strategy was directed towards the enclosure of Middle Claydon. Where copyholds were replaced by leases, or leases renewed, a standard clause was inserted giving the Verneys the right to enclose and to exchange the land cited in the deed for equivalent land elsewhere in the parish. One example in 1617 in a lease to Anthony Gibbes described the putative enclosure of waste and cow pasture as 'for Gibbes own good'. The consistency of practice during the century perhaps explains why there is no formal agreement document for any of the enclosures of Middle Claydon, including the final enclosure of 1654–6, which is otherwise exceptionally well documented. The Verneys' right to enclose was already established and no such agreement was necessary.[5]

Enclosure at Claydon was a lengthy process. At least some of the demesne was enclosed in the fifteenth century, probably for sheep, and 120 acres were indicted by the 1517 enclosure commissioners. By the seventeenth century all 650 acres of the demesne were enclosed. During the seventeenth century that process was extended to the waste, the woods, and finally to the open fields. As Claydon was situated in wooded country on the fringes of the ancient royal forest of Bernwood, some of its parish boundaries remained undefined until the early seventeenth century. In particular a large area known as the overlawn ('lawn' was originally a forest word meaning a clearing for deer) was intercommoned with the adjoining parish of East Claydon. In April 1613 Sir Thomas Lee, the Lord of the Manor of East Claydon, signed an agreement that divided the two parishes with a 'great ditch' six feet wide. Enclaves of Middle Claydon lordship which were claimed to be in East Claydon were eliminated and the line of the division on the ground

---

[4] S.E.V. (Sir Edmund Verney) to S.R.V. (Sir Ralph Verney), 4, 5, and 11 January 1635/6 R2. Throughout the chapter reference is to documents at Claydon House unless otherwise stated. The letter R followed by a number, e.g. R2, refers to the microfilm reel.
[5] Deeds 1617/4 dated 13 February 1616/17.

shared different qualities of ground between the two parishes. Nine days later, a further deed signed by the freeholders and copyholders of both East and Middle Claydon gave up all their claims to common rights in the overlawn. There is no evidence that there was any compensation for the village community.[6]

Two enclosures followed in the next forty years. In 1621, a year after making Claydon the family's main seat, Sir Edmund Verney set about further enclosures. Land from the common fields and meadows in the north of the parish was enclosed. Sir Edmund paid for the costs of enclosure and recompensed himself by eliminating common rights from the extensive woods at the southern end of the parish. In return, the tenants 'that had estates' (i.e. copyholders and long leaseholders) had the terms of their agreements doubled 'without any penny out of purse'. Some 300 acres of enclosed land were set out in new farms and the incoming tenants contracted to build houses in the fields. Further enclosure took place in 1635–6 involving land exchanges and quicksetting of new hedges, but its extent is not clear. However, as a result of these enclosures the open field system shrank to no more than 500 acres. During the first half of the seventeenth century it became necessary to make adjustments to the field regulations to accommodate the changes. The three great open fields were replaced by two rather smaller ones. Stints suffered: the parson complained that the stint of sheep fell from thirty to twenty per yardland in two years.[7]

The Verneys' strategy at Claydon in the pre-1640 period was one of gradualism. They eliminated common rights on the waste and turned copyhold to leasehold at every opportunity, with clauses permitting enclosure and exchange. They concentrated all freehold land into their own hands, by exerting claims to a pre-emptive right to buy, and then leased it out. They also enclosed sections of the open fields so as to change its operation markedly. The existing copyholders and lessees for three lives benefited from extended terms; it was only those farmers who took on new farms from outside the parish who paid the economic rents that estate policy was

[6] I. S. Leadam (ed.), *The Domesday of Enclosures 1517–18* (London, 1897), p. 174; PRO E179/424 (for 1566), C205/5/2 (for 1607). Deeds 1613 dated 11 and 20 April 1613.

[7] Bucks CRO D/A/GT Box 3; Lincs CRO. Terriers xv/29, xv/4, and 'bundle undated'; Deeds 1627 dated 2 February 1627/8; John Aris, Memorandum, n.d., ?1638 R2.

beginning to demand. The parson believed himself the greatest loser, citing the inferior quality of land on his exchanged strips and a loss of tithe. He claimed that his yearly harvest fell from thirty to seven or eight lambs. One result of the enclosure was that, from that time on, the incoming incumbent had to do a deal with the Verneys over what he should receive in lieu of tithe. The picture he paints is similar to Buchanan Sharp's scenario in the West Country forests of a cosy carve-up between landlord and farmers at his expense. Though the parson never said so, it was also at the expense of the poor.

The Civil War brought family tragedy, sequestration, exile, and huge financial loss to the Verneys, and it was not until 1648 that enclosure at Claydon was again considered. A piecemeal approach was again favoured by Sir Ralph. An enclosure of some 26 acres from the open fields was proposed and costed when the lease fell in. However, his advisers in England began to counsel general enclosure, not on the grounds of profitability or ease (though rents were rising fast and many copyholds had been vacated during the Civil War) but because the agricultural health of the community was endangered. In the late thirties Parson Aris had written of the consequences of the enclosure and reduction in size of the open fields. He claimed that 'the [open] fields winter very few sheep' and that the dunging of the open fields depended increasingly on 'foreigners who are long ere they come and gone betime; so soon as the field is done, which is commonly before men need give over their fold if their sheep were their own'. Sir Ralph's experienced farmer-bailiff, William Roades, gave his frank opinion that it would be 'wrong . . . to the town in general' and argued that:

> if I had a lease of any land there whether for lives or to pay a rack-rent, I should be better contented that you would inclose all the fields as any of it. First because I know the fields are so little already that they will not keep, without rutting, half sheep enough to fold half the land that should be folded every year, and for soil men can make but very little by reason they keep their cattle in pastures.

Sir Ralph's adviser and uncle, Dr William Denton, gave similar advice to 'inclose the whole'. He had consulted Parson Aris, who declared that although a small enclosure would 'little prejudice . . . the parson' such piecemeal activities 'would at length prove considerable injuries both to town and Parson, which makes him unwilling to it'. Despite agitations against enclosure at Brill, less than ten miles away, the worldly wise Dr Denton considered enclosure something 'I should heartily advice unto'.[8]

II

Piecemeal enclosure was forgotten, but Sir Ralph began a general enclosure soon after his return from exile in 1653. He quickly pressed on with the preliminaries, making lists of cottagers and the owners of common rights. William Roades was sent to evaluate 'Cousin Smith's West Country hedges'. A local surveyor was contacted and various field sizes were listed. There is no surviving enclosure agreement signed by all parties, and in all probability none ever existed. Sir Ralph owned all freehold land apart from the parson's, and enclosure clauses had been inserted in all copyholds and leases over the previous forty years. Cottagers and copyholders had to be persuaded to make the necessary exchanges willingly, and Sir Ralph needed the assistance of the leaders of village opinion to smooth the process. William Roades was already in his pocket, but Parson Aris was a trickier customer and could have become a rallying point for opposition. Sir Ralph remained diplomatically in London and waited until Aris was away from Claydon before setting Roades the task of cajoling the villagers into acceptance. Sir Ralph authorized him to brew 'twelve barrels rather than six' of ale to cheer the proceedings, and most of the tenants had agreed before the end of May 1653. However, Parson Aris was more difficult to deal with and held out until November 1654 before signing an agreement. Twelve clauses laid out the glebe exchanges in detail and compensated Aris for his lost tithe with a payment of £91 a year for his life. He had claimed his estate was worth £135 a year and asked for £112. By November it was already too late to break into the rhythm of the open field system, so enclosure was delayed until the following autumn.[9]

---

[8] B. Sharp, *In Contempt of all Authority* (London, 1980), esp. ch. 5; Lincs RO Terrier, bundle undated but from internal evidence *c.* 1679 and 1705–17. William Denton to S.R.V., 9 November 1648 R9; 24 May 1649 R10; William Roades to S.R.V., 20 December 1648 R9; 12 January 1649/50 R10; William Denton to S.R.V., 24 May 1649 R10; Edmund Chamberlayne to William Roades, 25 March 1654 R10.

[9] S.R.V. Memorandum, April 1653 R12; S.R.V. to William Roades, 23 May, 2 June 1653 R12; S.R.V. to William Roades, 9 and 12 May 1653 R12; Enclosure

During the autumn and winter of 1654–5 workmen began to bank and ditch the new fields. In the summer of 1655 much of the newly enclosed land appears to have remained in Sir Ralph's hands and, although there was a bean crop, the size of the hay harvest suggests that a considerable amount had already been laid down to grass. In the autumn posts and rails were added to the ditches to make better field divisions. When hedges were planted in the following spring the work was done not by local men, who had previously been employed picking stones, but by workers brought in from Towcester, Buckingham, and Radclive. The hedging was completed too late to let the land at Lady Day 1656, so most of the leases of the enclosure date from the early months of 1657, while the remaining land was let in 1658.[10]

The process of final enclosure was not quite as smooth and untroubled as the previous paragraphs suggest. Even after the main exchanges in May 1653 a few tenants held out and the last, Edwards, used Parson Aris to uphold his claims. When the final hedging took place the cottagers complained about the location of their common close and threatened to drive their livestock across the newly enclosed fields at morning and night. William Roades's advice was to change the location of the common close and so defuse the dispute. The greatest losers were not so much the owners of common rights, but their subtenants. Subtenants had no legal claim to compensation, yet in practice they exploited these rights in six out of seven cases. The Claydon labourers and smallholders who were logically the most available source of labour were thus the greatest losers from enclosure and hardly likely to cooperate in their own destruction. Direct action in response to the enclosure was, however, very limited and the one known case of hedge-breaking took place some five years later. Was more substantial opposition cowed by the local power and prestige of the Verneys and the active cooperation of the bailiff and better-off farmers? William Roades had established himself as a strong village spokesman in his own right during his master's absence as well as through his position as bailiff. The larger farmers had most to gain from the process. Con-

agreement dated 3 November 1654 E3/5; S.R.V. Memorandum, *c*. October 1654 R13.

[10] S.R.V. to William Roades, 8 February 1654/5 R13; William Roades to S.R.V., 30 July 1655 R12; S.R.V. to William Roades, 2 August 1655 R13, 29 March 1656 R14; William Roades to S.R.V., 31 March 1656 R14.

sidering the wider context of political ferment and considerable enclosure in the Midlands during the 1650s, the response to the changes at Claydon was weak and the Verneys could congratulate themselves on a most successful operation.[11]

What were the benefits of the enclosure of Middle Claydon to the Verneys? Improvement meant higher rents; during the first half of the seventeenth century Middle Claydon brought in an estimated total revenue that rose from c. £1,000 to c. £1,400–1,450 in the period before 1650. The rise cannot be attributed just to enclosure. Land was bought in, copyholds were replaced by leases, and shorter leases at economic rents became increasingly common. On the other hand, some leases were renewed beneficially to facilitate the earlier enclosure. These were the short-term hidden costs of enclosure. The potential profits were set out by William Roades in 1648:

> if there be 20 acres of arable land without grass ground that is worth to you . . . about 5s an acre which is £5 a year . . . enclose it and then it will be worth £20 a year.

Some of the increase came simply because the land was enclosed; more came from the premium which pasture and meadow held over arable ground. The evidence of the leases made in 1657–8, after the final enclosure, shows that the new enclosures were let for twenty-one years at approximately £1 an acre. No full rental of Claydon has survived for the 1660s, but on this basis the estate was producing close on £2,000 a year and the final enclosure had added somewhere between £250 and £375 a year. These increases represent a huge return on investment from what is known of the costs of enclosure. Parson Aris estimated that the cost of enclosure in the 1630s 'might be £300' for 300 acres, or £1 an acre. This sum looks about right if we compare it with William Roades's detailed costing for 26 acres in 1648, which amounted to £20. Even allowing for the legal costs of new leases, the brewing of beer, and the loss of rent during the enclosure, the return on capital was extraordinarily high, certainly exceeding 50 per cent, and on the most optimistic estimate approaching 100 per cent.[12]

[11] S.R.V., Memorandum, c. April 1653 R12; S.R.V. to William Roades, 29 December 1654 R12; Edward Butterfield to S.R.V., 22 October 1654 R13; William Roades to S.R.V., 29 April 1656 R12; Hugh Holmes to R. Kibble, 25 November 1661 R18.

[12] William Roades to S.R.V., 20 May 1648 R9; Edward Butterfield to S.R.V., 6 July 1663 and 26 June 1664 EC; S.R.V., Memorandum of c. 1655 in 5 July 1648

III

In the early seventeenth century the Verneys used enclosure as a tool for modernizing their estate management and maximizing income. At Claydon they created a consolidated estate let at rack-rent. On the outlying properties enclosure was also an important influence on rural life, but motives for enclosure were generally rather different. Most of the land acquired by the marriage of Sir Ralph Verney to the heiress Mary Blacknell in 1629, or by investment in Court schemes, had been sold off by 1665 to pay family debts. However, many of these properties were actively 'improved' by enclosing considerable portions of land before resale.

The manor of Mursley in Buckinghamshire had been owned by the Verneys since the fifteenth century, but much of the field land belonged to others. In 1611 Sir Edmund Verney joined with Sir Francis Fortescue to make an agreement with the tenants and farmers in the parish to enclose common and waste, specifying the number of acres of enclosed waste to be given to the tenants for every yardland held and setting aside additional land for the cottagers 'for their relief'. Sir Edmund Verney was to keep the residue for his own use. A 1614 lease of a large farm there also sanctioned the exchange of common field lands and included a statement that the lessee would receive a proportionate share of any enclosure, with the upwards adjustment of rent to be agreed by four local men or a mutually acceptable arbitrator. Between 1619 and 1623 various sales and leases show that enclosure of waste was in progress in 1619 and that there were considerable enclosures from the common fields in 1622. In 1624 the largest Mursley farm was sold with 'part of the Great common of Mursley as now fenced, mounded and enclosed'. Between 1619 and 1624 the Verneys actively enclosed in the parish and simultaneously sold off farms and land, leaving themselves only the manorial rights, which were apparently worth little and were sold to Sir Thomas Fortescue for a small sum in 1662.[13]

At the Restoration another Blacknell property, Preston Crow-

R9; J. Aris, Memorandum, n.d., *c.* 1638 R2; William Roades to S.R.V., 13 October 1648 R9.
[13] 1611 agreement R2; Deeds 1614/4 dated 9/3/1614; 1619/2 dated 9/11/19 Jas I 1619; 1621/10 dated 23/2/1621/2 19 Jac; 1624/1 dated 11 June 22 Jas I 1624.

marsh and Benson, underwent the same combination of enclosure and sale as had Mursley. Once again, earlier leases included the right of the Verneys to enclose. Leases dated 1659 specified the enclosure of waste at Little Marsh and North Mead and even how the enclosed land would be split, with four-fifths going to Sir Ralph Verney and one-fifth to the leaseholders and copyholders. The enclosure and sale followed in 1662–4. The manor itself went to one buyer, the main farm to another. In 1663 an enclosure agreement was signed with six tenants (or possibly more: there are two drafts), and North Mead and Little Marsh were divided in three parts, the tenants renouncing their rights of commonage. The same tenants then bought their own smallholdings from the Verneys, so that by 1665 the Verneys had profitably severed all connection with their Oxfordshire properties.[14]

Similar events took place at Wasing in Berkshire, part of Mary Blacknell's dowry, in the 1630s. Enclosures and cottage-building had taken place on Wasing Heath. Sir Ralph Verney took steps to ensure that he could reap the benefit by making the rector and inhabitants sign a deed admitting that turves removed from the Heath belonged to the Lord of the Manor. In the following year he forced the rector to grant him the tithes of the Heath 'being now in common' on a 120-year lease. Here too, the land would have been sold but for Mary Blacknell's insistence that Wasing be kept to provide an inheritance for her younger son John.[15]

In these three instances partial, piecemeal enclosure was the aim, not a grand design of total enclosure which would have been far more difficult given the spread of landownership. The Verneys used enclosure to justify increased rents and in consequence were able to obtain a higher price when they sold the land. They were taking a judgement on what investment would bring quick returns, not trying to complete the jigsaw of parish-wide enclosure. A similar rationale was applied to the lands the Verneys acquired through Court links. All the evidence suggests that even if such acquisitions had not been bought with the intention of selling at a quick profit, they were considered dispensable. The land acquired during the

---

[14] Deeds 1659/3, 1659/5 both dated 13/12/59; 1659/7 dated 21/12/1659; 1660/1 dated 3/4/1660; 1662/3 dated 9/9/62; 1663/2 dated 29/1/63/4; 1663/13 and 14 dated 26/1/1663/4; 1664/1, 11, 13, 16, and 19 all dated 11/6/1664; 1664/18 dated 8/7/64.
[15] St Malthus to S.R.V., 28 July 1634 R2; Claydon Deeds 1637/23 dated 17/11/37; 1638/5 dated 10/1/1638/9. M.V. to S.R.V., 6 and 13 May 1647 R7.

disafforestation of Bernwood in the late 1620s at Brill is a good example. There is clear evidence from Sir Ralph's notes on his inheritance in 1642, with their calculations on how he would pay the family debts, that he intended to sell the enclosed Brill forest lands quickly. Although the process was not concluded until 1654 the property fetched over 30 per cent more than had been expected in 1642. The share of Deeping Fen that Sir Ralph acquired from his friend Sir Nathaniel Hobart for £1,000 in 1635 was part of the land which Court 'projectors' were trying to drain on the Bedford level, and vast profits were expected. It was still in Verney hands in 1642 but was by then considered worthless, though when or how it was sold remains unknown. It, too, must be considered a quick and less successful speculation in land.[16]

IV

Up to 1665 the Verneys used enclosure to consolidate their main seat at Claydon and to develop outlying properties before resale. In the succeeding sixty-five years enclosure was less important in Verney estate policy, largely because the opportunities were few. Middle Claydon and Wasing in Berkshire were the only properties that remained in Verney hands throughout the period. From 1663 to 1709 they held a substantial but not dominating estate in neighbouring East Claydon as a result of Edmund Verney's marriage to Mary Abell. Because the Verneys had no lands that could easily be enclosed they had a very different perspective on enclosure and particularly on what other landowners around them were doing. The Verneys were affected by the period of falling rents after 1665. As they tried to maintain their own rents they feared that new enclosures would add to the supply of enclosed land, and further depress rents. Policy aimed to prevent nearby enclosures as a defensive measure.[17]

At the adjoining parish of Steeple Claydon the Verneys went to considerable lengths to prevent enclosure. There the Challoner family were struggling to recover from the losses they had suffered at the Restoration, when Thomas Challoner was executed because

---

[16] n.d. Estate papers Bundle 1630s; Deeds 1654/9 dated 29 March 1654.
[17] M. G. Davies, 'Country Gentry and Falling Rents', *Midland History*, IV (1977), 86–96.

he had signed Charles I's death warrant, and his heirs struggled with other local squires who were trying to take over their lands. The Challoners gradually brought under control some sixty of the eighty yardlands in the parish with the intention of enclosing the whole village. Sir Ralph told his son that he feared that this 'might not only cloak up your estate in point of hunting, hawking, coursing, riding and other pleasures . . . but it needs be a great loss to you in letting your grounds'. His son Edmund was instructed to discover if cows' commons could by custom be sold there without land. Eventually Edmund Verney bought one-and-a-half yardlands and half a cow's common, 'enough to prevent an enclosure, which is all you aim at'. He had to avoid letting the land to a farmer who owned the adjoining strips, or making leases more than two years in duration, in case the Challoners then bought up the lease and circumvented the impediments to enclosure. The purchase enabled Edmund Verney to prevent the enclosure of Steeple Claydon for 120 years at a cost of some £60. He also changed the pattern of the village's development. In defeat Challoner gave up his attempt to consolidate his grip on the whole parish and decided instead to sell out. In the course of 1683–4 he sold most of the farms and cottages that he owned, not to a single buyer, but piecemeal. The twenty-five different buyers were either the occupants or local farmers and yeomen intent on investment. When he sold the remnants of his estate in Steeple Claydon to the Verneys in 1704 only eight-and-a-half yardlands remained, compared with the sixty he had consolidated twenty-five years earlier.[18]

The defensive instinct to prevent others enclosing continued into the next century when in 1716 Sir John Verney wrote with concern to his son, the future first Earl, about the Lowndes family's land purchases in Shipton Lee, a hamlet of Winslow which they seemed likely to enclose. He commented 'I think Dr B[usby of Addington, the adjoining parish] did wrong not to buy somewhat in Shipton to prevent enclosing.' Although Steeple Claydon provides the most dramatic example, changing attitudes to common waste in East Claydon between the late seventeenth and mid eighteenth centuries

---

[18] Deeds 1683–4 and 1704/17 31/6/1704; S.R.V. to E.V. (Edmund Verney), 13 February 1672/3, 20 February 1672/3; E.V. to S.R.V., 17 February 1672/3, all R25. J.V. (Sir John Verney, first Viscount Fermanagh) to R.V. (Ralph Verney, second Viscount Fermanagh, first Earl Verney), 21 October 1716 R56.

neatly illustrate the element of self-interest. In 1673 Edmund Verney fought to prevent the Dormers of Quainton from promoting a division of the common wastes on Coppesley Hill between Quainton and East Claydon. He had the East Claydon freeholders on his side and his efforts were successful. At that time he was a substantial landowner in the parish but could not expect to enclose it himself, even though he was simultaneously undermining the functions of the manor court by supporting those larger farmers who did not want one called and attacking other common rights, including the vicar's right to cow commons. When, seventy years later, the Verneys had bought themselves back into East Claydon and become the dominant and enclosing landowners, they were able to complete the division of Coppesley Hill triumphantly with the proclaimed motive of 'the encouragement of future industry, good Husbandry and Improvement'.[19]

V

By that stage they had already enclosed East Claydon. This project was undertaken in 1741–3, and both the timing and method of enclosure pose interesting problems. The 1730s and 1740s are the classic age of Professor Mingay's 'Agricultural Depression'. The heavy Midland clays of north Buckinghamshire were particularly vulnerable to low grain prices and there was a general tendency to increase the proportion of grassland and pastoral agriculture, especially dairying, in the region. Higher rental values and lower management costs prompted landowners to make these moves. Three neighbouring villages, Ashendon, Wotton, and Twyford were enclosed in the same period; all were predominantly owned by major landowners.

As with Middle Claydon, the Verneys used enclosure by agreement to achieve their goal. Three neighbouring parishes in northwest Buckinghamshire provided simultaneous early examples of enclosure by Parliamentary Act before 1745, which were watched, examined, and discussed. The designation of John Millward, the Verney steward, as a commissioner in nearby Ashendon led to a

---

[19] E.V. to S.R.V., 26 May 1673, 29 May 1673, 9 June 1673, all R26; Lease dated 6 December 1673 R27; Deeds 1744–9 dated 15 September 1747; British Library, Add. MS 24737, fo. 200.

debate whether an Act was necessary at Claydon. The need to convert land to pasture was basic to many Buckinghamshire enclosures after 1650 and in East as in Middle Claydon at least one-third (over 800 acres) and perhaps as much as one-half of the open field land was already under sward. Much of this lay within old, piecemeal enclosures, and the terms of the 1737 stinting agreement, which reduced a cottager's common to one cow and five sheep, suggest that the tattered open field system was disadvantaged.[20]

It was a long drawn-out enclosure. Between 1737 and 1739 an enclosure agreement was drawn up, but not all those with land rights could be persuaded to sign. Farmer Thame insisted on enclosing his own share separately, thus considerably complicating the process. A separate agreement with the parson over tithes was still being discussed in 1739. There is no evidence of any particular drive to buy out small freeholders and copyholders before or during the enclosure. The Verneys are known to have spent at least £1,080 on such purchases in the 1730s and £780 in the 1740s, but these purchases were not concentrated in the period of enclosure. Few were made between 1737 and 1743, and land purchases continued haphazardly in the village until the 1760s.[21]

By 1741 agreement had been reached with the copyholders and freeholders, and in the autumn of that year the physical process of enclosure began. Ironically, the Verneys were laying the land to grass in a bumper harvest when Claydon grain yields (at 12:1 for wheat and 8:1 for barley) were the best for many years, while hay was short and the grass parched. At these ratios farmers understandably fought to protect their traditional right to plant winter wheat rather than spring barley, but the Verneys needed to clear the fields in the autumn and winter and intended to undersow grass with barley in the spring. Although this led to conflict, since 'a crop of wheat

---

[20] M. E. Turner, *English Parliamentary Enclosure* (London, 1980), ch. 6; J. Broad, 'Alternate Husbandry and Permanent Pasture in the Midlands, 1650–1800', *Agricultural History Review*, 28 (1980), 77–89; R.V.jr (Ralph, second Earl Verney) to R.V., 11 August 1741; R.V.jr to J. Millward, 24 January 1737/8 R58; R.V.jr to R.V., 13 December 1741 R58; 2 February 1741/2 R59; 28 January 1741/2 R58; R.V. to John Millward, 4 November 1737; 24 February 1738/9; 27 July 1739 R58; R.V.jr to R.V., 25 June 1741; 9 August 1741 R58; R.V. to J. Millward, 1 October 1737 R58.

[21] R.V. to J. Millward, 29 October 1737 R58; J. Millward to R.V., 12 May 1739 R58. On the tendency of parliamentary enclosure to promote an active land-market see Turner, ch. 7.

is almost as good again as a crop of barley', the Verneys' steward believed that farmers were more concerned to extract as much compensation as possible for their losses than to delay the enclosure. The future second Earl was particularly concerned that the huge fortune he and his brother had acquired by marriage should be kept secret so that the farmers would not set their demands too high. By 8 September all but two of the East Claydon tenants had agreed to the terms after four hours of wrangling. One eventually settled for cash; another was two years in arrears with his rent, and pressure could easily have been put on him. These few recalcitrants came under pressure not only from the Verneys, but from their fellow farmers, who petitioned for an early enclosure because they considered the conditions for such a move the best in fifty years.

The enclosure began with the fixing of the outside fences while teams ploughed the stubble and tenants dunged the fields in preparation for grass seed. The surveyor, Lee, arrived at the same time. The sum of £80 was spent on ploughing the fields, and details of the types of hedges to be planted were agreed. Crab was an important constituent because it grew so quickly and was mixed with aspen (a type of poplar) in the wettest parts of the estate. Elsewhere elm sets were mixed with crab, and a young oak tree was planted every two or three poles. The plants were obtained from a hedge nursery two miles from Syresham, just over the Northamptonshire border, and cost 3d a pole. In November ditching was under way on the Grandborough side of the parish. Eleven men were employed to dig a ditch 4 feet wide and 3 feet deep at the piece rate of 7d an 18-foot pole, a cost which Verney proudly announced 'is the lowest price it was ever done for in this county'.[22]

Four neighbouring villages were being laid down to grass simultaneously. The parallel timing of Wotton and Claydon enclosures led to a massive demand for grass seed for twenty or thirty miles around during the winter of 1741–2. The Grenvilles sent men to Brackley and Towcester markets to buy up any available seed, while the Verneys went as far afield as Hemel Hempstead and at one point considered enquiring about grass seed prices in Canvey Island. John Millward hoped that he would be unknown at Hemel and therefore be able to buy up grass seed cheaply and easily, but found that all the

---

[22] R.V.jr to R.V., 9 and 23 August 1741; 3 and 8 September 1741; 22 October 1741; 17 November 1741 R58.

seedsmen knew about the north Buckinghamshire enclosure and he had to pay a 25 per cent premium on his seed.

Enclosure and conversion were completed during the winter; new lettings were possible a year later in the winter of 1742–3. The enclosure was relatively smooth. Most of the opposition was bought out with cash payments, although one disgruntled farmer threw down his fences in 1745 and claimed he was entitled to because there had been no Act of Parliament to approve it. Perhaps he and others found that enclosure was bringing little benefit. The Verneys kept an eye on the financial results. In 1740, when negotiating a marriage settlement with Henry Herring, they had claimed that enclosure would increase East Claydon's income by £300 or more a year. No accounts or rentals have survived, but in 1746 the future second Earl reckoned that the enclosure had not yet paid for itself: 'As to the improvement of East Claydon, the Expenses attending the enclosure do yearly exceed the improvement, as the Books will make appear.' Enclosure was a long-term investment during the 1740s, a decade when farmers received low prices, and their herds were ravaged by cattle plague.[23]

During the period 1736–70 the first and second Earls Verney were buyers of land on a large scale. The first Earl preferred estates that had already been enclosed. Furthermore, he favoured pastoral land which he believed required less management and paid higher rents. In 1743 he wrote of an estate that it 'might be turned into Dairy bargains and hold rent, and all, or all but a trifle laid down, for surely if near half is ploughed, or but one fourth of it, it must needs have many barns and outbuildings to it which are great incumbrances'. The second Earl was a more active encloser, perhaps influenced by having personally supervised the process at East Claydon. He has left no general statement of his views, but his activities reveal a continuing preoccupation. In 1764 Westbury, a parish adjoining his temporary seat at Biddlesden, was undergoing parliamentary enclosure. Verney took the opportunity to seize and enclose woodlands that had previously been intercommoned by the two parishes, throwing out Westbury's commoners' livestock.[24]

[23] Henry Herring's estimate in a loose paper in the Middle Claydon churchwarden's accounts E2/3; R.V.jr to R.V., 6 October 1746 R59. J. Broad, 'Cattle Plague in England', *Agric. Hist. Rev.*, 31 (1983), 104–15.
[24] R.V. to John Millward, 27 January 1742/43 estate papers N4/2/3.

In 1765 he led a posse of gentry who charged 'levellers' who were attempting to dismantle the post and rails of the enclosures at Warkworth. This Northamptonshire village near Banbury was close to the second Earl's properties at Biddlesden and Syresham. He and his associates – Buckinghamshire friends of his, Joseph Bullock and Major Lovett – were, according to the *Northampton Mercury*, innocently dining as Astrop Wells, doubtless at the 'Great Room' that opened as a centre of local entertainment in the summer months. Verney's concern was not just the defence of property. At the time he was negotiating for an enclosure at Syresham. He claimed 20 of the 36 acres of waste, exaggerating his rights, and putting in additional cattle to press them. His name also appears in the parliamentary process involved in various enclosures in north Buckinghamshire. At Little Horwood, Shalstone, Grendon Underwood, and Soulbury, he was involved in the scrutinizing committee, and in each case the land was that of political allies or neighbours. In a quite different context he used his position as head leaseholder from the Duchy of Lancaster for the Honour of Pontefract in Yorkshire to exploit rights over waste. He appears to have taken the lease to try to exploit disputed mineral rights, for he sank considerable capital in coal mines for a number of years. He was thwarted in his plans but also tried to claim compensation for loss of waste in a number of Yorkshire enclosures.[25]

VI

The evidence of a consistent willingness to enclose on the main Verney estates and on their outlying and transiently owned properties over a period of two hundred years helps us to understand why partial and piecemeal enclosure in the pre-parliamentary enclosure era was so widespread and prevalent. It is more difficult to assess how important enclosure was in the process of economic

[25] *Northampton Mercury*, 16 September 1765; *Jackson's Oxford Journal*, 13 July 1754; E3/4 Green Folder 1765 letter – see also J. Millward to R.V., 4 April 1751 A15/8; Chest A/23, 29, 37, N4/1/2, N4/4/14; *Purefoy Letters*, ed. G. Eland (London, 1931), I, pp. 5–6; for evidence of Earl Verney's part in eighteenth-century enclosure bills see *CJ*, XXXI, 41 (Shalstone 1766); XXXII, 153 (Grendon Underwood 1769); XXXIII, p. 458 (Soulbury 1772); J. M. Martin, 'Members of Parliament and Enclosure: a Reconsideration', *Agric. Hist. Rev.*, 27 (1979), 101–9.

Table 1. *Estimates of the populations of the Claydons, 1524–1811*

	1524	1563	1603	1662/71	1676	1801	1811
Mid Claydon	30 families	113	200–16	200–37	217	103	129
East Claydon	c. 50 families	203	200–16	296–351	301	299	309
Steeple Claydon	c. 50 families	216	315–19	332–94	—	646	704

and social development at the village level, but the contrasting population figures for the three Claydon parishes between 1600 and 1800 suggest that a closer investigation of the relationship between enclosure, the organization of farms and estates, and population changes would be productive.

The figures in Table 1 suggest that in the sixteenth century Middle Claydon may have grown quite fast, but from 1600 onwards that growth was checked, and at some point between 1676 and 1801 it fell rapidly.[26] In this it differed markedly from its neighbours. East Claydon remained stable and Steeple Claydon advanced fairly rapidly. The extraordinary loss of population in Middle Claydon, unequalled in north Buckinghamshire, was the result of policy: in Middle Claydon the Verneys were able to establish a 'close' village with large farms, low poor rates and little in-migration. Such villages were not uncommon. Fourteen per cent of the parishes aggregated for the Wrigley and Schofield study had not exceeded their 1660s totals of baptisms by 1801. In north Buckinghamshire Middle Claydon was one of at least five parishes in Ashendon hundred that did not increase their populations between the Hearth Tax and 1801. None, however, underwent such a drastic fall in population. Yet a comparison of baptismal and burial registers indicates that although population was checked and stabilized after enclosure, the greatest fall occurred after 1750. This is confirmed by a precise population figure of 206 given by the rector in 1709. By contrast, in East Claydon, preliminary aggregate analysis of the parish registers suggests that the stabilization of population was

---

[26] These population figures are derived from the following: 1524: Buckinghamshire Lay Subsidy Returns (Bucks Record Society, vol. 8 (1950). 1563 and 1603: from ecclesiastical surveys using standard multipliers. 1662/71: from extant Buckinghamshire Hearth Tax returns, using 1662 list, but mediated by use of 1671 indications of numbers of exempt. 1801 and 1811: from Census returns.

Table 2. *Middle Claydon farm sizes by annual rent, 1646–1787*

	1646	1648	1688	1722	1787
Over £75 p.a.	0	2	7	12	11
£50–75 p.a.	4	6	8	6	2
£20–49 p.a.	11	11	10	4	2
£5–19 p.a.	24	25	7	2	5
Under £5 p.a.	19	9	15	7	9
TOTALS	58	53	47	31	29

Table 3. *Middle Claydon farm sizes by acreage equivalents based on a constant 2,000-acre farming area*

	1648	1688	1722	1787
Over 150 acres	2	2	1	8
75–150 acres	4	9	12	2
50–74 acres	5	5	5	2
20–49 acres	18	10	5	3
5–19 acres	18	6	1	5
0–4 acres	6	15	7	9
TOTALS	53	47	31	29

linked to enclosure. With this in mind it is worth analyzing the relative importance of other factors at work in the Claydons.[27]

One important aspect was estate policy on engrossing and optimum size of farms in the Claydons. Particularly good data exist for Middle Claydon. Tables 2 and 3 show the decrease in the numbers of tenants there over the period 1646–1787 and the distribution of farm sizes indicated both by rent paid (or in the case of 1648, estimate of rack-rent value), and an estimate of acreage equivalent.[28]

Although the final enclosure of 1653–6 led to fewer tenants overall in the next forty years, the reduction was considerably less than

[27] E. A. Wrigley and R. S. Schofield, *The Population History of England 1541–1871* (London, 1981), ch. 2; Christ Church, Oxford, Wake MS CCXXV, p. 449; for work on Buckinghamshire population totals I am immensely grateful to Dr Sue Wright. Middle, East, and Steeple Claydon parish registers are in Buckinghamshire County Record Office.

[28] The estate rentals are in the Muniment Room at Claydon House with the exception of part of the 1688 rental in Bucks CRO D/X 337; the 1646 rental includes small tenants but gives nominal rents for some properties, while the 1648 rate values all farms fully, but omits the small properties not paying rates.

in the succeeding thirty-five years when no equivalent upheaval took place. There is no way of telling how much of the reduction between 1646 and 1688 came during the 1650s. There were two departures at the time of Middle Claydon's enclosure in 1655. James Lea took his family with him; his reappearance at the time of the plague ten years later resulted in a village panic. The Tipping family also left *en masse* for London at the enclosure. Tipping had been offered a job as a drayman there and Sir Ralph Verney indicated his thoroughgoing approval of the decision. However, many tenants had left during the Civil War when empty farms were one factor which encouraged the Verneys to enclose. The picture that emerges from Tables 2 and 3 is that the most important part of the process of engrossing took place in the period 1688–1722. It was largely achieved by 'natural wastage' – the slow attrition of smaller farms caused by declining profitability and the Verneys' policy of evicting tenants who fell too far in arrears with their rent.[29]

Table 3 illustrates the way in which smaller farmers were squeezed. Farm sizes from 5 to 150 acres were affected progressively. The numbers of 5–19-acre farms were dramatically reduced between 1648 to 1688 and almost eliminated by 1722, only to achieve a slight and perhaps chimerical revival in 1787. These and farms of 20–49 acres bore the brunt of the reduction in the seventeenth and early eighteenth centuries. They were the equivalent of the half-to-two yardland farmers of pre-enclosure times, the traditional small farmers of Midland England. In 1648 there were thirty-six such farms, but by 1722 only six. For farms of fifty acres or more changes in the preponderance of various sizes are probable indicators of the economic size for pastoral farms in the south Midlands over two centuries. Farms of 50–74 acres changed little in number through the later seventeenth and early eighteenth centuries, but declined by 1787. Larger farms of 75–150 acres increased considerably in the period 1648–1722. Their numbers fell dramatically at some point in the second and third quarters of the eighteenth century. Large farms of 150 acres or more were relatively few in number in the later seventeenth and early eighteenth centuries, but by 1787 had come to predominate. These figures suggest that before 1750 farms of 75–150 acres were, or were considered to be, the

---

[29] S.R.V. to William Roades, 2 and 14 August 1655 R13; W. Roades to S.R.V., 6 August 1655 R13.

optimum size for the kind of farming practised in Middle Claydon. Later in the century, larger farms were increasingly viable (or alternatively fashionable) units of production.

For farm sizes above 4 acres, the impact of changing farm sizes can be seen in another way. In 1648 the predominant farm size groups were the 5–19 and 20–49-acre group. In 1722 the most important group was the 75–150-acre farm, while in 1787 the largest size of 150 acres or more predominated, with three farms exceeding 250 acres. Comparisons with East and Steeple Claydon are not available until the late eighteenth century, but 1780 and 1791 rentals and particulars of all three parishes show that rents paid in East Claydon were predominantly in the £100–200-a-year range, corresponding to the 75–150-acre farms in Middle Claydon. Those in Steeple Claydon were still smaller. The farm size differentials between the three villages, each enclosed at a different period and each dominated by the Verneys as landlords for differing lengths of time, provide a convincing mechanism linking concentration of ownership, enclosure, and the process of farm enlargement. In the Claydons this took place by gradual and piecemeal changes over a long period.[30]

The mechanism is well documented in the Verney correspondence. There are no indictments, petitions, or lists of depopulated houses such as exist for Stowe in the mid seventeenth century. At Claydon, as in many English villages in the seventeenth and eighteenth centuries, there were often empty houses, but whether they were pulled down, converted to use as barns, or refurbished, depended on circumstance. In one well-documented occasion immediately after the Restoration, Sir Ralph Verney ordered the pulling down of empty houses in an attempt to prevent John Butcher marrying and settling in the village.[31]

However, most demolitions were part and parcel of the changes in farm size and organization. In the late 1670s and early 1680s when Sir Ralph was short of tenants and invested considerable sums in rebuilding farmhouses at Middle Claydon, a number of houses were wholly or partially demolished. In 1681 he wrote about Widow

---

[30] Later eighteenth-century information on East and Steeple Claydon farm sizes from rentals in Chest A/1.

[31] Henry E. Huntington Library, Stowe MSS STTM Boxes 4 and 15; H. Holmes to S.R.V., 16 and 23 February 1662/3 R18.

Scott's house: 'I keep up that house only for her for 'tis not wanted there.' In 1678 Fimore Lodge, the old hunting lodge in the woods, which according to an observation on the Hearth Tax returns probably had six or eight hearths, was demolished and replaced by a more suitable farmhouse, while at least two if not three houses disappeared in the same period. In 1677 William Taylor's house was burnt down and Sir Ralph immediately offered to build a better house. He insisted 'I will set it where I please' and used the misfortune as an excuse for replanning the farm with an eye to amalgamating it with an ailing farmer's adjoining lands.[32]

A similar reshaping of farms and houses took place soon after Sir John Verney succeeded his father in 1696. He ordered his bailiff 'to neglect Mrs Parrott's house, if I should have that bargain fall, for there are too many houses press upon the Park and make incursions on it'. Houses were not demolished as an automatic response to any opportunity to engross holdings. When William Taylor died in 1713 leaving his farm vacant 'two or three of my tenants would take it but I can't let 'em for then the house would fall down, they all having other houses to live in'. Five years later a similar amalgamation was rejected on the grounds that 'if he should take it the house would soon fall'. The reduction in the numbers of houses on the estate was a gradual process, broadly in line with the declining numbers of holdings. No explicit statement exists, but the overall strategy appears to have been to relate rising farm sizes to the selective and spasmodic repairing and rebuilding of farmhouses.[33]

The demolition of farmhouses was a symptom of the process of farm enlargement which went on monotonously after 1650. It paralleled a leasing policy which sought, and received, economic rents and selected tenants on the basis of the capital and expertise that they could provide, rather than letting farms descend from generation to generation. It was also a policy which was relatively strict about rent arrears and did not hesitate to evict farmers who were unable to pay their way. One result was that there was a regular turnover of tenants on the estate. This is apparent from the correspondence, but can only be analysed in detail from the rent

---

[32] S.R.V. to W. Coleman, 10 January 1677/8 R31; 28 December 1676; 13 January 1680/1; 1 February 1676/7.

[33] J.V. to W. Coleman, 5 December 1697 R50; 9 March 1697/8 R50; J. V. to R. V., 1 February 1712/13 R55; C. Chaloner to R.V., 9 February 1717/18 R56.

rolls of the period 1679–94, which cover approximately two-thirds of the estate. They show that on only ten out of twenty-two holdings was there family continuity between 1679 and 1694. Furthermore, this was a period when Sir Ralph Verney reversed his policy of rapid eviction and tended to support ailing tenants with concealed subsidies, or on one occasion from the poor rate.

The continuous turnover of families between 1600 and 1800 is confirmed by the very few surnames that can be traced without a break through the family reconstitution of Middle Claydon. Of 400 reconstructed marriages analysed by family name (used crudely as an indicator of kinship), 148 (37 per cent) came from families with five or more apparent households over the period. However, only four family names produced more than ten apparent households (in total sixty-three reconstituted families (15.75 per cent)) over the 200 years. Quite a number of surnames survived over long periods. The Roades, for instance, first appeared in the 1630s and were present in large numbers until after 1800. The Kings (1562–1744), Butchers (1601–1800), Scots (1620–1721), Hintons (1618–1800), and Hicks (1588–1750) also maintained a presence in the parish for many years. However, all these names were common locally, and in no case can a direct line be traced with certainty for the whole period.[34]

In the Claydons enclosure was not the catastrophic agent of immediate social change, but there were immediate effects. The farming economy was rapidly altered by the replacement of the declining remnants of open field and mixed farming by pasture farming for fattening, dairying, and sheep-rearing. The earlier partial enclosures of Middle Claydon did not mean an immediate reduction in the number of farms. In 1635 Sir Edmund Verney altered the constable's return to Archbishop Laud's depopulation survey to say that he had:

> converted to pasture between thirty and forty acres of land by estimation which had until then been always used in tillage and that he is the user and owner of that land, but there is no decay of houses in the parish

and he commented that the statement was:

> all . . . truth . . . for though there be some houses down yet there are more erected in their places, of which he needs take no further

---

[34] This reconstitution involved the complete parish records of Middle Claydon, together with records of events in the adjoining parishes involving Middle Claydon residents where so named.

notice. I am well acquainted what is intended in this business of conversion, therefore let the return be made according to this direction, and let him make no other.

However, the change to pasture farming also meant that where the new farms were not occupied by tenants who needed resettling from their old holdings, they were offered on the open market. The new tenants were often outsiders with experience of the necessary pastoral management techniques. In 1623 two Whitchurch men took newly enclosed farms. In 1656–8 five farmers from outside the parish were given leases. All were from nearby: two had been farming the pastures of the long-deserted village of Hogshaw, one was from the enclosed parish of Grendon, and the other two came from East Claydon and Grandborough. That, and the changes to the landscape, the smaller fields, different farm buildings and stock, the hedges, and the greener tinge to the environment, were the immediate results of enclosure.[35]

Most other changes were more gradual, but enclosure was a turning-point in the affairs of all three villages. In Middle Claydon it brought the effective demise of old tenures and practices, even if their residual influence remained for a generation. It marked the end of one stage of the accumulation of property and the development of a great estate, but ushered in a much longer-term process of farm enlargement and population reduction. It also enabled the Verneys to replan farms and village away from their own house, preparing for the grandiose palace to be built by the second Earl in the 1750s. In East Claydon enclosure also followed the concentration of landownership, and there too it altered tenures. In the ten years after enclosure complaints about poverty in the parish became more common; by the end of the century population had been stabilized and farm sizes were rising. Steeple Claydon, where the Verneys made their successful bid to prevent enclosure in the 1670s, went a very different way. There the consequent fissuring of land ownership was followed by a swelling population in the late eighteenth century and the continuing predominance of small farms.

An overwhelming social contrast between the Claydons was

[35] Cl. H. Deeds 1623/3 and 1623/7 dated 30/3/23; 1658/1 dated 17/11/58; 1658/2 dated 2/8/58; 1656/4 dated 19/1/56/7; 1656/10 dated 3/12/56; 1656/12 dated 9/3/56/7. Memorandums and S.E.V. to S.R.V., 13 March 1634/5 R2.

apparent by 1800. Population and farm size had been affected by the long-term consequences of enclosure and estate policy, but so had the range of occupations in the three communities, as shown in the *Posse Comitatus* for Buckinghamshire in 1798. Middle Claydon's men were predominantly farmers, with farm servants and labourers supporting them. Steeple Claydon's men offered a wide variety of artisan trades and commercial services. East Claydon lay somewhere between these two extremes. In all three communities the role of women as economic providers was vital; and their profitable participation in lacemaking was one of the reasons why at the end of the eighteenth century dairying work in north Buckinghamshire was usually men's work, as Joseph Mayett's autobiography clearly shows. The structural change to a pastoral economy, with its lower labour requirements, which accompanied enclosure, provided the economic rationale for the transition to a 'close' village with large tenant farmers and few craftsmen and labourers, which was an ideal vehicle for estate management on the large aristocratic estate in the eighteenth century.[36]

[36] *The Buckinghamshire Posse Comitatus 1798*, ed. I. F. W. Beckett, Buckinghamshire Record Society, vol. 22 (Aylesbury, 1985); *The Autobiography of Joseph Mayett of Quainton 1783–1829*, ed. A. Kussmaul, Buckinghamshire Record Society, vol. 23 (Aylesbury, 1986), pp. 8, 11, 15–16.

3. Estate management in eighteenth-century England: the Lowther–Spedding relationship in Cumberland

JOHN BECKETT

In her report 'Large Estates and Small Holdings in England', written as a preliminary study for the Eighth International Economic History Congress held in Budapest, Joan Thirsk concluded that the increasingly positive attitude towards estate management on the part of the gentry by the later seventeenth and early eighteenth centuries 'was propelled by land stewards, who were becoming a more cohesive professional group, and who finished up in the late eighteenth century as the most highly paid of all professional men'.[1] As landlords were tempted to absent themselves from home for long periods, with regular meetings of Parliament, the growth of the London 'season', and a preference for urban life, the need to entrust their property to hired managers inevitably increased. Consequently, as Dr Thirsk acknowledged, these men played a vital role in the spread of agricultural improvement and efficiency. In his recent survey of post-Restoration landed society Christopher Clay has upheld this judgement, concluding that the movement towards 'ring fence' estates was largely due to 'the increasing tendency to employ the modern type of land steward, who saw his task not just as that of a mere rent collector but as an active manager whose business it was to improve his employer's property to the utmost'.[2]

[1] J. Thirsk, 'Large Estates and Small Holdings in England', in P. Gunst and T. Hoffmann (eds.), *Large Estates and Small Holdings in Europe in the Middle Ages and Modern Times* (Budapest, 1982), p. 74. For a similar view, expressed twenty years ago, see J. D. Chambers and G. E. Mingay, *The Agricultural Revolution, 1750–1880* (London, 1966), p. 202.
[2] Christopher Clay, 'Landlords and Estate Management in England', in Joan Thirsk (ed.), *The Agrarian History of England and Wales*, volume v, *1640–1750* (Cambridge, 1985), part II, p. 180.

Despite their acknowledged importance relatively little is known about individual eighteenth-century stewards. Edward Hughes wrote about them in 1949, but he persistently referred to the men involved as 'estate agents', a term inappropriate in the eighteenth century. G. E. Mingay produced a rather more substantial offering in 1967, but with the exception of comments by David Howell, and one or two pertinent case-studies, the pioneer estate managers have been relatively neglected.[3] Moreover, there is a contradictory tendency to hold with the view of stewards as playing a vital role, and yet to picture them as rapacious, untrustworthy, and weak-willed.[4] The latter view is undoubtedly derived from contemporary disparagement of venal stewards, but it has all too easily been pounced upon by historians anxious to introduce the odd juicy snippet into what might otherwise appear a rather dry account.[5] This somewhat jaundiced view of stewards as increasing efficiency while robbing the till is not necessarily very helpful to an understanding of the process of estate improvement, and in seeking a realistic assessment of change and development in English rural society during the eighteenth century it is useful to look once again at the much-maligned estate steward.[6]

[3] Edward Hughes, 'The Eighteenth-Century Estate Agent', in H. A. Croone, T. W. Moody, and D. B. Quinn (eds.), *Essays in British and Irish History* (London, 1949), pp. 185–99; G. E. Mingay, 'The Eighteenth-Century Land Steward', in E. L. Jones and G. E. Mingay (eds.), *Land, Labour and Population in the Industrial Revolution* (London, 1967), pp. 3–27; D. W. Howell, 'Landlords and Estate Management in Wales', in Thirsk (ed.), *Agrarian History*, V, II, pp. 252–97; Gary Firth, 'The Roles of a West Riding Land Steward, 1773–1803', *Yorkshire Archaeological Journal*, 51 (1979), 105–16; D. P. Gunstone, 'Stewardship and Landed Society: A Study of the Stewards of the Longleat Estate, 1779–1895', University of Exeter M.A. thesis, 1972; E. M. Jancey, 'An Eighteenth-Century Steward and his Work', *Transactions of the Shropshire Archaeological Society*, 56 (1957–8), 34–48; Joanna Martin, 'Estate Stewards and their Work in Glamorgan, 1660–1760: A Regional Study of Estate Management', *Morgannwg*, 23 (1979), 9–28.

[4] For an example of the disparaging view see J. J. Hecht, *The Domestic Servant Class in Eighteenth Century England* (London, 1956), p. 158.

[5] Corbyn Morris, *A Plan for Arranging and Balancing the Accounts of Landed Estates* (London, 1759); John Mordant, *The Complete Steward* (2 vols., London, 1761). Both Clay and Howell, writing about stewardship in Thirsk (ed.), *Agrarian History*, V, cite examples of incompetence, and note the contemporary reputation for dishonesty among stewards.

[6] The few published accounts of estate stewards usually depict men of integrity: see the items by Firth, Gunstone, and Jancey in n. 3 above, and also Peter Roebuck, 'Absentee Landownership in the Late Seventeenth and Early Eighteenth Cen-

On landed estates where the owner chose to devolve responsibility – and what this meant varied considerably in practice – the
steward became the linchpin of management. To him fell the tasks
of maintaining the house, gardens, and park, of letting farms,
collecting rents, surveying boundaries, drawing up accounts,
handling industrial enterprises, and even acting as electoral agent.
As agricultural improvement rendered the task increasingly complex, a body of literature appeared designed to inform the steward
of his responsibilities.[7] Experts believed that stewardship was a skill
which required careful nurturing, although landlords tended to
take a more sceptical view, favouring lawyers, tenant farmers, and
a host of other would-be stewards before men with any basic training. The poor reputation enjoyed by stewards in the eighteenth
century was largely a result of the disparaging comments made of
part-time and lawyer-stewards by so-called experts. In any case,
relatively few owners committed complete control into the hands of
an employee. Although the degree of initiative allowed to the
manager varied according to the landlord, most recognized the need
to visit, or at least to send instructions to the steward. Inefficient
management reflected on the landlord since it usually stemmed
from a failure to attend to the affairs of the estate or to ensure close
control of the steward. Contemporary commentators persistently
urged landlords to visit their estates frequently and to check
accounts regularly.[8] If, after so much encouragement, they failed to
do so, incompetence and even venality were at least in part their
own fault.

---

turies: A Neglected Factor in English Agrarian History', *Agric. Hist. Rev.*, 21
(1973), 1–17; J. V. Beckett, 'Absentee Landownership in the Later Seventeenth
and Early Eighteenth Centuries: The Case of Cumbria', *Northern History*, 19
(1983), 87–107.

[7] Giles Jacob, *The Complete Court Keeper or Land Steward's Assistant* (London,
1713); Edward Laurence, *The Duty of a Steward to his Lord* (London, 1727);
Mordant, *The Complete Steward*; Anon., *The Modern Land Steward* (London,
1801). The books grew in number and, individually, in size.

[8] *An Essay concerning the Decay of Rents and their Remedies, written by Sir
William Coventry about the year 1670*, in Joan Thirsk and J. P. Cooper (eds.),
Seventeenth-Century Economic Documents (Oxford, 1972), pp. 79–84;
Laurence, *The Duty of a Steward to his Lord*, p. 57; *Gentleman's Magazine*, 7
(1737), 104–6.

I

The ideal estate steward was competent at his work and honest. He was also committed to developing and improving his employer's estate; and one way of counterbalancing some of the more lurid accounts of venal stewards is to look in detail at the career of individuals who held such posts. Detailed analysis at a local level often helps to fill out our knowledge of wider issues, as Dr Thirsk's researches have shown over many years.[9] The case in question concerns the role played by John Spedding (1685–1758), steward for much of his life to Sir James Lowther (1673–1755), the West Cumberland landowner and coal entrepreneur. Edward Hughes noted that Spedding was a particularly good eighteenth-century example of an agent, but he did not appreciate the full value of the man, or the multiplicity of the roles that he played.[10] In fact, Spedding's career reveals the high level of competence which could be achieved, and the close relationship which could exist when an absentee owner had perforce to rely on a steward. As such he can be seen as an example of the genre, although his employer's lack of interest in agricultural improvements means that the case most clearly demonstrates the relationship which came into being on a minerals-based estate rather than one on which agricultural improvement was a priority.

In Cumbria, far distant from London, the majority of the larger landowners were absentee and relied on paid stewards. With its hostile climate the region was not particularly susceptible to agricultural improvement, although it was possible for progressive farming to take place even in the barren wastes of northern Cumberland, where the Earl of Carlisle's steward John Nowell was a pioneer. By comparison with Carlisle, landowners who were ready to improve estates they owned elsewhere in the country all too often disregarded their Cumbrian property. Sir James Lowther was such a man. His extensive estates in West Cumberland sat squarely on the coalfield, and the attitude taken towards farming was governed by this fact. Because many of the miners were part-time, the policy was

---

[9] Joan Thirsk, *English Peasant Farming: the Agrarian History of Lincolnshire from Tudor to Recent Times* (London, 1957); *Economic Policy and Projects: The Development of a Consumer Society in Early Modern England* (Oxford, 1978); *The Rural Economy of England* (London, 1984).

[10] Hughes, 'The Eighteenth-Century Estate Agent', p. 185.

to let the land in small parcels to men who would also work in the collieries. Improvement therefore became impossible, and although Lowther encouraged advanced farming methods on his Middlesex estate from the 1730s, and even on his Whitehaven home farm, he stubbornly resisted any attempts to introduce lease covenants which did anything more than ensure that tenants did not exhaust the soil. When marl was found on the estate in 1729 Spedding wrote to tell Lowther that its use in the area would be beneficial to farming, but he evinced no enthusiasm from London.[11]

John Spedding was not born with a silver spoon in his mouth. His father, Edward Spedding, was one of Sir John Lowther's tenants when John was born, but by 1687 he had taken up the tenancy of Akebank, one of Lowther's farms at Moresby, to the north of Whitehaven. He proved a less than adequate tenant, and by 1696 was in arrears with his rent. As a distant relation of one of Lowther's stewards he was found employment on or around the estate, and in 1700 he was appointed to a position in the customhouse. However, in 1706 Edward Spedding died in poverty.[12] Five years before this the fifteen-year-old John Spedding was hired by Lowther as a domestic servant, partly to increase the size of his establishment at Flatt Hall on his retirement to Whitehaven. Of Spedding's education and background little is known, but he clearly impressed his employer. He witnessed Sir John Lowther's will, and he organized and paid for the mourning following his employer's death in 1706.[13] In the months which followed, Spedding ruthlessly stepped over anyone who threatened his hopes of preferment in the Lowther management hierarchy. When in August 1706 Anthony Benn was shown to be incompetent, Spedding took over responsibility for the manor court books, while in October he wrote to Sir James Lowther informing him of the duplicity of John Gale, the colliery steward –

---

[11] Beckett, 'Absentee Landownership', 101; C[arlisle] R[ecord] O[ffice], D/Lons/W, John Spedding to Sir James Lowther, 26 Feb. 1729; Lowther to Spedding, 4 Mar. 1729.

[12] CRO D/Lons/W, Sir John Lowther's Commonplace book, fol. 57; Correspondence, William Gilpin to Sir John Lowther, 31 Oct. 1696; Lowther to Gilpin, 25 June 1698; James Lowther to Sir John Lowther, 16 Dec. 1699; Lancashire RO, Will of Edward Spedding, pr. 1706.

[13] CRO D/Lons/W, Miscellaneous correspondence, bundle 25, William Smith to Sir John Lowther, 18 Apr. 1700; Estate memoranda papers, bundle 6, bill for mourning; D/Lons/L Additional wills and settlements, 1565–1706, will of Sir John Lowther, 18 Oct. 1705.

his own uncle. Lowther was impressed, and told William Gilpin, his estate steward, in January 1707 that he was 'well satisfied with Spedding's diligence and capacity'. Gale's work, he added, would 'naturally fall to him in time', and in March 1707 Spedding was appointed colliery steward. Lowther offered him the same salary as Gale, £40 a year, with a proviso that it should be reduced while he continued to live at Flatt Hall. Spedding credited himself with the full amount, for which he earned a reprimand from his employer.[14]

When John Spedding became colliery manager in 1707 he held what was in effect the number two post on the estate. Traditionally overall responsibility was in the hands of the estate steward. Thomas Tickell was succeeded in this post at his death in 1692 by William Gilpin, who was a lawyer, and a member of a lesser gentry family with a small estate east of Carlisle. Gilpin (1658–1724) was primarily appointed to oversee Lowther's affairs in West Cumberland, but he also became a considerable local figure in his own right. He was appointed to the post of Comptroller of Customs at Whitehaven, and in 1718 he became Recorder of Carlisle.[15] By now he was aged sixty; his intention was clearly to hand on the Whitehaven business to his son Richard, who had also trained as a lawyer, and by 1717 was occasionally substituting for his father on Lowther's legal business. In fact, he turned out to be neither as efficient nor as competent as his father, and from the time he took over full responsibility in 1722 he fell foul of John Spedding's minute attention to business. He was frequently away from the town – he succeeded his father as Recorder of Carlisle in 1724 – and his accounts were often late in presentation. Spedding's letters through the 1720s were carefully designed to show Gilpin in the worst possible light.[16] This did not necessarily work to his advantage; indeed, in February 1728 Lowther mentioned a young man he had met in London whom he was considering as a replacement for Gilpin.

---

14 CRO D/Lons/W, James Lowther to William Gilpin, 17 Aug. 1706, 2 Jan., 21 June, 7 Oct. 1707; John Spedding to James Lowther, 27 Oct. 1706, 30 Mar. 1707.

15 CRO D/Lons/W, Memoranda books, indenture of 22 Apr. 1693; William Gilpin, *Memoirs of Dr Richard Gilpin of Scaleby Castle in Cumberland* (London, 1879), p. 14.

16 Carlisle Public Library, Whitehaven Town Book, entries between October 1717 and October 1729 concern Richard Gilpin's court keeping; CRO D/Lons/W, John Spedding to Sir James Lowther, 2 July 1721, 9 Nov. 1726; Lowther to

However, by taking over the estate steward's duties one by one Spedding eventually made himself all but indispensable.[17]

By contrast with Gilpin's slipshod performance Spedding had been a model of consistency. He had run the collieries with considerable skill and acumen through a difficult period during which Newcomen engines were first deployed in West Cumberland, gunpowder was introduced for blasting, and new methods of ventilation were brought into operation in order to overcome some of the problems which occurred with deeper mining. Above and beyond this he had stood in for the Gilpins during their frequent absences from Whitehaven; he had acted as an election agent; he had been treasurer for, and active in organizing the building of Holy Trinity Church in 1714 and 1715; and in the 1720s he had supervised alterations at Flatt Hall.[18] The result was that when Lowther finally decided to dispense with Richard Gilpin's services in 1730 he took the opportunity of changing the management structure in favour of Spedding. Since Spedding had no training in the law he could not inherit the whole mantle, so Lowther transferred the legal business to a part-time employee but left Spedding with all the other responsibilities of the estate stewardship.[19] At the same time John's younger brother Carlisle effectively replaced him as colliery steward, and the two brothers were to run the estate in tandem until Carlisle's death in 1755.[20]

Spedding, 2 Feb. 1727; Estate memoranda papers, box 6, Benson Highmore to James Lowther, 17 Aug. 1724. The rift opened up during the 1720s because of Richard Gilpin's failure to push forward the enfranchisement of Lowther's Whitehaven tenants, which was regarded as necessary if Sir James was to strengthen his electoral position in Cumberland.

[17] CRO D/Lons W, James Lowther to John Spedding, 10 and 15 Feb. 1728. Spedding's response to the suggestion of a young man from London was to suggest that he should take over part of the rent-collecting: Spedding to Lowther, 21 Feb. 1728. It is clear from the estate ledgers that Lowther allowed this change to take place: Ledger, 1723–37.

[18] CRO D/Lons/W, John Spedding to James Lowther, 18 Oct. 1710, 1 June 1720; Whitehaven papers, bundle 29; Whitehaven Public Library, bundle 41, Minute book re. Holy Trinity Church.

[19] CRO D/Lons/W, James Lowther to John Spedding, 31 Mar., 30 Apr. 1730.

[20] For an account of Carlisle Spedding's career see J. V. Beckett, 'Carlisle Spedding (1695–1755), Engineer, Inventor and Architect', *Transactions of the Cumberland and Westmorland Antiquarian and Archaeological Society*, 83 (1983), 131–40.

II

The range of John Spedding's activities on behalf of Lowther was considerable. On a day-by-day basis it was his role to collect rents and let farms, to supervise the tenants, and to ensure that they maintained an adequate standard of farming. Spedding was also expected to survey properties that Lowther had it in mind to purchase, and on occasion to contract for the land. In the case of small properties in the vicinity of Whitehaven it was not necessary to obtain Lowther's approval, although for substantial acquisitions he always referred to London for advice.[21] However, Lowther's concern with the coal-bearing propensities of the estate – rather than with its agricultural potential – probably explains why the normal succession through the administrative hierarchy was via the colliery stewardship. In addition to a general oversight of colliery affairs and accounts, Spedding was expected to take responsibility for promoting the mining and sale of Lowther's coal. This involved routine work such as drawing up colliery surveys, as a result of which he was able to point out in 1730 that he had been

> brought up from his youth in the management of collieries, and having for upwards of twenty-five years last past had the principal collieries in the neighbourhood of Whitehaven under his care and having made as good remarks in all that time as he was able to make of the nature and spread of the several coals in that part of the country is the better able to give his opinion of them.[22]

Spedding also had a variety of other tasks. In 1725 Henry Curwen of Workington asked Spedding to advise on the feasibility of mining coal on his estate. After inspecting the property Spedding encouraged Curwen to think of leasing to Lowther, a clear example of his employer's interests taking precedence.[23] Keeping an eye on the coal trade was also part of Spedding's role. From 1709 he was one of Lowther's nominated trustees on the Whitehaven Harbour

---

[21] CRO D/Lons/W, Estate papers, bundle 24, memorandums at Abbey Holm, 1731; John Spedding to Sir James Lowther, 6 Nov. 1734, 14 Oct. 1737, 10 Feb. 1744, 2 June 1745.

[22] Public RO PC1/4/106, fol. 72, evidence taken in the case of William Wood, 1730. For many years Spedding had demonstrated a willingness to take on other tasks when Lowther's employees left or died: CRO D/Lons/W, John Spedding to James Lowther, 25 Mar. 1709.

[23] CRO D/Lons/W, John Spedding to Sir James Lowther, 1 Sept. 1725.

Board, and from 1722 he kept the accounts. This enabled him to inform Lowther about the state of harbour finances, and about planned extensions and repair work.[24] Although Lowther generally refrained from active involvement in the coal trade, during the 1730s he invested in a number of vessels, and again it was Spedding's responsibility to acquire these.[25]

Apart from the estate and collieries Spedding undertook a number of other tasks on Lowther's behalf. In 1720 he supervised building alterations at Flatt Hall, and in 1729 he was elected to a governorship of St Bees school. The latter was a strategic position since Spedding was one of the three governors party in 1742 to a fraudulent lease granting coal royalties in the school lands to Lowther. On a number of occasions he acted as an election agent for Lowther, including the Appleby campaign of 1723 after Lowther had been unseated for Cumberland the previous year. In the 1740s he took charge of Lowther's negotiations to acquire burgages in Cockermouth which he hoped to turn into a pocket borough. On other occasions he was to be found distributing charity in White-haven on Lowther's behalf.[26] For these various roles he received a less than princely salary. From £40 in 1707 it was raised to £50 in 1721, and to £60 in 1728, at which it remained until Lowther's death. Carlisle Spedding received a substantial increase in salary when Sir William Lowther inherited the estate, and it is possible John also enjoyed a rise, although there is no evidence of his having done so.[27]

III

Although Lowther made little effort to improve the farming prac-tised on his Cumberland estates, the relationship with Spedding is significant because it illustrates how a close union could grow up

[24] CRO D/Lons/W, Minutes of the Harbour Trustees, 5 Apr. 1709, 22 July 1724, 26 Apr. 1726.
[25] CRO D/Lons/W, John Spedding to Sir James Lowther, 6 Nov. 1734.
[26] CRO D/Lons/W, John Spedding to Sir James Lowther, 1 June 1720, 24 Oct. 1729, 30 Jan. 1740; Lowther to Spedding, 28 Sept. 1710; D/Lec/170, Thomas Simpson to Thomas Elder, 22 Jan. 1747; J. V. Beckett, *Coal and Tobacco: The Lowthers and the Economic Development of West Cumberland, 1660–1760* (Cam-bridge, 1981), p. 24.
[27] CRO D/Lons/W, James Lowther to William Gilpin, 21 June 1707; Colliery Accounts, Midsummer 1721; Colliery Ledgers, 1727–32, entry for 25 December 1728; Beckett, 'Carlisle Spedding', 135.

between employer and employee, and how this could be used to the landlord's advantage. Spedding was Lowther's representative in Whitehaven, and he was expected to make known the party line. At a meeting of the ships' captains in 1720 Spedding 'entertained them so long . . . that a good many of them dropped off'. Letters sent from London often included specific instructions regarding the attitude Spedding was to convey in Whitehaven to certain proposals. In 1723, for example, Lowther wrote a long letter detailing the tactics he wanted to see pursued in the town in relation to the coal trade, and concluded by telling Spedding 'you will direct [your brother] how to talk'. A year later, when Lowther was considering moving the bulk of his interests to Scotland, Spedding was told to put his house up for sale as an indication of his employer's seriousness. On other occasions Spedding was instructed to read certain parts of Lowther's letters to individuals or to groups of people in the town.[28] He was expected to convey Lowther's views on harbour developments at meetings of the trustees, and to use the veto granted to his employer by the Whitehaven Harbour Acts of 1709 and 1712. He was even expected to forge Lowther's handwriting.

Spedding clearly did his job well. He was adept at getting information, and a hard bargainer. Over time, he became wholly attuned to Lowther's way of thinking, and when a colliery acquisition was in contemplation in 1731 Lowther noted that since Spedding was fully acquainted with his views on such matters there was little need for him to send instructions. Lowther was later to recognize that it was 'notorious in the country you are my agent in everything'.[29] Passing travellers could even conclude that Lowther knew nothing about the business of his estates, and relied entirely on paid servants – an assertion rapidly dispelled by even a cursory glance at the surviving correspondence.[30]

For Spedding there was a heavy price to pay in Whitehaven. His uncovering of John Gale in 1707 produced a lifetime of enmity with the Gale family, and he also made other enemies. His position,

---

[28] CRO D/Lons/W, John Spedding to James Lowther, 13 Nov. 1720; Lowther to Spedding, 21 Sept. 1723, 14, 21 Mar. 1724, 14 Oct. 1736.

[29] CRO D/Lons/W, James Lowther to John Spedding, 28 Sept. 1710, 6 Nov. 1731, 21 May 1751; Spedding to Lowther, 19 May 1728, 22 June, 2 Oct. 1743.

[30] W. A. J. Prevost, ' "A Trip to Whitehaven to visite the coal works there in 1739" by Sir John Clerk', *Transactions of the Cumberland and Westmorland Antiquarian and Archaeological Society*, 65 (1965), 312.

described by one opponent as that of 'mermidion', inevitably provoked resentment, and during the 1740s he had to fight a prolonged
legal battle with a local tobacco merchant, Walter Lutwidge.[31] His
willingness to accept such unpopularity was born out of a recognition that his time in Lowther's employment had given him
financial security, and a position locally that he could not have
expected in view of the family's circumstances at his father's death.
By 1745 he was recognized as being one of the leading townsmen.
This improvement in his fortune and status made it not surprising
that, as he told Lowther, 'the improvement of your estate . . . has
been the chief concern of my life'.[32]

There is no evidence to suspect Spedding of dishonesty, and he
claimed to have resisted efforts at bribing him into recommending
individuals to Lowther for preferment in the customs house.[33] In
any case, Lowther's attention to detail was such that no steward
could expect to survive unless he demonstrated loyalty. Apart from
the thrice-weekly correspondence, it is clear that Lowther went
through the accounts with a fine toothcomb. In the 1740s it was
reckoned that the two men took a full three weeks to sort out estate
business at the beginning of Lowther's annual summer visit to
Whitehaven.[34] When, on occasion, Spedding made a mistake,
Lowther was quick to pounce. In 1725 Spedding was asked to
explain a small error in the accounts; five years later Lowther was
unhappy with a lease he had drawn up; and in 1737 Spedding was
reprimanded for advancing money too readily in a mining project
undertaken by Lowther with Walter Lutwidge, and for buying an
unseaworthy collier on Lowther's behalf. The latter was *The Globe*,
which Spedding claimed after inspection was sound, but which
turned out to be worm-eaten and cost over £1,000 to be made
serviceable.[35] But these were forgivable instances in more than half
a century of devoted service.

[31] CRO D/Lons/W, John Spedding to James Lowther, 8 Jan. 1724; DX/524/1,
Lutwidge Letterbooks, Walter Lutwidge to John Cookson, 18 Jan. 1747.
[32] CRO D/Lons/W, Miscellaneous correspondence, bundle 44, letters from Sir
Everard Fawkenor, December 1745 and January 1746 re. the Jacobite uprising;
Spedding to Lowther, 8 Dec. 1742, 28 Dec. 1744.
[33] CRO D/Lons/W, John Spedding to Sir James Lowther, 25 Nov. 1742.
[34] CRO D/Lons/L, Miscellaneous letters 1550–1872, John Stevenson to Richard
Stevenson, 16 Mar. 1742.
[35] CRO D/Lons/W, James Lowther to John Spedding, 7 Dec. 1725, 28 Feb. 1730,
16 Apr. 1737; Estate Ledger, 1737–58, fol. 204.

Lowther responded to Spedding's loyalty by extending trust in the opposite direction. It became impossible to consult Lowther without Spedding being told, either through a copy of the offending letter, if this was the means of communication, or by a comment in one of Lowther's letters to his steward. Trying to denigrate the servant to the master became, in the opinion of Walter Lutwidge, like trying to move Skiddaw – the Lake District peak then thought to be the highest mountain in England.[36] John Stevenson, a close friend of Lowther's, told Spedding in 1750 that Sir James had frequently told him how thankful he was that he had met Spedding.[37] The two men developed considerable respect for each other. Lowther's letters included comments about the local gentry, London affairs, and his own relatives. He frequently expressed concern for Spedding's health, and in 1737 sent him 'spectacles to fasten by the side of your temples'.[38] Spedding ventured his own comments on occasion, as in 1723 when he 'greatly rejoiced to hear of Sir Thomas [Lowther's] being likely to match into so noble a family and heartily wish more of your family would take your advice and follow his good example' – a pointed reference to Sir James's own celibacy.[39]

Spedding's loyalty was purchased with a modest salary, but there were also important supplements. As Whitehaven harbour accountant he received £5 a year from 1722, rising to £10 in 1741.[40] Lowther's intention was that he should further supplement his income with a sinecure in the customs house. In 1726 negotiations began with Sir Robert Walpole for a position at Whitehaven, but Spedding finally had to be content with the post of searcher at Berwick on Tweed. Although reputedly worth between £80 and £100 annually, during his first six months the fees turned out to be less than £8, which made it hardly worth while. However, he held on to the post, and was finally rewarded with the collectorship of harbour duties at Whitehaven in 1746.[41] In addition to these income

---

[36] CRO DX/524/1, Walter Lutwidge to Sir James Lowther, 3 May 1747, 21 Mar. 1749, to Cousin Baynes, 12 June 1748.

[37] CRO D/Lons/W, John Stevenson to John Spedding, 23 June 1750.

[38] CRO D/Lons/W, Sir James Lowther to John Spedding, 23 Jan. 1735, 3, 5 Nov. 1737.

[39] CRO D/Lons/W, John Spedding to James Lowther, 3 Apr. 1723.

[40] CRO D/Lons/W, Minutes of the Harbour Trustees, 26 Apr. 1725, 26 Aug. 1741.

[41] CRO D/Lons/W, James Lowther to John Spedding, 1, 3, 13 Dec. 1726, 28 Jan.,

supplements Lowther may also have given Spedding one-off sums of money which did not appear as salary, as was the case with Carlisle Spedding.[42] But more significant for John Spedding were two considerations: first, Lowther encouraged him to develop his own business interests; and second, he was led to believe loyal service would be rewarded with family succession in the stewardship.

IV

Lowther's encouragement of John Spedding's business interests was clear from an early stage in the relationship. In 1715 Lowther invested £350 on behalf of his steward in the national lottery. Later he invested in South Sea stock for Spedding – on which the steward made a loss in the 1720 financial crisis. However, doubtless on Lowther's advice, Spedding had spread his investment portfolio, and had also put £400 into government redeemables. In 1723 Spedding still had £220 of South Sea stock which Lowther looked after for him, and he held on to this until 1738, when he transferred it to his son James. He also lent money on mortgage; in 1740, for example, to pay a portion of £500 on his daughter's marriage he called in a loan of £400 to a local landowner, Benson Highmore.[43] That Spedding does not appear to have expanded his London investments almost certainly came about because of the varied interests he built up in Whitehaven. In 1727 he leased from Lowther, jointly with three other partners, a Whitehaven ropery. Lowther bought his colliery ropes from the company. Problems arose during the 1740s when Walter Lutwidge claimed he had not been fully reimbursed for his expenses, and the partnership was dissolved in 1746. Thereafter Spedding carried on the works alone. The company was sold in 1765, seven years after Spedding's death, for £1,800.[44]

10 June, 2 Nov. 1727; Spedding to Lowther, 25 Feb. 1728; Minutes of the Harbour Trustees, 28 June 1746.

[42] Beckett, 'Carlisle Spedding', 135.

[43] CRO D/Lons/W, Cash transactions book, 1703–54, fol. 45; James Lowther to John Spedding, 8 Apr., 14 Nov. 1721, 15 June 1723, 19 May 1724, 9 Jan., 15 July 1725; Spedding to Lowther, 28 Dec. 1740.

[44] CRO D/Lons/W, Estate ledger, 1737–58, fol. 37; Sir James Lowther to John Spedding, 9 Nov. 1754; DX/448/14, Millbeck estate accounts 1774–88, unnumbered fol. re. Ropery Company.

Spedding also partnered his brother and Thomas Patrickson in a timber and brewery company. In 1737 they borrowed £630 from Lowther, and eight years later they leased part of a timber yard from him. The company expanded during the 1740s as Whitehaven's trade grew and its shipping requirements increased, although Spedding made his interest over to his son in 1748. The brewing part of the company benefited from the Lowther connection by acquiring cheap grain, which Lowther imported in the 1740s and 1750s to ease local supply problems. Finally, Spedding held a one-eighth share in the ill-fated Whitehaven glasshouse scheme of 1732.[45]

Spedding's loyalty was also encouraged by the prospect of his family inheriting the stewardship after his death. He informed Lowther in the autumn of 1715 that he intended to marry, but the ceremony is not actually recorded until July 1716, two months after the birth (and subsequent death) of a son to John and Ann Spedding. Two further sons, Lowther (1718–46) and James (1719–59) – the names are surely significant – and a daughter, Mary (1721–94), survived infancy.[46] Unfortunately neither of the two sons proved to be the successor that Spedding expected. Both sons were employed about the estates by 1737, and in 1740 Lowther became collector of harbour duties on a salary of £20 a year. By 1744 John Spedding was concerned that despite his best endeavours his elder son was not turning out to be capable of succeeding him because of his inattention to business. However, this never became a serious issue since Lowther Spedding died two years later.[47] James Spedding, to whom Sir James Lowther stood godfather, was employed by his patron in London from the summer of 1737. Lowther was pleased with his progress, but from the summer of 1739 James turned his attention towards the thriving Whitehaven tobacco trade. In November 1740 he sold his father's South Sea stock and annuities to finance a vessel to Virginia. Over the following years he became one of Whitehaven's most successful mer-

[45] CRO D/Lons/W, Estate ledger, 1737–58, fols. 85, 219; Sir James Lowther to John Spedding, 9 Apr. 1747; Beckett, *Coal and Tobacco*, pp. 138, 147–53, 198.

[46] CRO D/Lons/W, James Lowther to William Gilpin, 18 Oct. 1715; PR/84/1, Holy Trinity Church Registers, entries for 12, 29 May, 22 July 1716.

[47] CRO D/Lons/W, Sir James Lowther to John Spedding, 20 Nov. 1736, 7 June 1737, 3 Apr. 1740, 5 Apr. 1746; Spedding to Lowther, 7 May 1740, 6 Jan., 28 Dec. 1744.

chants.[48] Ultimately the succession from John Spedding passed to his brother Carlisle's son, also James.[49]

Although Spedding had failed to produce a son to succeed him in the stewardship the progress of his family had been considerable. From 1747 James Spedding began to acquire landed property at Armathwaite near Whitehaven, while his daughter Mary married into the Cumbrian lesser gentry in 1740. John Spedding himself was of no mean substance, leaving assets reckoned at £6,500 at his death – following a stroke – in 1758. Surprisingly, for such an organized and efficient administrator, he died intestate, but by this time the family fortunes had been transformed. His surviving son James was now a successful merchant and minor landowner, who, by the time he died in 1759, held the position of sheriff of the county. James's son, John (1747–81), was a country gentleman in his own right, with no attachment to the Lowther estate. Carlisle Spedding's son James, who succeeded to the stewardship on the deaths of his father in 1755 and his uncle in 1758, acquired Summergrove, a small estate in west Cumberland, in 1761.[50] The Speddings were now firmly established among the lesser gentry, a far cry from their straitened circumstances at Edward Spedding's death in 1705. If the salaries Sir James Lowther paid were apparently low, the overall result of stewardship for the Speddings was particularly impressive.

V

The role of estate stewards in eighteenth-century England was an important one which is often under-estimated. John Spedding's career helps to illustrate both the complexity and the significance of the task. From 1707 until 1730 he served Sir James Lowther in the post of colliery steward, a particularly critical period during which the first Newcomen engines were introduced at Whitehaven and important technological breakthroughs enabled coal production to be pushed to ever-higher levels. From 1730 he formally took over a series of other roles which he had gradually been filling during the 1720s through the inadequacy of Richard Gilpin. He now came to

---

[48] CRO D/Lons/W, Sir James Lowther to John Spedding, 24 May, 12, 23 July, 8 Nov. 1737, 13 Nov. 1740, 3, 12 Mar. 1741; Spedding to Lowther, 7 Nov. 1740.
[49] Beckett, 'Carlisle Spedding', 137.
[50] J. C. D. Spedding, *The Spedding Family* (Dublin, 1909), p. 99.

control the whole of the estate affairs, while his brother Carlisle acted as colliery steward. Spedding held this position until his death in 1758, at which point he had completed nearly sixty years' service to Sir John (d. 1706), Sir James (d. 1755), Sir William (d. 1756), and Sir James (1736–1802) Lowther. It was a remarkable record, and as far as the evidence allows he appears to have been honest, efficient, and committed to improving the Lowther properties in Cumberland.

The primary role John Spedding was expected to fulfil involved the collieries, and as such he was not representative of estate stewards in general. On Lowther's estates little attempt was made to introduce improved agricultural practice, largely because farming was regarded as secondary to mining. Sir James Lowther was not an agricultural improver in Cumberland, despite the efforts he made on his Middlesex estates, and this left Spedding little room for manoeuvre. Although Spedding accepted that land had to be made available in small parcels for men who would combine farming with work in the collieries, this did not mean he had no interest in agricultural improvement. In 1757, for example, he employed the Scottish agriculturalist Robert Maxwell to inspect the Lowther estates at Abbey Holm and to make suggestions for improving farming practice; and on the same visit to Cumberland Maxwell also inspected the Armathwaite property of James Spedding.[51] On an estate which abounded in minerals, however, the role of the steward was primarily that of looking after the resources, and developing them to the owner's specifications. Such was the significance of minerals that even after 1730 Spedding's letters to Lowther continued to be filled with information relating to the collieries and to the coal trade, with relatively little space being devoted to agricultural affairs.

The relationship which developed between Sir James Lowther and John Spedding was based on mutual respect and cultivated loyalty. By rewarding Spedding's ability and honesty, Lowther ensured that his steward would do all he could to promote the family interests at Whitehaven. However, there was no question of trusting to luck in these matters, and Lowther's handling of the relationship illustrates the care and concern that a sensible eighteenth-

---

[51] R. Maxwell, *The Practical Husbandman* (Edinburgh, 1757), pp. 248–67, 296–304.

century landowner took to ensure the best interests of his estate.[52] First, Spedding was gradually entrusted with additional responsibilities until his reliability was beyond doubt. It took time, since even in the 1720s Lowther was considering introducing a new estate steward from outside of Whitehaven, and it was only in 1730 that he showed how impressed he had been by Spedding's performance by altering the management structure in his favour.

Second, Lowther kept as close an eye on Spedding as was commensurate with residing for the majority of his life in London. He visited Whitehaven each summer, if his health permitted, at which point he went carefully through all the business transacted since the previous visit. Accounts and papers sent to him in London were scrutinized and errors highlighted. Letters were exchanged two or three times a week. Even allowing for the fact that Lowther was a particularly conscientious landlord, these were precisely the type of actions which contemporaries recognized as being critical for maintaining loyalty and honesty.[53] Third, Lowther upheld his steward's authority against whatever accusations were levelled at him, so much so that outsiders could even believe Spedding was the guiding force behind the estate administration.

Fourth, although Lowther did not pay Spedding a particularly impressive salary as a means of ensuring loyalty, he made sure that the steward had every opportunity of pursuing financially lucrative business interests of his own, even to the extent of putting up capital for the timber and brewery company. Such a policy was also employed by other eighteenth-century landowners. John Hardy, who was Walter Spencer-Stanhope's steward in the West Riding of Yorkshire between 1773 and 1803, was paid just £80, but he also enjoyed a favourable farm lease as well as having time to pursue a successful attorney's practice and to profit from investments in ironworks. Thomas Davis, steward on the Marquess of Bath's Longleat estate in the last quarter of the eighteenth century, also had a favourable farm lease as well as permission to undertake private business such as acting as an enclosure commissioner. By allowing

---

[52] Firth, 'The Roles of a West Riding Land Steward', pp. 108–9; Gunstone, 'Stewardship and Landed Society', pp. 26ff.

[53] Huntington Library, California, Montagu MSS, box 80, Mo 5978, Elizabeth Montagu to Sarah Scott, 28 July 1775; Martin, 'Estate Stewards and their Work in Glamorgan', 18; Roebuck, 'Absentee Landownership in the Late Seventeenth and Early Eighteenth Centuries', 1–17.

Spedding leeway to carry forward his own business enterprises Lowther not only had a trustworthy supplier from whom he could purchase colliery ropes, but also a steward with an intimate knowledge of industrial conditions in Whitehaven. Such a situation was in the interests of both men.

Finally, Spedding's loyalty was maintained through his family. Lowther stood godfather to his second son, James, and took him to London to introduce him to business affairs in the City. He also allowed Spedding to employ his sons on the estate, and to pay them for doing so, as well as making it clear that they could expect succession to the stewardship in due time. The fact that this did not occur was no fault of John Spedding. This ploy of offering the succession was found elsewhere; at Longleat, for example, Thomas Davis was succeeded by both his son and his grandson, and the family held the stewardship continuously from 1779 until 1839.[54]

What the Lowther–Spedding partnership illustrates is the all-pervading significance of finding a good man to run the estate and then ensuring his loyalty. When it succeeded, as in this case, it produced a situation where, over time, employer and employee came to enjoy a mutual respect, and to develop a genuine friendship. But it had to be worked at, and it was landlords who left too much to chance – by failing to visit the estate, failing to answer correspondence, failing to audit the accounts, or just by failing to take sufficient notice of what was happening on their estates – who suffered the perils of venal, disloyal stewards. Cases of maladministration are not difficult to find, but they reflect as much on the landowner's integrity as on that of the steward, and the progressive estates of the eighteenth century were certainly not those of landlords who chose to ignore the day-to-day running of their interests.

[54] Gunstone, 'Stewardship and Landed Society'.

4. 'Vain projects': the Crown and its copyholders in the reign of James I

RICHARD HOYLE

In the renewed prosperity of the late sixteenth and seventeenth centuries, English landowners were faced with the problem of devising ways of increasing the revenue they drew from their tenants, whose rights were often protected by custom and the common law. The study of the varying strategies they employed to overcome the inflexibilities in their income has been one of the preoccupations of early modern agricultural historians. Yet we are still some distance from possessing a wholly satisfactory understanding of the demands landlords made on their tenants, the extent to which the tenants resisted, and the success that each had in extending or defending their claims. And, strangely, we are almost entirely ignorant of the extent to which these same conflicts were fought over the ground of the Crown's own lands. The Crown, after all, was still the nation's largest landowner, and the income from the royal demesnes was still important in supporting the state. While the Crown had certain advantages over the private landowner, not least in its possession of a system of private courts which administered its estates, the problems it faced were common to all landowners – of eradicating custom, increasing fines, and if possible converting customary rents to market rents in the face of tenant resistance. The Crown's success – or failure – may therefore be indicative of the more general success or failure of English landlords in the early seventeenth century.[1]

---

[1] This chapter was written whilst I was still Joan Thirsk's doctoral student, and I am grateful to her – as always – for the suggestions and criticisms that arose from many discussions and her reading of an early draft. When she sees it here, I hope she will forgive the odd ruse to conceal why I was writing it. It is intended to open up a new area for research: many of the questions it raises will be considered in the collection of essays *The Estates of the English Crown, 1558–1640* (forthcoming).

Under Elizabeth, the Crown lands, like so many other aspects of Crown finance, were allowed to drift unsupervised, and the attempt to increase landed revenue in the reign of James I must therefore be seen against a background of general neglect. The story is, for the most part, unfamiliar, but something of it has long been known. Salisbury's apologist, Sir Walter Cope, wrote of Salisbury's industry towards all the Crown lands, his organization of surveys, the valuation of coppices, the increase in fines of copyholders for lives, and the sale of confirmations to copyholders of inheritance.[2] Of modern historians, Professor Campbell mentioned in passing Jacobean plans for the enfranchisement of its copyhold tenants.[3] Professor Kerridge appreciated that the management of the Crown's estates was put on a new, more professional footing in the early years of the reign, while Professor Youings contributed a short section on 'The Failure of Efforts at Reform [on the Crown Estates] in the Reign of James I' to the fourth volume of the *Agrarian History*.[4] Of the purely local writers, Dr Tupling published a fine account of the Crown's treatment of its copyholders in eastern Lancashire as long ago as 1927, while Dr Pettit ranged far beyond the purlieu of his Northamptonshire forests to discuss the Crown's attempts to increase its woodland revenue.[5]

As it happens the full story cannot be told. The documentation is fragmentary and dispersed. Promising lines of enquiry fade away after time in much the same way as the executive initiatives they describe. There is valuable material in the Jacobean State Papers, especially for the period of Salisbury's Lord Treasurership. For other periods – Dorset's Lord Treasurership and the entire 1610s – there is little or nothing. Dorset's own records seem to be lost, as are those of the Treasury Commissioners of 1612–14. Even the Privy

---

[2] Sir Walter Cope, 'An Apology for the Late Lord Treasurer Sir Robert Cecil, Earl of Salisbury', in J. Gutch (ed.), *Collectanea Curiosa* (2 vols., Oxford, 1781), I, pp. 119–33. G. Goodman, 'Aulicus Coquinariae' (1650), printed in *The Secret History of the Court of King James I*, ed. Sir W. Scott (2 vols., Edinburgh, 1811), I, pp. 151–3, merely paraphrases Cope.

[3] M. Campbell, *The English Yeoman* (New Haven, 1942), p. 138.

[4] E. Kerridge, 'The Movement of Rent', *Econ. Hist. Rev.*, 2nd ser., VI (1953), 29–33; J. Youings in J. Thirsk (ed.), *The Agrarian History of England and Wales*, IV, *1500–1640* (Cambridge, 1967), pp. 268–74.

[5] G. H. Tupling, *The Economic History of Rossendale* (Chetham Soc., new ser., LXXXVI, Manchester, 1927), ch. 5; P. A. J. Pettit, *The Royal Forests of Northamptonshire: A Study in their Economy 1558–1714* (Northamptonshire Record Soc., XXIII, 1968), *passim*.

Council Registers for the first part of the reign are destroyed, burnt in the Whitehall fire. There is valuable material in Caesar's papers and Cotton's collections, and in the records of the Exchequer itself.[6] Admittedly the low premium placed on paper documents by the early custodians of the archives of the Exchequer and Duchy of Lancaster has allowed much to be lost, yet there are pickings in the land revenue papers, especially in the so-called 'auditor's memoranda' (LR9). That said, the archives of the Duchy of Lancaster contain few informal papers. The records of the administrators of the Queen's jointure are almost all gone. In these circumstances a great deal must remain to be learnt from the records of individual manors, much of which passed into private hands in the later years of the reign. This chapter hopes to establish a framework which the history of such manors may amplify and modify.

I

The point might be made that there was not one Crown estate in the early seventeenth century, but several. The body of the Crown's lands were in the charge of the Exchequer with smaller estates managed by the administrators of the Duchies of Lancaster and Cornwall. From the Exchequer's lands was carved the Queen's jointure: in 1610 the grant of the reconstituted estates of the Duchy of Cornwall to Henry Prince of Wales, as Dr Croft has recently shown, precipitated a crisis in the royal finances.[7] Only the experience of the estates of the Exchequer and Duchy of Lancaster will be considered here.[8] While the estates were independent, each with its own staff of administrators, there was almost certainly an element of common political direction over their management, but it remains most convenient to describe the progress of reform on the Exchequer and duchy estates separately.

It would be widely agreed that the Elizabethan legacy of estate

---

[6] All manuscript references in this chapter (unless otherwise stated) are to sources lodged in the Public Record Office, Chancery Lane, London. Quotations have been modernized.

[7] P. Croft (ed.), 'A Collection of Several Speeches and Treatises of the Late Lord Treasurer Cecil . . . ', in *Camden Miscellany*, XXIX, Camden Soc., fourth ser., XXXIV (London, 1987), pp. 257–9.

[8] The management of the Duchy of Cornwall's estates will be described by Dr G. D. Haslam in his contribution to *The Estates of the English Crown*.

management was not a happy one. There was a general weakness of direction. Too great a responsibility was placed on the Lord Treasurer, and Burghley's concern was inevitably with the smooth receipt of rents rather than the improvement of revenue. (It must be remembered that the control of the Crown's landed revenues was a small component of the duties of all Lord Treasurers.) The Crown's officers were lightly supervised. An obvious tension existed between the interests of the Crown and the concerns of its stewards and bailiffs: in the sixteenth century opportunities for peculation, especially of fines, were rife. Few surveys were made during Elizabeth's reign, but then, surveys were unnecessary when the administration was geared to collect the same rents year after year. The rent of individual properties was rarely, if ever, increased. The fines on leases (which were negotiated centrally) remained fixed at low levels, usually two years' rent, from the mid 1560s onwards. Fines on copyholds were normally equally low. It had also been usual for the Exchequer and duchy to confirm the fines it received from its customary tenants, especially those in Northern England.

The contrast between the old regime and the new was not merely that between corruption and reform, or a parsimonious queen and a profligate king. Given that the Exchequer was in surplus for much of Elizabeth's reign, the stimulus for a more businesslike approach to the landed revenue was absent. There can be no doubt that a shortfall in income was inevitable when a single monarch was replaced by a royal family.

The reform of the Exchequer and the King's finances is usually dated from the appointment of Salisbury to the Lord Treasurership on the death of Dorset in May 1608. Perhaps Dorset has suffered two posthumous misfortunes: firstly that his papers are lost and secondly, that he had for his memorialist his chancellor, Sir Julius Caesar. Caesar, unquestionably, was a reformer and Dorset, in Caesar's eyes, was not. It was his desire to have 'a man of under-standing and wisdome, some religiously wise, irreproveably honest, uncorrupt, stout, and chasteminded Joseph' to bring order to the Exchequer. His Joseph was Salisbury, whose frantic labours in his first few weeks as Lord Treasurer Caesar recorded at length.[9] Yet Dorset was not without policies towards the Crown lands.

---

[9] L. M. Hill (ed.), 'Sir Julius Caesar's Journal of Salisbury's First Two Months and Twenty Days as Lord Treasurer: 1608', *Bull. Inst. Hist. R.*, XLV (1972), 312.

It was Dorset and not Salisbury who instituted the Jacobean survey of Crown lands; his surveyors were active as early as 1604. That a general survey was in progress clearly came as a surprise to Salisbury and Caesar: after they heard of it at a meeting on 11 May 1608, the most prominent of Dorset's surveyors, John Hercy, wrote to Salisbury to explain the background and circumstances of his work, and to defend himself from allegations of its excessive cost.[10] Hercy explained that Dorset had made warrants to him in the summer of 1607 for the survey of Crown manors where the tenants held copies of inheritance or for lives. In February 1608 Dorset had issued a further warrant to make surveys of manors in Hampshire, Wiltshire, Somerset, Dorset, and Devon.[11] By May 1608 Hercy had surveyed 300 manors in twenty-five counties. Hercy estimated that the paper books of these surveys stretched to 10,000 pages, most of which had been engrossed, save for those nine counties, the fair copying of which Hercy had deferred on the instructions of Dorset. Nor was Hercy the only surveyor in the Exchequer's employment in these years: John Johnson and John Goodman had surveyed the north-western manors of the Crown in the spring of 1604.[12]

While commentators such as Sir Robert Johnson argued that the making of surveys was the prerequisite to bringing the Crown estates to some order, Dorset's surveys were designed to go hand in hand with a general enfranchisement of the estates.[13] A commission

---

[10] SP14/32 nos. 85 and 85I. Hercy's work as a surveyor appears to have been previously unnoticed. Hercy was of Cruchfield, near Maidenhead in Berkshire, and claimed descent from the Nottinghamshire family of his name (*Victoria County History, Berkshire*, III (1923), p. 101; *The Four Visitations of Berkshire*, I (Harleian Soc., LVI (1907), p. 97)). I owe this identification to Sara Gillot together with the observation that Hercy and his son, John, with whom he made surveys, was in the service of the Earl of Shrewsbury. For correspondence between the Hercys, father and son, and Shrewsbury, see *Catalogue of Arundel Castle Manuscripts* (in Sheffield City Library) (Sheffield, 1965), pp. 206, 207, 209, 212, 217, and Historical Manuscripts Commission, *Manuscripts of the Marquis of Salisbury* (24 vols., 1883–1974), XVIII, pp. 328–9. John Younger was BA Oxon and admitted as a Barrister at Lincoln's Inn in 1607. He made surveys in the company of his father and had his own commission in the Midlands in 1608. Joseph Foster, *Alumni Oxonienses 1500–1714* (4 vols., Oxford, 1891–2), II, p. 697.

[11] SP14/31 no. 28.

[12] CRES40/19A no. 6 (a breviate of their surveys).

[13] For Johnson, see *Calendar of State Papers Domestic 1602–3* (1870), pp. 176–9, discussed by S. J. Madge, *The Domesday of Crown Lands* (London, 1938), pp. 51–3. I hope to publish a later version of this letter addressed to King

to sell copyholds had been made to Dorset as early as October 1603, and in 1606 Dorset calculated on raising £40,000 in this way.[14] When Johnson and Goodman reported on the north-western manors in 1604, they took care to assess the value of the lands if sold in fee farm and the willingness of tenants to buy.[15] Hercy was expressly instructed to negotiate with tenants willing to purchase their copyholds in fee farm in his commission of February 1608,[16] but the evidence of his surveys shows he had been engaged in this work much earlier. Hercy's survey of Tidmarsh (Berkshire) of January 1604 is little more than a book of the offers made by tenants to buy their fee simples. The survey of Clewer Brocas (Berkshire) of the following March contains the signed offers of tenants as marginalia.[17] The survey of Bulford (Wiltshire), made by Hercy in March 1604, contains for each messuage three memoranda of offers to buy in fee farm, one undated (but possibly of 1604), one of September 1606 and one of April 1608. The agreements made in 1606 also offer to double the rent of each tenement.[18] The tenants of Rowington (Warwickshire) in a note appended to the survey made in August 1605 indicated their willingness to buy their freeholds on reasonable terms.[19] Copyholders' offers to buy their tenements are marked in a number of surveys made in 1608 (for example Sanderville (Buckinghamshire) and Frodingham (Hampshire)).[20] In his letter to Salisbury on the latter's appointment as Lord Treasurer, Hercy reminded him that the Crown had to accept these offers by midsummer 1608 or else they would lapse. Salisbury rejected the option of enfranchisement explored by Dorset – for a time.

Dorset also appears to have attempted to limit the possibilities of peculation by stewards. In the summer of 1607 Hercy carried instructions from the council to the stewards of manors that they were to admit tenants only in the company of the surveyor of each county and a Justice of the Peace dwelling nearby. In a letter dated 31 July, Dorset asked the Custos Rotulorum of Essex that the

James I. The link between enfranchisement and the need to survey was made by the surveyor Ralph Agas in a memorial in Caesar's papers, Brit. Lib., Add. MS 11,497, fol. 342r–v.

[14] C66/1611 dorse; SP14/4 no. 31; F. C. Dietz, *English Public Finance* (2 vols., London, 1964), II, p. 145.

[15] CRES40/19A no. 6 (unfoliated).   [16] SP14/32 no. 85 (fo. 160v).

[17] LR2/209 fols. 20–52.   [18] LR2/203 fols. 369–82.

[19] LR2/228 fol. 178   [20] LR2/209 fols. 183–92; 203 fols. 20–31.

county justices might assist stewards in the assessing of copyhold fines. No copy of the directions given Hercy is known, but the Essex letter shows that their purpose was to reduce the possibilities for stewards' peculation rather than increase fines.[21]

So, when Salisbury became Lord Treasurer, he inherited from Dorset well-developed plans to survey the estates, enfranchise copyholders, and limit the possibilities for peculation. In his turn, Salisbury introduced two innovations, both of which will, on inspection, be found to be more closely related to Dorset's policies than might otherwise be supposed.

In the first place Caesar tells us that Salisbury discovered 300 surveys, 'which before lay scattered in corners, which have already and will hereafter prove to the King's exceeding advantage in the leasing of lands'. Salisbury ordered that the surveys were to be lodged with the Lord Treasurer's Remembrancer. All auditors receiving a warrant to draw up a particular for a lease of surveyed property were to send word to Hercy in the Remembrancer's office, who was to search out details from his surveys and send them to the auditor to engross on the particular for the information of the commissioners for leases.[22] He then charged fourteen surveyors with making surveys of the other Crown manors which remained unsurveyed, suspending the leasing of tenements within these manors until the surveys were made and returned to the Exchequer.[23] Warrants were formally issued on 11 July, and at least some of the surveys were being actively engrossed in December.[24]

Secondly, in the Exchequer Chamber on 30 May, Salisbury rejected the 'vain projects' for enfranchisement which had been entertained by Dorset. His alternative policy was to place the granting of copies on a new footing. To this end, he ordered the dispatch to all 202 of the Crown's stewards and neighbouring justices of books of printed instructions (606 in all) for the assessing of fines.

---

[21] SP14/32 no. 85 (fol. 160v). Essex RO Q/SR 181/100, a copy of the calendar of which I owe to the kindness of the county archivist.

[22] LR9/9/1280/2.

[23] Hill, 'Sir Julius Caesar's Journal', 316 (where Hill reads 'sovereigns' for 'surveys'), 322 (where fourteen surveyors are dispatched), 325 (where twenty-one are mentioned), and 326. The surveyors were arranged in twenty-one commissions, listed in SP14/31 no. 29 (of ? July 1608 rather than the date in the calendar).

[24] Hill, 'Sir Julius Caesar's Journal', 322. Brief certificates for a number of the surveyors are in Brit. Lib., Lansdowne MS 166.

Caesar was impressed; he estimated that this would bring in to the Exchequer £6,000 for every £1,000 of fines collected previously. And, in a step which established the direction of his future policy, he declared the fines of the manor of Edmonton (Middlesex) to be arbitrary, and then confirmed them by decree at one year's value.[25]

The book of 'Directions for commissioners with the steward of each manor to assess fines of copyholds . . . ', often referred to as the 'printed instructions', became the basis of Crown policy for at least the next decade and a half.[26] The commissioners (normally the county surveyor with a JP, or two JPs – the echoes of Dorset's instructions are clear enough) were to assess fines in the company of the stewards. The important feature is that the book attempted to cut through all customary levels of fining. The commissioners were to assess the value – the yearly profit of the tenement – and satisfy themselves of its tenurial status. Where the copyhold was held for lives and paid a heriot, 9 years' *value* was to be taken for a new demise for three lives, 7 years' for two lives, and 5 years' for one life. Where by custom no heriot was due, 10, 8, and 6 years' value were to be taken.

In the case of copyholds of inheritance, the commissioners were again to gauge the value of the tenement and where the copyhold paid a heriot, they were to take fines at the rate of 1.5 years' value, and where not, 2 years' value. Where the tenants claimed a certain custom of fining, it was to be accepted by the commissioners only if it was evidenced by the court rolls of Henry VII and earlier. Where the tenants maintained their custom in the absence of such proof,

---

[25] Hill, 'Sir Julius Caesar's Journal', 317–18, 323, 325, 326. At Edmonton Salisbury confirmed the existing custom, but altered the rate of fines from the one year's rent claimed by the tenants to one year's value as established by a survey made by Hercy in 1604. No fine was taken for the composition. E126/1 fols. 109v–110v, Greater London RO Acc. 695/42, confirmed by Act 7 James private no. 2.

[26] It is not certain that the printed book of instructions was issued to duchy stewards, but there are indications that it was. DL41/15/3 is a bundle of steward's certificates, mostly of late 1608, describing customs and in some cases referring to attempts to implement a policy of higher fines. (DL30/80/1088 is a stray from this bundle.) One (no. 4, for Whitbeck in Cumberland) refers to the Chancellor's letters of 23 July with 'a book of directions'; other stewards held courts in the company of two JPs. DL41/15/8 is a list of fines abated in Pontefract in 1616 from 1608 onwards suggesting fines were substantially increased in the latter year. At Clitheroe, the tenants refused to pay fines after September 1608 because they were assessed at much greater values than customary. J. T. Swain, 'Industry and Economy in North East Lancashire 1500–1640', Ph.D. thesis, Cambridge University, 1983, 107.

the tenants were to be admitted but the fines respited until the King's counsel had been satisfied as to the tenants' claims. In every case the stewards were to send estreats to the Exchequer. A letter to stewards of March 1609 makes clear the value of the surveys made during the summer of 1608 and earlier for this project. The engrossed surveys were in the process of being sent to individual stewards, and any who had not received a copy of the new survey for their manor were to have one on request. The valuations of improved values in the surveys were to form the basis of subsequent assessments of fines on tenants.[27] This explains why the original surveys in the Public Record Office are entirely on paper sheets; they are Hercy's drafts, written in the field. As evidence of this deduction, it may be seen that they often bear the signatures of jurors, signed offers to buy tenements, and more occasionally, notes as to how the surveys were to be engrossed. The engrossed texts were returned to the counties for the use of the stewards.

In retrospect the audacity of Salisbury's policy is astounding. At a stroke he cut through the problems traditionally faced by the Exchequer. He completely ignored local manorial customs in favour of taking fines at the market rate. By drawing his assessment of value from Hercy's surveys, involving commissioners, and insisting on the return of estreats, he removed the possibilities for corrupt behaviour by stewards. But one also suspects a failure to appreciate the practical difficulties of enforcing the executive will.[28]

II

How the printed instructions were received by tenants is more difficult to establish. At least two abstracts were made of the

[27] SP14/44 no. 4. The date of this letter is given as 24 Mar. in the copy at E163/15/33 fol. 11 and SP14/51 no. 19 at fol. 25r. A further order of 30 Nov. 1609 reminded the stewards to assess the fines in accordance with the values in the surveys. The auditors were asked to inspect the estreats to ensure that this was done. Any stewards who had not yet had their surveys were to have them on request. SP1/51 no. 19, another copy LR1/12 fol. 40v. As early as December 1608 Salisbury had a request for a copy of one of Hercy's surveys to allow a steward to hold a court. HMC *Salisbury*, XX, p. 283.

[28] There also appears to have been an attempt to invite copyholders to attend Salisbury to surrender their copies for leases for forty years or six lives. Such a letter was sent to the steward of the manor of Ombersley and drew objections from the Crown's lessee, Sir Samuel Sandys, of unjustified interference. SP14/43 no. 56.

certificates returned by stewards during late 1608, and these showed that many tenants claimed certain fines, some by prescription; but others, especially in the North, cited decrees made by the Exchequer under Elizabeth.[29] In either of these circumstances, the stewards appear to have handed the problem to the Exchequer to resolve. Only a few manors sued in the Exchequer court.[30]

It may be envisaged that Westminster in the autumn of 1608 was filled with Crown tenants arguing the fine detail of their manorial customs, and this may have prompted a change in tactics. The discovery that many tenants were prepared to stand by the familiar practice of their manor necessitated an investigation of their customs. In late 1608 a set of draft instructions was circulated amongst the auditors which envisaged the responsible auditor, county surveyor, and steward of each manor meeting together in the auditor's office to search the court rolls for evidence of uncertainty, passing doubtful cases over to the King's counsel.[31] By mid December a circular letter had been prepared for dispatch to the stewards of twenty-seven manors warning them that the tenants should come up to London with their court rolls to compound for their copyhold fines during Hilary term; and another circular was contemplated to all stewards along the same lines.[32] A further circular to stewards dated only to March enclosed the draft of a decree to confirm the customs of copyholders whose fines were (or had been declared to be) arbitrary.[33] Describing this policy in a memorandum to the King, Salisbury announced that where fines were acknowledged to be uncertain by custom, or where uncertainty could be proved, he intended to make them certain by decree in the Exchequer. Given that most tenants claimed their fines to be certain, Salisbury wrote that he foresaw great difficulties in discovering whose claims were genuine and whose not; he had therefore given instructions for all court rolls to be brought down to the Exchequer, where they were to be searched for evidence of variations in fining.

[29] SP14/37 no. 21, 20 Oct. 1608; no. 80, 17 Nov.

[30] See below, p. 84.

[31] LR1/12 fol. 1r, undated, but the next item in the book is of 30 November 1608.

[32] SP14/38 no. 25I, associated with letter of 14 Dec. SP14/44 no. 5, is a short note of copyholders summoned between 26 Jan. and 2 Mar. [1609]. SP14/58 no. 57 is a note by Bartholomew Haggatt dated only to 3 Dec. of the problems of obtaining a general composition.

[33] SP14/44 no. 4.

Where the claims could be justified by reference to the court rolls they would be allowed, but where deviations from the alleged custom could be found, even, in the case of monastic lands, from before the dissolution, the fines were to be declared arbitrary.

The memorandum continued by explaining that Salisbury had sent letters to those manors where copyholders of inheritance held by uncertain fines inviting the tenants to appear before Salisbury, Caesar, and the barons of the Exchequer to negotiate compositions for the payment of their fines at a lower rate than was stipulated by the book of directions. The resulting agreements were to be decreed by the Exchequer.[34] The tenants called before them had been charged by the printed book with fines of two years' value in place of which they had agreed to pay fines of one year's value in perpetuity with a down payment of two years' value as the price of the Exchequer's concession. Hence, in Salisbury's example, a copyhold worth £10 'upon the racke' (i.e., at a market rent, but not including the Crown's rent, which might be an additional 20s) and which was not liable to pay a heriot, whose tenant was by the book of orders to pay £20 for his fine, was to pay £20 for the privilege of paying fines of £10 in perpetuity.[35]

Salisbury had found a way of achieving an increase in recurrent income whilst claiming an extraordinary windfall, but it could not successfully be put into effect. In November 1609 Hercy was acknowledging the 'unexpected slowness' of copyholders to compound and was offering Salisbury advice as to how to persuade more to come forward.[36] The failure of the project is plain when the evidence of receipts for compositions is examined. Only in the two years following Michaelmas 1609 were any significant sums received by the Exchequer, in all less than £3,500. (Detailed figures are provided in Table 1.)[37] In the last year of Salisbury's life, no money

---

[34] To encourage confirmations to be made, the Parliament of 1610 enacted a government bill to give statutory confirmation to decrees made in this way in the duchy or Exchequer courts. This was to remain operative for three years; 7–8 James c. 21 (*Statutes of the Realm*, IV, part 2 (1819), pp. 1180–2).

[35] SP14/43 no. 113.

[36] SP14/49 no. 60. The advice appears not to survive.

[37] I am grateful to Dr D. L. Thomas of the Public Record Office for pointing out to me that the auditor's receipt books were the appropriate place to search for evidence of the success of Salisbury's initiative. Table 1 is based on the receipts recorded under the head of payments by customary tenants for compositions. It includes receipts from the tenants of Tynemouth who were probably tenants by

was paid to the Exchequer for the purchase of compositions of Exchequer copyholds. In all, the tenants of only twenty-six manors appear to have taken advantage of the offer to compound for fixed fines (for the names of which see Appendix 1). An undated gazetteer of the Crown's manors in the view of the Exchequer (but of 1611 or 1612) lists only fourteen manors which had succumbed to the temptation of composition, eleven where fines had formerly been arbitrary and were now confirmed as certain, and three where certainty had now been confirmed. Only a dozen or so decrees can be found on the Lord Treasurer's memoranda rolls. The offer to compound produced an abysmal response.[38] In the last months of his life, Salisbury moved towards a new enfranchisement of Exchequer copyholders. A commission to this end was granted in November 1611, but there is no evidence of its being put into effect.[39]

III

The commission for enfranchising copyholders of 1603 was empowered to negotiate with the tenants of the Duchy of Lancaster. By April 1604 an approach had been made to Richard Molyneux, the duchy's steward of the Honour of Clitheroe in Lancashire, proposing the enfranchisement of tenants in the honour, a proposal which Molyneux sought to discourage on the grounds of the tenants' poverty. There were, he reported, fewer than ten tenants within the honour who could afford such expenditure.[40] This offer was repeated in April 1607, but resulted in a composition to confirm copyhold.[41] In late 1606 the duchy proposed to the steward of its Forest of Knaresborough that the tenants there should pay either larger fines or compound for their entry fines, but as the tenants were able to point to an Elizabethan decree establishing their

tenant right, but I have discounted sums paid in by the tenants of Middleham and Richmond (Yorkshire) for the renewal of their leases. For their difficulties, see R. Fieldhouse and B. Jennings, *A History of Richmond and Swaledale* (London, 1978), ch. 6, part 2.

[38] Brit. Lib., Lansdowne MS 166, fol. 274; SP14/51 no. 19. The decrees are listed in Appendix 1 below.

[39] C66/1915.

[40] Swain, 'Industry and Economy', 120, citing Wigan RO D/DZ/A4 (collections by Christopher Towneley), fols. 56r–v.

[41] Discussed below, p. 86.

customs, the duchy's interest appears to have petered out.[42] The Earl of Shrewsbury is to be found writing to his servant, the surveyor John Hercy, seeking to have Hercy head off some duchy tenants in the Peak who were enquiring about purchasing their fee farms.[43] In February 1606 the Privy Council wrote to the tenants of the duchy's manor of Newby in Yorkshire (who held by tenant right rather than copyhold) stressing the weakness of their estates since the unification of the kingdoms. The tenants were invited to confer with the commissioners for the enfranchisement of duchy copyholders to buy their estates in fee farm. The tenants chose to stand by their tenant right, sending a delegation to Dorset to plead that their tenant right estates be respected; but a faction within the tenants also petitioned Dorset enquiring what terms would be offered for their purchase. Nothing further appears to have come of this.[44] The copyholds of the manor of Wakefield were surveyed in the spring of 1607 and the tenants agreed to compound for their copyholds in the autumn, usually offering around seventy years' rent for the freehold. For reasons which are not clear, this was not proceeded with and the tenants finally compounded.

The attempt to raise capital from the duchy by enfranchisement was abandoned in the lifetime of Lord Treasurer Dorset. Between 1607 and 1610, the duchy tried to raise money by calling into question the validity of the copies of its tenants on its large northern manors. Copyhold was a customary tenure; copies could not be legally valid unless they met the acid test of a custom – that they had existed from beyond the memory of man. The duchy had on a number of occasions in the sixteenth century granted new copies of freshly disafforested lands or newly enclosed wastes, copies which, while administratively convenient, were technically insecure. So, the copyhold lands of the Honour of Clitheroe fell into two parts, the ancient copyholds which had existed from time immemorial,

---

[42] B. Jennings (ed.), *A History of Nidderdale* (Huddersfield, 1967), pp. 122–4. SP14/37 no. 107 may date from about this time.

[43] HMC *Salisbury*, XVIII, pp. 328–9.

[44] Leeds City Archives, Acc. 1448 (Clapham Parish Records in photocopy), nos. 214, 217. In July 1608 Auditor Fanshaw wrote that the Lord Treasurer was willing to take one course with those who would 'compound' and another with those who would not, but the context is far from clear: *ibid.*, no. 222. For the manor during the sixteenth century, see R. W. Hoyle, 'Lords, Tenants and Tenant Right', *Northern History*, XX (1984), 52–9. I hope to write further on Jacobean attitudes to Tenant Right.

and the 'Newhold', where copies of disafforested lands and vaccaries had been granted in 1507. In Wakefield copies had been granted of waste land throughout the sixteenth century.

In April 1607 five Privy Councillors (Ellesmere, Dorset, Suffolk, Northampton, and Salisbury) wrote to the duchy's auditor, Thomas Fanshaw, and a neighbouring gentleman, Mr Assheton of Leaver, pointing out that the copies of the Newhold were invalid. Fanshaw and Assheton were to call together all the tenants of the honour, whether they held by new or old copies, to tell them of the King's willingness to enfranchise and report the tenants' response to London.[45] The tenants' reaction is unknown, but the duchy sought to put pressure on the tenants by instituting a survey of the Newhold in January 1608 and suspending the admittance of all tenants to the manorial court. By May 1608 a delegation of eight tenants had negotiated the terms of a confirmation of the Newhold copyholds with Salisbury and the chancellor of the duchy, Parry, at a cost to the tenants of twelve years' rent (although the Crown demanded twenty years'). This agreement was confirmed by a fictitious suit in the duchy's own court. A bill alleging the illegal occupation of the Newhold was introduced by the Attorney General in November and a decree formalizing the agreement was made on 10 February 1609. The same claim of the illegal occupation of duchy lands by invalid copies granted in 1507 was made against Sir Richard Molyneux for lands in Croxteth and Symondswood, for which, like the tenants of the Clitheroe Newhold, he paid a confirmation of twelve years' rent and had a decree in his favour in May 1610.[46]

In the manor of Wakefield, following its change of heart over enfranchisement, the duchy moved to make a joint confirmation of copyhold fines and of those copies made of wastes. In November 1608 the Privy Council accepted the offer of the tenants to pay thirty-five years' rent for a confirmation, which was to include a doubling of all copyhold fines. A decree in the duchy followed, which was given the sanction of statute.[47] Pressure was placed on

---

[45] Lancs. RO DDKe/5/86 fol. 2r. This contains all the documents subsequently referred to. The account that follows is largely based on Tupling, *The Economic History of Rossendale*, ch. 5 and Swain, 'Industry and Economy', ch. 4.

[46] Lancs. RO DDM 17/105.

[47] Discussed in general by M. J. Ellis, 'A Study in the Manorial History of Halifax Parish in the Sixteenth and Early Seventeenth Centuries', *Yorkshire Archaeological J.*, XL (1959–62), 259–61 (although she thought that the initiative came

other duchy tenants whose titles were insecure. The tenants of Manningham hamlet in Bradford petitioned Salisbury to be allowed to proceed to a confirmation, but having attended the chancellor of the duchy in Michaelmas 1610, they were allowed to return home until recalled, which, so far as can be told, they never were. Those of Slaidburn likewise petitioned Salisbury for a confirmation, their copyhold having been called into question by the duchy, but again nothing came of the request.[48]

A further, more general campaign to bring the duchy's copyholders to enfranchisement or composition commenced in the late spring of 1611, the impetus for which may well have come from Salisbury and Caesar. In September 1610 Caesar had before him a project for copyholds, subscription to which was to be enjoined on the chancellor of the duchy, which did little more than develop the principles of the printed instructions of 1608. Where fines were acknowledged to be arbitrary, no action was to be taken. Where the tenants claimed to possess fixed fines, the steward, auditor, and surveyor were all to search for evidence of their past variability which they were to certify to the Exchequer; but where certainty was acknowledged, the tenants were to be offered a composition.[49]

Within six months these plans had been abandoned for something more radical; a general enfranchisement of the duchy's northern manors. On 12 March 1611 Thomas Fanshaw, the duchy's general auditor, was given instructions for a general survey of the duchy's copyholds, during which he was to establish the details of the tenants' customs.[50] His 'private instructions' authorized him to treat with the copyholders for the purchase of their estates in fee farm with the reservation of ancient rents, suit of court, the enfranchised lands to be held in socage. But, while this was the preferred course, if the tenants wished to remain copyholders, then he was to offer

---

from Wakefield itself); Bodleian Library, Oxford, MS Top Yorks c. 12, fols. 13r–15v. The decree is printed in J. Charlesworth (ed.), *Wakefield Manor Court Book*, Yorkshire Archaeological Society Record Series, CI (Wakefield, 1939), pp. 17–35. The resulting Act was 7–8 James private no. 1. A further duchy decree followed in May 1611. DL5/26 fols. 60v–69v.

[48] DL5/25 fol. 275; SP14/61 no. 85.

[49] Brit. Lib., Lansdowne MS 166, fols. 276–7, docketed by Sir Julius Caesar to 1 Sept. 1610. The propositions made by Mr Auditor Fanshaw on 23 August, *ibid.*, fols. 278–9, another copy of which is SP14/61 no. 67, follow the same conservative lines.

[50] Brit. Lib., Lansdowne MS 166, fols. 280–3; the quotation is from fol. 282v.

confirmations under the terms of the Act of 1610, confirming or reducing fines to certainty. Irregular copies of demesne and waste lands were to be confirmed. Where the tenants had commons by the explicit grant in their copies, or by prescription, Fanshaw was to offer either enclosure, with the reservation of a share to the King, or the sale of the commons to the tenants. And, the instructions continued,

> in which intreaties you shall not make any conclusion, but concealing from the tenants that you have not any power to conclude, you shall show unto them all the defects of their estates and the uncertainty of their fines and customs, acquainting them also (as you shall find fit occasion) that if his Majesty's occasions be not furnished by sums of money to be raised by the copyholders themselves, either for the purchase of their estates or settling of their customs, he shall then sell the same to other persons, from whom they cannot expect any such offer of favour and security as is now offered. And thereupon you shall press to understand from them what is the uttermost which they be persuaded to give unto his Majesty upon your said treaties.

Neither the surveys Fanshaw was to make nor the books of proceedings he was to keep survive. However, his accounts show him travelling about the north of England from 27 May to 26 August and about the north Midlands from 24 September to 11 October. It appears that he first made surveys, moving from Duffield Frith and other Derbyshire manors to Clitheroe (Lancashire), Bradford, Pontefract, Tickhill (Yorkshire), and Long Bennington (Lincolnshire), then Tutbury (Staffordshire) and Halton (Cheshire). He then repeated this circuit to take the answers to the King's propositions. Hence, he impanelled surveys at Wirksworth on 6 June and returned there on 19 July. In the autumn he travelled about to bring the tenants of the Honours of Bolingbroke, Tutbury, and Leicester and the manor of Long Bennington to composition.[51]

The duchy's tenants were generally hostile to these proposals. The reports of the local commissioners appointed for Clitheroe and Pontefract suggest that Fanshaw's bringing of 'his Majesty's great grace and favour' and his willingness to raise sums by confirmation rather than 'questioning their estates and customs' which he would have to do if he were 'not pleased graciously to deal with them' was

[51] DL41/33/14A.

received with little enthusiasm. The Clitheroe tenants made a 'great show of unwillingness to deal with us at this time', asked for further time, and thought that their customs and commons were as secure as could be made by decree. In the end an unwilling consent to proceed with composition was obtained. The Pontefract commissioners wrote that they 'did not find at the first any great desire the tenants had to deal with us'. After much persuasion the tenants made an offer of thirty years' rent for the purchase of their freeholds. At the end of the year Molyneux asked that the tenants of Westerby (Lancashire) should have further time to send a delegation to Salisbury. None of these hopes came to pass. A search of the duchy receiver's accounts and the Exchequer auditor's receipt books reveals no income from confirmations and only one case of duchy tenants – those of Whitley and Cogeshall in the Honour of Halton in Cheshire – taking their fee farms.[52]

IV

On Salisbury's death, the Exchequer was placed in the hands of commissioners for two years. Evidence for their management of the Crown estates is somewhat sparse. Salisbury's initiatives were probably allowed to lie fallow; it is noticeable that the commissioners' report on the possibilities 'for the repair of the king's estate and raising of monies' of about August 1612 neglects copyholders as a source of revenue, and no instances have been found of tenants compounding in 1613 or 1614.[53] Both Cotton and Bacon proposed to raise further income by enfranchising copyholders and the commission to enfranchise was renewed in June 1612.[54] A group of Exchequer officials, including the ubiquitous John Norden, toured

---

[52] SP14/64 no. 37; 65 no. 75; 67 no. 6; DL28/11/6 (unfoliated, recording payments from the tenants); DL44/903, SP14/104 no. 73. W. Beamont, *A History of the Castle of Halton and the Abbey of Norton* (Warrington, 1873), p. 105.

[53] J. Spedding (ed.), *The Letters and Life of Francis Bacon* (7 vols., London, 1861–74), IV, pp. 314–27. The same is true of other place papers of about this time, e.g. the undated and unsigned 'Considerations propounded . . . ', SP14/70 no. 44 and Brit. Lib., Lansdowne MS 165, fols. 233–6, 207–10, dated to 1612 and 1613.

[54] Cotton's proposals are: Brit. Lib., Cottonian MS Cleo. F VI fol. 44v; Bacon's: Spedding (ed.), *Letters of Bacon*, IV, pp. 327–37. The manuscript is undated, but may be that referred to in Bacon's letter to the King of 18 September, in Spedding, pp. 311–12; C66/1953 no. 27.

ten manors in Hampshire, Wiltshire, and Devon in March 1614, where they contracted to sell copyholds to the value of £11,928.[55]

Under the direction of Suffolk (Lord Treasurer 1614–19) and Sir Fulke Greville (chancellor 1614–21), the Exchequer attempted to enforce the provisions of the printed instructions whilst working towards (in the first instance) a further enfranchisement. Suffolk's device to obtain conformity was a letter sent to stewards in August 1615 which became known, because it prohibited the holding of courts, as the Great Restraint.[56] This described how some stewards had wrongly taken credence of customs pretended by tenants and others had allowed a backlog of fines to develop. In future they were to apply the book rigorously to any unassessed fines and seize the lands of any tenants who refused to pay the fines laid down. To assist the execution of the commission for enfranchising copyholds, all stewards were forbidden to keep any court barons or make admittances.[57] The immediate result was to revive old grievances over fines as at Holme Cultram (Cumberland), where the tenants had bought a confirmation (of an already certain custom) from Salisbury, and in the words of their steward would 'not condiscend to the printed instructions'.[58] At Ennerdale (Cumberland) the tenants refused to accept either the uncertainty of their fines or purchase their fee farms and petitioned Suffolk directly.[59] The plans for the enfranchisement appear to have been dropped. By 1618 Suffolk could describe the Great Restraint as having been introduced 'in expectation of some special service intended by his Majesty which by reason of other occasions was afterwards thought fit to be deferred'.[60]

Further instructions were issued in 1618 for the enforcement of the printed instructions. Where fines were acknowledged to be

---

[55] Their report is CRES40/18 fols. 187–93 and their book of agreements with tenants LR2/203 fols. 39–71v. A list of tariffs from this period is Brit. Lib., Cottonian MS Cleo. FIV, fol. 120. See also *The Narrative History of King James for the first Fourteen Years* (London, 1651), p. 56.

[56] Cumbria RO, Carlisle, PR122/254f. The warrant of 1618 cancelling the Great Restraint dates the initial letter to August 1614, but no letter of that date has been found. The text used here is dated August 1615, the month after the commission for enfranchisement was granted; the two are clearly connected. The commission is C66/2078 dorse (cf. *Calendar of State Papers Domestic 1611–18*, p. 298).

[57] Cumbria RO, Carlisle, PR122/254f.

[58] LR9/107, file of letters to the Earl of Suffolk as Lord Treasurer 1614–15.

[59] LR9/83, Ennerdale file, letters of 1615.   [60] LR9/9/1309.

uncertain, the book was to be implemented; where fines were 'pretended' to be certain, the tenants were to attend on the Lord Treasurer and chancellor to prove their claims and have their customs regulated by Exchequer decree.[61] There survives a list of manors whose tenants were called to the Exchequer in the summer of 1618 for this purpose. At least two northern manors had their claim to certain fines accepted, in the case of Warton (Lancashire) after their proofs had been scrutinized by Yelverton, the Attorney General.[62]

A further commission of 1623 empowered the confirmation of customary fines or the enfranchisement of copyholds, but, as I shall show, it attracted little business from the Crown's copyhold tenants.[63]

Whilst tenants certainly came to prove their customs before the Exchequer in 1618, there is no evidence that any of them bought confirmations at this time.[64] In this respect the duchy was more successful, but not exclusively so. In the thirty months between February 1618 and July 1620, no fewer than seventeen decrees were enrolled in the duchy's records for the confirmation of customs and fixing of fines. The manors involved are listed in Appendix 2; they included estates in Lancashire, Staffordshire, Leicestershire and Northamptonshire.[65] In most cases the tenants paid forty years' rent to have their fines fixed at a year's rent, but the duchy occasionally took a greater fine for the confirmation of copies of roodland,

---

[61] LR9/9/1309. In a substantial number of manors, no fines appear to have been taken between 1614 and 1618, for instance LR9/1/46.

[62] SP14/104 no. 72; Lancaster Public Library MS 230 unfoliated; LR9/9/1307 (discharge of Muchland). On a number of manors the Great Restraint continued into the 1620s. In July 1621 the Lord Treasurer and chancellor again ordered that fines were to be taken on all manors, but at the rates set down in the 1608 instructions. LR1/140 fo. 39. At Newby (Yorkshire) a similar order was made in 1619 but had not been put into effect by 1628. Leeds City Archives acc. 1448/223; PRO C21/B44/10, responses to plaintiff's question 9 (and DL5/29 fol. 55).

[63] See below, p. 99.

[64] A search of the Lord Treasurer's memoranda rolls about this time found no decrees; nor were payments traced in the auditor's receipt books, E401/2429, 2430.

[65] For the experience of one manor, Raunds (Northamptonshire), see Roger B. Manning, *Village Revolts: Social Protest and Popular Disturbances in England, 1509–1640* (Oxford, 1988), pp. 121–4, although Manning does not appreciate the extent to which the treatment of these tenants was part of a larger campaign.

demesnes, or former waste land.[66] The composition in every case was due in two instalments, one on the making of the decree and the other on its statutory confirmation. While the composition fines in the decrees total £17,984 3s 4d, only half was immediately gathered in, and the balance was often still outstanding in 1649.[67] As an inducement to the tenants, the commons were often sold to them as part of the general confirmation.

Although the duchy made a number of decrees, there is copious evidence of its tenants refusing to cooperate. The tenants of Westerby, in common with other Lancashire manors, refused the commissioners' overtures. The duchy agreed to sell a confirmation to the tenants of Chatburn, Worston, and Pendleton, save two who declined, and to the tenants of West Derby and Wavertree, on condition that a majority of the tenants would agree to be party to it. In the last case, the tenants, perhaps for want of numbers, failed to proceed to a decree. The penalty, either for individuals or whole communities who rejected the offer of confirmation, was the enforcement of the book of printed instructions.[68]

V

Jacobean policy towards copyholders on the estates in the view of the Exchequer and duchy veered between attempts to improve fines and bids to sell either confirmations of customs or enfranchisements.[69] In this they mirrored the policies of gentry the country

---

[66] Roger Kenyon was active making surveys of Lancashire manors in 1617, apparently to distinguish oxgang land from roodland. Lancs. RO DDKe/5/45, 46, 62.

[67] As on the Lancashire manors, Tupling, *Economic History of Rossendale*, pp. 158–9. The total is based on Appendix 2.

[68] Lancs. RO DDKe/5/66, 74; DL5/27 fol. 1308; 28 fols. 106r, 282; Leeds City Archives acc. 1448 no. 223. M. Gregson, *A Portfolio of Fragments*, ed. J. Harland (Manchester, 1869), pp. 145–9. The duchy decree and order books were searched until mid 1622 (the end of DL5/28) without any further decrees being found.

[69] The same devices were used on the estate of the Queen's jointure and Charles, Prince of Wales. Grants of confirmations by the queen are recorded in SP14 no. 50; 67 no. 28; 68 no. 50; 76 nos. 29, 106; LR2/326 fol. 46. The Prince of Wales made compositions in the Barony of Kendal, C78/504 no. 8; at Cheltenham, see Gwen Hart, *A History of Cheltenham* (Leicester, 1965), p. 92; and Bromfield and Yale (the tenants of which were not copyholders), statute private 3 Charles I c. 6 (noticed but not printed in *Statutes of the Realm*, V (1819), p. vi.).

over.[70] The incompatible policy options chosen by successive Lord Treasurers reflected a tension between irreconcilable aims, between increasing regular revenues and obtaining windfall sums by liquidating capital assets to pay off debts. Can their activities finally be judged a success?

All Crown administrators faced certain disadvantages. The most important was the sheer scale of the estates and the need to motivate and control innumerable minor officers. They also faced the problem of the Elizabethan legacy: the belief amongst tenants that past maladministration was really a display of the Crown's love for its tenants. When the duchy's commissioners went to Pontefract in 1611 and stressed to the tenants that their fines were uncertain in law, they reported that the tenants believed that if there was any uncertainty, 'it was so small that they would not believe that the King's majesty would take any advantage thereof'.[71] It was doubtless hard for the Crown to persuade away its image of sanctity.

Equally damaging was the inconsistency of purpose that the Crown displayed throughout the period. Not only did every attempt to sell confirmations, whether by Salisbury in 1608–12 or the duchy in 1607–11 and 1618–19 restrict the capacity of future Lord Treasurers to milch the estates, but from the tenants' point of view vacillation bred confusion, uncertainty, and scepticism. The tenants of Holme Cultram might not have been exceptionally troubled by successive projects. They possessed fixed fines. In 1608 they refused to pay the fines demanded by the book of instructions and in 1610 paid £300 to have their fines placed beyond reproach. In 1615 they were invited to enfranchise. In 1618 their fines were again challenged and in 1623 they were asked to purchase their fee farms.[72] The results of this constant tacking between raising fines and selling confirmations or freeholds was acknowledged by an anonymous writer of Salisbury's time or just after:

This business hath been often set in hand by the lords, and by themselves upon solemn debate with the barons of the Exchequer laid down again, when many tenants were ready to have gone that course which has made the tenants conceive that either good

---

[70] For some preliminary comments on this see Hoyle, 'Lords, Tenants and Tenant Right', 38–44.
[71] SP14/65 no. 75.
[72] SP14/37 no. 80; E368/536 ro. 211; Cumbria RO (Carlisle) PR122/254f; SP14/104 no. 72; LR9/6/712/1, LR9/9/1201.

assurance cannot be made to them, or that the state affecteth it not further then as a business which necessity enforceth, and thereupon many tenants who once did desire it, are now afraid therein.[73]

In this way, the tenants of Pontefract in 1611 remembered the cavalier treatment of the tenants of neighbouring Wakefield four years earlier.[74]

It is difficult to ascertain the success of the book of printed instructions without undertaking a large search through the surviving court rolls, now scattered through many repositories. There are indications that it met with real resistance. A good number of stewards cited decrees settling customs to the tenants' advantage in the estreats they made late in 1608: the steward of Rowington (Warwickshire) searched the court rolls, satisfied himself that the tenants possessed a custom of fixed fines, and returned a certificate accordingly.[75] Elsewhere the stewards attempted to implement the instructions to the letter and ran on to the rock of tenant intransigence. At Knowle fines were respited whilst the matter was passed to the council to decide, whilst in the Honour of Clitheroe the tenants refused to pay their fines assessed by the book of instructions: the resulting impasse lasted ten years until they had a confirmation of their custom.[76] Much the same happened at Newby.[77] It is true that few tenants complained to the Exchequer court, but others petitioned Salisbury.[78] Even where the principle of fining at one-and-a-half or two years' value was accepted, complaints could be made of the assessment of value in royal surveys.[79] The tenor of

---

[73] SP14/59 no. 44.   [74] SP14/65 no. 75.

[75] See above, p. 78; Warwicks. RO CR 1008/70. The steward (in the company of two JPs) examined court rolls dating back to 25 Henry VI.

[76] Knowle, Warwicks. RO CR 1886/2310 *passim*. The case was finally decided when the steward, John Hercy, attempted to take fines according to his own survey and the tenants sued the Attorney General; E112/128 no. 170, E134/9 James I/Hil. 21, E126/1 fols. 323v–324r. For Clitheroe, see Swain, 'Industry and Economy', 107.

[77] See above, p. 85.

[78] A search of the relevant Exchequer decree and order books revealed only the case of Knowle (n. 76 above) and that of Hemel Hempstead, E126/1 fols. 141v, 142r, 145r–148v. For petitions, see SP14/40 no. 21; 58 no. 43.

[79] LR9/61 pt 2 (auditor's memo. book) fol. 17v (petition of the tenants of Bishop Wilton, Yorkshire, requesting a new survey because of over-valuation); LR12/34/1260, petition of 1615 by a tenant of Fulborn (Cambridgeshire) to Lord Treasurer Suffolk. Allegations of over-valuation were also made at Knowle, where Hercy's working methods were unattractive. E134/9 James I/Hil 21.

the Great Restraint, that unassessed fines had accumulated in recent years because the tenants would not cooperate with stewards, rings true of much of the evidence. Indeed, the Exchequer seems to have been barely aware of events on any particular manor. After it cancelled the Great Restraint in 1618, a further order repeating the first had to be sent to auditors in July 1621.[80]

Earlier it was suggested that the proposal of late 1608 to allow tenants to compound arose from the practical difficulties of persuading them to accept the implementation of the printed instructions. Besides the cost of purchasing the confirmation, the fines established by Salisbury's decrees were the rack-rented values given in the surveys rather than those customarily paid: accordingly the confirmation may not have been an attractive proposition. The confirmations offered at other times were merely for the existing fines (although at Wakefield fines were doubled).

VI

Some more forward-looking tenants might have realized that accepting arbitrary fines calculated on the value of the tenement allowed future governments to revalue the tenement, a possibility which the purchase of a confirmation nullified. Yet there is copious evidence that the offer made to the tenants was but infrequently accepted; in some places only a minority of the tenants compounded.[81] The tenants of Wakefield who declined to compound in 1609 were offered a second chance in 1623. In the case of West Derby and Wavertree in 1620, the duchy was willing to proceed to a composition if half the tenants would assent: but nothing came of it. Considerable evidence from the same campaign reveals a general indifference to the duchy's overtures.[82] There could also be open hostility on the tenants' part. At Wakefield, where the negotiation of compositions was entrusted to Sir John Savile, antagonisms reached such a pitch that Savile sued a tenant in Star Chamber for slander and the circulation of libellous bills and rhymes.[83] Where

---

[80] LR1/140 fol. 39.
[81] It was accepted that some tenants, notably widows and minors, would be unable to compound.
[82] DL41/15/8; DL5/28 fol. 282 and above, pp. 88–9.
[83] Manning, *Village Revolts*, pp. 148–9, citing STAC8/258/5.

the Crown was able to claim that the tenants' very title was insecure, the reasons for coming to a rapid agreement were all the more cogent, but here Crown policy is revealed in all its full nakedness. The selling of compositions was little more than the sale of protection from the further attentions of the Crown's administrators and lawyers. The Crown was in the business of extortion.

It is still more difficult to know how many tenants obtained their enfranchisement during the reign. Each successive commission was enjoined to keep records of its meetings, but save for some scraps, all is lost. A full assessment must therefore await the publication of the patent rolls. The argument therefore proceeds largely from silence. While Dorset collected many offers from tenants, there is no evidence that any grants were made by him. Nothing is known of the success of the commission granted in 1611, but offers to purchase were actively solicited in the West Country in 1614. The commission of 1615 was acknowledged to have been abortive and that of 1621, on the evidence of its records, brought not a single agreement. Accordingly, many commentators were pessimistic about the plausibility of enfranchisement, but the option always remained open for an impecunious Lord Treasurer to explore.

The attraction was inevitably the possibility of releasing the capital value of the lands. One commentator thought that enfranchisement could raise £150,000.[84] Without doubt such sums were not beyond the bounds of possibility; the 1614 commission raised £11,928 from ten manors in a season's work. This compares favourably with the £12,000 Thomas Fanshaw claimed he had brought to the Exchequer in seven years of bullying the duchy's tenants.[85] But fee farming, as commentators thought it should be practised, brought the additional reward of enlarging the King's revenues by granting the freehold at double or treble the customary rent. Some of Hercy's bargains were made on the basis of doubling the rent. Sir Robert Johnson, Sir Robert Cotton, and Sir Francis Bacon all proposed granting fee farms at double or treble the customary rent in about 1611 or 1612. Indeed, Bacon went so far as to suggest granting

[84] Brit. Lib., Cottonian MS Titus B IV, fol. 256 (undated; probably a draft petition).
[85] CRES40/18 fol. 192v; F. Devon, *Issues of the Exchequer, being Payments Made out of His Majesty's Revenue during the Reign of James I* (London, 1836), p. 314.

all the royal lands in this way.[86] Yet they deluded themselves. Johnson outlined four options in his tract: to continue taking customary rents but with fines at a market valuation, fee farming upon the old rent, selling the fee simple without reservation, or selling in fee farm with improved rents. He preferred the first option, but if not that, the last. Johnson acknowledged that the tenants might not be interested in fee farming, but he thought that their doubts would be nothing once they realized that it would make an end to fines. When the people came to apprehend the advantages, he believed that they would praise it 'as the greatest favour that ever proceeded from a prince to a people'; indeed, discreetly handled, it might become the petition of the people themselves.[87]

Other commentators had their feet more firmly placed on earth.[88] Two anonymous and undated writers identified a wide range of problems. Not all tenants would wish, or be able, to enfranchise. There would be a need to maintain officers and courts and problems were envisaged in the collection of rents. The interest of any Crown lessees would have to be bought out. Tenants would require time to pay their compositions. Provision would have to be made for the transfer of commons and other customary perquisites. There were procedural problems and doubts about conveyances, and one of the writers (as we saw earlier) offered his opinion that much good will had been spent by previous vacillation.

Moreover one of these writers was sceptical that the tenants would be willing to pay a respectable sum for their fee simples. Tenants, he explained, would never pay forty or fifty years' rent when the contractors for the sale of Crown lands had bought the fee simple of copyhold lands for twenty-five years' rental value, or less for chantry lands.[89]

---

[86] For Hercy's work, LR2/203, marginalia of 1606 in his survey of Bulford, Wiltshire, fols. 365–82. For Johnson, see below; Cotton: Brit. Lib., Cottonian MSS, Cleo F VI fol. 44v (based on Johnson's figures); Bacon: Spedding, *Letters of Bacon*, IV, pp. 327–36.

[87] Johnson's thoughts on enfranchisement survive in two texts, one based on the other. The first, Brit. Lib., Lansdowne MS 165, fol. 146v, was docketed by Sir Julius Caesar to 25 Jan. 1611; the other, Cottonian MSS, Cleo. F VI, fol. 110v, dates from after the death of Salisbury. The quotation is from the latter text.

[88] SP14/59 no. 44, placed in the state papers under 1610 for no obvious reason. SP14/104 no. 74 is based on this text. SP14/104 no. 73 is incomplete. Its references to the Lords Commissioners probably makes it of 1612–14.

[89] SP14/59 no. 44.

This view contained many grains of truth. Even where Hercy negotiated the sale of copyholds for lives, his contracts appear to have held the promise of only small sums entering the Exchequer. At Frodington (Hampshire) some tenants offered over fifty years' rent, but others placed a very small valuation on their lands. Henry Ridge would give only £30 for the fee simple of the copyhold he rented at £3 4s 10d or £20 for the fee farm, but was outbid by a gentleman who offered £100 for the fee farm.[90] In 1606 at Bulford (Wiltshire) tenants by copy for lives offered paltry sums, for instance 20 marks and a double rent for a tenement valued to be rented at £10 or £20 and a double rent for sixty acres valued at £26 and rented for 33s 6d. Other tenants expressed themselves content for another man to buy the fee farm. The 1614 commission in the West Country was able to make sales at between forty and fifty years' old rent or between six and ten years' value. But both Hercy and the 1614 commissioners were selling tenements held by copies for lives, and the considerations taken for the fee farms were in the same range as the fines on new demises ordered by the book of instructions. Moreover, even at cheap rates, it is clear that neither Hercy nor the commissioners were able to liquidate entire manors. At Frodington only six tenants accepted in 1614 (including a lease-holder). At Bovey Tracey nineteen tenants contracted to buy their tenements, but seventeen refused and their freeholds were sold to a neighbouring gentleman.[91] The commissioners themselves thought they could have sold a third more tenements but for doubts over title and if longer days of payment had been offered.

Copyholds of inheritance were an even less attractive prospect for purchase, whether by the outsider or tenant. For the tenant there was little advantage in buying the fee simple of a copyhold of inheritance when the right of alienation and inheritance was admitted and (as was normal on Crown manors notwithstanding the book of instructions) fines were fixed. There was no interest in fee-farming copyholds in the Honour of Clitheroe, although some handsome rates of composition were offered in Wakefield before enfranchisement was abandoned. In short, copyholders of inherit-ance lacked that element of insecurity that made copyholders for

---

[90] LR2/203 fol. 20.
[91] CRES40/18 fols. 187–93 *passim*, LR2/203 fols. 20–31.

lives amenable to persuasion. Accordingly the former were likely to put a much smaller valuation on their freehold.

The disparity between different assessments of worth is exhibited in the scrappy proceedings of the 1623 commission for enfranchising.[92] The practical business of negotiating with tenants was placed in the hands of Exchequer officials sitting in London rather than itinerant commissioners as had previously been the norm. The tenants of Ditton and Datchet (Buckinghamshire) appeared and offered five years' old rent for their fines to be made certain, and ten years' to be enfranchised. The commissioners demanded sixty years'. The tenants of Hampton offered forty years', those of Twickenham thirty years'; again sixty years' was demanded. A tenant of Shitlington (Bedfordshire) offered ten, twelve, or at most fifteen years' on behalf of his fellow tenants. He was turned away. A few more offers were made, including some for single tenements, but none was offered at a satisfactory value.

VII

For most of the Crown's tenants, their landlord's persistent need to raise money did not represent an opportunity for liberation from feudal obligations. Instead, it was a time of confusion and contention, from which some tenants bought their peace by acceding to the King's demands. It is impossible to speak of a general tenant experience. The costs of fines, or compounding, or enfranchisement, were proportionately a much greater cost to small tenants than large. For many tenants, the Crown's new impositions represented a substantial increase in their costs. At Mere (Wiltshire), Kerridge found that the new policy imposed fines ten times as great as the old.[93] At Knowle the tenants claimed, apparently with justice, to pay a year's rent for a fine. To give but one instance, the new regime demanded a fine of £11 19s 1½d for three cottages and five acres of land, the rent of which was 7s 3d.[94] At Ledbury it was reported that the poorer tenants were having to sell cattle and

[92] LR9/6/712/1–9, various papers, of which 712/3 is the commissioners' notebook.
[93] Kerridge, 'Movement of Rent', 33.
[94] E112/128 no. 170. The court roll for 1 April 1611 shows that the fines originally demanded were often substantially marked down. Warwicks. RO CR 1886/2310 fol. 27v.

borrow money to meet their composition fine.[95] Nor was this special pleading. An anonymous commentator assumed that an enfranchising tenant would have to sell part of his lands to buy the rest.[96] Nor did the cost to the tenant end with his share of the purchase of a confirmation or his freehold. There were in addition the costs of negotiation and conveyancing. The tenants of Holme Cultram estimated their costs in obtaining a confirmation at £500, but only £300 was paid directly to the Exchequer.[97]

The Crown, doubtless, made some profit out of all these doings. It did not make a large profit. Salisbury's confirmations brought in £3,500. Fanshaw's work was on his own estimate worth £12,000. The duchy Receiver-General's accounts which survive for nine years between 1605 and 1620 show an income from fines for compositions and grants of fee farms of £14,494.[98] Of course, there was in addition a lasting improvement in annual revenue.

The problem the Crown's administrators faced was simply that no matter how insecure the claims of their tenants were in law, especially where tenants held copyholds of waste or demesne lands or claimed customs of fixed fines where past variability could be shown, the Crown was constrained to work along lines which favoured the tenants. So tenants could not be dispossessed in the Newhold of the Honour of Clitheroe any more than the demands of the book of instructions for market fines could be implemented: instead the politically expedient course in the face of the tenants' willingness to obstruct and litigate was to sell compositions. In taking this line, the Crown admitted the sheer impracticality of obtaining the strict enforcement of the law at a time when the need for funds was both immediate and desperate. The solution to a massive shortfall of income was, as Dorset saw and Salisbury came to appreciate, not the improvement of the profits of customary tenure, but the release of capital through enfranchisement. Indeed, in the face of the inability to enforce the book of printed instructions and raise fines without querying the customs of each and every manor, the implementation of the book became little more than a

---

[95] Campbell, *English Yeoman*, p. 141.

[96] SP14/59 no. 44.

[97] F. Grainger, 'The Chambers Family of Raby Cote', *Trans. Cumberland and Westmorland Anti. and Arch. Soc.*, new ser., I (1901), 213.

[98] DL28/11/3–15 (omitting duplicate accounts). The next two years' accounts contain no extraordinary revenue.

spur to cajole tenants to look more favourably on the possibilities of purchasing their tenements.

Exactly the same difficulties faced a myriad of private landowners who in the early seventeenth century found themselves with their lands in the hands of copyholders. If the Crown could achieve so little, what chance had they? The fact that the continued existence of copyhold was a problem that exercised Victorian and early twentieth-century law reformers is in its way evidence of the impossibility of extirpating the copyholder in the early modern period. And where the copyhold did disappear, we need to recognize that its loss frequently came from landowners taking the line of despair – enfranchisement – rather than by its legal abolition.[99]

VIII

The 'vain projects' of James's reign were sometimes bold, frequently muddled, and occasionally short-sighted attempts to raise revenue from the Crown lands. To a degree they were successful, but the sums they produced could never have paid a king's ransom and certainly not James's debts. They were a poor reward for so great an endeavour, but perhaps form a true reflection of the costs of improving the revenue from copyhold lands in early modern England.

[99] I hope to write on these matters at greater length in the future.

Table 1. *Payments for compositions recorded in the Auditor's Receipt Books, 1607–12*

	Exchequer manors	Duchy manors	Termly total
October 1607–September 1608	nil	nil	nil
October 1608–March 1609	nil	£3,553 19s 5d	£3,553 19s 5d
April–September 1609	£1,070	£1,520 0s 11½d	£2,590 0s 11½d
October 1609–March 1610	£739 13s 2d	£4,025 13s 5d	£4,765 6s 7d
April–September 1610	£1,191 18s 7½d	nil	£1,191 18s 7½d
October 1610–March 1611	£466 19s 8d	£458 2s 9½d	£925 2s 5½d
April–September 1611	nil	nil	nil
October 1611–March 1612	nil	£408 6s 3d	£408 6s 3d
April–September 1612	£2 17s 0d	£114 1s 5d	£116 18s 5d
TOTALS	£3,471 8s 5½d	£10,080 4s 3d	£13,551 12s 8½d

Source: Public Record Office, auditor's receipt books, E401/2408–2418

Appendix 1: Compositions by Exchequer tenants, 1609–11

This Appendix provides a list of all Exchequer manors found in the Auditor's Receipt Books for 1608–12 (E401/2408–2418) making payments to the Exchequer for the confirmation of customs (excluding Richmond and Middleham (Yorkshire), for which see pp. 83–4 above). Explicit references are not offered. Where a decree is to be found in the Lord Treasurer's memoranda rolls (E368) or elsewhere, this is noticed.

BUCKINGHAMSHIRE: Ditton (E368/540 ro. 114), Great Missenden, Holmer Green (E368/537 ro. 143), Langley (E368/359 ro. 102), Taplow, Upton (E368/546 ro. 185), Wyrardisbury.

CUMBERLAND: Holme Cultram (E368/536 ro. 211).

DORSET: Gillingham.

ESSEX: Orsett.

HERTFORDSHIRE: Hemel Hempstead (E126/1 fols. 141v, 142r, 145–148v), Pinchfield, Redbourn, Rickmansworth.

HUNTINGDONSHIRE: Colne, Earith, Fenton, Pidley, Somersham (decree for the Soke of Somersham E368/359 ro. 103).

LINCOLNSHIRE: Baston (E368/536 ro. 214), Crowland.

NORTHAMPTONSHIRE: Torpell (in Ufford?).

NORTHUMBERLAND: Tynemouth (E368/537 ro. 142, also LR1/195 fols. 95r–97v).

SUFFOLK: Brandon (Ferry), Glemsford.

WILTSHIRE: Corsham (E368/358 ro. 102).

YORKSHIRE: Hatfield (LR1/195 fol. 157r–v, printed J. Tomlinson, *The Level of Hatfield Chase and Parts Adjacent* (Doncaster, 1882), pp. 195–6).

Appendix 2: Compositions made on the Duchy of Lancaster estates, 1618–21

DERBYSHIRE: Wirksworth cum membris (Decree 5 July 1620, DL5/28 fols. 368v–380v), fine £1,193 16s 5¼d.

LANCASHIRE Accrington, Oswaldtwistle and Haslington (Decree 14 February 1618, DL5/27 pp. 1125–34), fine £793 17s 6d. Huncote and Accrington (Decree 16 May 1618, *ibid.*, pp. 1215–24), fine £166 0s 0d. Tottington (Decree 16 May 1618, *ibid.*, pp. 1225–38; 1338–40), fine £1,420 13s 4d and £80 for the confirmation of enclosed lands. Colne (Decree 20 June 1618, *ibid.*, pp. 1312–28), fine £1,050 9s 2d. Ightenhill (Decree 20 June 1618, *ibid.*, pp. 1341–62), fine £2,141 10s 10d. Wapentake of Blackburn (Decree 10 Feb. 1619, DL5/28 80r, 107r–113v), fine £205 11s 8d and £163 6s 8d for enclosures. Chatburn, Worston, and Pendleton (Decree 10 May 1619, *ibid.*, fols. 106r–v, 144v–151r), fine £1,179 8s 4d.

LEICESTERSHIRE: Desford (Decree 6 Feb. 1618, DL5/27 pp. 1135–42), fine £782 11s 4d. East Shilton (Decree 6 Feb. 1618, *ibid.*, pp. 1143–52), fine £859 5s 10d. Smeeton and Foxton (Decree 5 July 1620, DL5/28 fols. 364v–368v), fine £385 1s 6¾d.

LINCOLNSHIRE: Brocklesby (Decree 7 May 1619, DL5/28 fols. 151v–154v), fine £273.

NORTHAMPTONSHIRE: Irchester (Decree 26 Nov. 1618, DL5/27 p. 1308; 28 fols. 50r–6r), fine £723. Rushden (Decree 28 Nov. 1618, DL5/27 p. 1309; 28 fols. 68r–73r), fine £2,165 19s 10d. Raunds (Decree 28 Nov. 1618, *ibid.*, 73r–78v), fine £1,640.

STAFFORDSHIRE: Newcastle under Lyme (Decree 10 June 1619, *ibid.*, fols. 456r–461v), fine £1,373 5s.

YORKSHIRE: Slaidburn (Decree 22 Nov. 1619, DL5/28 fols. 237r–243v), fine £1,630 12s 6d.

5. Rural society and agricultural change: Ombersley 1580–1700

PETER LARGE

Amongst the many contributions Joan Thirsk has made to our understanding of the economy and society of early modern England, two themes have been most clear. First, the changes which took place were not uniform or simple but were the complex consequences of the inter-relationship of social, economic, legal, and geographical characteristics. Secondly, the examination of these changes is most clearly illuminated by detailed study. It is only from the particular that realistic generalizations can be shaped and continually refined. By an examination of rural society and agricultural change in the Worcestershire manor of Ombersley this chapter offers some refinements to the understanding of the relationship between manorial custom and agrarian change during the seventeenth century and to the realities of small farm viability during this period.

The general explanation of the relationship between rural society and agricultural change rests upon the steady growth of landed estates and the spread of leasehold tenure during the sixteenth and seventeenth centuries. The process which 'turned lordship into absolute ownership'[1] has been examined by many historians from both a legal and an economic viewpoint.[2] Out of this research a clear

---

[1] H. J. Perkin, 'The Social Causes of the British Industrial Revolution', *Trans. R. Hist. Soc.*, 5th ser., XVIII (1968), 135.

[2] R. Brenner, 'Agrarian Class Structure and Economic Development in Pre-industrial Europe', *Past and Present*, LXX (1976), 29–75; D. C. North and R. P. Thomas, 'The Rise and Fall of the Manorial System: A Theoretical Model', *Journal of Econ. Hist.*, XXXI (1971), 771–803; A. Jones, 'The Rise and Fall of the Manorial System: A Critical Comment', *Journal of Econ. Hist.*, XXXII (1972), 938–44; W. Letwin, 'The Contradictions of Serfdom', *Times Literary Supplement* (25 March 1977), 373–5; C. G. A. Clay, *Economic Expansion and Social Change: England 1500–1700* (2 vols., Cambridge, 1984), I, pp. 62–84.

message has emerged about the nature of manorial custom and the fortunes of the small landowner, the descendant of the medieval peasant. In the arable areas, continuing economic and legal pressures threatened the existence of the small landowner. The attempts of landlords to extract increasing rents and to challenge customary rights during the late sixteenth and seventeenth centuries presented one threat.[3] The economic pressures placed on small arable farmers by bad harvests in the 1590s and 1620s and falling prices combined with rising taxation in the later seventeenth century represented a second and perhaps more dangerous challenge to the small landowner, particularly where inheritance customs produced a progressive fragmentation of holdings.[4]

Whilst no single force was at work, it remains clear that the partial elimination of the small landowner occurred during the early modern period. The engrossing of smaller holdings into larger farms, freed from the rigid communal regulations of the manor, is regarded as an important part of the improvement in agricultural productivity. The financial resources of the larger farmer and the greater flexibility of the enclosed leasehold farm were clearly important elements in the development of certain arable regimes, most notably the arable vales. However, we must remember that manorial holdings, and heritable copyholds in particular, remained one of the principal forms of land tenure during this period. In the seventeenth century, the manor was still a reality in much of western England and open field systems were adapted or enclosed within the structure of communal regulation.[5]

Ombersley provides a classic example of a manor which remained a vital and highly relevant institution throughout the seventeenth and early eighteenth centuries. It is the story of a large community

---

[3] J. Thirsk, 'Enclosing and Engrossing', in J. Thirsk (ed.), *The Agrarian History of England and Wales*, IV, *1500–1640* (Cambridge, 1967), pp. 200–12; R. H. Tawney, *The Agrarian Problem in the Sixteenth Century* (Oxford, 1912), pp. 201–64; B. Manning, 'The Peasantry and the English Revolution', *Journal of Peasant Studies*, II (1975), 133–58; P. Bowden, 'Agricultural Prices, Farm Profits and Rents', in Thirsk (ed.), *Agrarian History*, IV, pp. 679–80, 683–4.

[4] M. Spufford, *Contrasting Communities: English Villagers in the Sixteenth and Seventeenth Centuries* (Cambridge, 1974), pp. 58–119; H. J. Habakkuk, 'La Disparition du paysan anglais', *Annales*, XX (1965), 649–63; Clay, *Economic Expansion and Social Change*, I, pp. 87–97; G. E. Mingay, *Enclosure and the Small Farmer in the Age of the Industrial Revolution* (London, 1968), p. 17.

[5] Clay, *Economic Expansion and Social Change*, I, pp. 87, 114–15.

of small farmers which survived the economic and legal challenges of the seventeenth century and whose inhabitants were amongst the more progressive agricultural innovators of the period. It is an example of a type of rural society in which a resilient but flexible body of manorial customs both preserved the social structure and accommodated agricultural change.

Ombersley was a large manor, lying between the city of Worcester and market town of Kidderminster and extending westwards to the banks of the river Severn. The manor was conterminous with the parish and until the Dissolution it belonged to the Abbots of Evesham. During the second half of the sixteenth century it was granted to a succession of lessees and finally, in 1582, to Samuel Sandys. Throughout most of its history as a monastic and Crown property the manor did not have a resident lord, and until 1590 it was administered by a group of tenants who formed the backbone of the manorial jury, the homage.[6]

Apart from being effectively self-governing, an important characteristic of the manor of Ombersley was that custom established an estate of inheritance for the copyholders. Almost all land in the manor was held as copyhold of inheritance, and custom dictated that copyholds descended to heirs by seniority, the eldest son taking the most productive or largest holding and younger sons or daughters any remaining holdings by seniority. Once copyhold land descended to an heir it was deemed 'descent land' and could not be surrendered to a 'stranger'; it passed to the heir either on the death of the copyholder or by relinquishment while he was living. If any land was escheated to the lord it could be purchased by 'whatsoever persons for such fyne as the lord and the taker can agree upon'. The land so purchased could pass to a 'stranger' as 'surrender land' until an heir inherited, and then it became 'descent land' once more.[7] This inheritance custom dictated that land was dispersed amongst the heirs, but it prohibited the fragmentation of holdings into minute parcels. Consequently, Ombersley remained a community of small landowners into the nineteenth century. The configuration of copyhold lands in Ombersley during the early seventeenth century clearly displayed the outlines of the standard medieval yard-

---

[6] *Victoria County History of Worcestershire*, III (London, 1913), p. 462.
[7] Worcester Record Office (hereafter WRO), Sandys MSS, BA 3910/29; Survey of the Manor of Ombersley.

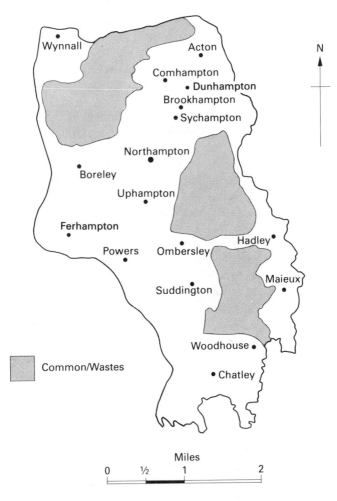

Figure 1 The manor and parish of Ombersley

land and half-yardland holdings. A survey of 1605 recorded 4,500 acres of copyhold land divided between 188 tenants. Only 7 tenants had holdings in excess of a thirty-acre yardland, 57 copyholders had holdings between twenty and thirty acres, and 124 tenants had 'half yardlands' of under twenty acres. The remainder of the manor comprised some 300 acres held by free tenants, plus the demesne lands and three vast areas of common waste which covered almost 2,000 acres. This distribution of land ownership remained unchanged during the seventeenth century, and the rental of Lady Day 1722 recorded the same holdings and a total of 188 copyhold tenants.[8]

Whilst little value can be placed on the evidence of surveys or rentals as a measure of farming units, since they do not reveal any subletting or consolidation of copyholds to form larger farming units, it is clear from other sources that Ombersley was a community of small owner-occupiers. An analysis of summer inventories which include full crop acreages indicates a median of fifteen acres of arable land per farm in both halves of the seventeenth century.[9] Moreover, Ombersley was the most densely populated of the north Worcestershire agricultural parishes according to the Hearth Tax assessment of 1664, which recorded 70 per cent of the inhabitants assessed at one or two hearths.[10] In the 1690s one inhabitant indicated nothing had changed when he described Ombersley as a community of customary tenants 'many of them not poore though not any of them very rich'.[11]

This chapter examines the nature of customary law and how it operated within the manor of Ombersley; the challenges to this legal and social framework; and the adaptability of manorial custom to the requirements of agricultural progress. Finally, it describes the changing agricultural regime and improvement in sheep and corn husbandry achieved in Ombersley during the period.

I

The recognition of copyhold property rights at Westminster is now well understood by historians.[12] Prof. Kerridge has described the strong legal position of customary law and the importance of the concept of reasonable customs in shaping customary practice.[13] Contemporaries had no doubt about the status achieved by the

---

[8] WRO BA 3910/29; Sandys MSS, BA 3792/10. Rental of Ombersley.

[9] WRO Probate Inventories, BA 3585; Ombersley has extraordinarily good probate coverage. For the whole of the seventeenth century 136 summer inventories have been examined. Out of this total, 19 provide full crop acreages.

[10] PRO Exchequer King's Remembrancer, Subsidy Rolls, E179/201/312.

[11] PRO Exchequer King's Remembrancer, Bills and answers, E112/706/28.

[12] C. M. Gray, *Copyhold, Equity and the Common Law* (Cambridge, Massachusetts, 1963), *passim*.

[13] E. Kerridge, *Agrarian Problems in the Sixteenth Century and After* (London, 1969), pp. 17–31, 67–8.

copyholder of inheritance. Edward Coke's assertion in *The Compleate Copyholder* that 'the favourable hand of time hath so infranchised these Copyholders'[14] was a view shared by other lawyers.[15] Coke argued that the 'enfranchised' copyholder who held a customary estate in fee had a more valuable property than a freeholder.[16] Other writers were more forthright: Nicholas Breton's 'Countryman' declared, 'I had rather hold it in a coppy of a good Tenure, than by the title of an idil braine to keepe a fooles head in Freehold.'[17] Many landowners clearly shared this preference for copyhold, and where entry fines were fixed and other tenurial exactions light, a copyhold estate could be superior. Often copyholds had more valuable common rights attached to them, and as all transactions were recorded on the court rolls, there was less fear of 'fraudulent evidences'.[18]

What is less fully recognized is that the acceptance of copyhold by the common law courts did not undermine the integrity and relevance of customary law. On the contrary, the strength of the heritable copyhold estate lay in its relationship with the manor as the legal entity which administered the customary law. In Coke's words, 'Manor is as the body and copyholds certaine members of this body.'[19] Whilst manorial custom was increasingly accepted by the common law courts during the fifteenth and sixteenth centuries, 'on common law of custom' was established and customary law remained in essence a local and particular legal framework for which the individual manorial jurisdiction was responsible.

Whilst the common law required customs to be reasonable, consistent, and to be practised from 'time immemorial', this did not

---

[14] Edward Coke, *The Compleate Copyholder* (London, 1644), pp. 5–15, 71, 74.

[15] Charles Calthorpe, *The Relation betweene the lord of a mannor and the Coppy-Holder his tenant* (London, 1635), pp. 15–16; *A Commentary on the Tenures of Littleton Written Prior to the Publications of Coke upon Littleton*, ed. H. Cary (London, 1829), pp. 163–4.

[16] Coke, *Copyholder*, pp. 155–8.

[17] Nicholas Breton, *The Court and Country, or a Briefe Discourse betweene the Courtier and Country-man; of the Manner, Nature and condition of their lives* (London, 1618), p. 188.

[18] M. Campbell, *The English Yeoman* (New Haven, 1942), pp. 137–9; R. Gough, *Antiquities & Memoirs of the Parish of Myddle, County of Salop* (Shrewsbury, 1875), pp. 85–6; G. H. Tupling, *The Economic History of Rossendale*, Chetham Soc., n.s., LXXXVI (1927), pp. 133–4; G. Batho, 'Landlords in England: The Crown', in Thirsk (ed.), *Agrarian History*, IV, p. 269.

[19] Coke, *Copyholder*, p. 1.

serve to codify custom.[20] In reality, the issue of 'time immemorial' was fraught with difficulties of interpretation. From the lawyers' perspective the meaning of 'time immemorial' changed during the sixteenth and early seventeenth centuries, although by the early 1600s it was firmly established that copyhold estates were 'fixed' by 'long custome and continuance of time'.[21] Uncertainty over the concept of 'time immemorial' was accentuated by the range of antiquity of manorial custom. Inheritance customs had very deep roots stretching back before the advent of manor court rolls and copyhold tenure. Other customs emerged as copyhold developed out of villeinage, and those relating to agricultural practices were generally of shorter duration and often changing.

If lawyers were unable to rationalize manorial customs by a strict interpretation of 'time out of mind', they were also unable to establish a common law of custom because of the remarkable variety of manorial customs. Coming rather late into the central courts, the copyholder brought with him a body of customary law which the common lawyers could not sweep away.[22] Coke was candid enough to admit that 'should I goe about to make a catalogue of severall customs, I should . . . undertake an endlesse peece of worke'.[23]

Whilst custom and common law had a resemblance through the maintenance of the same concept of 'reasonable' practice, they could differ markedly in what they allowed. In the case of heritable copyholds, customs had to fit into a mosaic of related rights and regulations, and what was reasonable in one case might not be in another. Moreover, the determination of what was reasonable was not the exclusive privilege of the common lawyers, and equity considerations were especially important in matters of copyhold and custom from the earliest stages of their recognition at Westminster.[24] Both Chancery and Exchequer had a significant involvement in copyhold matters during the sixteenth and seventeenth centuries, but in these courts a body of substantive law was slow to

[20] *Ibid.*, pp. 80–3; Calthorpe, *The Relation*, pp. 21–44.
[21] Gray, *Copyhold, Equity and the Common Law*, pp. 63, 71–84, 199–201; Calthorpe, *The Relation*, pp. 3–6, 15–16; BL Harl. MSS, 1588, Reports 37 Eliz. I, fols. 5r–5v.
[22] Coke, *Copyholder*, pp. 130–2; E. Coke, *The Reports*, IV (London, 1777), fol. 22b.
[23] Coke, *Copyholder*, p. 78.
[24] Gray, *Copyhold, Equity and the Common Law*, *passim*.

emerge.[25] In the early seventeenth century, equity was not administered according to a rigid set of rules and judicial precedents, but
remained a fluid system of justice based on the principles of juris-
prudence.[26] In manorial matters, the notion of reasonable customs
was the central tenet of equity jurisdiction and, in the case of
heritable copyholds, customs had to fit into a jigsaw of related rights
and economic obligations.

The inability of the common law to subsume custom and the
recognition of the particular and local characteristics of customary
law by the equity courts ensured that manorial jurisdiction
remained vital and relevant whenever copyhold estates continued
to exist. The body of customary law was administered through the
manorial court baron. Coke described this court as 'the chiefe prop
and pillar of a manor which no sooner faileth but the manor falleth
to the ground'.[27] The court was constituted by the manorial lord or
his steward and the manorial homage, a group of tenants represent-
ing the whole tenurial population.[28] The homage was responsible
both for making presentments to the court and for acting as a jury;
it effectively determined the issues raised in the court and passed
verdicts on them.

In the early seventeenth century the standing of the manorial
homage was fully recognized by the central courts. As the customs
of every manor were to some degree a unique body of law, both the
equity and common law courts often directed the appropriate
homage to settle disputes over customs. In the first decade of the
seventeenth century, the Court of Common Pleas left the settling of
reasonable fines to the manorial homage in a number of cases.[29]
When no documentary evidence existed the homage was often

[25] W. J. Jones, *The Elizabethan Court of Chancery* (Oxford, 1967), pp. 266–86;
W. H. Bryson, *The Equity Side of the Exchequer* (Cambridge, 1975), pp. 18–19.

[26] Bryson, *The Equity Side of the Exchequer*, pp. 7–8; Jones, *Elizabethan Chancery*,
pp. 2–4, 420–1; G. W. Thomas, 'James I, Equity and Lord Keeper John
Williams', *Eng. Hist. Rev.*, XCI (1976), 512–13; G. W. Thomas, 'Archbishop
John Williams: Politics and Prerogative Law, 1621–1642', D.Phil. thesis, Oxford
University, 1974, 43–6.

[27] Coke, *Copyholder*, pp. 62–3.

[28] Traditionally, the court baron was held every three weeks and the homage was
the entire tenurial population owing suit. By the early seventeenth century quar-
terly courts were more frequent and the homage had become representatives of
the tenants as a whole.

[29] R. Brownlow and J. Goldesborough, *Reports of Cases in Law* (London, 1651),
pp. 132–3.

made responsible for defining the manorial custom. In 1602 the custom of escheat was in dispute at Ombersley and, as the court rolls shed no light on the matter, the court of Exchequer observed that it was 'most fittest to be decided and determyned by the seaventeene Tythingmen representinge the homage of the said Mannor at and in the Courte of the said Mannor'. The case was therefore dismissed and referred to 'the tyrall of the homage . . . to be by them determyned', and whatever they were 'to fynde and present upon their oathes' was to be accepted by the lord of the manor.[30]

Given the key position held by the homage, it is not surprising that its members were drawn from amongst the most substantial tenants. At Ombersley in 1600, the typical homager had lived all his life in the manor and was considered to be a 'yeoman'. All had been about forty years old when first chosen for the homage and only four had served for less than 5 years, whilst three had served continuously for over 20 years.[31] The stability of the homage remained a salient feature throughout the seventeenth century and no court saw the introduction of more than three new homagers; in each decade a core of six or seven tenants served throughout.[32] In essence the homagers of Ombersley were not only the representatives of the manorial tenants but also the embodiment of the local customary heritage. Their lineage added weight to their judgements on customary matters and gave them much greater authority in the courts baron, where they were the custodians of manorial custom. The seventeenth-century homage differed markedly from H. A. L. Fisher's 'small knot of rustics' whose 'bucolic mind' was in need of guidance.[33]

Whilst customary law and manorial jurisdiction maintained a clear identity within the wider legal framework of early modern England, there is no doubt that customary jurisdiction was subjected to increasing challenge by manorial lords during the late sixteenth and early seventeenth centuries. The increasing opportunities for commercial farming allied to the forces of inflation encouraged a search for an improved return from manorial lord-

[30] PRO Exchequer King's Remembrancer, Decrees and Orders, Series 1, E123/28, fol. 108.
[31] WRO BA 3910/30; PRO E134, 43 Eliz., Hilary 2.
[32] WRO BA 3910/19, 25, 43; PRO Star Chamber Proceedings, Jas 1, Stac 8/269/31.
[33] H. A. L. Fisher, *Pages from the Past* (Oxford, 1939), pp. 119–21.

ship. The rise in agricultural prices gave landlords an added incentive to grasp the commercial opportunities, and many extended their demesne by engrossing and enclosing customary holding and waste land.[34]

Throughout England, customary estates for years or lives largely disappeared during this period as progressive landlords consolidated holdings and let their land at competitive rents. The rents and fines paid by leaseholders were greatly increased on many private estates between the 1570s and 1640s, and the Crown was constantly being advised to convert copyholds to leases. In some cases landlords, including the Crown, challenged the titles of copyholders of inheritance in an attempt to persuade tenants to exchange their copies to leases.[35] In general, however, landlords did not challenge heritable estates but looked to improve the tenurial revenue, particularly entry fines. This challenge was made through the central courts, especially the equity courts, and the key issue for historians is whether the concept of reasonable fines meant that heritable copyholds were given the financial protection which could sustain inheritance or whether, as R. H. Tawney argued, arbitrary fines were ultimately forced up to a commercial, rack-rent equivalent.[36]

Ombersley provides a good example of the process of manorial conflict. From the mid 1590s Samuel Sandys, the manorial lord, embarked on a determined effort to exploit the manor 'for his best profit' by increasing customary revenues and reletting the demesne land 'to the very uttermost value'.[37] This was the great age of the assiduous steward, searching the court rolls for forgotten services, lapsed titles, or irregular admittances which might warrant forfeiture, often with a share of any profits.[38] Sandys employed one

[34] J. Thirsk, 'Enclosing and Engrossing', in Thirsk (ed.), *Agrarian History*, IV, pp. 200–12; Tawney, *Agrarian Problem*, pp. 201–64.

[35] L. Stone, *The Crisis of the Aristocracy, 1558–1641* (Oxford, 1965), pp. 309–13, 320; P. Bowden, 'Agricultural Prices', in Thirsk (ed.), *Agrarian History*, IV, pp. 269–70; Manning, 'Peasantry and the English Revolution', 134–9.

[36] Tawney, *Agrarian Problem*, pp. 296–8, 304–10.

[37] PRO Exchequer King's Remembrancer, Decrees and Orders, Series IV, E126/1, fol. 84r.

[38] Thomas Clay, *Briefe Easie, and Necessary Tables . . . together with A Chorologicall Discourse of the well ordering, disposing and governing of an Honorable estate or Revenue* (London, 1622), pp. 21–36, 40–2, Statutes of the Realm, 1 Jac c. 5. In 1604 a statute was passed forbidding profit-sharing arrangements between lords and stewards since this practice had resulted in tenants being 'unjustlie vexed and by grievous Fynes and amercements undulie punished'.

Thomas Ainsworth to search for such sources of income and prepare evidence for suits in the Court of Exchequer.[39] Having been overruled in 1602 by the manorial homage, in his attempt to contest the customs of escheat and forfeiture, Sandys turned his attention to entry fines.[40]

Entry fines were potentially the most valuable source of revenue at Ombersley, but throughout the sixteenth century fines had been levied at a nominal rate of two years' customary rent.[41] In 1571 fines were formally fixed at this rate in an agreement between the copyholders and the manorial lessee, Sir John Bourne.[42] The agreement was ratified by the Court of Exchequer in the same year, and in the manorial survey ordered by Sandys in 1605, the homage confirmed entry fines as two years' customary rent.[43]

In 1606, with the manorial survey completed and new copyhold valuations made, Sandys challenged the custom of fixed fines. Fines of one year's rentable value were demanded by his steward in open court, and when the homage ruled that only two years' ancient rent was payable on admittance, Sandys petitioned the Court of Exchequer. In October 1607, on the evidence of court rolls from the fifteenth century, it was decreed that the entry fines were arbitrary. The decree of 1571 which seemed to exclude any decision unfavourable to the copyholders was declared void. As a decree made to verify a private agreement, it was not allowed the status of an order resulting from judicial proceedings, and, as it was made between the tenants and a Crown lessee, it could not bind the Crown or any succeeding owner. Sandys was advised that he could take 'such reasonable and arbitrary ffynes for their admittance unto their said copyholds and everypart thereof as shall be reasonably taxed and assessed'.[44] The court did not set a maximum level for reasonable fines, and initially Sandys demanded about one year's full value, which caused little hardship to the tenants.

Nevertheless, the copyholders considered the decree to be an injustice. Their natural inclination was to reject ancient documentary evidence and to accept the usage 'time out of mind', which they

[39] PRO Exchequer King's Remembrancer, Depositions taken by Commission, E134, 38 Eliz, Easter 4; E123/23, fol. 35r; E112/132/155.
[40] PRO E123/28, fol. 108.
[41] WRO Sandys MSS, BA 1910/19, 21, 42, 43: court rolls.
[42] WRO Sandys MSS, BA 1910/7.
[43] WRO Sandys MSS, BA 3190/29.   [44] PRO E126/1, fols. 83r–86v.

believed was guaranteed by the decree of 1571. Indeed, the custom of fixed fines might not have been overturned if the tenants had prepared their defence more thoroughly, since the equity courts were not bound by the revelations of 'ancient evidences'. But in 1605, faced with Sandys's challenge, the copyholders had hastily exhibited a cross bill making the contradictory claim that fines had been fixed at two years' old rent or *less* from before the Dissolution.[45] This admission of variable fines counted heavily against the tenants when the suit came to hearing.

Sandys feared that the testimony of ancient witnesses might take precedence over the court rolls in an equity court, and he waited until most of the oldest inhabitants who had been party to the 1571 agreement were dead before demanding larger entry fines.[46] Thomas Nash was the most influential of these tenants. He had solicited the agreement of 1571, had been among the group of leading copyholders who leased the manor and its court baron between 1587 and 1590, and had served as a homager for over thirty years. Sandys made his first claim to arbitrary fines at the very next meeting of the court baron after Thomas Nash's death, when George Nash was presented as heir to his father's holding.

The copyholders were outmanoeuvred. Their first reaction was to question the validity of the fifteenth-century court rolls, suggesting that the fines recorded were for admittance to demesne copyholds.[47] When this had failed, they exhibited five bills between 1607 and 1613 in which they appealed to the provisions of two deeds allegedly made by the Abbots of Evesham in 1533 and 1537. All the bills were dismissed because neither deed constituted proof of fixed fines.[48] In January 1613, the court finally ordered the tenants to refrain from challenging the 1607 decree and the evidence on which it was made.[49]

Sandys's success in 1607 owed much to his adroit timing and the initial confusion prevailing amongst the tenants. But the way in which the Court of Exchequer dismissed the copyholders' pleas con-

---

[45] PRO E112/132/124.

[46] PRO Chancery Proceedings, Series 11, C3/369/1.

[47] PRO E112/132/155; Exchequer King's Remembrancer, Decrees and Orders, Series 11, E124/37, fol. 257r.

[48] PRO Stac 8/269/31.

[49] PRO E134, 11 Jas 1, Easter 3; Stac 8/259/6; E124/7, fol. 104v; E124/12, fols. 215v–16v; E124/14, fols. 333v–4v; E124/16, fol. 224.

trasts sharply with their more circumspect approach in 1571. The Commissioners appointed to arbitrate between Sir John Bourne and the tenants during 1571 had been equally aware of the discrepancy between the 'usage and custom' of the tenants and the ancient court rolls, but they had accepted the usage and adjudged the fines to be fixed.[50] The almost cavalier way in which the court abrogated the 1571 decree reflects a less favourable disposition towards fixed fines in general. Ombersley was not the only manor in which an Elizabethan equity court decision fixing fines was set aside during the early seventeenth century, and it is likely that as agricultural prices rose through the 1580s and 1590s the equity courts saw the justice of variable fines which allowed landlords to reap some of the fruits of inflation.[51] A more critical appraisal of the documentary and oral evidence on which fixed fines were based became general in the first twenty years of the seventeenth century. John Norden the surveyor believed that some copyholders had originally enjoyed fixed fines, but that as prices rose they were obliged to accept variable payments.[52]

Equity considerations took precedence over both oral and written evidence in such cases, and a recognition of inflation by the courts undermined fixed fines in the late sixteenth and early seventeenth centuries. The thrust of this change coincided with attempts to improve the management of Crown lands at the beginning of James's reign. Proposals to enfranchise royal copyholds and to convert uncertain entry fines into certain ones depended for their success as a financial venture on initially proving that fines were uncertain. If fines were arbitrary, large composition payments could be demanded in exchange for fixed fines or freehold possession. The Crown relied on equity considerations and ancient documentation to the exclusion of accepted usage in most of its claims to arbitrary fines.[53] The Crown's advisers did not have much respect for manorial customs and some believed most customs were

[50] WRO Sandys MSS, BA 3910/32.
[51] A. B. Appleby, 'Agrarian Capitalism or Seigneurial Reaction? The North-West of England, 1500–1700', *American Hist. Rev.*, LXX (1975), 590.
[52] John Norden, *The Surveiors Dialogue*, 2nd edn (London, 1618), p. 106.
[53] G. Batho, 'Landlords in England', in Thirsk (ed.), *Agrarian History*, IV, pp. 269–70; Manning, 'Peasantry and the English Revolution', 136–9; J. Porter, 'Waste Land Reclamation in the Sixteenth and Seventeenth Centuries: The Case of South-Eastern Bowland, 1550–1630', *Trans. Hist. Soc. of Lancs. & Cheshire*, CXXVII (1977), 13.

riddled with 'untruth and uncertainty'.[54] The equity courts were influenced by these attitudes and by the Crown's quest for improved revenue in the opening twenty years of the seventeenth century.

A hardening in the Exchequer's attitude is also suggested by their willingness to declare a maximum reasonable fine of three years' value at Ombersley in 1615. Behind this decision lay an agreement made between Sandys and the Crown. Sandys offered to pay £2,500 for the purchase of the fee farm of the manor on condition that the Exchequer commissioners, who organized the sale of Crown lands, arranged with the Barons of the court for three years' 'true' value to be authorized as a reasonable fine. The court considered that 'special reasons', including the provisions for freebench, which entitled a widow to her husband's copyhold during her widowhood for the payment of one penny, warranted a substantial entry fine on admittance of an heir.[55]

In addition to fines, the copyholders had to carry the burden of two heriots, and, even before the ruling of 1615, many tenants had thought it prudent to take out bonds to cover this outlay.[56] Higher entry fines on top of the burden of heriots threatened the economic viability of farming in Ombersley. The copyholders practised a sheep and corn husbandry. Farming units were small and such small farmers were especially vulnerable when prices fluctuated widely. As barley prices fell after 1615 to a trough in 1619 and 1620, the tenants faced considerable hardship.[57] Early in 1622 they complained to Chancery that fines were being assessed from estimates of improved value made by the manorial surveyor in 1605 which were no longer applicable because 'these times are cheape'. However, instead of requesting a moderation of fines, the copyholders asserted that manorial custom authorized 'a ffine certeine of two yeres old rent or under'.[58] As the tenants insisted on reopening the controversy over fixed fines which had already been determined in Exchequer the bill was dismissed.[59] The tenants were also

[54] Batho, 'Landlords in England', p. 270.
[55] PRO Stac 8/269/31; C3/369/1; E124/37, fol. 162r.
[56] WRO BA 3585. Probate Records.
[57] P. Bowden, 'Agricultural Prices', in Thirsk (ed.), *Agrarian History*, IV, pp. 631–2; C. J. Harrison, 'Grain Price Analysis and Harvest Qualities, 1465–1634', *Agric. Hist. Rev.*, XIX (1971), 150, 154.
[58] PRO C3/369/1.
[59] PRO Chancery, Judicial Proceedings (Equity Side) Entry Book of Decrees and Orders, C33/141, fol. 570r.

refused a hearing on the same issue in Exchequer during Easter term 1625. The court confirmed 'three yeares fynes at the full value to bee reasonable to bee taken upon earlie admittance' and ordered the copyholders not to exhibit any more bills regarding the certainty of fines.[60]

Whilst the tenants as a group were appealing to the equity courts about the old issue of certain fines, individual copyholders with the support of the homage were refusing to pay three years' value for admittance. Sandys once more resorted to the Exchequer to uphold his demands. In 1622 the manorial steward demanded £25 from Henry Collier as an entry fine for a copyhold tenement called Reynolds and Goodmans. Collier refused to pay for two reasons. First, he claimed that the property was not worth £11 per annum, as estimated by the bailiff, but only £6 per annum. Moreover, parodying the arguments employed by Samuel Sandys in the original case concerning fines in 1606 and 1607, he suggested that he was not bound by any decree of 1607 or the order of 1615 because he had not been a tenant when the fines were adjudged uncertain. Thus, Collier argued that, regardless of the value of his holding, he was only liable to pay a fine of two years' ancient rent. The Exchequer denied this privilege to Collier and appointed a commission to examine witnesses about the value of the holding.[61]

Before the dispute over Collier's fine was settled a suit was filed against Thomas Amphlett, who was heir to copyhold land worth £7 per annum. At the court baron held on 12 April 1625 the steward set an entry fine of £21, but Amphlett 'absolutelie refused to paie the same'.[62] When examined by the Barons of the Exchequer he said that he was willing to pay a fine of two years' improved value, which he hoped the court would consider 'reasonable'. He claimed that any greater sum would be unreasonable because his father had left him poor, the manorial bailiff had taken three heriots by 'vyolence', and these were the only cattle his father had been able to provide for him.[63] Two weeks after this examination, on 21 November 1626, the court ordered that 'in regard of his povertie' Amphlett was to pay

[60] PRO E124/37, fols. 256r–7v; E125/1, fols. 16r–18v.
[61] PRO E124/37, fol. 162v.
[62] WRO Sandys MSS, BA 3910/36: copy of an Exchequer affidavit, 14 August 2 Chas 1.
[63] PRO Exchequer King's Remembrancer, Depositions taken before the Barons of the Exchequer, E133/105/76.

£13 6s 8d for his fine. The Exchequer stressed that setting the fine at slightly less than two years' value was an *ad hoc* decision made to guarantee Amphlett's right of inheritance after the bailiff had taken an extra heriot. However, on the same day, the court gave a group of copyholders, including Collier, leave to exhibit a bill concerning the general 'unreasonableness' of fines in Ombersley. The only condition imposed was that the bill should 'medle with no things wch hath been already decreed'.[64] In their bill the tenants accepted uncertain fines as one of the 'sentient and laudable' customs of the manor but argued that Sandys had demanded large entry fines which were unreasonable impositions on copyholders who held estates of inheritance.[65]

When the Exchequer eventually brought Collier's case to hearing in May 1627 they had clearly accepted the tenants' arguments about unreasonable fines. The copyhold tenement in question was valued at £11 per annum, but Collier was ordered to pay £20 for his entry fine rather than the £25 demanded by the steward. Moreover, whilst the court confirmed the decree of 1607 and the lord's right to arbitrary fines, they directed Sandys to accept two years' full value as the maximum reasonable fine.[66] The economic difficulties faced by the tenants in the depression in the early 1620s and the copyholders' appeals for relief from unreasonable fines were responsible for the abrogation of the 1615 order. But the events in Ombersley in 1626 and 1627 were part of a more general reaction by the equity courts against the implacable decisions regarding entry fines which characterized the first twenty years of the century. They illustrate a more liberal approach to the problems of custom and time immemorial. After the Chancery decision of 1625 which distinguished tenant-right and customary estates, a similar generosity towards prescriptive rights was shown in the cases concerning border tenure.[67] As the equity courts were swayed by the Crown and other landlords between 1600 and 1620, they were influenced by tenant opposition in the wake of economic depression during the 1620s.

Whilst the Exchequer, and the equity courts generally, had no rigid concept of how many years' value represented an appropriate

---

[64] PRO E128/2, fols. 283v–284r.   [65] PRO E112/256/10.
[66] PRO E126/3, fols. 151r–153r.
[67] Manning, 'Peasantry and the English Revolution', 137.

entry fine, they were guided by the principle of reasonable customs. In the case of heritable copyholds, fines and other customs had to be consistent with the right of inheritance. Anyone inheriting customary land also acquired a series of rights such as that of common pasture. These rights were also protected by the equity courts. In 1596, Samuel Sandys's right to free warren throughout the manor of Ombersley was restricted to a modest part of the waste called Linehold and Ouldfield in order to protect the copyholders' common grazing which the court recognized was an integral part of the communal inheritance.[68] Again, in 1622 Sandys tried to exercise his right of free warren throughout the entire manorial waste. He claimed that the former decree was made whilst he was 'farmer for yeares' and since he now held the inheritance of the manor he was no longer restricted by the judgement. Notwithstanding Sandys's purchase of the fee farm, the Court of Exchequer upheld the decree of 1593 and limited the free warren in order to protect the copyholders' estates.[69]

In a society which was predominantly agricultural, land was the principal means of holding, generating, and transmitting wealth. The central developments in land law between the fifteenth and seventeenth centuries were a growing recognition of this property in land and an increasing concern to guarantee the rightful inheritance of land.[70] In the case of heritable copyholds all customs relating to tenure had to be compatible with the inheritance customs which determined the nature of the estate held by the tenant. But the precise form of all manorial customs depended on the local economic and social situation. In the case of entry fines the basic feature of a reasonable fine was not that it should conform to a standard multiple of annual value but that it guaranteed the copyholder of inheritance a substantial surplus above the minimum return on which a man would farm the land. In other words copyholders of inheritance were not subject to rack-rents.

Tawney argued that the variation in reasonable fines adjudged by the courts indicated that no notion of reasonable fines existed independently of market forces. As inflation demanded some adjustment, arbitrary fines were forced up and customary tenants ulti-

---

[68] PRO E134, 37 and 38 Eliz., Michaelmas 48; E123/23, fol. 35r.

[69] PRO E112/133/251; E126/61, fols. 274–275r; E124/33, fol. 95v.

[70] A. W. F. Simpson, *A History of the Land Law* (Oxford, 1986), *passim*.

mately paid the full competitive price for their holdings. The surplus, capitalized in the entry fine, passed from the tenant to the landlord, and the interest of the copyholder depreciated to that of the leaseholder.[71] In fact, copyhold fines were generally set between one and two years' value and fines of more than two years' value on the admittance of an heir were generally considered unreasonable.[72] This was the case in Ombersley, even though the benefit of widows' freebench was also conveyed by custom. Fines of two years' full value compare favourably with the standard rack-rent lease which was for twenty-one years determinable on three lives, leaving heritable copyholders with a significant proportion of the rack-rent value.[73]

The commitment which the equity courts showed towards heritable copyholds ensured that the forces of social change, in the form of new aggressive landlords like Samuel Sandys, were curbed. The hereditary right or estate held by a copyholder was the fundamental determinant of his tenure. The copyholder of inheritance, unlike the copyholder for lives, had a guarantee of reasonable fines, and this allowed him to retain his status as a family farmer and remain distinct from the leaseholder. The copyholders of Ombersley were acutely aware of their social position and in complaining about excessive fines in 1622 they claimed that their 'estates of inheritance' were being reduced to worse estates than 'anie particular estates'.[74]

But the underlying assumptions of seventeenth-century law and society were not enough to ensure the survival of heritable copy-

---

[71] Tawney, *Agrarian Problem*, pp. 296–8, 304–10.

[72] *Ibid.*, p. 296) Kerridge, *Agrarian Problems*, p. 39.

[73] If a copyhold tenement changed hands three times in twenty-one years, and two years' rack-rent was payable on the admittance of each tenant, a maximum of six years' rack-rent would pass to the lord. Heriot payments would add further to the capitalization of rent, but each payment accounted for no more than a half of one year's annual value. Thus, on the adverse assumption of fines at two years' annual value and genuine heriots, only about 7.5 years' value or 36 per cent of the rack-rent would be transferred to the landlord. The true rent cost of copyhold land was rather greater because entry fines represented an advance payment. On the unfavourable assumption that the copyhold fine was paid in one sum at the commencement of the term, rather than as three fines and three heriots, the capitalized rent would still have been less than the capital value of the rent paid by a rack-rent lease. In 1600, at an interest rate of 10 per cent, the capitalized rack-rent of property discounted over twenty-one years was 8.2 years' value.

[74] PRO C3/369/1.

holds. Equity jurisdiction was still to some extent unpredictable. At all times the equity courts faced difficulties in interpreting the concept of time inherent in custom, and in assessing the validity of conflicting evidence drawn from the depositions of living witnesses, the written testimony of the distant past, and the rulings of recent custumals. Samuel Sandys was aware of these problems and he waited until influential copyholders had died before he challenged the custom of fixed fines in Ombersley. The uncertainties of evidence helped to produce a rich crop of tentative litigation upon which the growing population of lawyers thrived. George Norburie, an informed early seventeenth-century critic of Chancery, thought that only 30 per cent of the bills exhibited had 'any colour or shadow of just complaint'.[75] Yet some speculative suits based on tenuous evidence were successful. Tenants had to be skilful litigants in order to protect their customs, and copyholders who were badly organized could lose their rights.

In Ombersley the copyholders displayed the tenacity and cohesion necessary to protect their inheritance after being defeated in the 1607 suit. The opposition to Sandys was directed by George and Thomas Nash, sons of the Thomas Nash who died in 1606. George was at the centre of litigation from the outset because of his refusal to pay an arbitrary fine for admittance of his father's copyhold. Thomas Nash was made custodian of the 'customary booke' in which all the provisions of the 1571 decree were written.[76] He was a champion of 'honest farmers' and averse to grasping landlords, asserting that 'the original and first moving causes of many of those felonies, robberies, burglaries and murthers, which are now adayes comitted, proceeds from the Arch-Enemy to our Plowe, the Engrossing Depopulator'.[77] Sandys, on the other hand, referred to him contemptuously as one of the 'comon solicitors, followers and abettors' of the tenants.[78]

The suits which Nash solicited were financed by taxing the copyholders according to the annual value of their holdings. In 1607 he

---

[75] G. Norburie, 'The Abuses and Remedies of the High Court of Chancery', *A Collection of Tracts Relative to the Laws of England*, ed. F. Hargreaves (London, 1787), p. 434.

[76] PRO E133/42/12.

[77] Thomas Nash, *Quarternio, or a Fourfold way to a Happy Life* (London, 1633), pp. 6–7.

[78] PRO Stac 8/269/31.

organized the collection of over £200 from the tenants as a 'common purse' to support litigation. In 1608 a second levy was made by two other homagers, John Bourne and William Pardoe, to pay for suits based on the Evesham Abbey deeds, and in 1610 a further £55 was gathered, 'the better to mainteine the p(ro)ceedings'.[79] In 1613 Thomas Nash formalized the procedure by drawing up articles of agreement for the assessments and levies. In that year £600 was raised from the copyholders.[80]

Other successful attempts to protect manorial customs were associated with good organization and financial strength. At Willingham in Cambridgeshire, the tenants collected 'great somes of money amongst themselves' to finance suits over entry fines and common rights, and they were successful in restraining their rapacious lord, Sir Miles Sandys, the brother of Samuel Sandys.[81] But not all manorial tenants were able to organize themselves so effectively and some suffered from the twin disabilities, poverty and ignorance of the law, which Tawney illustrated.[82] For example, the copyholders of Wark and Harbottle in Northumberland failed to uphold strong claims to customary status because they did not coordinate their defence in Chancery or form a common fund to sustain litigation.[83] Although the central courts did much to protect customary estates of inheritance, copyholders had to present their case competently, and this demanded leadership and finance.

In Ombersley, the cohesion and legal awareness of the copyholders was not an exceptional feature but an integral part of the customary culture in seventeenth-century England. The tradition there of self-government by the manorial homage, so well established in the second half of the sixteenth century and formalized in the 1571 decree, clearly strengthened these powerful customary bonds. Samuel Sandys encountered a unified tenant population, well organized by the leading homagers and capable of defending their customs in the central courts.

Once the challenge of the first quarter of the seventeenth century had been met, the copyholders of Ombersley faced no further legal

---

[79] PRO E134, 2 Jas 1, Hilary 11; E133/152/3; Stac 8/289/6.
[80] PRO Stac 8/269/31.
[81] Spufford, *Contrasting Communities*, pp. 121–5.
[82] Tawney, *Agrarian Problem*, pp. 252–3, 302–5.
[83] S. J. Watts, 'Tenant-Right in Early Seventeenth Century Northumberland', *Northern History*, VI (1971), 75, 79–80.

threats to their customary estates or tenures. On the other hand, they failed during the upheavals of the 1640s in an opportunistic attempt to restore the 1571 decree.[84] In Ombersley the manor remained a powerful force and the returns from land were shared by the lord and the tenants by virtue of reasonable entry fines and 'fair portion' of waste land. As we shall see, the guarantee of reasonable customs also facilitated agricultural development in Ombersley.

II

In general, the manor, its customs and communal controls, are portrayed by historians as restraints on change. Areas of rural industry and rapid population growth were often areas in which manorial control was tenuous and tenurial freedom extensive. Whilst the absence of manorial control facilitated the emergence of rural industry in certain pastoral areas, the presence of customary regulations are thought to have been barriers to agricultural improvement in areas of mixed and arable farming. Despite the evident flexibility of some open field systems in accommodating complex crop rotation,[85] communal farming and manorial custom are still regarded as fossilized institutions which were gradually buried by enclosure and agricultural progress. The growth of landed estates, the steady consolidation of farms, and the spread of leasehold are considered to have provided the stability and capital required for the adoption of new methods which were crucial to agricultural progress.[86] Accordingly, the stability offered by copyhold property rights, the significance of capital channelled into farming by reasonable entry fines, and the contribution made by the communal regulation of common wastes to the supply of animal feed have received little attention.

Ombersley is a clear example of agricultural change within the customary and communal setting. The manor lies on light soils produced by an outcrop of Bunter and Keuper sandstone with a scattering of light alluvial deposits on the banks of the river Severn. These

---

[84] PRO C6/4/34.
[85] M. A. Havinden, 'Agricultural Progress in Open Field Oxfordshire', *Agric. Hist. Rev.*, IX (1961), 73–83; J. Thirsk, 'Farming Techniques', in Thirsk (ed.), *Agrarian History*, IV, pp. 177–9.
[86] E. L. Jones, 'Editor's introduction', in E. L. Jones (ed.), *Agriculture and Economic Growth in England 1650–1815* (London, 1967), pp. 9–10, 12–17.

light soils provided the natural environment for sheep and corn husbandry drawing on common wastes for additional sheep pasture.

In this extensive manor, the hamlet was the primary form of settlement. Ombersley embraced sixteen hamlets apart from the parochial village. All were drawn together by the manor and each settlement provided one homager or tythingman at the courts baron. In the early seventeenth century each township had a separate field system and the 1605 survey indicates that all of the hamlets possessed sufficient fields to warrant some communal organization, although the extent of open field tended to diminish in the outlying hamlets. The central part of Ombersley, including the villages Uphampton and Northampton, contained regular fields, whereas the outermost hamlets, Woodhouse, Acton, Ferhampton and Boreley, were by 1605 already characterized by fragmented fields and closes.[87] Extensive common wastes survived until enclosure in the early nineteenth century.[88]

The significance of the wastes lay in their importance as sheep pasture. The sandy soils of these wastes were ideal for sheep grazing and sheep were fundamental to the success of light soil arable farming.[89] This common pasture played a crucial role in arable fertility since sheep grazed on the commons during the day were folded on the arable land at night. In the early seventeenth century, the common land was most valuable to the small farmers in Ombersley where extensive open fields left little provision for pasture closes. Little could be gained in terms of arable productivity by enclosing these wastes, and their integrity was protected by strict communal control.

In 1596 an Ombersley inhabitant, testifying before commissioners appointed by the Exchequer, stated that 'the cheif livinge and maintenance of the customary tenants consisteth wholly in their tillage and keeping of sheep upon the commons'.[90] The arable, sheep, and corn emphasis of the manor was clearly displayed by the survey of 1605. The inner townships of Ombersley, Northampton and Uphampton had between 80 and 90 per cent of

[87] WRO BA 3910/29.

[88] J. A. Yelling, 'Open Field, Enclosure and Farm Production in East Worcestershire, 1540–1870', Ph.D. thesis, Birmingham University, 1966, 30, 129–37.

[89] Thirsk, 'Farming Techniques', in Thirsk (ed.), *Agrarian History*, IV, pp. 179, 188.

[90] PRO E134, 37/38 Eliz. Michaelmas 48.

their lands in arable open fields. Only in the outlying villages of later settlement did open arable fall below 50 per cent of the lands.[91] Probate inventories confirm the pre-eminence of tillage and sheep in Ombersley. The traditional rotation within the open fields was rye, barley, and fallow in equal proportions. The evidence of the division of copyhold land between the fields, particularly in the townships of Ombersley and Uphampton, suggests that this rotation was the one anciently followed within the manor.[92] By the early seventeenth century, however, a greater variety of crops was being grown. Pulses and oats were introduced, sometimes at the expense of barley as a spring crop, and gradually in place of fallow. Wheat appeared also, at least from 1623, as a supplement to rye in the winter field. But despite these developments, rye and barley remained the most important grains.[93] Sheep were the natural accompaniment to light land tillage. The median number of sheep per farm was twenty-nine, but the mean stood at thirty-five sheep since some copyholders had quite large flocks and at least three men met the commonable limit of eighty sheep.[94]

Small sheep and corn farmers like those in Ombersley appear to have faced considerable hardship between the early 1590s and the early 1630s as a consequence of the wide fluctuation in grain prices. Indeed Dr Spufford has argued that small arable farms of between 20 and 30 acres became unviable during this period of volatile price movements, and she has documented the disappearance of the small landowner of Chippenham in Cambridgeshire following the poor harvests of the 1590s.[95] This research has endorsed the general conclusions reached by Dr Bowden, who examined the problem on the basis of a schedule of costs and output for a 30-acre hypothetical farm. According to this model, small arable farms operated on very slim margins and were unable to adjust to harvest fluctuations. As a result of these characteristics, a succession of abundant or very poor harvests 'could hardly fail to bring complete ruin to small

[91] WRO BA 3910/29.
[92] WRO BA 3910/29; Yelling, 'Open Field, Enclosure and Farm Production', pp. 387–99.
[93] WRO BA 3585, 1606/5; 1609/143; 1613/210; 1614/70; 1624/97; 1638/129. PRO E134, 20 Jas 1, Michaelmas 28.
[94] WRO BA 3585, 1617/7; 1624/97; 1638/129.
[95] Spufford, *Contrasting Communities*, pp. 58–119.

cultivators'.[96] This was not the case in Ombersley. The farmers were certainly buffeted by the volatile price movements of the period; in the opening years of the seventeenth century they referred to the 'Late Dearth & Scarcytie' of the late 1590s, and in the early 1620s they were complaining that 'these times are cheape'.[97] They were also subjected to the additional strains of high mortality in the 1590s and 1610s.[98] But, despite these difficulties, the number of copyholders did not decline and Ombersley remained a community of small farmers.

In essence their survival can be attributed to the preservation of a delicate agricultural equilibrium through the system of customary property rights which regulated both the common pasturage and the level of 'rent' payments in the form of entry fines. The common wastes were immensely valuable. Primarily, they were a source of much-needed manure for the arable fields, provided by sheep, fed on the wastes and folded in the fields.[99] The sheep themselves were a direct source of income. Short-fleeced, Ryeland sheep were bred in Ombersley, and the sale of fine wool and lambs for fattening on richer pastures was a lucrative if seasonal business.[100] The commons were also a source of fuel and building materials in the shape of furze, fern, turves, clay, and stone. The tenants were well aware of the value of their commons and they knew that without the rights of pasturage and the other benefits of common they would have 'to leave theire ploughes and laye down tillage'.[101] Through the courts baron and equity jurisdiction at Westminster, the tenants protected

---

[96] Bowden, 'Agricultural Prices', in Thirsk (ed.), *Agrarian History*, IV, pp. 650–63, esp. p. 659.

[97] John Gardner referred to the dearth in his will of March 1603 and his executors echoed him in the inventory made in April 1603, WRO BA 3585, 1603/41; PRO C3/369/1.

[98] WRO Parish Archives, BA 3572: Register of baptisms, marriages, and burials in the parish of Ombersley. Mortality peaks occurred in 1593, 1597, 1610, 1613, 1615, and 1616. In these years deaths were most numerous in the last summer and early autumn and were clearly the result of sickness rather than food shortage.

[99] Sheep manure was the richest form of manure for light soils, and particularly suited to barley ground.

[100] PRO E134, 5 William & Mary, Michaelmas 54; in 1614 a witness examined at the consistory court testified to the importance of sheep-breeding in Ombersley and observed 'the tythes of lambes is one of the best tythes belongesth to the vicar of Ombersley'; WRO Diocesan archives, BA 2102: Consistory court deposition books, vol. VI, fol. 128v.

[101] PRO E134, 37 & 38 Eliz., Michaelmas 48.

the commons from over-stocking, enclosure, or encroachment by rights of free warren. The level of 'rent' payment was equally important. During the difficult 1590s, when the combination of poor harvests and increased mortality placed a significant economic burden on the Ombersley copyholders, entry fines were of only nominal value. Later in the early 1620s, when conditions were again difficult, the Court of Exchequer intervened to enforce reasonable fines of two years' value.

The importance of common pasture rights and reasonable entry fines in increasing income and containing costs can be seen by comparison with the farmers of Dr Bowden's hypothetical farm.[102] Significantly, the unviable farm was one on which all earnings came from the sale of grain and no income was derived from the sale of wool, lambs, or mutton. This model approximates to the conditions examined by Dr Spufford: in Chippenham, copyholds tended to be subdivided through semi-partible inheritance and the tenants lost the right to graze sheep on the wastes as early as 1544. Like Dr Bowden's hypothetical farmers, they kept no sheep.[103]

Reasonable entry fines and the sanctity of the wastes were fundamental to the economic viability of small sheep and corn farmers in the early seventeenth century. They provided a cushion against the effects of fluctuating grain prices to which farmers in Ombersley were exposed because their agriculture was founded on the production of grain on light soils which could not be readily converted to grazing land. Moreover, during the course of the early seventeenth century this communal and customary society proved sufficiently flexible to foster improvements in farming practice.

During the late sixteenth century the farmers of Ombersley were hampered by a chronic shortage of good pasture and meadow. Contemporaries observed that 'most lands lye open togeather one man's with another in the common fields', and there were few pasture closes except in the outlying hamlets.[104] Apart from the common wastes, the fallows were the major source of pasture and tenants often had to resort to agisting 'their cattle of husbandry' on rented pastures outside Ombersley. The scarcity of good pasture discouraged the keeping of dairy cattle and consequently the copyholders grazed 'not in general as many cattel upon the saide com-

---

[102] Bowden, 'Agricultural Prices', in Thirsk (ed.), *Agrarian History*, IV, pp. 653–5.
[103] Spufford, *Contrasting Communities*, p. 64.   [104] PRO E112/49/80.

monable places as by the rate is allowed'.[105] During the first quarter of the seventeenth century, however, the copyholders made significant improvements by introducing pulse crops in place of fallow and by adopting convertible husbandry. Both these changes disrupted the traditional crop rotation and provided more feed for the cattle.

The first signs of these improvements appeared in 1604. In July, Richard Taylor had six acres of rye and six acres of barley, the traditional crop combinations, and in addition one acre of pulse growing on land which would otherwise have been fallow. Part of his arable land was under leys and valued for 'grass on the ground'.[106] By the 1620s the system of convertible husbandry was well established and in 1628 Lady Sandys observed that throughout the manor the copyholders 'plowed their land untill it is out of heart [then] lett it lye untilled for some few yeares to gather heart againe'.[107] The adoption of convertible husbandry was not accompanied by formal enclosure but by temporary exchange and consolidation of land within the common fields. The court baron played an important part in this procedure; all exchanges were registered in the court rolls and conducted after payment of a nominal entry fine.[108] In January 1630, for example, John Guch and Francis Lambe exchanged some land temporarily through the court baron and a standard entry appeared in the court roll:

> a Licence is granted to John Guch to exchange three acres of arable land being in Patch headland, being parcel of his customary lands, with Francis Lambe for three acres of his customary lands whereof one acre and a half doe lye in either field and the rest doe lye in nyther crofte, fine a couple of fat hens.[109]

In this way the customary court adapted smoothly to the need to break away from the simple rotations of the open field and embraced a complex system of exchanges and consolidation.

As tenants in different townships freely exchanged lands, convertible husbandry spread widely and fallows were replaced by a three-crop rotation in which pulse and oats figured as feed for cattle and horses. In the summer of 1638, for instance, John Pardoe had eight acres of wheat and rye, six of barley, and six of pulse and oats.[110] These changes reinforced each other and improved pro-

[105] PRO E134, 37 & 38 Eliz., Michaelmas 48.
[106] WRO BA 3585, 1604/53.
[107] PRO E112/91/16.
[108] WRO BA 3910/20, 21, 25, 26.
[109] WRO BA 3910/21.
[110] WRO BA 3585, 1638/129.

ductivity in numerous ways. The pulse crops added nitrogen to the soil, and in conjunction with ley farming, enriched the arable and sustained higher grain productivity, particularly for barley and wheat. Since pulse crops and leys also provided animal feed they partially compensated for the scarcity of natural pasture and facilitated a modest increase in the number of dairy cattle kept by the copyholders.[111] Thus, by 1640 the small farmers of Ombersley had already placed their agriculture on a stable foundation and were less exposed to fluctuations in grain prices. Nevertheless, corn production and sheep grazing remained the foremost commercial activities and the common wastes retained their central importance.

During the first half of the seventeenth century arable production increased in Ombersley in response to the growing markets for grain in the west Midlands. The rise in cereal production was underpinned by the regulated grazing of the common wastes and the cultivation of pulse crops which together facilitated an increase in the number of sheep and thereby improved the supply of manure. Sheep folds sustained and enhanced arable productivity and in particular supported more intensive barley cultivation. The introduction of convertible husbandry was an additional prop to arable productivity but it did little to improve fertility since livestock grazed on natural grass leys tended to take out as much as they put in.[112] Only by feeding sheep on the wastes and folding them on the arable, or by growing leguminous crops like pulses as animal feed, could farmers transfer fertility to the arable land.

In the second half of the seventeenth century, however, these sources of fertility were supplemented by the introduction of clover, which improved leys dramatically and by increasing the supply of fodder allowed more sheep to be kept and better fed, thus producing more manure. Heavier applications of manure enhanced the yields of fodder crops as well as cereals and facilitated a further increase in livestock. Clover was particularly suited to light soils which were dry

---

[111] The mean number of dairy cattle recorded in the inventories increased from 1.6 per farm in the period 1601–20, to 2.4 in the years 1621–40; WRO BA 3585.

[112] Kerridge saw convertible husbandry as one of the most important aspects of agricultural improvement, responsible for a doubling of productivity: E. Kerridge, *The Agricultural Revolution* (London, 1967), pp. 39, 207–9. This claim has been conclusively refuted by Professor Jones: E. L. Jones, 'Agriculture and Economic Growth in England, 1660–1750: Agricultural Change', *Journal of Econ. Hist.*, XXV (1965), 4–5.

enough for sheep to be kept on the land during winter to feed off the fodder crops, thus returning manure for the next cereal crop.[113]

Clover was introduced into Ombersley during the middle years of the seventeenth century. Andrew Yarranton, one of the early advocates of clover, lived in Astley, just across the Severn from Ombersley. Writing in 1663 he referred specifically to the light soils of north Worcestershire and claimed that he wished 'to give my countrymen a remedy for this gravelly, dry, sandy or rye land which is worn out with tillage and liming'.[114] Clover had its greatest impact on land with little natural pasture or meadow, and farmers in and around Ombersley were amongst the first to adopt clover in place of natural leys in this region. Yarranton stressed the benefits of clover on arable land and newly laid down pasture which would not support natural grass for the first two years. He suggested that, on balance, 'six acres of land in clover will keep as many cattle as thirty acres of natural grass'.[115] In 1656, Philip Burlton was one of the first Ombersley farmers to use clover. He sowed clover seed on six acres of barley and in the spring of 1657 'mowed the same ground being then with clover grasse'. The tithe due on this ground was 'well worth twenty shillings' according to contemporary witnesses.[116] This suggests a return of £1 13s 4d an acre, so on the assumption that the tithe was rather less than a full 10 per cent, Burlton was probably achieving the forty shillings per acre return which Yarranton suggested for 'Rye land' leys.[117]

Burlton was one of the most substantial copyholders in Ombersley. In 1664 he was listed as having five hearths in the Hearth Tax returns when 70 per cent of the inhabitants were assessed on only one or two hearths. He was exceptional in having possession of three copyholds in Ombersley; when he died he had a

---

[113] Jones, 'Agriculture and Economic Growth', 3–5, 10–11; E. L. Jones, 'English and European Agricultural Development, 1650–1750', in R. M. Hartwell (ed.), *The Industrial Revolution* (Oxford, 1970), pp. 6–11, 72–3; C. Lane, 'The Development of Pastures and Meadows during the Sixteenth and Seventeenth Centuries', *Agric. Hist. Rev.*, XXVIII (1980), 24–30.

[114] A. Yarranton, *The Improvement Improved by a second Edition of the Great Improvement of land by Clover* (London, 1663), p. 33. There appears to be no first edition of this book on clover, and it is possible that the published work is a revision of a manuscript guide to clover husbandry.

[115] *Ibid.*, p. 12.

[116] PRO E134, 13 Chas 2, Michaelmas 21.   [117] Yarranton, p. 19.

personal estate valued at £640.[118] Burlton's enterprise was emulated by Walter Moyle, who sowed two acres of 'tillage' with clover in 1659 and a further five acres in 1661.[119] Moyle was not as affluent as Burlton, but he was a homager and had joined with Burlton in 1653 to organize a Chancery bill of complaint concerning heriot payments.[120] Both Burlton and Moyle held copyholds in the hamlet of Hadley and it seems to have been here, on enclosed lands, that clover was first sown. By the 1670s, however, the use of clover to improve leys was commonplace throughout Ombersley and was promoting a substantial increase in piecemeal enclosure.

During the first half of the seventeenth century the adoption of convertible husbandry had prompted the exchange and temporary enclosure of land. These exchanges increased in frequency and became much more ambitious from the 1650s as clover leys were introduced. In the 1630s, for example, enclosures rarely exceeded three acres, but by the 1660s it had become commonplace to enclose up to ten acres at a time after a series of five or six parcels of land had been exchanged.[121] The temporary enclosure of land so exchanged was effected with great economy by planting hawthorn quicksets. By the 1680s whole hamlets rather than individuals were involved in the process. In 1685 'great quantitys' of Burnhill and Greefield and a large part of a common field in Lower Northampton were enclosed and sown with clover. At about the same time, 'one inclosure . . . was made of a great part of a Common Field called Awford by several Customary tenants . . . and sowed with clover'.[122] Since Awford field covered 250 acres, the enclosure must have been substantial.

Large-scale enclosures were a further manifestation of the long tradition of communal activity which was most apparent in the regulation of common pasturage on the waste lands. In contrast to the control of the common wastes, however, the exchange and enclosure of land for clover was increasingly undertaken outside the

---

[118] PRO E179/201/312; WRO BA 3585, 1672/274. After 1660 inventories housed at the St Helen's Record Office in Worcester are not indexed individually, but are catalogued by year and stored in numbered boxes. Probate references henceforward are by year and box number only.

[119] PRO E134, Chas 2, Michaelmas 21; E134, 15 Chas 2, Hilary 11.

[120] PRO C5/41/9.

[121] WRO BA 3910/25, 26; PRO E134, 5 William & Mary, Michaelmas 54.

[122] PRO E134, 5 William & Mary, Michaelmas 54.

manorial court. Following the disagreements with the Sandys family over heriot payments in the 1650s, the homage instituted an alternative system of temporary land transfer which by-passed the court baron and deprived the manorial lord of his fee for the exchange. Land was exchanged by word of mouth in the presence of a member of the homage, thus leaving no record of the transaction. Throughout the 1680s and early 1690s the homage refused to present such exchanges at the courts baron until they were obliged to do so by the Court of Exchequer in 1697.[123]

Despite the extra-curial exchange of lands and the more complex relationship between farms and copyholds which inevitably resulted, the customary bonds remained secure and were reinforced by the Exchequer decree of 1697. Copyhold tenements remained the reference point for all exchanges and the corpus of manorial custom was not disturbed. In 1693, one of the homagers explained to the Court of Exchequer that all exchanges were at 'the will of each party exchanginge' and that 'noe alteration of the tenure or other customs or services' took place as a result of making the exchange.[124] Moreover, the rights of pasture on the wastes were still of fundamental importance, and customary regulation continued to protect the wastes from enclosure or encroachment.[125]

The introduction of clover and the piecemeal enclosure of arable for leys reinforced the traditional rural economy of Ombersley in which the sheep fold was the central pillar. Indeed, sheep numbers increased; in the first half of the seventeenth century the mean number of sheep per farm was thirty-five, whilst in the period 1670 to 1700 the mean was fifty-four. Through the release of some of the conventional leys for sheep grazing, the spread of clover facilitated the increase in sheep numbers, but the major contribution of clover was as feed for horses and cattle. The mean number of dairy cattle recorded in the inventories increased from 2.4 per farm between 1621 and 1640 to 4.5 in the years 1671 to 1700.[126] The increase in fodder allowed more livestock to be overwintered and thus a farmer

[123] PRO E112/706/28; E134, 5 William & Mary, Michaelmas 54; WRO BA 1476: copy of an Exchequer decree.

[124] PRO E112/706/28.

[125] Some 863 acres of common waste survived to be enclosed by Act of Parliament in 1814.

[126] WRO BA 3585.

like Thomas Nayer, with the aid of hay and clover 'in tabletts', could keep twelve cows and heifers through the winter of 1681.[127] More livestock produced more manure and, in conjunction with the leguminous qualities of clover, this improved the fertility of arable land. The yields of the traditional crops of rye and barley were thereby increased and in some cases farmers were encouraged to introduce wheat into the winter crop by the improved potential of the arable lands.[128]

The copyholders claimed that the introduction of clover and the related enclosure of arable land improved the value of copyholds in Ombersley by between 30 and 50 per cent during the final quarter of the seventeenth century.[129] Good corroboration of this view can be found in the level of entry fines recorded in the court rolls. Entry fines, assessed on two years' value, were rising during the later seventeenth century at a time when agricultural prices were tending to drift downwards. Entry fines seem to have increased in all the townships and across a range of absolute values. Philip Burlton's holding in Uphampton was assessed at £23 in 1673 and at £26 in 1691. A copyhold in Northampton was valued at £26 in 1661 and at £32 in 1687; the fine for a holding in Chatley was £15 in 1670 and £18 in 1685, whilst a copyhold in Powers was assessed at £12 in 1673 and at £16 in 1701.[130]

This significant improvement in agricultural productivity was achieved within a regime of customary property rights and communal regulation which proved to be both supportive and, where necessary, adaptable. In its essentials the customary society remained unchanged; land was subject to a greater degree of exchange but the copyholds retained their integrity as units of ownership and cultivation. Similarly the common wastes remained an integral part of this farming system. Here, communal regulation continued as assiduously as ever, as one William Lamb discovered when he was amerced for keeping more than eighty sheep on the wastes of Ombersley in 1703.[131]

---

[127] WRO BA 3585, 1681/297.
[128] WRO BA 3585, 1675/281, 1678/283, 1697/352, 1698/353.
[129] PRO E112/706/28.
[130] WRO BA 3910/23, 27, 43.   [131] WRO BA 3910/23.

III

Ombersley is an example of a rural society in which the customary institutions and traditional landowning structure prevailed despite the legal and economic pressures exerted on it during the seventeenth century. It would be incorrect to assert that the resilience of this community was representative of agrarian society in seventeenth-century England, but it does provide a refinement to our understanding of the forces which were steadily undermining the small customary landowner.

The developing relationship between customary law and the central courts strengthened rather than undermined the position of copyholders of inheritance during the seventeenth century. Undoubtedly historians must look elsewhere for the forces of change, since perhaps half the customary tenants in seventeenth-century England enjoyed a secure estate of inheritance. The integrity of customary law and the failure of the central courts to subsume its particular and local characteristics gave the manor a continuing significance. The efficiency of this jurisdiction and the ability of customary tenants to protect their property rights clearly varied from manor to manor. Whilst seventeenth-century England was a litigious society, the strength and determination of the Ombersley homage was representative of a community accustomed to independence rather than domination. Further research into the ecclesiastical manors, many of which were left to their own jurisdictions after the Dissolution, would no doubt provide more evidence of tenant self-determination.

Heritable copyhold estates and a strong communal spirit could offer protection against the most vehement legal challenges, but only a partial protection from the economic threats posed by volatile grain prices. The nature of inheritance customs was of critical importance. Where, as in Ombersley, custom protected against the fragmentation of holdings and in manors where the common wastes were strictly controlled, the small landowner could achieve economic security with a holding of fifteen to forty-five acres. Elsewhere, partible inheritance and the loss of common waste undermined the viability of small sheep and corn farmers during the seventeenth century.

In Ombersley small landowners did more than survive: they prospered. This Worcestershire parish provides further evidence of the adaptability of communal and open field regimes. Historians have emphasized the importance of large-scale farming and landlord capital to the agricultural advances of seventeenth-century England. With the stimulus of the growing demand for grain in the nearby markets of the west Midlands, the farmers of Ombersley were quick to adopt clover leys and to make significant improvements in agricultural productivity without the benefits of large-scale capital. They provide another example of the relatively small scale of much of the progressive enterprise of seventeenth-century England.

6. *The limitations of the probate inventory*

MARGARET SPUFFORD

In 1895, Mr J. H. Round published his collected essays under the title *Feudal England*.[1] The index entry for 'Freeman, Professor' is justifiably famous. It runs to two columns: some of the entries run as they are set out below.

Freeman, Professor:
his 'certain' history . . . his
'undoubted history' . . . his
'facts' . . . underrates feudal
influence . . . overlooks the
Worcester relief . . . influenced
by words and names . . . his
bias . . . confuses individuals
. . . his assumptions . . . his
pedantry . . . misconstrues his
Latin . . . imagines facts . . .
his supposed accuracy
. . . his guesses . . . his
confused views . . . evades
difficulties . . . his
treatment of authorities
. . . misunderstands tac-
tics . . . his special weakness . . . necessity of
criticising his work . . .

This index entry seemed likely to remain unique in the annals of criticism. However, it has recently been equalled if not surpassed, by an even longer entry in a biography of Scott.[2] This runs, in part

Scott, Robert Falcon:
early flirtations . . . runs
aground . . . unimpressed by
other Polar explorers . . .
endangers ship through
ignorance of ice . . . failure
of first attempt at sledge
travel . . . belated study
of Polar literature . . . inadequate preparation . . .
ignorance of snowcraft . . .
risks comrades' lives in
determination to achieve
southern record . . . Admiralty
mistrust of his ability . . .
his scientific knowledge
criticised . . . quarrels and
tension with companions . . .
collapses as leader . . . last
camp and immolation in

[1] J. H. Round, *Feudal England* (London, 1895), pp. 580–1.
[2] Roland Huntford, *Scott & Amundsen* (London, 1979), pp. 658–60.

139

tent . . . farewell letters . . . self-justifying message to public . . . creation of legend . . . as heroic bungler . . .

Characteristics: absent-mindedness . . . agnosticism . . . command, unsuitability for . . . criticism, refused to accept . . . depression, bouts of . . . emotionalism . . . impatience . . . improvi-

sation, belief in . . . inade-quacy, sense of . . . insecu-rity . . . insight, lack of . . . irrationality . . . isolation . . . jealousy . . . judgment, defective . . . leadership, failure in . . . literary gifts . . . panic, readiness to . . . recklessness . . . respon-sibility, instinct to evade . . . sentimentality . . . vacillation.

These index entries, which appear to have nothing whatever to do with the subject in hand, came to mind simply because I was considering the bland and pallid prose of my own index to a book on pedlars and their goods.[3] It runs, in part

Inventories, probate:
dowries omitted from:
goods omitted from: mis-
leading nature of . . .

The limitations of the probate inventory have been much in my mind since the work on pedlars, which largely rested on them, was completed. I was led to crystallize my doubts by a day conference on the probate inventories as a source, run by the ESRC in London in the autumn of 1984. Professor Cole of Swansea was then launching a project to 'explore the possibilities of using probate inventories as a source for the study of long-term economic growth in England and Wales'. The immediate objective was 'to identify a representative sample of areas in England and Wales from which long-running series of inventories have survived in sufficient abundance to form the basis of a . . . project designed to produce and analyse series illustrating the occupational distribution of the labour force, the level and consumption of household wealth, and changes in the pattern of consumption in the period from about 1529 to the mid or late eighteenth century'. In the discussion on the project, it appeared that Professor Cole's pilot study was confined to the values of household goods in inventories. These values are free

---

[3] *The Great Reclothing of Rural England: Petty Chapmen and their Wares in the Seventeenth Century* (London, 1984) (henceforward, *The Great Reclothing*).

from most, but not all, of the dangers of the source that most worry me.[4] But this chapter is the fruit of general reflection on probate inventories as a source, and further work which I have been led to carry out as a result, to see if some of the limitations of inventories could be corrected from other documents.

If this chapter concentrates on the limitations of the source, it only does so because the English can be regarded as an expert audience. English economic, social, and local historians probably know more about probate inventories as a source than any other Europeans. Ever since William Hoskins pioneered the use of inventories in 1950[5] and Joan Thirsk followed him up with her essay 'Fenland Farming in the Sixteenth Century' in 1953, inventories have been familiar. Dr Thirsk followed up her work on the Fens by her much more major study of Lincolnshire, in which for the first time she attempted to delineate agricultural regions by the analysis of inventories. They must be one of the most used sources for the *Agrarian History of England and Wales*, IV, *1500–1640* (1967). Its companion volume, V, laid the regional farming boundaries of England firmly on the map, using the same analytical techniques. The trickle of work based on the probate inventory has become a flood, demanding its own bibliography.[6] English work on agrarian history, and on vernacular architecture, also based on probate inventories, has led the field. It is astonishing that the probate inventory has only recently been 'discovered' as a new source on the continent.[7] Because the use of inventories has been pioneered in England, and they are known to be both valuable and irreplaceable, largely thanks to Dr Thirsk's work, it seems appropriate also that their disadvantages should be stressed in England, to an audience already fully aware of their potential. It is a good moment to do so, for if anything the fashion for using these convenient documents, which are so readily susceptible to analysis, is growing. This paper concentrates on one disadvantage, the omission of debts owing by the dead

---

[4] See below, pp. 144–5, for reservations.

[5] W. G. Hoskins, *Essays in Leicestershire History* (Liverpool, 1950).

[6] Mark Overton, *A Bibliography of British Probate Inventories* (Dept. of Geography, Newcastle upon Tyne, 1983). Dr Overton's own work is probably the best introduction to recent developments in the field.

[7] A. G. Bijdragen, *23, Probate Inventories: A New Source for the Historical Studies of Wealth, Material Culture and Agricultural Development*, ed. A. Van der Woude and A. Schuurman (Wageningen, 1980). The 'newness' of the source is stressed not only in the title, but in the Introduction, pp. 2–3.

person from the inventory, but it seems convenient to itemize other disadvantages, before concentrating on the omission of debt.

I

Every economic historian knows that real estate is not included in an inventory. The inventory only legally listed goods belonging to the administrator, or executrix, of an estate.[8] These included movable goods and leasehold land, but not real property. Real property included copyhold land, which would descend according to the custom of the manor if it was not bequeathed in a will, and freehold land, which descended according to common law, if it, similarly, was not bequeathed. Some of the omissions of an inventory can therefore be repaired if a will survives. Even so, only two-thirds of freehold land could be willed, although all leasehold and copyhold could. There was no necessity to bequeath any property at all if the testator desired it to go to the executrix or executor. In this case, it would not appear in either will or inventory. However, the two documents together do give a much more balanced picture. It is often one which is much at variance with the picture of a man's prosperity drawn from the inventory alone.

The will, which may accompany the inventory, is not nearly so readily broken down, nor does it lend itself to computer analysis, yet the total, brutal, differences between the individuals who look so alike from an analysis of their inventories can only be demonstrated from these documents taken in conjunction with each other. The most striking example among the group of inventories on which I have recently been working, those of the petty chapmen, or pedlars, also happened to be that of a man who appeared from his inventory to be the most outstandingly successful of them all. Charles Yarwood of Macclesfield had money and goods worth, according to his inventory, a total of £9,226 4s 8d. This included 'shop goods' valued at £497 8s. He had in the house and 'att London' at his death, the colossal sum of £3,454, and was also owed over £5,000 in good and bad debts. However, Charles Yarwood's will told a very different story. It laid down that his debts owing at his

---

[8] Both nouns have appropriate feminine forms. I have not wished to use four nouns to replace two, and cover all the variables, and have therefore deliberately used the masculine version of one and the feminine of the other here.

death to Francis Dashwood of the City of London should be paid out of the 'monies which I have Lodged in his hands, and such as there shall bee found in my owne custody soe farr as itt will Extend'. If, on the other hand, 'these monies shall fall short to discharge the said debt . . . the residue thereof to be paid out of my Personal Estate'. If, in turn, 'that bee not sufficient for that purpose' then his debts were to be paid out of the sale of the burgage in Macclesfield he lived in, and the messuage of which he had a lease in Upholland, Lancashire.

Patently, his financial affairs were not in the straightforwardly healthy state the inventory would give the reader to suppose. He was himself a worried man, because the provision for payment of his debts 'if what I have before appointed for payment to my debts shall fall short to discharge them all' is repeated three times in different wording in the will.

Charles Yarwood may have provided the most dramatic, but he did not provide by any means the only example of the way inventories can mislead. For instance, when they died in 1663, 1712, and 1714, Thomas Large of Foulsham in Norfolk, Walter Martin of York, and John Young of Brasted in Kent left gross estates which from their inventories were worth £73, £65, and £71 respectively. Thomas Large, from his inventory, had a well-furnished house, and was totally dependent on his chapman's trade. He had a good stock, worth £49, and presumably travelled to sell it. However, his will left his widow all his goods, land, tenements, and 'shoppes' in Foulsham on the condition that she was 'to be Carefull in the paying of my debts, according to the trust I have reposed in her'. Walter Martin of York had selling goods worth £62, more than those of Thomas Large, listed in his inventory of 1712, and his gross estate was worth £65. There was no indication of indebtedness at all. His will, unlike that of Thomas Large, not only failed to reveal the existence of any real property, but also stated 'I am indebted to Mr. John Dickinson of the City of York, Linen Draper for a Considerable Sum of money.' It left all the goods to him in at least part-payment. The selling wares of John Young were worth £50 a couple of years later. He looked at first sight much less prosperous than Walter Martin, except for his hopeful debts. This will revealed not only that he was not, like Thomas Large and even more, Walter Martin, heavily indebted, but also that he was in a position to bequeath 'messuages, lands and appurtenances' lying both in Leigh and in Tonbridge, as well as the residue which presumably included his shop and house at Brasted. Yet both the selling wares and the gross estates of Martin and Young look very comparable.[9]

Here, then, are examples of estates in which comparison of the will with the inventory reveals something of the real estate omitted by the inventory, and demonstrates that the financial standing of men who from their inventories look extremely similar is, in fact, very different indeed. The inventory alone is a seriously misleading document.

Its most major defect may be in the omission of the freehold or copyhold land, the real property, which may appear in part in the wills. But the inventories also mislead in other ways. They do not reveal occupations properly. We are becoming more and more conscious of the importance both of dual occupations and of the family budget. The probate inventory throws no direct light on a man's second occupation, unless by inference from his tools. It also frequently reveals a difference of opinion about a man's social status made by his neighbours in the inventory and his own opiniion, or his scribe's opinion, revealed in his will.

The legal scope of an inventory, which included only movable goods, that is those which belonged to the administrator or executrix, explains two other possible omissions in the inventory, both of which could be serious to historians using household goods as an index of spending power and consumption. The bequests made in a will were sometimes not included in the inventory. These were often the testator's most precious possessions. Edward Chew of Lancashire, for instance, left his 'Clock and Chimbs' to a son in 1697. A clock is one of the really significant possessions in the late seventeenth century, but the possession of this one could only be deduced by the wary historian from the existence of a room called 'the Clock Chamber' in the house. The clock itself, separately bequeathed, had been removed by the time the inventory was made.

John Uttinge of Great Yarmouth appears to have worried about the possible abstraction of goods not specifically bequeathed by him from his inventory. He was a linen-draper-cum-chapman, who left over £65 in bequests 'in goods out of my shop' when his will was made on 20 February 1627. He appointed four appraisers in the will,

---

[9] *The Great Reclothing*, pp. 37–9.

and said his goods were to be appraised within seven days after his death. After the appraisal, the key of the shop was to be delivered to his supervisor: the goods bequeathed were to be handed over at the shop within two months. However, although three of the four men Uttinge wanted as appraisers did in fact act for him, they did not make their inventory until 9 April. The whereabouts of the key meanwhile has to be borne in mind. It is almost certain that £65 worth of goods bequeathed in the will were not included in the total of £100 worth of goods the appraisers did list. Omission on this scale, if it was common, would seriously distort conclusions drawn from the household goods remaining within an inventory, since there is no reason to suppose that the habits of testators were uniform.

Yet another possible omission affecting the household goods and consumables in an inventory concerned the widow's property. My work on the pedlars drew my attention to peculiar examples of men who appeared from their inventories to be itinerant pedlars with nothing but their selling wares and the clothes they stood up in, who appeared from their wills or administrations to be married. There were also cases in which the wife's original dowry was separately listed in the inventory.[10] There is no indication of how often her possessions, or portion, were excluded altogether, if she was not the executrix.[11] Without her goods, the house would appear very scantily furnished indeed.[12]

Despite these disadvantages, the household goods in inventories do provide an index of domestic comfort and consumption which

---

[10] Amy Louise Erickson, of Corpus Christi College, Cambridge, tells me she has found examples of widows' inventories including goods which were not in the earlier inventory of the husband.

[11] The inclusion of goods originally belonging to the wife seems to have been debatable. Her apparel, her bed, and any personal ornaments, later called *paraphernalia*, were, according to Burn, to be omitted from the husband's inventory by law. Different authorities disputed this, but, he eventually summarized, 'if we shall respect what hath been used and observed . . . widows have been tolerated to reserve to their own use, not only their apparel and a convenient bed, but a coffer with divers things therein necessary for their own persons; which things have usually been omitted out of the inventory of the dead husband's goods . . . '. Richard Burn, *Ecclesiastical Law* (1st edition, London, 1763), pp. 649–51. Individual appraisers may well have been confused, or cajoled.

[12] *The Great Reclothing*, pp. 40–1, for Chew, Uttinge, and omission or separate listing of the wife's property.

show change over time, just as the crops on the ground or in the barn, and the stock in the yard, provide information on farming practices. Mrs Rachel Garrard's work comparing interior furnishings in Suffolk between the late sixteenth and the late seventeenth centuries[13] and Dr Lorna Weatherill's work[14] examining the distribution of certain key household goods by period, region, and social status both show inventories providing the material for broad brush-strokes to draw outlines.

But there are maddening omissions of goods by the appraisers, either for legal reasons or because of the low value of the items. These goods omitted for legal reasons could be extremely significant. 'Corn growing upon the ground, ought to be put into the inventory; seeing it belongeth to the executor: but not the grass or trees so growing; which belong to the heir, and not to the executor', ran the legal direction.[15] In the same way, grass ready to be cut for hay, apples, pears and other fruit on the trees, shall not go to the executors because they come 'merely from the soil, without the industry or manurance of man'. The protagonists of arboriculture and the orchard growers of the seventeenth century[16] were therefore engaged in labours not yet recognized as such by the law in the eighteenth century. As a result the spread of orchards and their fruit cannot be traced in inventories, which listed only the 'executors'' goods. Hops, saffron, and hemp came in a different category 'because sown; shall go to the executors', said the law. These therefore should, and often did, appear in inventories. However, the logic applied by legal maxim is bewildering to the modern mind. The 'new' root crops were also sown, yet one judgement was recorded that 'roots in gardens, as carrots, parsnips, turneps [sic] . . . and such like, shall not go to the executor, but to the heir', since they could 'not be taken without digging and breaking the soil'. Of roots in the open fields nothing was said, but the same judgement

---

[13]   Rachel P. Garrard, 'Patterns of Conspicuous Consumption and Spending on the Domestic Environment in England, 1560–1700', Cambridge Ph.D. thesis in progress, 1982. See her paper 'English Probate Inventories and their Use in Studying the Significance of the Domestic Interior, 1570–1700', A. G. Bijdragen 23, pp. 55–82.

[14]   L. M. Weatherill, *Consumer Behaviour and Material Culture in Britain, 1660–1760* (London, 1988).

[15]   All quotations from Burn, *Ecclesiastical Law*, pp. 646–7; Wills, ch. 5, para. 10.

[16]   Joan Thirsk (ed.), *Agrarian History of England and Wales*, V (Cambridge, 1985), pp. 309–11.

may have applied. They might therefore not be found in an inventory. It seems highly likely that the historian might search as hopefully, but quite as vainly, for root crops in inventories as for fruit, egged on by mentions of saffron, hops, and hemp. Awareness of the legal distinctions involved, which are by no means self-evident, is very necessary. Moreover, the law was, in some ways, attempting to bring itself up to date, and was, therefore, even more confused. There was nominal awareness that improved grassland did involve the 'industry and manurance of man', even if arboriculture was as yet unrecognizable as the fruit of human industry. According to the textbook, for '*clover*, *sain foin* and the like, the reason of manurance, labour and cultivation is the same as for corn; but no case hath occurred, wherein these matters have come in question; this kind of husbandry having been in use only of late years'. It seems that, at least in theory, clover, sainfoin, and lucerne should have appeared in inventories along with hops, saffron, and hemp, whereas fruit could never, and roots very rarely, be found there. Here, however, yet another set of disadvantages comes into play, on top of the legal ones. The appraisers, as well as not necessarily being informed of the exact detail of the law, were extremely unlikely to bother to list goods which were insignificant in value. But goods of small size and trifling value can be extremely significant to the historian looking for clues in all sorts of areas, from agriculture, to literacy, to the 'growth of the consumer society'. Such goods could well be covered by the frequent use of 'etc.' or 'and other things', or 'other lumber'. Seed for improved seventeenth-century grassland, for instance, is usually missing, although it was of vital agricultural importance. Dr Thirsk discusses the spread of ideas and information amongst the gentry after 1649 on the cultivation of clover, sainfoin, and lucerne, but it is not possible to underpin this discussion with the spread of these seeds amongst non-gentle society, because their possession cannot be demonstrated from the inventories.[17] Only if a man had an unusually large quantity of seed would it appear in an inventory. Michael Havinden's elegant and convincing demonstration of improvement in the open fields of Oxfordshire, which showed the median sheepflock in the inventories there increasing fourfold in size from fourteen between 1580 and 1640, to sixty between 1660

---

[17] Joan Thirsk, 'Agricultural Innovations and their Diffusion', in *Agrarian History*, V, pp. 553–6.

and 1730, rested on the spread of improved grassland within the open fields to support these extra animals.[18] It is fortuitous but remarkably useful that Robert Plot, with his maddening fixation for only describing the unusual and the abnormal, wrote in 1677 in his *History of Oxfordshire* of the new grasses that they were grown everywhere, 'so nothing of it'. Mr Havinden's discussion did not, and could not, rest on direct evidence from inventories. As he wrote on another new crop, 'the earliest reference to turnips which I have come across in examining thousands of probate inventories from Oxfordshire is in 1727, when John Deane, a cordwainer of Brize Norton, had twenty bushels of turnip seed worth 10s. a bushel'.[19] He deduced from this an absence of turnip husbandry in Oxfordshire. However, in view of the legal attitude to roots, at least in gardens, as part of the freehold, we can probably draw no conclusions at all about the presence, or absence, of the turnip and its like from the open fields of Oxfordshire, or anywhere else either. The additional unwillingness of the appraisers to list goods of small value meant that seed in stock, rather than crops in the ground, would only appear in an inventory if, like John Deane's turnip seed, it was present in usually large quantities. Therefore, although the 'seedsmen' who appear in the fifth volume of the *Agrarian History* as such important figures as the source of supplies for these new crops are frequently discussed, they, and their customers, remain shadowy figures, because the possession of such seeds cannot be demonstrated. Amongst the itemized goods of the petty chapmen whose surviving inventories were collected by me only two mention seeds specifically. Roger Carrington of Lincoln had 'onion seed' which must have been a large enough quantity to bother with, because it was worth 20s in 1613. John Bibbie of Manchester had 'garden seed' lumped together with worsted yarn and other selling goods in 1661. Inventories cannot be used either for evidence of the cultivation, or diffusion, of many of the new crops: yet the absence of these from them has sometimes been taken as evidence. Indeed, the sneaking suspicion arises that the relative lengths of the sections devoted to various new crops in works of agricultural history may in

[18] M. A. Havinden, 'Agricultural Progress in Open Field Oxfordshire', *Agric. Hist. Rev.*, 9, part 2 (1961), 73–83. See also M. A. Havinden (ed.), *Household and Farm Inventories in Oxfordshire, 1550–90* (Oxfordshire Record Society, 1965).

[19] Havinden, 'Agricultural Progress', 77.

some way relate not to the relative importance of these crops, but their legal status, as well as their relative overall value, in the minds of the appraisers who drew up the inventories on which such works to some extent depend.

In a completely different area of interest, the historian of literacy likewise finds it impossible to trace the spread of cheap print from the probate inventory. Almanacs, chapbooks and ballads, items worth 1d to 3d when new in the seventeenth century, stood no chance of being listed as old, whereas a family's expensive bound bible might. So the spread of reading habits amongst the barely literate, those who could read but not write, is untraceable.[20]

The historian working on the 'growth of the consumer society' finds it is equally impossible to trace the spread of the humble shirt, or indeed any other clothing, since items of clothing are so rarely separately appraised in England. A shirt would be a particularly useful index of domestic comfort and consumption.[21] Yet 349 Suffolk inventories made between 1570 and 1599 yield thirty-seven references to shirts and none to shifts. Three hundred and ninety-seven inventories made between 1680 and 1700 yield only thirteen references to shirts and three to shifts. It is inconceivable that shirts and shifts were becoming less common, in the light of a set of Suffolk overseers' accounts for the 1630s, as well as the accounts of detailed expenditure on children's clothes discussed below.[22] The overseers' accounts list the clothing made for children for whom the parish was responsible. They were fitted up with one 'suit' of outer clothing, or a petticoat and waistcoat, one or two canvas bodices for girls, one pair of hose knitted of grey yarn, and one pair of shoes apiece. But they all had two shifts, made of two yards of linen each, or two linen shirts. The girls had two coifs each. The linen, in this

---

[20] Margaret Spufford, *Small Books and Pleasant Histories* (paperback edition, Cambridge, 1985), pp. 48–9.
[21] For what follows, and the limited appearances of clothing in inventories, see *The Great Reclothing*, pp. 125–9. Dr Weatherill did what could be done on the lump sums given by appraisers in a paper given to the Pasold Conference on the Economic and Social History of Dress in September 1985, 'Consumer Behaviour, Textiles and Dress: The Evidence from Probate Papers and Household Accounts, 1670–1730'. She then stated that clothing was not mentioned at all in about a fifth of her sample of 2,902 inventories. It was as likely to be omitted in the inventories of the rich as in those of the poor. Moreover, only half of the inventories valued clothes separately from cash and other personal possessions like saddles, watches, and jewellery. Details of individual items were very rare.
[22] See below, p. 171.

case, was lockram. If even 'parish' children had a change of shifts or shirts by the 1630s in Suffolk, the probate inventories have to be misleading here. Moreover, Gregory King's unpublished table of the 'Annual Consumption of Apparell' of 1688 includes no fewer than ten million shirts and smocks, at 2s 6d or 2s each. This figure was only equalled by that for stockings, and exceeded by that for shoes. It indicates that every family in the kingdom was acquiring over seven new shirts or smocks a year. Such garments were, then, commonplace. It seems much more likely that the increasing cheapness and spread of the garments made them objects for appraisers to ignore. An increased rarity of comment thus perversely argues a spread of usage. The paradox is that as an article becomes commoner and cheaper, it appears less often in inventories, once it has fallen below a certain value. A new, or still unusual, object would attract attention, however. Window curtains were another very useful index of increasing comfort. They were also cheap. Yet the proportion of inventories in which window curtains were recorded grew rapidly from 7 to 21 per cent from 1675 to 1725.[23] Some labourers had them.[24] It seems therefore quite possible logically to claim that the disappearance of the shirt from Suffolk inventories has nothing to do with the disappearance of the garment from Suffolk backs, but on the contrary, argues its increasing ubiquity.

II

Lastly, I come to the second most important drawback of inventories after the omission of real estate, and the one on which this chapter focusses. In 1974 I wrote of the way English rural society, like the French rural society of the Beauvaisis, was underpinned by a complex system of debt and credit, and the powerful motive to learn reading that the ubiquity of the bill or bond must have provided.[25] In the following year, Dr Holderness's first article drawing attention to inventories as a source for credit appeared.[26] 'Infor-

---

[23] Weatherill, *Consumer Behaviour*.

[24] *The Great Reclothing*, pp. 115–16, especially nn. 26 and 27.

[25] Margaret Spufford, *Contrasting Communities* (paperback edition, Cambridge, 1979), pp. 78–82, 212–13. The 'forthcoming article' cited as n. 48, p. 80, was made redundant by Dr Holderness's work. See also below, p. 173.

[26] B. A. Holderness, 'Credit in a Rural Community, 1600–1800: Some Neglected Aspects of Probate Inventories', *Midland History*, III (1975–6), 94–115.

mation about debts which they reveal has so far been neglected', he wrote. But inventories, although they draw our attention to debt, only do so by revealing good, or bad, debts due to the dead man. Only a minority record his debts to others. Indeed, they should not have done so. 'Debts, which the deceased owed to others, ought not to be put in the inventory, because they are not the goods of the deceased, but of other persons', wrote Burn.[27] Dr Holderness said tentatively in 1975 'One must assume that a proportion of the "credits" revealed would have been offset by "debits" if only a balanced account existed . . . the inventories reveal neither the real extent of borrowing within particular communities nor the complex network of credit amongst various social groups in the country-side . . .'[28]

The magnitude of the problem and the way in which probate inventories can mask the actual state of a man's finances, even excluding the most major item, real estate, was brought home to me by the study of a tiny group of citizen-stationers of London. The aim was to establish the profitability of their businesses. This tiny group of people provided two extreme examples.[29] Josiah Blare and Charles Bates were men whose total movables, the value of which could be established in their inventories, were worth £341 and £400 in 1707 and 1716. They looked extremely similar in financial standing. But they left real net estates, the value of which could be established from the Orphans' Accounts of the Freemen of the City of London, of £3,274 and £236 respectively. The difference was accounted for by Josiah Blare's very considerable investments. My sense of caution, and of moving on quicksand in the use of inventories to establish net wealth, even excluding real property, was increased by these two men. The prospect of documents like this being treated even as 'semi-complete' indices of a person's net movable estate alone is an alarming one. There seems to be no reason why there should be any consistent pattern in habits of indebtedness or in savings, which should cancel each other out.

Alarm was not allayed by work on the pedlars. A total of 127 probate inventories for petty chapmen were found, but it was only possible to establish a net estate for 23 of these after their debts had

---

[27] Burn, *op. cit.*, p. 646.   [28] Holderness, 94, 95, 108.

[29] See Spufford, *Small Books and Pleasant Histories*, pp. 85–90, for a full discussion of Josiah Blare and Charles Bates, and the misleading nature of their inventories.

Table 1. *Gross and net values of chapmen's movables in the sixteenth and seventeenth centuries*

Rank order (gross)	Total inventory value	Value of goods	Debts owed to him	Name	Place	Date	Debts owed by him	Net value	Rank order (net)
1	£411	£13	£398	Richard Trendall	Norfolk	?1595	£396	£16	9
2	£402			Thomas Teisdale	Lincoln	1619	£236	£166	2
3	£282	£260	£22	James Pilkington	Lincs.	1635	£35	£247	1
4	£161	£104	£57	Thomas Walker	Lancs.	1662	£15	£147	4
5	£160	£93	£67	Robert Marler	Lancs.	1558	c. £10	c. £150	3
6	£117	£10	£107	John Crosby	Bristol	1674	£58	£60	5
7	£86	£83	£3	Robert Wilkinson	Lincoln	1678	£115	−£29	20
8	£83	£18	£65	Robert Chadwick	Rochdale	1661	£47	£37	7
9	£65	£65	nil	Walter Martin	York	1712	More than estate	Nega-tive	16?
10	£65	£65	nil	John Tomkins	Bristol	1661	£23	£42	6
11	£61			William Wilson	Boston	1666	£73	−£12	19
12	£53	£43	£10	John Poynton	Notts.	1658	£80+	−£37+	23
13	£39			Reece Barratt	Salop	1675	£32	£7	11
14	£35	£21	£14	William Davies	Bucks.	1588	£68	−£33	22
15	£33	£33	nil	John Smith	Herts.	1615	£26	£7	12
16	£31	£25	£6	Roland Johnson	Penrith	1683	£28	£3	14
17	£28	£28	nil	John Hollinshead	Macclesfield	1688	£29	−3s	17
18	£28	£12	£16	Samuel Dewhurst	Rochdale	1680	£3	£26	8
19	£27	£19	£8	Anne Hall	Cumberland	1670	£18	£10	10
20	£18	£18	nil	Christopher Dalton	Holderness	1695	£50+	−£32+	21
21	£18	£7	£11	William Davidson	Tweedmouth	1663	£18	12s	15
22	£11			Charles Cutliffe	Lincs.	1625	£15+	−£4+	18
23	£11	£8	£3	Oliver Jones	Hereford	1665	£7	£5	13

All figures are rounded to the nearest pound.

been collected, and above all, their creditors paid. Even this 'net estate' was, of course, the value of movable goods and cash only, excluding any real estate. These twenty-three were listed in rank order of the total assessed value of their movables downwards (see Table 1). Then, after calculating the net estate after collection, and payment, of debts had been made, a new rank order of their estates in terms of movable goods was established. This new rank order was frequently very different from the first one.[30] Furthermore, whereas the median gross wealth of all 127 chapmen, excluding debts, was £28, the median net estate of the 23 for whom a net estate could be established after their creditors were paid off was only £6 19s 8d, though the group included some of the more substantial men.[31]

It could well be objected that the changes in rank order of financial status among the pedlars are too small to be of any significance, especially since the group were almost all worth under £100 gross. However, the fact that no reliable economic hierarchy could be established amongst them from the inventories alone suggested that there might well be equally misleading examples over a much wider economic span of people. Indeed, the nasty warning provided by Josiah Blare and Charles Bates, worth £341 and £400 from their inventoried wealth, but £3,274 and £236 in reality, showed the real adjustments to be made are very great indeed. These adjustments might mean not only that an inventory cannot be trusted to establish the true net economic worth of any individual's estate, but also the standing of whole social groups within the population for which inventories were made might be affected. An essay for Joan Thirsk seemed a very suitable place to explore not only the disadvantages of the inventory, but any documentary source which might redress these disadvantages.

Such a source does indeed exist, in the form of the barely known and little exploited[32] final document in the probate series required by the ecclesiastical courts, the probate, or administrator's account. These listed all the expenses paid out of the deceased's estate, usually a year after death, but sometimes more. The account began by stating the amount recorded at the foot of the inventory as 'the

---

[30] See, for instance, nos. 5, 9, 14 and 18.

[31] *The Great Reclothing*, pp. 43, 69–70.

[32] As far as I know, these documents have been used exclusively by Clare Gittings, *Death, Burial and the Individual in Early Modern England* (London, 1984).

charge' or money at the disposal of the executor or administrator. So whether or not the inventory survives, its total is still known. The account continued by listing all payments outwards by the executor or executrix, from the physic and funeral expenses, through those of raising minor children or paying bequests to those who had attained their majority, the payment of back debts, rent, parish expenses, and the court costs. They finish by recording the sum left in the hands of the executor or administrator, or possibly the amount by which he or she was overspent, by deducting this expenditure from the credit sum in the inventory. Directions are sometimes recorded by the court on the way this final remaining sum is to be divided to support the widow and heirs. The probate accounts do, in fact, meet the need expressed by Dr Holderness in 1975, when he lamented the lack of 'a balanced account'. Moreover, they most certainly do 'reveal the real extent of borrowing within particular communities', as well as 'the complex network of credit amongst various social groups in the countryside'.[33]

Although the probate accounts are rare, they are not as rare as has been supposed.[34] At least 27,000 of them survived. Happily, one of the largest groups is in Lincoln. For reasons of *pietas*, this was the most suitable county to work on, since Dr Thirsk's own work on inventories was based there. Moreover, Dr Holderness's work on credit was also, felicitously, based on Lincolnshire.

An investigation of the probate accounts for Lincolnshire to explore the relationship between inventoried wealth and the final probate account wealth further therefore seemed the ideal subject for this chapter. Groups of seventeenth-century probate accounts for Lincolnshire labourers, husbandmen, and yeomen were

---

[33] See above, p. 151.

[34] I became interested in probate accounts during my work on chapmen, and suggested they might form a fruitful source to Amy Louise Erickson for her thesis, 'Property Ownership and the Financial Obligations of Women in Early Modern England' (Cambridge PhD. thesis, submitted 1989). Erickson's preliminary survey of surviving accounts shows there are at least 27,000 in various record offices in England, mostly concentrated from the mid sixteenth to the late seventeenth centuries. My husband, Dr Peter Spufford, and I have submitted (autumn 1986) a joint proposal to the ESRC which, if it is accepted, will enable us to produce an index to these survivors in the *British Record Society* series. We hope if the proposal is accepted that the volume may appear in 1993. Meanwhile, I would like to thank Amy Erickson very warmly for her help with this project so far, and for collecting the sample of probate accounts for Lincolnshire which form the basis of the following discussion.

examined. Twenty-nine accounts were found for labourers, thirty-five for husbandmen, and thirty-five for yeomen.[35]

The immediate aims were firstly, to discover whether the final credit sum given in the probate inventory bore any predictable relationship to the final net estate of the dead man given at the end of the probate account. Secondly, I wanted to know whether the initial financial status of individuals in each social group, in relation to each other, gave any reliable guide to the final size of their estates and their ultimate financial standing, or whether the inventoried sums were as wildly misleading for other social groups in the countryside as they had been for the migrant chapmen. That is, did the degree of indebtedness of individuals vary so much that their relative prosperity within the group changed violently in relation to each other, and was it very different from that which the reader would deduce from the inventory? Thirdly, even if the rank order of individuals within each group in relation to each other did change wildly, did the financial relationship of each group to other groups remain constant, or did that also change? In other words, just how much ultimate economic difference was there between rural groups labelled by themselves, or described by their neighbours as 'yeomen', 'husbandmen', and 'labourers'?

The twenty-nine labourers' accounts showed that from the assets included on their probate inventories at their deaths, they were worth from £12 to £89. The lower quartile ran from £12 to £20 and the upper from £42 to £89. The median inventory wealth was £29. The accounts themselves showed a very different picture. After funeral and sickness expenses, the court expenses, the debts, rent, and necessary charges for the upkeep of minor children had been deducted from the inventory values, the administrators of these

---

[35] The ninety-nine inventories and accounts examined came from the early 1630s, and from 1660 to the mid 1680s. There were thirteen from the 1630s, nearly forty from the 1660s, thirty from the 1670s, and just over a dozen from the 1680s. Despite the disparity in dates, it seemed fair to compare the values of the probate inventories given in each, since a graph of decennial averages of agricultural products from the 1590s to the 1740s, taken from the statistical Appendices to the *Agrarian History*, IV (1967) and V (1985), shows rough comparability between the beginning of the decade of the 1660s and the end of the 1680s, despite a drop of five index points to the mid 1670s. The figures obtained from table XIII of the *Agrarian History*, IV, p. 862 were reduced to the same level as table XII of *Agrarian History*, V, p. 856. Agricultural prices were obtained by multiplying all figures by 104/644, and industrial prices by multiplying by 97/306.

Table 2. *Gross and net value of labourers' estates in Lincolnshire in the seventeenth century from probate inventories and probate accounts*

Order (gross)	Gross wealth: inventory total	Name	Place	Date (inventory or account)	Net wealth: account total	Order (net)
1	£89 5s 0d	Jo. Hanson	Burgh-in-Marsh	1680	£60 17s 7d	2
2	£79 2s 2d	Ric. Charles	Asklackby	1669	£64 17s 1d	1
3	£73 19s 4d	Will. Anthony	Helprioryhorn	1665	£50 4s 1d	3
4	£68 11s 8d	Hammond Craven	Boothion	1678	-£2 15s 0d	25
5	£62 4s 8d	Steph. Drust	Wrawby	1662	£29 17s 0d	5
6	£44 4s 6d	Wm Walton	Gainsborough	1676	£21 3s 0d	6
7	£42 9s 6d	Chris. Picklington	Cumberworth	1669	£38 19s 4d	4
8	£36 16s 8d	Ed. Mason	Scremby	1669	£20 2s 0d	7
9	£34 7s ?d	Fra. Martin	Little Panton	1670	£20 0s 1d	8
10	£34 3s 4d	Thos Roweth	Swineshead	1670	£17 ?s ?d	10
11	£33 13s 6d	Jo. Chapman	Poynton	1670	£4 5s 6d	22
12	£33 6s 8d	Thos Lyson	Ashby cum Fenby	1680	£17 3s 0d	12
13	£32 10s 4d	Nic. Collingwood	Lincoln	1669	12s 7d	24
14	£31 16s ?d	Jo. Froth	Croft	1672	-£7 3s 0d	28
15	£29 7s 6d	Matth. Burtoft	Burringham	1666	£5 16s 8d	21
16	£28 2s 0d	Thos Brown	Horncastle	1670	£12 19s 4d	14
17	£27 3s 8d	Chas Johnson	Swineshead	1670	£15 6s 2d	13
18	£25 0s 2d	Will. Reader	Flixborough	1667/8	£17 3s ?d	11
19	£23 9s 10d	Geo. Martin	Awborne	1669	£9 8s 0d	16
20	£23 0s 0d	Dan. Hardell	Coulsterworth	1631	£17 12s 0d	9
21	£21 4s 8d	Robt Hall	Skirbeck	1630/1	£7 10s 4d	19
22	£21 1s 0d	Walt. Jebb	Deeping St James	1667	£7 9s 0d	20
23	£20 0s 0d	Jo. Morgan	Saleby	1678	£11 1s 2d	15
24	£19 8s 0d	Will. Townend	Haxey	1671	-£3 8s 1d	27
25	£17 7s 6d	Hen. Bauger	Brigend, Horbling	1632	£8 3s 10d	18
26	£16 6s 4d	Tobias Chapman	Croxby	1632	£8 19s 2d	17
27	£15 7s 8d	Will. Michaill	Wrangle	1666	-£3 2s 6d	26
28	£13 0s 0d	Will. Clapham	Weston	1683	-£10 14s 4d	29
29	£11 17s ?d	Godfrey Wood	Willoughton	1678	£3 15s 4d	23

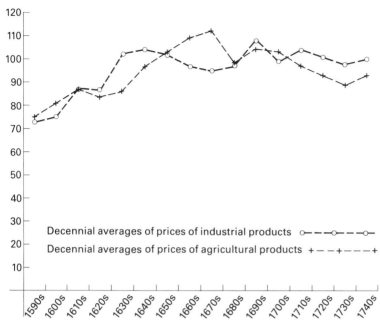

Figure 2 Decennial averages of prices of industrial and agricultural products (source: *The Agrarian History of England and Wales*, IV and V; 1640–1749 = 100)

labourers generally ended up at least £20 worse off then the totals in the inventories would have led the reader to expect. The labourers' estates ended up in a range, from the unfortunate administrator who was £11 out of pocket after paying all the charges, to the man who still had a net credit of £65 after all debts were paid. The lower quartile now ran from −£11 to £4 in credit, and the upper from £20 to £65. But there was no predictable relationship between the total value of the labourer's probate inventory and the net value at the end of his account. The labourers' degrees of indebtedness and their family and demographic circumstances varied so much that it was quite impossible to tell from the figures at the end of the inventory how any individual estate would end up. Just under a third of the twenty-nine labourers' estates moved six places or more either up, or down, in order of value between the first, probate inventory, value, and the final probate account value. The median value of the labourers' probate accounts was that of the estate of John Morgan of Saleby, £11 1s 2d (see Table 2 and Figure 3).

Substance is given to these rather bleak figures by considering further the situations of Matthew Burtoft, the labourer with the median inventoried wealth, and John Morgan, the labourer with the median net probate account wealth. Matthew Burtoft of Burringham, in the Lincolnshire fens, had had goods valued at £29 7s 6d in 1667. His inventory survived and showed him living in a two-roomed cottage with a 'parlour' for sleeping and a 'house' fulfilling all other functions. The place was in considerable domestic disorder, with a strike of rye and a straw skip as well as a wheel and yarn in the parlour, and the coulter and share of a plough in the 'house', which was meagrely furnished with essentials. There were only three pairs of sheets and a single blanket to go with the standing bed and the trundle bed in the parlour, although it did have bed curtains. The only modest signs of comfort were the three cushions in the 'house'. The stock in the yard suggested that Matthew had common rights, for he had seven cows, yearlings, and calves as well as two little pigs, geese, hens, and a cock. He also had two old horses and a cart and the gears. These, along with the ploughshare in the hall and 'hemp, hemp seed and wheat' in store suggested that he did hold an acre or two of land and did not depend only on wages. He also had a stock of peat in the yard and part of a 'small moore' valued at £3. But the number of his tools suggested employment as an agricultural labourer as well, for he possessed forks, spades, pruning hooks, and mole-catching equipment. All in all, then, the inventory indicated that Matthew and his household ploughed some land and cultivated wheat and rye, grew and spun hemp and yarn, dug and stacked peat, ran cattle on the common and raised calves, possibly with a little dairying on the side, kept pigs and poultry, and indulged in a multiplicity of skilled agricultural tasks.

The inventory was one of the very rare ones which give any indication of debts owed outwards: the appraisers made a list of sixteen debtors, including the landlord's rent of £4. The total debts, a little larger in the account, were £13 6s 4d, or nearly half the value of the inventory. Interestingly Matthew owed 1s as 'chimney money', so we know both that he had one hearth in his two-roomed house, and also that he was not exempt from the Hearth Tax on the grounds of poverty. Apart from the £4 he owed as rent, his other debts were all owed to Burringham men and women, except one to a relation of his landlord who lived in Gainsborough and one to a man who came, like his landlord, from Messingham. The account gave no idea of the reasons for his borrowing, except for the two forks and scythes he had bought, but not paid for. Matthew also had family problems which may have helped account for the indebtedness. His wife was dead, his administrator lived elsewhere, and the account included expenses for 'nursing' and clothing the children, 'looking to' the dead man's house and land, ploughing the land, and removing the goods by water to the administrator's village. These were all responsibilities the widow, as administratrix, would have undertaken. There were four children. The eldest, a thirteen-year-old boy, Thomas, had been bound apprentice since his father's death at a cost of £3. Mary, one of the three little girls, had died, and interestingly, more was spent on her funeral than on her father's, although both were meagre in the extreme, and cost only 6s 8d and 5s respectively. The surviving two girls, Anne and Sarah, were eleven and six when the account was drawn up, and received 13s 4d apiece as their children's portions. The reader wonders about the sleeping habits of this family. When their mother was still alive, did the 'standing bed' in the parlour serve as a sort of *letto matrimoniale* for the whole family, or did the trundle bed under it take more than the youngest of the four children? However the family slept, they had inadequate covers with only one blanket. The last group of expenses in the Burtoft account were the ecclesiastical court fees involved in obtaining letters of administration, and finishing off the business, including travelling and apparitors' fees. These were roughly standard in all probate accounts, whatever the size of the estate, or social status, of the dead man. However, they naturally represented a much greater proportional expense of the value of the inventory goods on a labourer's probate account than on a yeoman's. In Matthew Burtoft's case, they amounted to £3 19s 10d, or over an eighth of the inventory value. His administrator ended up with £5 16s 8d in his hands, and two little girls to look after. The estate was reduced to this both because of the dead man's indebtedness, and also because of the expenses of a young family left motherless. The final net value of a man's estate may, then, have been as much related to his stage in the family life-cycle, and his demographic situation, as to his degree of indebtedness. These may, of course, have been strongly connected. It is pure surmise to suggest that the wife of a labourer may usually have contributed considerably to the family budget, and it was the absence of his dead wife's earnings which led to Matthew's running up so many local debts, but it is still a potentially

useful suggestion for exploration. Certainly, the expenses of keeping a family between the date of the inventory and the date of the
final account were the second major category of expenditure to
influence the final net value of the account. Because of the combination of debts and family expenses since his death, Matthew
Burtoft's estate ended up at only twenty-first place amongst the
twenty-nine labourers.

The suggestion that indebtedness and the stage a man had
reached in rearing his family may have been strongly interconnected
is reinforced by considering the probate account of the man who
emerged as holding the median net figure for labourers on the final
values retrieved from the probate accounts. John Morgan of Saleby
had only £20 worth of goods in his inventory of 1677, and stood
twenty-third in order amongst the twenty-nine labourers. His inventory also survived, and showed him living in a five-roomed house. It
had a hall, a parlour, and chamber, with two service rooms, a dairy,
and a buttery as well. His furnishings were also adequate, but not
luxurious, and he only had two pairs of sheets with the bed in the
parlour. There were fewer beasts in the yard. The three cows and a
calf there suggested both common rights and dairying. This time the
suggestion was borne out by the cheese tub and nine bowls in the
dairy indoors. The swine in the yard were for domestic consumption, judging from the flitch of bacon in the dairy. Nothing in the
yard suggested that John Morgan had any land or grew his own flax
or hemp. But the implication of spinning made by the 'two wheels'
in his chamber is amply borne out by the two webs of cloth 'at the
weaver's' worth £1 10s 0d. The probate account demonstrated John
Morgan's carefulness, and his different family circumstances. His
widow was his executrix, and he had no debts at all, apart from his
rent of £4 15s 0d. After his funeral expenses and his mortuary were
paid, the only charges on his estate were his widow's travelling to
Louth twice on business connected with the court, getting letters of
administration, and getting the account passed, as well as the court
fees. Either his family was grown, or he had none. His wife's spinning was an asset, judging from the webs at the weaver's. Whether
the lack of a family, or having a grown family, accounts for his lack
of indebtedness must remain open. But it is not surprising that the
final value of his estate from his account was over £11 and brought
him up to fifteenth place.

III

The totals of inventory values recorded in the thirty-five husband-men's accounts showed that, from their assets at their deaths, this social label was applied to men who had movables valued at as little as £9 to as much as £388 at their deaths. The lower quartile of inven-toried value ran from £9 to £32, and the upper from £112 to £388. The median of inventoried wealth was £62. Again, the probate accounts themselves showed a very different picture. After all the deductions were made, the husbandmen's administrators usually ended up £60 worse off than the inventories had indicated. The final range ran from those overspent by as much as £64 to those in final credit of £319. The whole lower quartile of husbandmen's adminis-trators varied from being out of pocket by £64 and just in credit by £2. The upper quartile was very wide, from £38 in credit to £319 in credit. So the median net estate for husbandmen was finally as low as £13, only just over that of a labourer. The relationship between inventoried wealth and net wealth was even less predictable for 'husbandmen' than for labourers. Nearly half the husbandmen's estates moved more than six places up or down the rank order between the value of goods when the inventory was drawn up, to the time the final account was made. Examples of this movement, and its reasons, may not come amiss (see Table 3).

The goods of William Presgrave of Steddington, for instance, were appraised at £291. He was the second most prosperous amongst the husbandmen from his inventory. But the account of 1674 included amongst his debts arrears of rent of over £140 to two landlords, as well as an allowance for losses for one hundred sheep which 'dyed the last Rott' and cattle and horses which died since the taking out of letters of administration. He was a hirer of labour, but he had not paid his wages either: he owed two maidservants, two menservants, and a shepherd sums of money. When all was paid off, the two sons who acted as his administrators ended up £12 out of pocket, or so they claimed. The net value of the estate placed William Presgrave only thirty-first amongst the thirty-five husband-men. Here the cause of the trouble may have been the disease amongst the livestock which may have caused the arrears of rent. Yet the inventory indicated the scale of Presgrave's farming activities accurately, although it was no guide at all to the ultimate solvency of a man who was deeply financially embarrassed.

Table 3. *Gross and net value of husbandmen's estates in Lincolnshire in the seventeenth century from probate inventories and probate accounts*

Order (gross)	Gross wealth: inventory total	Name	Place	Date (inventory or account)	Net wealth account total	Order (net)
1	£387 13s 10d	Thos Hudson	Melton Ross	1679/80	£318 11s 2d	1
2	£291 4s ?d	Will. Presgrave	Steddington	1668	−£11 14s 0d	31
3	£239 8s 6d	Hugh Dickinson	Billinghay	1671	−£12 9s 10d	32
4	£174 17s ?d	Robt Dance	Ryby	1666	£38 15s ?d	9
5	£150 10s 4d	Robt Bettison	Glenthorn	1632	£100 19s 8d	3
6	£133 0s 0d	Ric. Thornton	Arncotts	1667/8	£81 15s 8d	5
7	£122 0s 10d	Thos Parrett	Hallington	1678	£26 19s ½d	12
8	£112 19s 10d	Jo. Godsave	Fenton	1680	−£64 18s ?d	35
9	£112 8s 4d	Anthony Duke	Lutton	1678	£81 11s 4d	6
10	£111 0s 0d	Thos Waterland	Craisland	n.d.	£102 13s 2d	2
11	£101 12s 0d	Robt Chapman	E. Kirby	1632	£93 12s 0d	4
12	£92 1s 0d	Will. Turnard	Brothertoft	n.d.	£45 15s 0d	8
13	£82 15s 0d	Ric. Tenby	Foxhill	1666	£38 14s 2d	10
14	£78 6s 0d	Hen. Goodman	Fleet	1666	£6 4s 2d	22
15	£77 11s 4d	Wm Parkes	Norton Disney	1673	£13 2s 6d	18
16	£69 11s 4d	Ed. Cooke	Bicker	1678	−£48 0s 4d	34
17	£68 5s 10d	Peter Grainger	Harpswell	1668	£11 2s 4d	20
18	£62 6s 0d	Math. Wilkinson	Tottle	1679	£46 6s 8d	7
19	£61 0s 10d	Ric. Pepper	Pinchbeck	1669	£1 8s 0d	24
20	£59 1s 9d	Wm Tysedale	Tydd St Mary	1683	£11 1s 8d	21
21	£54 0s 0d	Wm Coopeland	Dogdike	1664	£24 18s 0d	13
22	£50 4s 4d	Thos Lawrence	Nether Toynton	1678	−£2 13s ?d	27
23	£38 3s 0d	Robt Lawrence	Froddingham	1669	£15 3s 6d	16
24	£36 13s 1d	Thos Stennet	Moulton	1681	−£8 19s 11d	30

25	£35 16s 2d	Will. Fox	Bottesford	1673	£27 15s 2d	11
26	£35 7s ?d	Jo. Taylor	Digby	1673	−£7 9s 0d	29
27	£31 15s 8d	Stephen Burd	Hallington	1669	£13 8s ?d	17
28	£29 3s 0d	Robt Doulton	Carlton-in-Moreland	n.d.	£6 12s 2d	23
29	£27 8s 11d	Will. Abraham	Leake	1632	£22 14s 7d	14
30	£26 0s 11d	Ric. Chatterton	Snitterby	1673	£22 2s 11d	15
31	£25 10s 0d	Fra. Charity	Dembleby	1667	£12 1s 2d	19
32	£21 8s 4d	Robt Smyth, Snr	E. Halton	1666	−£26 4s 0d	33
33	£16 16s 10d	Thos Hardy	Fishtoft	1683	−£7 6s 6d	28
34	£12 10s 0d	Jo. Whelston	Wainfleet	1669	−9s 4d	25
35	£8 10s 2d	Barth. Onn	Wigtoft	1632	−£2 0s 9d	26

There were other examples, which were almost as dramatic, in the other direction. Richard Chatterton, husbandman, of Snitterby, had goods worth only £26 when his inventory was taken in 1673. His estate came thirtieth amongst the thirty-five husbandmen. His hall and parlour were reasonably comfortable. He had more sheets, which usually seemed to provide a fair index of comfort and possibly surplus purchasing power,[36] than either of the labourers discussed above. From the inventory, the reader would guess at both the existence of a wife, and domestic by-employment. There was a woollen wheel and a spinning wheel in the chamber, with half a stone of hemp. The four yards of hempen cloth, and six yards of harden in the parlour, therefore could have been either bought or made. The stock and farm tools in his yard likewise indicated that he held more land than the labourers: he had three mares and a foal as well as his cattle, and two wains, three yokes, and a plough and harrows. There was a little grain in his barn with the hay. Yet his goods were still worth less than the inventoried value of the median labourer. The reader could not possibly guess that when his adult son, who was the administrator, came to the final accounting, there would not be a single charge on the estate apart from 13s 4d for the funeral, 6s 8d for a mortuary, and the inevitable court charges. There was not a single debt to be paid, no rent in arrears, no expense on other minor children, and no evidence of a widow. Despite the low value of Richard Chatterton's goods in the inventory, his frugal habits and domestic situation as someone unencumbered with any other person and yet still an active man, meant that the net value of his estate was as much as £22. It was fifteenth, not thirtieth, and came well above the median for husbandmen. His son, improbably, inherited more in terms of cash from his father than did the sons of William Presgrave.

Despite the wide range of inventory values for husbandmen, the median of £62 was significantly different from that of the labourers, as the scale of operations of the husbandman also seems significantly different. They quite frequently owed more than one rent in the accounts for land, and they also quite frequently owed wages.

---

[36] *Yeomen and Colliers in Telford*, ed. B. Trinder and J. Cox (Chichester, 1980), pp. 36–7. This study regards the capacity to change the bedlinen as 'one of the best indicators the inventory gives of steadily rising standards of comfort' in the 1680s. See also my discussion of the resources to change one's shirt, above, pp. 149–50.

Although there is no evidence of the acreages they farmed, the whole 'feel' of their enterprise is that of the tenant of half a yardland or a yardland in the seventeenth century. The 'median' husbandman from the inventories, Matthew Wilkinson of Tottle, owed £8 4s 0d in rent, double that for a labourer, and also owed wages to one man and one girl. He, like Richard Chatterton, owed no other debts and there were no minors to establish. His widow had remarried by the time she had put the account in. The estate ended up with a net value of £46, over triple the median value for the probate accounts for husbandmen. William Parkes of Norton Disney, whose estate in 1673 was worth the net median of £13, had had goods worth £78 originally on his inventory. He had owed two rents, house repairs and some wages, as well as payments for grazing. The main charges on his estate had been payments of £13 18s 0d to each of his three daughters, however. These were very much more substantial than the marriage portions payable by any labourer's estate and had actually been paid out before the account was drawn up. The scale of farming operations and provision for sons and daughters made by husbandmen who emerged as 'median' on the probate inventories and the probate accounts respectively was indeed much more considerable than in the case of the labourers, although the whole range of 'husbandmen' overlapped so heavily with that of the 'labourers', and the median account value was so little higher.

IV

In the same way, the thirty-five yeomen's probate accounts showed another leap in the scope of their operations. The totals of their inventory values brought forward to the probate accounts showed a range of movables valued at between £18 and £2,583. The lower quartile ran from £18 to £55, the upper from £287 to the very substantial £2,583 worth of goods and chattels left by John Forman of Bardney Dairies in 1673. The median of inventoried wealth was that of George Bartrum of Pickworth, whose goods were appraised at £149 in 1669. An increased scale of indebtedness and family obligation went with this increase of inventoried wealth. The probate accounts showed an overall drop between the inventory and account which varied between as little as £4 and as uch as £598. The median drop was £59. The final range of value of yeomen's estates in their accounts varied from that on which the unfortunate administrators showed a loss of £188 to the £2,580 still left in the hands of John Forman's sisters and administratrixes. The lower quartile of yeomen's administrators ended up almost entirely over-spent: the top of the quartile was just in credit at £4. The upper quartile ranged from £114 to Forman's £2,580. But the median plummeted between inventory and account, from the £149 in George Bartrum's inventory to the £26 in the account of Stephen Trigot of Haburgh. Even though this was double the median of the husbandmen's accounts, it still demonstrated a really startling drop between inventory and net value. It was very noticeable that of the yeomen with really substantial farms above the median inventory value, also almost all indulged in transactions involving their credit very heavily. The median drop in value between inventory and account for yeomen with inventories worth over £161 was as much as £217, whereas for the yeomen below the median inventory value, who overlapped so heavily with the group of husbandmen, the median drop was only £29. Borrowing power was then immediately related to the size of the large-scale farmer's operations. The debts were likely to be to scale. The extent of the deductions meant the yeomen's final financial position in relation to each other was even less predictable than for any other group. Nineteen of the thirty-five, or over half of them, changed six places or more in relative order between inventory and account (see Table 4).

Individual examples again illustrate the scope of yeomen's farm-ing activities, their use of credit, and the scale of their endeavours to provide their daughters with portions at marriage or majority, and their sons with land or money to set up. The two yeomen who had the median inventory, and the median account wealth, George Bartrum and Stephen Trigot, also had disappointingly brief records. There was no surviving inventory for Bartrum in 1669, although the account of course recorded the inventory total of £149. The widow, the executrix, was recorded as 'having noe children'. There were no debts, as well as no portions to be paid, or expense for young children. George Bartrum was not even in arrears with his rent. So the widow's sole expenses after paying £3 for the funeral were the court fees. She was left with £142 in hand. The combined absence of debt and family charges meant that the estate ended up seventh, rather than eighteenth, in order of net value. In exactly the same way, Stephen Trigot, whose inventory of 1632 showed him in possession of merely £36 of goods, which only put him thirtieth in order amongst the thirty-five yeomen, had no family obligations and only minor debts. His widow, after paying these, his funeral expenses, and the court costs, was still left with £26 in hand, which astonishingly made the estate eighteenth in value and gave it the median final account value for the sample of yeomen. In both these cases, the childlessness and carefulness of the yeomen concerned seem to have been the overriding factors which put men farming in a relatively modest way disproportionately high amongst their fellows in the same social group.

The reader might suppose, from these yeomen, that childlessness was the overriding factor which brought the final value of the yeoman's estate in the probate account up in relation to that of his fellow yeomen. But this is not so. There are examples of childless yeomen who have plunged deeply into debt. There are also examples of yeomen with families who had managed to establish their heirs, or paid the expenses of their minor children, without running deeply into debt. Moreover, both these indebted childless yeomen and those who had successfully established families occurred at all economic levels in the wide range covered by the yeomen. Robert Holmes of Markby was worth £562 according to his inventory, which did not survive. His widow ended up out of pocket by £36 in 1683. Yet she had paid nothing to support any of his children, although there was admittedly a deduction of £100 left in his will to her five children by an earlier marriage. The back rents, at £40 a year at least, alone amounted to over £270. His 'servants'' wages at over £5 a quarter and 'labourers'' wages for threshing, hedging, sheep-washing, and shearing, and the mowing, cocking, and 'leading' of hay and corn were also unpaid, as was his bill to the smith and the carpenter. He owed poor rates, constables' charges, church lays, and assessments for the repairs to the old and the new sea banks at Sutton. The account was a mine of detail for farm and parish charges. There were small debts due for purchases of barley, pigs, and calves, as well as larger unspecified ones due upon bond. Robert Holmes was in arrears with everything, and the value of all his movables, which no doubt would have looked very substantial indeed in the inventory, was gobbled up by these numerous debts. The establishment of his own children, and even the £100 to his stepchildren, had nothing to do with this. His widow may have looked fifth most prosperous amongst the yeomen from the inventory, but

Table 4. *Gross and net value of yeomen's estates in Lincolnshire in the seventeenth century from probate inventories and probate accounts*

Order (gross)	Gross wealth inventory total	Name	Place	Date (inventory or account)	Net wealth account total	Order (net)
1	£2,583 1s 10d	Jo. Forman	Bardney Dairies	1673	£2,579 10s 6d	1
2	£1,093 17s 0d	Hen. Boulton	Bardney	1632	£850 15s 2½d	2
3	£1,015 16s 4d	Thos Appleby	Thornton Curtis	1664	£435 1s 10d	4
4	£624 19s 2d	Thos Lockin	Laughton	1666	£448 16s ?d	3
5	£562 3s ?d	Robt Holmes	Markeby	1683	-£36 4s 8d	32
6	£426 6s 8d	Jo. Harrison	Canwicke	1670	£118 4s 0d	8
7	£290 12s 10d	Jas. Mabbut	Sutton St Ed.	1684	£145 15s 4d	6
8	£287 5s 7d	Thos Christian	Kitlington	1686	-£5 17s 9d	28
9	£253 18s 5d	Hen. Maltby	Crowland	1679	£226 12s 10d	5
10	£218 2s 0d	Will. Tebbutt	Gt Hale	1666	£6 15s 5d	25
11	£210 15s 0d	Thos Squire	Washingborough	1666	£97 1s 0d	11
12	£205 9s 2d	Simon Pennell	N. Kelsey	1673	-£7 15s 5d	30
13	£194 11s ?d	Chas Milnes	Normanton	1690	-£34 10s 10d	31
14	£193 7s 0d	Thos Pawling	Hindleby	1666	£114 15s 8d	9
15	£191 3s 4d	Vincent Russell	Bassingham	1679	-£71 7s 4d	33
16	£179 17s 4d	Jo. Creswell	Wragby	1663	£127 11s 4d	10
17	£161 4s 2d	Jo. Hodgson	Kirton	1683	-£188 2s 10d	35
18	£149 1s 0d	Geo. Bartrum	Pickworth	1669	£142 9s 8d	7
19	£101 7s ?d	Fra. Short	Dunholm	1676	£72 13s 0d	12
20	£84 14s 4d	Geo. Deyne	Swineshead	1632	£26 4s 2d	17
21	£80 13s 0d	Will. Watkinson	Reepham	1683	£49 4s 0d	13
22	£79 10s 10d	Thos Crainton	Heckington	1666	£21 10s 8d	19
23	£78 7s 0d	Geo. King	Sereby	1672	-£7 15s 8d	29
24	£69 9s 0d	Wm Simpson	Gosbertowne	1632	£10 16s 2d	22

25	£68 13s 0d	Nic. Leach	Raceby	1683	£48 ?s ?d	14
26	£61 8s 0d	Jo. Seamor	Caythorpe	1664	£8 7s 8d	24
27	£55 3s 0d	Will. Rodgers	Crowle	1669	£33 0s 8d	15
28	£46 8s 4d	Jas Harnson	Burnham	1669	£32 5s 0d	16
29	£38 8s 0d	Thos Johnson	Gedney	1666	£4 5s 0d	26
30	£36 0s 0d	Steph. Trigot	Haburgh	1632	£25 17s 10d	18
31	£29 12s 2d	Jo. Raven	Northwitham	1631	£20 10s 0d	20
32	£29 11s 0d	Arthur Wilkinson	Boston	1666	£4 3s 11d	27
33	£28 12s 10d	Will. Nichols	Hareby	1669	£15 6s 4d	21
34	£22 17s 0d	Thos Obbington	W. Keale	1668	–£73 11s 0d	34
35	£18 8s 0d	Ric. Hardy	Skidbrook	n.d.	£8 15s 0d	23

she ended up thirty-second amongst the thirty-five on the accounts. There was no necessary causal connection between the indebtedness and the demographic circumstances or the family structure of the dead man.

Other yeomen's accounts also demonstrated this, from their proven ability to establish the next generation, or sustain the expenses of minor children between the time of their deaths and the final account. An example shows the way adult sons and daughters had been successfully established. Thomas Appleby of Thornton was the third most prosperous of the Lincolnshire yeomen when his inventory was taken in December 1664. The most substantial item in his inventory was 'corn in the barne and stackes in the yard' worth £467 10s 0d at this point immediately after harvest. There were three teams of plough horses in the stable, with their gears. He also had a flock of over 160 sheep and lambs, ten mares and colts and over thirty dairy cattle, calves, oxen, and three bulls. The possession of bulls was usually as certain a sign of economic prosperity in an inventory, as was the desire to be buried inside the church in a will an index of social status. There were two different sets of 'servants' beds'. The widow's disbursements in her account showed practically no indebtedness apart from the massive rent due of £250, which she had already paid. Apart from the court charges and the funeral, her only other expense had been even more massive, £300 'paid to Laurence Appleby, the deceaseds sonne being oweing to him . . . upon the Solemnization of a marriage betweene the said Laurence and one Mary Smyth, his now wife'. So we know that this yeoman's son had been financially established on his marriage, not with land but with cash, which was actually paid by his mother. Moreover, the notes made by the court official demonstrated much more fully just how successful this yeoman had been. There were four sons and a daughter, aged 33, 31, 29, 27, and 25 at the time of the account. Each of them received 5s as a token, since each of them had already had £150 in cash in his or her father's lifetime. Although she paid out £581 before the account was drawn up, the widow still ended up with £435 in hand, fourth most prosperous of the administrators. Her husband's provision for his grown children had been realistic, as well as lavish, and had not led to indebtedness. This widow was indeed in comfortable circumstances.

Two other yeomen's accounts in this sample give rare and invaluable examples of the expenses of bringing up minor children, and again demonstrate that these did not necessarily reduce an estate proportionately very much. Thomas Lockin of Laughton, indeed, was fourth most prosperous amongst the yeomen, from his inventory. When all expenses were deducted, and the account drawn up, he ended up third most prosperous. The inventory, worth £625, showed Thomas Lockin lent money on a very considerable scale. Nearly £330 was due to him on 'specialty'. But he was still actively farming as well. His flock of over 350 sheep had no fewer than eight rams to serve it. From the account, he was, as one would expect, a respected local figure and parish official. A small sum was due to the town, outstanding from his accounts at the time of his church-wardenship. He owed a year's rent, and wages to a maidservant, a manservant, and two labourers. His executor paid out the family legacies in Thomas's will, and painstakingly accounted for the uncollectable debts amongst those due to Thomas. But the major expenses were for the 'diet, maintenance and other necessaries' laid out for the young, only son, William. These came to just over £100 for four years, and were broken down in minute and fascinating detail. From them, exact costs for food, clothing down to the price of broadcloth per yard and tailor's bills, individual bands (collars) and shoeties, hats, pocket money, and entertainment can all be worked out. But young Master Lockin, who was well dressed and well mounted, had his hair cut regularly, attended cock fights, and had a new knife in his pocket, along with his pocket money, was by no means too expensive for his father's estate. It seems he inherited it in good heart. The final account showed a surplus of £448.

In the same way, the two little daughters of Jonas Mabbut of Sutton St Edmunds, Sarah and Joan, were not too expensive for their father's estate. It was worth £291 according to the inventory. The administrator put in three years' accounts for all the expenses of the two children, ranging from board for them to minute details of their clothes, down to straw hats, stockings, and all the various types of linen to make them clothes, to medical expenses, a 'Testament' for Joan, and Sarah's schooling at 2d a week. Just as William Lockin had his pocket knife, so these girls had black whisks and ribbons, and Sarah obtained the dignity of a 'Mantua Gowne', as well as boarding in Wisbech for a year, possibly at school. The accounts finished £146 in credit in 1684, despite the educating of two girls who would have been extremely well treated and dressed.

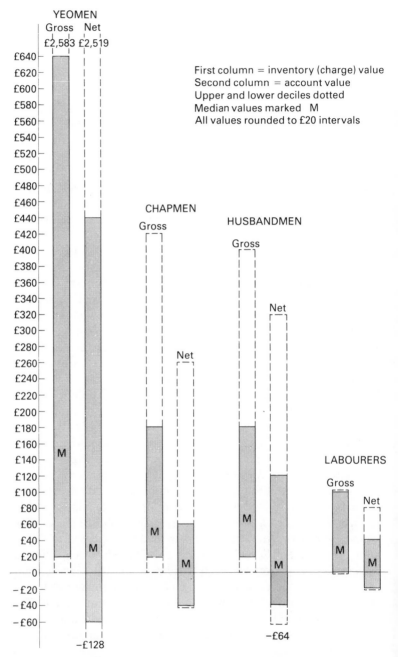

Figure 3 Comparison of inventory and probate account valuations

V

It seems from these examples that neither child-rearing nor the payment of portions to adult daughters, or cash sums to adult sons,
were themselves the cause of indebtedness. There could be, but was
not necessarily, a relationship. Such expenses were, however, one
of the major categories of expenditure in many of the probate
accounts, and certainly form one of the headings for future analysis,
just as indebtedness formed another. This cursory survey of a small
sample of probate accounts for Lincolnshire shows how much work
needs to be done. It also shows how much new material there is in
the accounts, from information on inheritance customs and settlements down to exact expenditure on servants' wages, and on the
hitherto inaccessible subject of clothing below the gentry level.
Most of all, the accounts demonstrated that the probate inventory
alone is no guide to a man's relative financial standing within his
own social group. Indeed, the net wealth of groups in relation to
each other is very different from that which the relative values of the
movables within each group would indicate.

The sum which appears at the foot of the probate inventory cannot be taken to indicate any individual's real net wealth, even in any
approximate manner not only because it does not include, as we all
knew, real estate, but because it carries no clue to the extent of his
indebtedness. Rural credit underpins the whole of English rural
society so completely that the humblest individuals above the levels
of vagrants, and possibly even they, were involved in the network.

I argued much better than I knew in 1974 when I suggested the
necessity to be able to read the bill or bond must have been as
powerful an incentive to learning the skill of reading as any pressure
to read the Holy Scriptures. Not only is the sum at the foot of the
inventory no guide to the individual's net wealth, but it is no guide
at all even to his relative financial standing within the same occupational or social group. We are all familiar with the nebulous
nature of these same social groups, comprehending, as they do,
wide extremes of inventoried wealth. Now this nebulous nature is
stressed even more when the median net wealths of labourers,
husbandmen, and yeomen are compared with their inventoried
wealths. Certainly the 'median yeoman' from the Lincolnshire
probate administrators' accounts, Stephen Trigot of Haburgh, was
worth, with his £26, more than the 'median husbandman', William

Parkes of Norton Disney, with his £13. He, in turn, was worth a little more than his fellow 'median labourer', John Morgan of Saleby, with his £11. But such distinctions are so very much a matter of niceties, when compared with the glaring differences in the medians, £149, £62, and £29, taken from the probate inventories for these same social strata, that we are entitled to ask whether these groups do in fact have any economic reality at all. Do they lack economic cohesion to the point at which they are meaningless? Close reading of the inventories and administrators' accounts taken together suggests that although the former must be disbelieved as guides to wealth more strenuously than ever before, the groups called 'labourers', 'husbandmen', and 'yeomen', with all their huge economic overlaps and lack of distinction, probably still act as good guides to a man's scale of operations, his social pretensions, and possibly quite explicitly, his borrowing power. Labourers owed the rents of their cottages and were owed a year or in some cases half a year's wages. They borrowed within these limitations, and, in the manner of individual personalities at all times, some of them were much rasher than others. These men, or rather their widows, came out much worse than their more cautious brethren. Yeomen owed rents of land, possibly to many different landlords in many different parishes. They also owed wages to the labourers or servants they employed. Their scale of borrowing was explicitly adjusted to their scale of farming, and to their pretensions within the community. Indebtedness might therefore increase in direct proportion to the inventoried value of the yeoman concerned. Inventories must still be used, but their air of spurious exactitude, and their quantifiability, must be taken no longer with pinches of salt, but with whole salt-cellars of disbelief. Some of these inexactitudes can be corrected with the complementary probate account.

We owe to Dr Thirsk's work over the last thirty years the wholesale exploiting of the probate inventories as sources to draw the map on which the regional boundaries for the agrarian history of England can be laid out. The inventories have yet to be fully exploited for household interiors and domestic furnishings, to give us the guides to consumption that they could. But the next thirty years should partially be spent by social and economic historians exploiting the 'new' and complementary sources of the surviving probate accounts, which add so much new information on both social and economic customs.

7. Freebench and free enterprise: widows and their property in two Berkshire villages

BARBARA TODD

That the widow should have a share of her deceased husband's estate has been a remarkably powerful tradition in English life. Law, custom, contract, and sheer good will have guided men of property as they have provided for their widows. As a result a substantial proportion of the wealth of each generation has fallen into the hands of some widows, even while poverty was the lot of many others. Historians are gradually becoming aware of how the widow's share could affect families and communities. But although the powerful dowager is a familiar figure, and the medieval peasant widow is becoming better known,[1] the effects of the widow's estate on the women and families of rural England in the early modern period are still far from clear.[2]

The form of the widow's share, and the consequences of women's ownership, have varied widely according to local tradition, the nature of the economy, and family circumstances, and can best be studied in a particular local setting. This is especially true of free-bench, the rule by which a widow succeeded to all or part of her husband's land held by customary tenure. Not only did it vary from place to place in its precise effects; freebench was rapidly disappear-

---

[1] See, e.g. Rowena E. Archer, 'Rich Old Ladies: The Problem of the Late Medieval Dowagers', in A. J. Pollard (ed.), *Property and Politics: Essays in Later Medieval English History* (Gloucester, 1984), pp. 15–35, and J. Ravensdale, 'Population Changes and the Transfer of Customary Land on a Cambridgeshire Manor in the Fourteenth Century', in R. Smith (ed.), *Land, Kinship and Life-Cycle* (Cambridge, 1984), pp. 197–225.

[2] Although a number of studies have outlined what husbands proposed in the light of custom as their widows' share (among the most recent, see H. C. F. Lansberry, 'Free Bench See-Saw: Sevenoaks Widows in the Late Seventeenth Century', *Archaeologia Cantiana*, 100 (1984), 291–93), none has shown how custom, as adapted in practice, actually affected widows' later lives.

ing entirely in some localities as customary tenures were converted to leasehold and freehold. Even where it persisted as custom, it was liable to be adjusted or ignored by families trying to balance the right of the widow against the claims of children. This must have been especially common where the strong form of freebench prevailed which allowed the widow to have all of her husband's lands for life. But even this form of freebench survived intact in many communities.[3] It survived because it was useful, adding the widow's life to the husband's life estate, and at a time when men still often died young, providing security for the widow acting as head of her family in the hiatus between male generations.

Long Wittenham, a village in the Vale of Oxford where traditional agrarian and tenurial practices seem to have been particularly durable,[4] provides a good setting for studying this strong form of the widow's estate. The following account asks first what proportion of the land came into widows' hands under this version of freebench, and then how widows' ownership worked in practice. Finally it compares the situation of widows in Long Wittenham with the role of widows in the neighbouring village of Sutton Courtenay, where a diversified and innovative economy had developed, and where freebench was absent. The comparison gives some sense of how widows fared when they lacked traditional rights, how they were affected by the local economy, and how the presence or absence of widows' property rights affected the situation of women in general.

I

Long Wittenham lies on the banks of the Thames to the south-east of Abingdon. Between the 1520s and the 1660s its population grew from about 125 to about 300.[5] The economy was almost wholly

---

[3] E. P. Thompson's discussion of freebench ('The Grid of Inheritance', in J. Goody, J. Thirsk, and E. P. Thompson (eds.), *Family and Inheritance* (Cambridge, 1976), pp. 349–58) is based in good part on Berkshire evidence, and may thus reflect regional practice that this chapter from the same geographical perspective only further emphasizes.

[4] J. R. Wordie, 'The South: Oxfordshire, Buckinghamshire, Berkshire, Wiltshire and Hampshire', in J. Thirsk (ed.), *The Agrarian History of England and Wales*, V, *1640–1750* (Cambridge, 1984), pt I, pp. 325–6.

[5] Based on assessments for the lay subsidy of 1524 (Public Record Office (hereafter PRO), E. 179/73/134) and the 1664 Hearth Tax (PRO E. 179/75/38). Since

agrarian, based on the mix of arable and dairy production that was typical of the clay Vale of Oxford; barley was the main corn crop.[6] The manorial history of the village is complex, but by the mid sixteenth century St John's College, Oxford, was in possession of the two surviving manors (Strangeways-De la Pole and Pudsey's) and of the farm called Louches,[7] about two-thirds of the village lands. The rest was divided between the rectory (belonging to Exeter College, Oxford) and a number of freeholds (fourteen in the 1580s). Holdings were in half-yardland units, the yardland measuring about twenty acres. An assessment list from the early 1580s shows 87¾ yardlands divided amongst thirty-seven owners, of whom twenty-six had a yardland or more, the largest holding being the 6 yardlands of Widow Webb.[8] Over the course of the seventeenth century there was little change in the sizes of customary holdings although a few families acquired new land, a few divided theirs, and a few cottage holdings were created on customary land. The increased population seems to have been housed on fragments of freehold land beyond manorial control.[9] What follows is based primarily on a study of the families who held land subject to the customs of the manors owned by St John's.[10]

Following a pattern common in this area, holdings on the Long

households headed by widows are seemingly under-represented in the former (only one as opposed to fourteen in the Hearth Tax listing), the earlier population may well have been somewhat higher, perhaps about 150.

[6] Based on a study of all the Long Wittenham probate inventories between 1540 and 1720 held in the records of the Berkshire Archdeaconry, in the Berkshire Record Office (hereafter Berks. RO). Long Wittenham fits the pattern of agrarian practices of the region as described in J. Thirsk, 'The Farming Regions of England', in J. Thirsk (ed.), *The Agrarian History of England and Wales*, IV, *1500–1640* (Cambridge, 1967), p. 66 and Wordie, 'The South', pp. 324–5, 338.

[7] *V.C.H. Berkshire* (London, 1906–24), III, 384–9.

[8] St John's College, Oxford, Muniments (hereafter St John's), Box XII, no. 14. I am very grateful to Mr Howard Colvin for his kind assistance in making it possible for me to examine the Long Wittenham material held by St John's College, and to the President and Fellows for their permission to cite it here.

[9] Based on the reconstruction of the history of tenements discussed below. At the time of enclosure in 1809 there were still thirty-three holdings, but the large holdings were much larger. Bodleian Lib., MS Top. Berks. 32 (B. Morrell, Papers Regarding Enclosure of Long Wittenham), fols. 102–9.

[10] The manors also included freeholds and possibly some leasehold tenements, but except for a period of about thirty years in the early seventeenth century, the descent or transfer of these properties is not recorded in the court books, and the extent to which they were subject to manorial custom is unclear.

Wittenham manors were granted as copyholds[11] 'at will according to the custom of the manor' for two of three lives, with the children of good tenants having preference in renewal of the tenancy. Copyholds were transferred by surrender in the yearly courts baron, and were never devised by will. Comparison of manorial and probate records indicates that the court books present quite an accurate picture of landownership, although some people obviously owned more than their customary lands.

Until the 1580s the widow's freebench was in the form of a life estate, with the lives of the taker, his wife, and another (usually a child) entered on the copy.[12] Wives thus held their land by right of widowhood, but in as full a tenure as any one else, and on at least one, and perhaps both, of the St John's manors, they could remarry without forfeiting freebench (a right that was uncommon in this area at this period). Many did so. At least four of the ten widows who held freebench between 1560 and 1590 on tenements studied below took new husbands.[13] But since the incoming husband normally took the holding in his own name, remarriage threatened the rights of succession of children of the first husband, and in the 1580s freebench was modified in favour of stronger principles of inheritance.

Like most changes of custom this new rule was the result of a compromise advantageous to both lord and tenants. The College wanted to avoid renewing the lease of the Sawyer family, its very difficult tenants at Louches Farm,[14] which the College had already

---

[11] Customary tenants referred to their holdings as copyholds (see, e.g., the will of Thomas Lovegrove, Berks. RO, D/A1/18/fol. 31) and despite the fact that they were occasionally called leases (see the will of James Jennens, Berks. RO, D/A1/87/19), they were clearly administered as copies for lives subject to custom and renewed only when a life fell.

[12] Based on sixteenth-century copies, St John's, Boxes XI, 9 and 10, and copies listed in an unnumbered MS Notebook of Copies, 1499–1604 (hereafter Notebook of Copies).

[13] Remarriages were traced in a combination of probate and manorial records and in the parish register (Berks. RO, D/P153/1, or Bodleian Lib., MS Film dep. 198).

[14] In addition to causing waste and damage to College houses, withholding rents, and failing to do tenants' service, they had sued to overthrow the customs of the manor, and worse, inspired other tenants with ideas inimicable to sound manorial control: 'Sawyer has many times sought the Colleges disinheritance as now his widdowe doth by seaking to worke a state of free holde to all College tenants . . . assuring them thereof so as they neaded not to seek theyr land lords favors' (St John's, XII.20, 'Reasons why Widow Sawyers Lease should not be Renewed').

let in reversion to William Russell, one of the Fellows.[15] Since the Sawyers held Louches as a result of the remarriage of a widow in an earlier generation,[16] a version of freebench that prevented remarriage would reduce the validity of their claim to a new lease. At the same time the villagers had been made sensitive to the dangers to succession inherent in freebench by other events: the displacement of the children of Joan Rolland because of her remarriage,[17] and by the case of the Webb family, who lost their large farm when the son who was to succeed to the copyhold died unexpectedly during his mother's long widowhood.[18]

The new custom, which allowed a widow to hold freebench only *dum sola et casta* (the version of freebench typical in this region), was first used in a new copy for Joan Rolland's farm,[19] and was then formally stated as the rule in the grant of a new copy for the Webb's estate, given to former Fellow and future President of St John's, Ralph Hucheson.[20] The College gained its immediate objective when the Sawyers were replaced by William Russell, although Widow Maud Sawyer fought hard for her lands.[21] Sitting male tenants lost nothing by the change. In fact the usefulness of free-

---

[15] *Ibid.* Granting holdings to Fellows was against the spirit but not the letter of the College statutes: see W. H. Stevenson and H. E. Salter, *The Early History of St. John's College, Oxford* (Oxford Historical Soc., n.s., I, Oxford, 1937), p. 248.

[16] See leases to Hugh Smith and Richard Sawyer, St John's, XI.10.21; Notebook of Copies, no. 20; wills of Hugh Smith, Berkc. RO, D/A1/4/fol. 34v, Elizabeth Sawyer, Berks. RO, D/A1/115/16, and survey, PRO, L.R. 2/187/427–8.

[17] St John's, Notebook of Copies, nos. 41, 46, and Joan Rolland's will, Berks. RO, D/A1/10/fol. 106v.

[18] Richard Webb, Berks. RO, D/A1/133/46.

[19] St John's, Summary notebook of customary tenants (unnumbered), p. 16, roll 138, 23 April 1578, entry of Robert Bishop. Agnes Keate held 'for widowhood' according to a survey made in 2 Ed. VI (PRO, L.R. 2/187/426), but there seems to be no other reference to such a limitation, if indeed this means a prohibition of remarriage, before 1578.

[20] St John's, Summary notebook of customary tenants, p. 20, roll 155, and XI.10.155. He was soon to marry Mary Wodeson, stepdaughter of then President Willis (Mary Prior, *Fisher Row: Fishermen, Bargemen and Canal Boatmen in Oxford, 1500–1900* (Oxford, 1982), p. 87), and the grant preserves her right to remarry, a privilege that was not to 'infringe the Custom of the Manor with respit to the Widows of other Tenants'.

[21] For a brief account of this case and the unsuccessful outcome of Maud Sawyer's suit (which she pursued all the way to the Privy Council), see Stevenson and Salter, *Early History*, pp. 246–9. See also PRO, STA.C. 5/S.16/7, and for a similar case at Frilford, in which Widow Sawyer joined, STA.C. 5/H.62/26 and STA.C. 5/H.49/5.

bench to them was increased. What they gained appeared in a restatement of customs in 1590 and 1591. In addition to the prohibition of remarriage, any wife of a tenant of Strangeways would now be able to take freebench, not just the wife whose life was named in the copy (in the smaller Pudsey's manor it continued to be the rule that only the first wife of the taker could have freebench). It was also confirmed that on Strangeways manor heriot would no longer be paid on the death of a widow, nor would lands be granted in reversion.[22]

The change shows the extent to which family succession had become the guiding principle of freebench, and how much the widow's scope for independent action was subject to that end. Widows still held life estates, but the custodial nature of their tenure was now much clearer. Not surprisingly, after 1590 remarriage by freebench holders became much less common. Two women of the next generation remarried and the new husbands took their holdings, and another woman remarried when she was forced to surrender her land for other reasons,[23] but thereafter no remarriages are recorded in the court books. It is of course impossible to say that no other freebench holder remarried. But of the other forty-five widows whose freebenches ended between 1590 and 1692 only nine are not known to have died as widows. Even if all these nine remarried, which is most unlikely given the advanced ages of many of them, the proportion remarrying would have been much lower than in the years before 1590.[24]

---

[22] St John's, XII.16 (Notes on customs abstracted from court rolls).

[23] Mary Wise, whose only child was a daughter whose life had never been put into the copy, holding one yardland, married John Barnes, who took the holding (will of John Wise, Berks. RO, D/A1/133/182; St John's, Notebook of Copies, nos. 74, 82); Agnes Child (one-and-a-half yardlands) married Richard Truelock, and her son by her first marriage was named as the second life when Truelock took the holding in 1610 (St John's, Court Book I, L.6.56, p. 47); Elizabeth Hyde surrendered her three-and-a-half yardlands to William Finmore under an earlier arrangement, having recently married Francis Keeblewhite, one of the men to whom Finmore was then authorized to sublet his land (see n. 38 below).

[24] In fact remarriage by freebench holders was so rare that in 1835 (surely one of the last of these incidents) when a freebench holder became pregnant, the court books were searched to ascertain the custom. Widow Stevens did then forfeit her estate, which was granted to the baby's father, who in the mean time had married the widow (St John's, Court Book IX, L.6.64, p. 3). On the general decline in the likelihood that a widow would remarry see my 'The Remarrying Widow: A Stereotype Reconsidered', in Mary Prior (ed.), *Women in English Society, 1500–1800* (London, 1985), pp. 54–92.

II

Of course, even without the power to take the property into a new marriage, freebench in the whole of one's husband's lands was still a strong right. To measure its effect on widows' ownership of customary land I have reconstructed the histories of twenty-four holdings from the early or mid sixteenth century to about 1700, using manorial records, supplemented by reference to probates.[25] Widows who succeeded to their husbands' lands held title to these properties not quite 20 per cent of the time at a minimum,[26] and if daughters holding in their own right are added, women held them almost 24 per cent of the time. If this is expressed in terms of 'yardland years', widows held 1,139 out of 5,899 years, or more than 19 per cent. Listings of tenants are rare, but in 1659, the only occasion in the seventeenth century in which all tenants are listed in the court books, there were seven widows out of a total of thirty-five tenants, or 20 per cent.[27] That this should correspond to the 21 per cent reported at the manor of Mardon in Hursley, Hampshire in 1707 may be a coincidence,[28] or it may suggest that about one-fifth

---

[25] Holdings were identified at their first appearance in the St John's Court Book I (L.6.56) beginning in 1606. They were then traced back in the contemporary notebooks of copies and tenancies and in filed copies, and forward through subsequent court books to 1692. If a family acquired more than one holding after 1606, which occurred in two instances, I have continued to trace and count the holdings separately, but separate holdings combined before 1606 to make up one estate were considered to be a single holding throughout. The longest period for which a holding was traced was 187 years, and the shortest 75 years. Probates were used to identify terminal dates of tenancies when these were missing from court books or notebooks, but the next life had taken the holding, and the dead tenant had clearly died in possession. Probates used in this study include all those proved in the Archdeaconry Court of Berkshire between 1540 and 1720 (Berks. RO, D/A1 series), and all proved in the Prerogative Court of Canterbury between 1540 and 1700, 182 in all. I have not seen the five Long Wittenham probates from these years in the files of the Salisbury Consistory Court now in the Wiltshire Record Office.

[26] Where either of the terminal dates of a widow's tenure are unknown (eight cases) I have counted it as lasting only one year, except in the three cases in which widows held beyond 1692; their tenures were calculated as ending at that point. I have ignored the four instances in which freebench occurred in small cottage holdings broken off to provide for younger sons in this calculation, but not in subsequent discussions based on the numbers and histories of freebench holders.

[27] St John's, Court Book IV, L.6.59, p. 53, 13 Sept. 1659. There are no rentals for this period.

[28] Thompson, 'Grid of Inheritance', p. 356, n. 67, citing M. Imber, *The Case, or an Abstract of the Custom of the Manor of Mardon in the Parish of Hursley* (London,

female ownership may be a good estimate for the effect of this version of the freebench rule, something to be tested by studies of other localities. In 1664 the Hearth Tax assessors listed widows as heads of 26 per cent of the households in Long Wittenham (not all were freebench holders), a higher proportion than in neighbouring villages.[29]

It appears that few Long Wittenham widows were discouraged or prevented from taking at least part of their freebench. Of the ninety-three male tenants of these holdings, fifty-eight were succeeded by widows.[30] Seven widows did not take their freebench either because they died or remarried before the next manorial court (two), were given other lands (three),[31] or were ineligible by being second wives of holders in Pudsey's manor (two cases). Another seven male holders were not succeeded because they were widowers and one was a bachelor. Five or six more men were non-residents and clearly transferred their holdings for financial reasons. When these are eliminated, fourteen or fifteen instances remain in which it is unclear if a widow survived but did not hold freebench. Some twelve of these men had once been married. If they all died as widowers it would be more than one would expect,[32] but freebench may have created a prejudice against remarriage by

1707). However, in the subsidy assessment list from the 1580s, when remarriage was common, only two of the thirty-six free and customary tenants were widows (St John's, XII.15).

[29] PRO E. 179/75/38. In Sutton Courtenay, for instance, widows were only 13 per cent of those listed as liable or not liable to pay the tax: PRO, E. 179/75/381.

[30] It is at least a suggestive coincidence that this should correspond to the figure obtained using a different method of calculating female (largely widows') succession in late medieval manors: R. H. Hilton, *The English Peasantry in the Later Middle Ages* (Oxford, 1975), p. 100.

[31] In two cases a widow took freebench in only one of her husband's two holdings, and another was given land in Little Wittenham instead of her freebench: William and Joan Lyde als. Joiner, St John's, Court Book I, L.6.56, p. 126, II, L.6.57, p. 19, and PRO, PROB. 11/137/229 and PROB. 11/219/129 and the wills of Thomas Barnes, Berks. RO, D/A1/39/161, and Thomas Lovegrove, D/A1/18/ fol. 31.

[32] Although there is little information on this subject, the parish register of Stanford in the Vale, where a similar freebench rule was followed, records the marital status of men buried, and shows that married men outnumbered widowers by nine to one: Berks. RO, D/P 118/1, or Bodleian Lib., MS Film dep. 159; see also V. M. House, *Stanford in the Vale: Parish Record* (Stanford, n.d.), and for a case arising over widow's estates, PRO, E. 134/41/2 Eliz. M.18 (*Knowles* v. *Church*); and B. J. Todd, 'Widowhood in a Market Town, Abingdon 1540–1720', D.Phil. thesis, Oxford University, 1982, 82, 122.

widowers as well as widows[33] (five of the twelve held in Pudsey's manor where there was no tenurial advantage to remarriage). If indeed all died as widowers, then all eligible widows took up some widow's estate. But even in the unlikely case that all these men whose marital status is unknown died married to eligible wives, still 80 per cent of eligible women entered their estates.

Surrendering lands early in favour of the heir was one way of avoiding freebench, but this was not done in Long Wittenham. In other localities farmers often retired in this way,[34] but the court books for Long Wittenham contain no retirement agreements, and the probate records yield only one (by a couple who were not customary tenants).[35] There were seven instances in which men surrendered all their lands *inter vivos*, but in only one of these is a widow known to have survived, and she was later reported (although perhaps erroneously) to have entered her freebench anyway.[36] Surrendering early meant the loss of two lives from the copy, and forced an immediate renewal, for which fines were variable and sometimes high.[37] Freebench was thus just too valuable to forfeit in this way. A more attractive alternative, surrender to the use of one's will, was not part of Long Wittenham custom.[38]

Limiting freebench by surrendering part of the holding was a

---

[33] The opposite practice of late marriage by elderly tenants to young wives in order to lengthen estates has been described by J. H. Bettey, 'Marriages of Convenience by Copyholders in Dorset during the Seventeenth Century', *Dorset Natural History and Archaeological Society Proceedings*, 98 (1976), 1–5.

[34] M. Spufford, 'Peasant Inheritance Customs and Land Distribution in Cambridgeshire from the Sixteenth to the Eighteenth Centuries', in Goody, Thirsk, and Thompson (eds.), *Family and Inheritance*, pp. 173–5, summarizes some of the evidence.

[35] Thomas and Elizabeth Yate, Berks. RO, D/A1/16/p. 405 (1632) and D/A1/142/82.

[36] Martha Strange, St John's College, Court Book IV, L.6.59, p. 77 (1663), V, L.6.60, p. 6 (1669). There is no record of her death, and her son Richard retook his holding in 1677, p. 6.

[37] Fines were recorded regularly only in the later sixteenth century (St John's Notebook of Copies), and ranged from less than a year's rent up to £40 for a holding rented at £2 2s. The normal range seems to have been three to ten times' rent.

[38] One copyholder, Thomas Hyde, did assert that he had the right and could use it to deprive his wife. Nonetheless he made her his executor and she took her freebench, although Thomas had apparently already made some agreement to transfer the property to the man to whom Elizabeth Hyde eventually resigned the holding under pressure seven years later. See PRO, PROB. 11/116/113v; St John's, Court Book I, L.6.56, p. 61 (25 Sept. 1611); p. 97 (26 Sept. 1614); p. 126 (22 Sept. 1617); and see n. 23 above.

more popular way of adjusting it to the needs of both widow and heir: about a fifth of the widows took freebench in only part of their husbands' tenements.[39] When holdings were divided this way it was always into half-yardland or yardland components, the older couple and then the widow normally taking the larger part, and the waiting heir the other. The holding was then reunited upon the death of the widow, perhaps to be redivided again in the next generation. For instance Richard Finmore surrendered one of his three yardlands to his son in 1591. When he died in 1608 his widow Margery had her freebench in two yardlands and at her death in 1620 the holding was reunited until 1623, when Richard's son divided it again with his own son John, a division that lasted until 1654.[40] Whether this was merely a division of title or if the lands were separately farmed is unclear. Thomas Child, who owned tenements at each end of the village, certainly divided his lands, giving one part to the husband of his daughter by his first marriage, and keeping for himself the part that later passed to his widow and then to his son by his second marriage.[41]

It was uncommon for a family to divide its holdings permanently to provide for a child, although on a few occasions cottage holdings, an acre or two and up to a half-yardland, were broken off for a son. These then became permanently separate tenements, following their own descent. Such subdivided cottage holdings were never used to substitute for freebench for the widow.

What to do with the waiting heir was certainly a matter of some concern to Long Wittenham tenants. On at least one occasion, the waiting son provided for himself by marrying a widow and taking her holding,[42] but this was unusual, and although women who held in their own right invariably remarried, it was rarely to sons of other copyholders. It is clear nonetheless that heirs did not wait to marry until they entered their lands. In at least half of the fifty-three cases in which freebench occurred in families with children, the succeeding child married before the parents died or surrendered title

---

[39] In addition to the two who took freebench in only one of two separate holdings (n. 31 above).

[40] St John's, Notebook of Copies, no. 68; Court Book I, L.6.56, pp. 32, 147; II, L.6.57, p. 19; IV, L.6.59, p. 11.

[41] St John's, Notebook of Copies, no. 48 (1580), and Court Book I, L.6.56, p. 39 (1609), and see n. 23 above.

[42] Mary Wise and John Barnes (n. 23 above).

(eleven before the father died, sixteen before the mother died or gave up ownership). Unfortunately there is little evidence as to how the young family was housed.[43] One or two men's wills show that the young couple were expected to share the widow's home,[44] and that may have been a common practice. Yet one young Long Wittenham man, who reported in reply to an accusation in archdeaconry court that 'he liveth from his wiffe because he doth his mother her husbandrie',[45] obviously shared the work of the farm without establishing a two-family household.

Whether widows actually possessed and managed the farms they formally owned is a more pertinent concern here. If they did not, the economic and social impact of women's ownership would have been greatly reduced. Farm wives, we know, were expected to excel in husbandry as well as housewifery.[46] There seems no reason to assume that widows would not have been capable of farming successfully, and examples cited below show it could be done. When tasks were beyond the widow's strength she could hire help or rely on her sons, as men often did. In the widow's case the economic cost would have been less, since her outlay for labour was partially balanced by the absence from her household of a male adult.[47] On the other hand, as a woman dealing in a man's world, the widow-farmer was handicapped in subtle ways, symbolized by the fact that freebench holders were never included in the homage jury,[48] and apparently had no formal say in decisions of the manorial court. True, important issues of farming policy were doubtless discussed

---

[43] There is no residential listing, and the Hearth Tax assessment lists are unenlightening.

[44] Among customary tenants Robert Webb was the only testator to do so (Berks. RO, D/A1/132/195); also see William Sawyer of Louches Farm, D/A1/115/167, and William Broke, D/A1/39/207.

[45] Berks. RO, D/A2/c. 31, *Ex officio* Act Book, 1591–3, fol. 84. The Stevens family were not copyholders.

[46] On widows' ability to manage see Hilton, pp. 101–2.

[47] It may be that very small holdings were less economical for a widow to run on her own since a family could be supported only by a combination of farming and by-employment income from a second adult family member. In the New College manor of West Drayton to the west of Long Wittenham, where most holdings were a half-yardland or smaller, widows were much more likely to surrender their holdings than in Long Wittenham (based on a study of records at New College, Rolls nos. 4037, 4040, 4044, Rental 4058 and Book of Extracts, 4059; my thanks to Mrs C. Wilson-Pepper for assisting me to see these documents).

[48] On two occasions widows were listed amongst those essoined: St John's, Court Book IV, L.6.59, p. 53 (1659) and V, L.6.60, p. 16 (1670).

and decided outside the court and a widow farming six yardlands presumably had to be consulted; but did the opinions of a woman with only a small farm matter very much?

Whether the widow was capable was only part of the equation. Fathers were also concerned about the ambitions of their sons and heirs, deprived of control of the copy by the widow's freebench. As we have seen, a few formally divided their holdings. It seems to have been more common for men to use their wills to encourage their widows and sons to share control of undivided farms. How husbands conveyed their livestock and farm implements gives a good indication of how they expected their farms to be run. But since Long Wittenham tenants rarely made specific bequests of their agricultural goods, which instead were almost always part of the residual estate going to the executor, it is to the naming of the executor that we must look to assess men's intentions. If the wife were to take freebench and run the farm, the obvious step was to make her the sole executor as well, and so convey the farm implements to her. It was in fact normal in Berkshire for men to make their wives their only executors. In Abingdon, for instance, 74 per cent of testators with surviving wives did so (83 per cent of testators who died in the sixteenth century), as did some 70 per cent of married men in a sample for the whole county.[49] Given the practicality of relying on one's wife, and the difficulties inherent in choosing anyone else, this is not in fact very surprising.[50]

One would expect that in Long Wittenham executorships by widows would have exceeded these proportions. This was not the case. Wills were made by forty of the fifty-eight copyholders whose wives took freebench, and of these only 52 per cent made their wives sole executor (only one-third of those dying before 1600 did so). But 33 per cent made their wives coexecutor with a son or daughter

---

[49] Todd, 'Widowhood', 81–6. The county sample is based on the first one hundred wills in the following Berkshire archdeaconry court probate registers: Berks. RO, D/A1/5 (1545–9); D/A1/14 (1608–9); D/A1/19 (1722–33).

[50] This is a much higher proportion of widows named sole executors than N. Evans found for a somewhat earlier period in four localities in Essex (2 per cent to 49 per cent), but there a higher proportion were joint executors (28 per cent to 43 per cent): 'Inheritance, Women, Religion and Education in Early Modern Society as Revealed by Wills', in P. Riden (ed.), *Probate Records and the Local Community* (Gloucester, 1985), p. 66. In Sevenoaks, 1660–85, two-thirds of married testators made their wives sole executors (Lansberry, 'Free Bench', pp. 283–4).

(compared with 9 per cent of Abingdon testators, and 12 per cent of the county sample). These men expected their wives to share the implements and livestock of the farm, and thus its management, with their sons (or in two cases daughters) who would later have the land. Sharing of management was an important aspect of freebench in Long Wittenham.

It is instructive to look in more detail at some of these wills. When Thomas Lovegrove made his wife Elizabeth his executor in 1570, he forbade his son to meddle with the horse and plough until after her death, and Elizabeth still had the holding when she died in 1580.[51] William Bedford (holding one-and-a-half yardlands) made his wife his executor, and although he gave his plough, plough team and carts to his son, he was not to have them until after the widowhood of his mother. She farmed the holding for more than fourteen years.[52] In 1609 William Sadlar asked his wife to till and plough certain plots on behalf of a poor brother and his wife, and she continued to farm with apparent success for some ten years.[53] These men plainly expected their wives to farm and be in full charge. On the other hand when wife and son were made coexecutors, it was with the expectation that they would live and work cooperatively if possible. Robert Webb expected his wife and his son to dwell together as coexecutors, sharing his copyhold as well as the lease of the parsonage. But as was usual whenever Berkshire testators planned this, he made alternative plans 'if they cannot agree to dwell together', the widow to take the copyhold, and the son the parsonage.[54] Who was to have the dominant role in these cooperative arrangements seems to have varied. Nicholas Sawyer, holding three yardlands, made his wife and son coexecutors, and asked his son to live with his mother, 'to be hir husband to husband all thyngs to the best for them bothe'.[55] But John Barnes, holding four yardlands, urged his children to be 'dutiful and obedyant to their aged mother', and not to contest the will.[56]

---

[51] Berks. RO, D/A1/9/fol. 235; D/A1/10/fol. 244.

[52] Berks. RO, D/A1/40/62; D/A1/41/12.

[53] Berks. RO, D/A1/117/32, and see n. 79 below.

[54] Berks. RO, D/A1/132/195.

[55] Berks. RO, D/A1/116/124. She continued to hold freebench for twelve years: see St John's, Court Book I, L.6.56, p. 32.

[56] PRO, PROB. 11/117/219. She surrendered her freebench after three years: St John's, Court Book I, L.6.56, pp. 61, 97.

A husband who did not make his widow his executor when she was to take freebench had to make even more specific arrangements. Normally the will gave the wife the right to dwell on the copyhold to which she in fact held title.[57] Without ownership of the implements of farming or livestock, and sometimes without even household goods, the title to freebench was decidedly hollow.

It seems then that of those copyholders who made wills and who were succeeded by their wives, about half (a third of all those whose wives took freebench) showed by their choice of executors that they intended either that their widows would not farm, or that they would share control of the land. Many of those who made their wives sole executors may have done so only because they had no adult children. Thus while most Long Wittenham fathes sought to preserve the principle of freebench as a useful protection for the widow and her children, they adapted it to the needs of the succeeding son and his family. The effect of women's ownership was thus considerably modified. Nevertheless at least eleven of those who made their wives their sole executors had complete faith in a woman's ability. They ignored the claims of an adult son, and reinforced freebench with ownership of the tools to farm the holding, leaving their wives in full control. It can also probably be assumed that those who did not make wills were aware that their wives would be made administrators of their estates.

III

Before considering how widows in Long Wittenham fared once they had taken freebench, it is enlightening to compare their husbands' expectations with the evidence of probate records in neighbouring Sutton Courtenay, where freebench was not practised.[58] If Long

---

[57] See, e.g., the will of James Jennens, Berks. RO, D/A1/87/19 (1667); his wife took the copy, holding it for nine years before she surrendered it to her son shortly before she died (St John's, Court Book V, L.6.60, p. 78; PRO, PROB. 11/352/172). Jennens gave his wife his household goods, but not any corn, cattle, or goods in the outhouses. Thomas Weston, whose wife took freebench in one of his two yardlands, gave her only 40s in his will (Berks. RO, D/A1/138/99; St John's, Court Book V, L.6.60, p. 130).

[58] Probates in the Archdeaconry Court of Berkshire, 1540–1720, and Prerogative Court of Canterbury, 1540–1700 (273 in all); eighteen probates in the Consistory Court of the Diocese of Salisbury were not examined. I have included the hamlet of Sutton Wick but not the chapelry of Appleford.

Wittenham can stand as an example of a village where traditional ways remained viable and acceptable, and were maintained with strong manorial supervision, Sutton Courtenay is a good example of how weak manorial control allowed a varied and innovative economy to develop. For much of the sixteenth century the manor there was part of the Crown estates, granted successively to several different holders.[59] In the resulting instability most residents began to claim to hold in free tenure. A survey made in the 1620s shows that only two men still acknowledged holding by copy. Free tenants had 'dismembered their yardlands in to half acres, acres and roods', and many holdings were very small.[60] Deeds and wills suggest that there was an active market in these small pieces of land.[61]

The general pattern of agriculture was the same as in Long Wittenham and other villages in the clay vale, but in Sutton Courtenay there were many more smallholders who combined farming with non-agrarian pursuits. Some worked on the river as boatmen, or in the transshipment of goods, since the village lay at the head of navigation of the Thames. Others supplied the river trade as ropemakers. There was also a paper manufactory and a brickworks, and the population was large enough to support a fair-sized contingent of tailors, shoemakers, carpenters, and butchers. The barley that grew in abundance in neighbouring villages supplied the most important industry, malting. Almost two out of three of the households liable to pay the Hearth Tax had a kiln, and women's main contribution to the family economy came from work on the malt floor rather than at the spinning wheel or in the dairy.[62] However, none of these were industries that were particularly labour-intensive. Sutton Courtenay's population grew from about 340 in the 1520s to about 580 in the 1660s.[63]

As holdings were enfranchised, most of the customs of succession were lost, including any freebench rule that once may have

---

[59] *V.C.H. Berkshire*, III, 373.

[60] PRO, E. 163/15/33, fols. 24–27v. See also L.R. 2/196/fols. 102–6.

[61] Deeds in Berks. RO, e.g. D/N1 2/23; D/Ex 17/4 T6) D/EBr T23; and wills, e.g. William Hawkins, D/A1/80/83 (1658); John Martin, D/A1/97/52; William Middleton, D/A1/97/199; Thomas Dyer, D/A1/61/205; Edward Tyrrell, D/A1/129/95.

[62] PRO, E. 179/75/381. On women's work in malting in the area see Todd, 'Widowhood', 48–56.

[63] Calculated from the lay subsidy assessment of 1524 (PRO, E. 179/73/134) and the Hearth Tax of 1664 (E. 179/75/381), including Sutton Wick, but not Appleford.

applied.[64] In the sixteenth century, however, it was still unclear which if any of the lands of the village were still liable to custom, and if a tenant could devise his lands away from the customary heir by his will. Without a freebench rule it was therefore uncertain if a landowner could give his lands to his widow at all. Cases arising from contested wills in 1567 and 1595 seem to have determined that widows could succeed under their husbands' wills, but unless a husband made a specific bequest the lands would go by default to the customary heir.[65] When it later became less certain what was customary land, men may have more often used other ways of conveying land to their wives; but it seems reasonable to presume that when men in Sutton Courtenay intended their wives to have their lands, they would be reasonably likely to say so in their wills.

For this comparison I have selected from the 118 wills of married men proved between 1540 and 1720 those of the sixty-two men whose inventories indicate they were farming a half-yardland or more. Of these, eighteen (or 29 per cent) gave their wives all their lands for life or widowhood, an estate comparable to freebench in Long Wittenham. Seven left the widow all their property until the heir came of age, or for some other limited term, and nine more gave a life estate in half or a third of their lands, or specified a separate property. Thus at least 55 per cent wanted their wives to have some portion of their lands for some period, as compared to a minimum 80 per cent succession to copyholds in Long Wittenham. Of the others, one excluded his wife explicitly, and sixteen did so implicitly by leaving only keep or household goods. Eleven made their wives executor without further reference to land, possibly masking a settlement by jointure.[66]

---

[64] There is no evidence of freebench for customary tenancies recorded in the eighteenth-century court book of the manor, Berks. RO, D/EC M148.

[65] Wills of William Truelock and Thomas Truelock, Berks. RO, D/A1/126/81 and D/A1/126/180, and PRO, E. 134/41 Eliz. H. 14, which explains what happened in the earlier case.

[66] The situation of widows in Sutton Courtenay resembles that in Kibworth Harcourt where, despite a freebench rule, tenants devised their lands by will. Thirty-five per cent of testators with surviving wives there left the widow a life estate or estate until the son was twenty-one as compared with 40 per cent in Sutton Courtenay, and 21 per cent gave part of their lands, as compared with 15 per cent in Sutton Courtenay. Recalculated from C. Howell, *Land, Family and Inheritance in Transition* (Cambridge, 1983), p. 256; on widow's continued ownership there see p. 260.

The widows of the farmers of Sutton Courtenay thus seem to have held a fairly substantial share of their husbands' lands. But as in Long Wittenham when a widow succeeded to full control it was often for lack of an alternative. Of the eighteen who took an estate of inheritance or a life estate, thirteen were childless or mothers of minor children only. Women with adult children were much more likely to receive no interest in lands at all. Or if they received a life estate, they were often coexecutors with their sons. As might be expected, the reasons that led men to modify freebench in Long Wittenham had stronger force when widows lacked customary rights as in Sutton Courtenay. But the practicality and justice of the widow's estate were still a strong force, perhaps the more so because freebench was common in the area.

IV

It remains to assess how widows fared as landholders in Long Wittenham, and to enquire if the persistence of freebench gave widows a stronger economic presence there than in Sutton Courtenay.[67] It is relatively easy to determine if they retained formal title to their lands. Of fifty-nine freebench holders on the holdings reconstructed, forty-eight can be traced to the end of their tenures.[68] Of these, thirty-four held until they died,[69] on average for almost twelve years. The other fourteen, those who surrendered their titles before they died, held their lands for an average of almost seven years.[70] Five of these gave up their lands when they

---

[67] Thompson speculates that freebench may have enhanced the 'feminine presence' in village societies where it pertained ('The Grid of Inheritance', pp. 349, 356–7), a hypothesis which has stimulated the following discussion, even though the suggestion that the feminine presence increases with ownership of property implies that women are somehow less present without it.

[68] The outcome of six women's tenures was not recorded and five held beyond the end of the period studied. The number of freebench holders differs from the number of men whose widows succeeded them because in three instances the first tenant discoverable for a holding was a widow.

[69] Including Frances Harford, who surrendered about a third of her holding six years before she died after having held freebench for forty-eight years (St John's, Court Book III, L.6.58, p. 20; V, L.6.60, p. 130; and PRO, PROB. 11/415/156v).

[70] On average those who surrendered had slightly larger holdings (2.5 yardlands) than those who died in possession (1.98 yardlands). But if those who disappeared and those who retired (below) are considered to have surrendered, there is virtually no difference in the average size.

remarried,[71] while the rest seem to have retired from farming and surrendered ownership to the heir, or, in two cases, to a man not apparently related. Widows did not often sublet their properties. The court books regularly recorded that male holders had been granted leave to take subtenants, but on only one occasion in this period did a widow receive permission to do so.[72] It appears that widows did not automatically, or even readily, give up formal title.

Did they also continue to farm their land? The probates which survive for twenty-three of the thirty-four widows who died holding freebench give some idea of how many were still owners of the equipment of a working farm, and how many had disposed of their livestock, ploughs, and carts, and reduced their possession to household goods alone. Two probates give too little information to determine the woman's situation. Of the rest, thirteen women had crops, implements, and stock equivalent to what one would expect, considering the size of their holdings and taking account of five cases in which the widow was coexecutor for her husband. Three more widows had the crops one would expect, but no livestock, and were probably not farming; while five probates indicate that the woman was clearly not farming and owned only household goods or personal items. Thus slightly more than half of those whose estates reached probate continued to work as farmers, or one-third of all those who held title when they died.[73] The Hearth Tax assessment gives a further sense of this, since of the six women who should have been holding freebench according to manorial records, two are missing from the list of heads of households.

When these women gave up control, and why, are questions not easily answered. Some, like Agnes Sangwyn, who executed a deed

---

[71] Only Agnes Slater, with one-and-a-half yardlands, appears not to have surrendered her land at once when she married John Weston, another copyholder, in 1568; she took a new copy to herself and a cousin, Peter Slater, who eventually succeeded her: St John's, Notebook of Copies, no. 38, Court Book I, L.6.56, p. 84.

[72] Margaret Bishop, 1618, St John's, Court Book I, L.6.56, p. 134. One other woman, Alice Seamon, 1629, Court Book II, L.6.57, p. 63, was presented for having a subtenant. The court books so routinely record subletting by men that I see no reason to assume that if widows took subtenants it went unrecorded.

[73] It seems reasonable to assume that women whose estates were not proved were probably not farming.

of gift immediately upon taking her freebench,[74] may have abandoned *de facto* control at once. But she was the only woman to take this formal step, and it seems likely that most women continued to manage their estates for some period at least. Marriage of the succeeding child was clearly a factor. When sons married it was eventually at the cost of the widow's control of her land. In every case except one in which a succeeding son married before the death of his mother, the property was divided, or she surrendered her lands early, or she retired informally while retaining title (assuming that widows who died without probate had probably already retired). In only one case is a mother with a married son known to have been farming her own freebench when she died.

Not surprisingly, women who were not their husbands' executors were more likely than others to surrender their titles or to retire informally (although one held for fourteen years, and another for nine, before doing so). But whether a woman was executor or coexecutor of her husband's will seems to have had little effect on whether she would continue to farm. The *modus vivendi* of cooperation between executors seems to have worked, yet women left in full charge do not seem to have foundered for lack of assistance, or to have given up at once in the face of pressure from anxious heirs.

The interesting question of why some women gave up control of their lands cannot be answered from extant sources, nor can we know if they felt they had 'retired' when they limited their responsibilities to the duties of the household. Whether the decision to withdraw reflected the plight of women in a male-dominated world, or female weakness, or whether the mother's sensitivity to the claims of a son and heir is positive evidence of women's responsible participation in the complex web of family succession, is something that must be explored further elsewhere.

The fact that some women eventually surrendered freebench and others gave up management of their lands does not of course prove that women failed at farming, or that they were without influence in their community. The manorial court records give no indication that

---

[74] Berks. RO, D/A1/16/p. 236; her entry into freebench is not recorded in the court book, but her husband took a new copy in September 1622 (St John's, Court Book II, L.6.57, p. 12) to himself and his daughter, she made her deed of gift to her son-in-law in July 1623, and her death as freebench holder was presented September 1631 (p. 84), the deed of gift having been executed in June of that year.

widows normally had trouble meeting their obligations: only two women were presented for failing to repair a bridge or scour their ditches.[75] On the other hand they appeared quite as frequently as their numbers warranted among those presented for over-stocking the common or for pasturing pigs in the fields too early, although only one woman was presented more than once.[76] Frances Harford, who held her freebench for almost fifty years, was guilty for several years of blocking the church way with a mud wall, but it is unclear what led her to do this.[77] Her name, alone among Long Wittenham women, appears more than once amongst those witnessing wills. She and the unfortunate Maud Sawyer, who lost Louches Farm, are the only two widows who emerge from the records as assertive women.

Nor does comparing probate inventories of husband and widow (in the seventeen cases where comparable pairs exist) show that widows were failures. It is possible that three or four widows were having trouble and had had to sell oxen, or were planting less than their whole holdings. But while the totals of other widows' inventories were smaller than those of their husbands, the discrepancies arose from the fact that the widow was only a coexecutor, or no longer owned goods bequeathed by her husband. On the other hand, four widows' inventories totalled substantially more than those possessed by their husbands (almost double in two cases). But again, in all but one of these cases the difference was due to the season, or to the technicalities of making inventories.[78] Only Elizabeth Sadlar, who held three yardlands, really seems to have enhanced her property: she doubled her worth between 1609 and 1620, by substantially increasing her flock of sheep and accumulating £20 in savings.[79]

Yet while they were apparently competent farmers, no freebench holder achieved notable success, nor did any take initiatives to

[75] Margaret Slater, 1619, St John's, Court Book I, L.6.56, p. 143 and Dorothy Withrington, 1637, Court Book II, L.6.57, p. 128.

[76] Alice Seamon (three yardlands), St John's, Court Book I, L.6.56, p. 154; II, L.6.57, p. 6.

[77] St John's, Court Book IV, L.6.59, pp. 34, 45, 53.

[78] E.g. including the value of the executor's year, something never included in the inventory of a husband whose widow-executor was to take freebench (see, e.g., Dorothy Finmore, Berks. RO, D/A1/68/98).

[79] William Sadlar, Berks. RO, D/A1/117/32 and Elizabeth, D/A1/118/24.

enhance her estates. No widow of a copyholder records the purchase of free land in her will. None appears in the manorial records as acquiring an additional customary holding, although five took new copies.[80] Elsewhere the role of the widow in generating credit and capital was increasingly important,[81] but only two Long Wittenham widows appear to have been lending money.[82] The strongest impression one receives from their wills and inventories is of good but very careful management. In the conservative world of the manorial village, within the limits imposed by holding a life estate, widows played their role efficiently enough, sustaining and maintaining their farms for the next generation, but risking no initiatives to expand their fortunes. In Long Wittenham freebench did not produce a community dominated by a group of village matriarchs.

This record can well be compared with a different picture in Sutton Courtenay. Without manorial records the accomplishments of widows there can only be observed in their probates and in the chance survival of deeds, evidence which tends to highlight the active and successful and obscure those who failed. Proportionately fewer Sutton Courtenay widows were people of economic consequence; widows' probates constituted 18 per cent of all probates there, as compared to 25 per cent in Long Wittenham. The difference was even greater amongst widows of landholders. Fifty-five per cent of the widows of copyholders in Long Wittenham who did not remarry left probated estates, but only 21 per cent of the widows of the Sutton Courtenay landholders discussed above. A com-

---

[80] Five took new copies for their holdings: Agnes Slater, n. 71 above; Alice Sadlar took a new copy in 1591 for her widowhood and for her son for reasons that are unclear, St John's, Notebook of Copies, no. 67; Agnes Sawyer, no. 88 (1604) replaced a dead son with a son-in-law; Elizabeth Sadlar replaced one son's life with another for reasons that are unclear, St John's, Court Book II, L.6.57, p. 127, III, L.6.58, p. 20; Emma Weston, 1630, II, L.6.57, p. 73 took a new copy to herself and her son-in-law, and in Marion Child's time, a reversion was given to her granddaughter Ann Taylor (1668), IV, p. 112, while the son who previously had the reversion was still alive. Widows must have exercised some initiative here, although the dynamics of these changes are unclear.

[81] B. A. Holderness, 'Widows in Pre-industrial Society: An Essay upon their Economic Functions', in Smith (ed.), *Land, Kinship and Life-Cycle*, pp. 435–42.

[82] Elizabeth Barnes als. Carter, Berks. RO, D/A1/43/144, and Joan Strange (not a freebench holder), 1625, D/A1/118/82. Three others (Agnes Andrews, D/A1/36/146, Dorothy Finmore, D/A1/68/98, and Elizabeth Keeblewhite, PRO, PROB. 11/173/68) held credits that probably belonged to the estates of their husbands who had died only a year before.

munity like Sutton Courtenay was also likely to produce more poor widows. Although there were landless men in Long Wittenham whose widows must have been desperately poor, it is in Sutton Courtenay that one finds a charity for widows (before 1641)[83] and later (1818) widows' almshouses.[84] The establishment of charities indicates the poverty of many widows, but at the same time it suggests that the people of Sutton Courtenay were aware of the widows in their midst.

Yet for widows of men of wealth and property, the economy of the open village offered opportunities that they were in a position to exploit. Fewer Sutton Courtenay widows held land, but since their successors were more often provided with other lands as well, those who held land did so with fewer constraints than widows in Long Wittenham. When widows were given their share in cash instead, they could enter the lively market in credit. Thirteen of the thirty-four widows for whom inventories survive from 1600 to 1720 had money on loan (nine of nineteen after the Restoration). Surviving deeds also show that they invested in mortgages, and that some bought land in Sutton Courtenay and neighbouring villages, including Long Wittenham.[85] They found investing in the malt trade profitable.

A few examples of economically active women will have to suffice here. One of the most successful was Christian Tirrold, widow of a yeoman who died in 1608. In a widowhood that lasted forty years, she bought several pieces of land to add to her holdings, built and furnished an additional house on her lands, lent £100 on mortgage to a man in neighbouring Steventon, advanced other money on bond, stood surety for the administration of her son-in-law's estate (something that was highly unusual for a woman to do in Berkshire), and when she died at the age of 96 was still actively engaged in farming.[86] The presence in her probate inventory of a malt house

---

[83] Will of William Andrews, PRO, PROB. 11/188/38v (1641) and monument in All Saints', Sutton Courtenay.

[84] *V.C.H. Berkshire*, III, 378.

[85] Margery House, whose husband died in 1692, leaving her with debts to pay, reports in her will of 1708 that she has put one son's life into an estate in Long Wittenham held of St John's, provided a 'very sufficient portion' for one daughter, and passed on to two other sons lands her husband left her; she made her unmarried daughter her executor (Berks. RO, D/A1/197/140, D/A1/83/183).

[86] Berks. RO, D/A1/126/246, D/EBr T22, D/A1/128/26, D/A1/183/13 (Richard Curtis).

and malting equipment (absent in her husband's) suggests that the profits of malting had contributed to her success. Later in the century Martha Saunders, a widow of a farmer who had apparently retired before he died in 1661,[87] came out of retirement when her son mortgaged his yardland holding for £150 and then failed to redeem it. She acquired the mortgage deed, and when she died in 1705, she owned the property.[88] Martha Hibberd, widow of a maltster-farmer who died in 1695, continued her husband's practice of lending money. Amongst her clients was Dorothy Bartlett, widow of an impoverished gentleman, who repeatedly borrowed funds on mortgage, first to pay off her husband's debts and then, apparently, to settle her children. Ultimately she had to sell her jointure lands.[89] Whether successfully or unsuccessfully, all these women were moving with some confidence in a credit market in the interests of themselves and their families.

V

Although women like Christian Tirrold can scarcely be said to be typical of Sutton Courtenay widows, there were enough women like her, and together they are sufficiently different from women revealed by Long Wittenham records for one to begin to suspect that there were fundamental differences between the two villages in the widow's role and, indeed, in the situation of all women. It is obviously difficult to measure the relative status of women in two communities of the past, but a number of things confirm the general impression given by the widows' probates. On the one hand there is little evidence that freebench gave widows a greater public presence, or improved the situation of women in general. As I have already pointed out, freebench did not convey to widows in Long Wittenham the right to participate in manorial court, something that might have enhanced women's public status there. Further, although it is difficult to quantify the treatment of children in wills, it also appears that there was little difference in the value of bequests to daughters where freebench existed and where it did

---

[87] William Saunders, Berks. RO, D/A1/214/134 (his inventory totalled only £7 17s 4d).

[88] Berks. RO, D/A1/122/141.

[89] William Hibberd, PRO, PROB. 11/426/96. Bartlett Deeds, Berks. RO, D/EB T98, William Bartlett, Berks. RO, D/A1/179/11 and Dorothy, D/A1/48/177.

not.[90] Nor were daughters in Long Wittenham favoured in succession to land. Local custom in both villages clearly favoured sons, although not necessarily the eldest. Daughters succeeded to land on seven occasions in Long Wittenham, and in two cases they clearly did so in preference to male offspring.[91] This was paralleled in Sutton Courtenay, however, by fathers who gave their real property to daughters in preference to sons.[92]

By other criteria, it was Sutton Courtenay people who seem to have shown the greater respect for women's talents, and public presence. For example, husbands in Sutton Courtenay were marginally more likely overall to make their wives their sole executors (62 per cent) than were the men of Long Wittenham (58 per cent). If testators did not appoint their wives, there was an increasing tendency in this area for them to name women rather than men as an alternative.[93] This occurred in both Sutton Courtenay and Long Wittenham, but the proportion of the alternative executors who were female was higher in Sutton Courtenay (30 per cent in women's wills, 22 per cent overall) than in Long Wittenham (7 per cent and 12 per cent). Equally noticeable was the difference in the tendency to use women as witnesses to wills. Fully a quarter of Sutton Courtenay probates after 1660 involved one or more female witnesses, but only 14 per cent in Long Wittenham.[94] It was a Sutton Courtenay woman, too, who appeared in the highly unusual role of surety in an administration bond, and a Sutton Courtenay woman who asked a woman to oversee the execution of her will.[95] Neither of these things occurred in Long Wittenham.

[90] In Long Wittenham two fathers and one mother showed a sensitivity to women's situation by creating a separate income for a married daughter, while only one Sutton Courtenay man did so: William Cowdrill, PRO, PROB. 11/264/372v (1656); Thomas Lovegrove, Berks. RO, D/A1/18/fol. 31 (1710); Joan Lyde als Joiner, PRO, PROB. 11/219/129 (1641); Richard Small (Sutton Courtenay), Berks. RO, D/A1/18/fol. 183v (1714).

[91] In 1596 Edward Keate put his daughter's life into his copy, and despite the subsequent birth of several sons she took the holding in 1633 (Berks. RO, D/A1/89/14 and St John's, Notebook of Copies, no. 80, and Court Book II, pp. 63, 101). See also the case of Marion Child and Ann Taylor (n. 80 above).

[92] James Billingsley, Berks. RO, D/A1/44/148; Daniel West, D/A1/137/124 (1665); George Middleton, D/A1/18/fol. 256 (1715) divided his lands amongst his sons and daughters.

[93] Todd, 'Widowhood', 86–7.

[94] Not counting scriveners' wives, omitting nuncupative wills, and counting more than one female witness to a will as a single instance.

[95] Catherine Keate, Berks. RO, D/A1/90/44.

Inadequate though these things are as a measure of status, they do suggest that women in Sutton Courtenay were in some sense more fully accepted in affairs of business than were their freebench-holding neighbours. What explanations are there for the difference? The fact that freebench was only a life estate is one possible factor, although most Sutton Courtenay widows who succeeded to land also had only a life interest. One might also assume that because of impartible succession to land, Long Wittenham widows would have been more heavily burdened with paying portions in cash and kind to their daughters and younger sons, and therefore less able to exercise initiatives. But the patterns of husbands' bequests in cash and kind in the two villages were very similar, and in Long Wittenham there was a tendency to make any large payments the responsibility of the heir once he had entered his lands. Perhaps the difference is in part more apparent than real, and resulted from a decline in farm income in Long Wittenham as corn prices fell in the later seventeenth century.[96] At the time when increasing prosperity in the malt trade, for instance, gave Sutton Courtenay widows greater opportunities to show their mettle, economic difficulties may have plagued widows in Long Wittenham and forced retrenchment rather than expansion. In the period of agricultural prosperity in the late sixteenth century, successful widows in Long Wittenham were likely to remarry and so be lost to the historian. But is also seems that there was an element of real difference. An independent productive role, as in malting, may have given women a greater public economic presence than did working as farm wives, even where freebench gave widows strong rights of succession. In that case, this evidence would suggest that work roles, rather than property rights, were more influential in determining women's social position.

In conclusion, it appears that freebench did convey substantial rights of ownership of land to women, and that many widows did exercise their powers as owners, although only a minority retained full control of their estates until they died. But the sense of free-bench as a bridge between generations rather than an individual woman's right of ownership, a sense that went beyond the differ-

---

[96] Probates from the period 1660–1720 make up a much smaller proportion of all probates 1540–1720 in Long Wittenham than in Sutton Courtenay – 32 per cent as opposed to 51 per cent.

ence between a life estate and an absolute estate, imposed its own logic on Long Wittenham widows, and they responded with careful management rather than economic initiatives. By contrast, the particular economic structure of Sutton Courtenay enhanced propertied widows' ability to fuel the economy, even though fewer of them succeeded to control of their husbands' lands. They responded to the economic opportunities that came their way. In the economy of Sutton Courtenay, as in free enterprise economies everywhere, there was less security for most women, but far greater scope for a few.

8. Wives and wills 1558–1700

MARY PRIOR

Wills are amongst the most useful sources for the study of ordinary people in the early modern period. For married women, if we exclude the writings of the literate, often extraordinary, minority, they are almost the only source. Considering the position of married women under common law the marvel is that any wives made wills.

According to the common law the married woman's identity was absorbed into that of her husband. She was covert, veiled, clouded, living within the shadow of her husband, and under obedience to him. So far as property went, for this is the concern of wills, the married woman could do nothing without the consent of her husband. Her personal property became her husband's when she married, and other forms of property passed under his control for the duration of the marriage. How, then, could wives make wills at all?

And yet, some did. It is the purpose of this chapter to plot the incidence of wives' wills (using Prerogative Court of Canterbury (PCC) wills and Oxfordshire wills for the period), to examine samples of their wills to learn what we can of the wives, and to consider such changes as are to be found over the period.

I

First, however, it is essential to sketch the powers which enabled wives to make wills. It must be pointed out that what is laid down by law and what is found in these wills are often hard to reconcile. It would be quite impossible by induction from the wills themselves to reconstruct the law which governed their making.

The attitude to wives making wills changed over time. In the thirteenth century it had been regarded by the church as a sacred duty for all adults to commit their souls to God, and to make provision of some sort for the soul's health by leaving money for prayers and alms by means of their last will. The canon lawyers agreed with the common lawyers in holding that the wife's personal property passed to her husband on marriage, but also held that, if the wife died before her husband, it was fitting that the husband gave the wife consent to make provision for her soul out of that third of the husband's personal property (the widow's third) that was her legal right in widowhood. This, however, was challenged by the common lawyers from the thirteenth century. They held that wives could not leave by will what they did not own.[1] After about 1440 wives' wills became very rare in many areas, but there seem also to have been pockets of resistance, such as the archdeaconries of Buckinghamshire and Sudbury.[2]

The oldest, and at all times the commonest, way for a wife to make a will was by the permission of her husband. This in no way controverted the husband's authority. By consent the wife was entitled to dispose of personal property,[3] and also leasehold and (where manorial custom allowed it) copyhold land which she had inherited. In the case of copyholds, though, her husband retained a life-interest. She was, however, expressly forbidden to devise freehold land by a law of Henry VIII's reign (34 and 35 Hen. VIII c. 5). This law, which seems so definite, was perhaps less so than it

[1] Michael M. Sheehan, 'The Influence of Canon Law on the Property Rights of Women in England', *Medieval Studies*, XXV (1963), 119–22; Anne Kettle, ' "My Wife shall have it": Marriage and Property in the Wills and Testaments of Later Medieval England', in *Marriage and Property*, ed. Elizabeth J. Craik (Aberdeen, 1984), p. 94; Kay E. Lacy, 'Women and Work in Fourteenth and Fifteenth Century London', in *Women and Work in Pre-industrial England*, ed. Lindsey Charles and Lorna Duffin (London, 1985), pp. 31–4; Sir William Holdsworth, *History of English Law* (17 vols., London, 1966), III, pp. 542–4.

[2] *Index to Wills in the York Registry 1389–1514*, Yorkshire Archaeological and Topographical Association, Record series, VI (1889); *Wills etc. from the Dean and Chapter's Court 1321–1636*, Yorks. Arch. Assoc., Record ser., XXXVIII (1907); *Calendars of Lincoln Wills*, I, 1320–1600, British Record Soc., Index Library, XXVIII (1902); *Index of the Probate Records of the Court of the Archdeaconry of Buckingham, 1483–1523*, Buckinghamshire Record Soc., XIX (1975); *Index of the Probate Records of the Court of the Archdeacon of Sudbury 1354–1700*, I, XCV (1984).

[3] Henry Swinburne, *A Treatise of Testaments and Last Wills* (London, 1590), p. 48; Holdsworth, III, pp. 543–4.

seems. One finds wives devising freehold, and the wills being proved, despite statutory pronouncement.[4]

Consent might be acknowledged in the will itself; sometimes the husband signed the will as well as the wife; sometimes it was expressed in practice by the husband's being appointed executor and proving the will, or by his allowing it to be proved by some other executor. The husband had, however, the right to withdraw consent to the will after his wife's death, even to the moment of probate. How often wills were simply ignored we shall never know. An example of a husband refusing to allow another man to prove his wife's will appears in the Oxford Caveat Book in an entry for 1674, and the husband's letter is tucked between the pages of the book.[5]

There were exceptions to the rule that a wife needed consent to leave personalty. The medieval claim to leave paraphernalia had long been lost,[6] but bequests of pin-money (the yearly allowance a husband might make his wife during her lifetime) were allowed.[7]

Wills made on the basis of contracts allowing the wife freedom of testation over certain property may be regarded as a form of consent. Essentially these amounted to pre-marital guarantees of permission, and they were usually accompanied by bonds for their performance. As it was argued that a contract between a man and woman was voided by their subsequent marriage, contracts had to be drawn up between the husband and a third party. Such contracts might stand on their own, or be incorporated in a wider set of marriage covenants, as was the case when Margaret Cranmer married Bartholomew Scott. They were used increasingly throughout our period, and were recognized by common law. Frequently, however, it is not possible to tell from a will whether it is made on

---

[4] PROB 11/45/32 (will of Thomasine Fanshawe, wife of the MP, Henry Fanshawe); T. E., *The Lawes Resolution of Women's Rights* (London, 1632), p. 123; C. S. Kenny, *A History of the Law of England as to the Effects of Marriage on Property and on the Wife's Legal Capacity* (London, 1879), p. 101.

[5] Oxfordshire Record Office, MS Wills Oxon 307.89, 90.

[6] Holdsworth, III, 543.

[7] *Baron and Feme. A treatise of law and equity . . . the third edition in which are added many cases in law and equity, from the best books of reports*, 3rd edn (London, T. Waller, 1738), p. 82. In 1699 Lady Kemeys left her son japan dressing boxes and white china she had bought with her allowance (PROB 11/450/76).

the basis of a contract or a trust. Sometimes both were involved in a marriage settlement.[8]

We now turn to wills which could be made without the permission of the husband. In such wills the wife herself is not, strictly speaking, involved in the transmission of property directly, though she might cause property to be transmitted. Theoretically at least, the position of the husband as owner and controller of her property was maintained.

A wife was entitled to make a will as the executor of a will, simply to appoint a new executor in her place. If, however, she used her will to carry out the terms of the will of which she was executor, then she required her husband's permission as she had taken the property into her own hands.[9] In an age where remarriage was common, women often had responsibilities outstanding as executors of a first husband's will when they took a second husband.[10] It was, though, uncommon for a wife to appoint an executor other than her husband, and especially without his permission. The eighteenth-century will of Jane Lenthall of Burford provides an example. This seems to have been made behind her husband's back.[11]

A second reason for a wife to make a will which did not require consent was in the disposal of choses in action. Choses in action included such things as debts and legacies, monies or other property which was not, for some reason, in her possession during her marriage, but was due to her.[12] Such a will was made by Susan Egleston, wife of Thomas Egleston, mayor of Winchelsea, and sometime its MP, disposing of 'the portion or debt due to me by the heirs, executors or assigns of Sir James Hales my late brother'.[13]

Finally we come to wills made without consent by wives who benefited from trusts giving them a separate estate which, though

---

[8] Holdsworth, V, 310–12; PRO C3/217/30. For forms of contract see William West, *Symbolaeographia: The Art, Description or Image of Instruments, Covenants, Contracts &c.* (London, 1590), sig. B iv, K v; PROB 11/65/5. This will is apparently based on both a contract and a trust.

[9] Swinburne, p. 49; *Baron and Feme*, p. 235; according to T. E., *The Lawes Resolution*, p. 144, she could not be an executor without her husband's permission.

[10] PROB 11/44/25, the will of Alice Blackwell, wife of Richard Blackwell, and executor of her late husband John Preest.

[11] MS Wills Oxon 213/352. I am grateful to Mrs Greta Darke for information on this testator.

[12] Swinburne, p. 48, says that she must make her husband executor, but *Baron and Feme* in the early eighteenth century said it was not necessary.

[13] PROB 11/85/14.

not recognized by the common law, was recognized by the Court of Chancery,[14] which, by tradition and conscious policy, sought the protection and development of women's interests. Trusts may be regarded as the most substantial way of not having one's cake and yet eating it. Here the wife benefited from property which was legally vested in trustees who were morally obliged to use it for her benefit. A separate estate could provide a wife with an income for life, and her interest in this estate was devisable. Women's freehold land could not be devised by will, but if it were in trust the interest in it could be devised.[15]

Trusts were still only being developed as a method of property management in the sixteenth century to replace the medieval use. Uses could be used to evade feudal dues, and the government had taken steps in Henry's reign to limit their applicability. From the very time of the enacting of the Statute of Uses in 1535 an alternative had been sought.[16]

Occasionally uses had been established by wealthy medieval women to preserve their economic freedom before marrying.[17] Lack of such means left such sixteenth-century wives vulnerable. This is very evident from the will of the Essex gentleman Henry Fortescue made in 1576:[18]

> Forasmuch as my daughter Dorothy Nokes cannot enjoy quietly anything I should bequeath to her in certainty (being under covert baron and the yoke of matrimony, but that the same may be taken from her by her husband, of whom I have no good opinion), I request my wife to use her godly and good discretion to dispose of

---

[14] Kenny, pp. 99–101; Maria L. Cioni, 'The Elizabethan Chancery and Women's Rights', in *Tudor Rule and Revolution*, ed. DeLloyd J. Guth and John W. McKenna (Cambridge, 1982). At present Ms Amy Erickson, of Corpus Christi College, Cambridge, is doing research on separate estate. I would like to thank her for discussing the subject with me, and letting me read a preliminary paper on equitable trusts for married women.

[15] 'A woman that hath a husband cannot devise lands by the Statute of 32 H. 8, but if landes be settled in others in trust for her use and to be at her disposing, then she may dispose as she will in equity.' This statement of the law occurs in advice to a client in 1635 (Kenny, p. 101, quoting Cambridge University Library, Patrick Papers, vol. XXIII, p. 34).

[16] Kenny, p. 51; Holdsworth, V, pp. 303–10.

[17] N. H. Nicholas, *Testamenta Vetusta* (2 vols., London, 1826), II, pp. 482–4 (Duchess of Norfolk, 1472).

[18] F. G. Emmison, *Elizabethan Life: Wills of Essex Gentry and Merchants* (Chelmsford, 1978), pp. 84–5.

her benevolence hereafter as well towards the relief and comfort of my daughter as to every of her children.

Whether inadvertently or not, the testator here had given the executor of this will something of the responsibilities of a trustee as far as his married daughter was concerned. Wives' wills made in the period 1558–83 include several cases of proto-trusts.[19] The outcome of cases in Chancery involving separate estate was uncertain up to the eve of the Civil War. Thereafter it was generally recognized.[20]

By the end of the seventeenth century trusts had developed so fully that a wife could have considerable freedom. This can be seen in the will of Lucy Lewes, the wife of a wealthy Aleppo merchant whose will was proved in 1698.[21] Lucy Lewes was the widow and executor of Roger Hatton, and she had two wons at the time she married Thomas Lewes. Before marrying she sold her deceased husband's estate to Lewes and placed the money in the hands of trustees. From the interest, money was allocated for her own separate use and also for the education and maintenance of her sons, who would receive their shares on reaching their majority. Five years later, perhaps because the couple separated, her husband agreed to pay her trustees £6,000. He failed to pay the full sum, the remainder was treated as a debt, and she lent a further sum to make up £9,000, on which interest at 5 per cent was paid. Property at West Wycombe and Stokenchurch was secured to the trustees against the debt. After the debt was repaid she bought an estate and by her will settled it on her elder son, and the residue of her estate, which included certain investments she had made, went to her younger son, apart from some minor bequests. Given biddable trustees Lucy Lewes was pretty well mistress of her own fortune. We have moved a long way from the view of the husband as his wife's baron and guardian.

II

So much for the powers (and constraints) under which a wife could make a will; but how far did wives avail themselves of them? In this

---

[19] Examples include the wills of Margaret Lane, wife of Thomas Lane, gent. of London (PROB 11/45/9, 1562), and Dame Dorothy Butler, wife of Henry Butler of Prittlewell, Essex, esquire (PROB 11/65/13, 1581).

[20] Holdsworth, V, pp. 312–14; Kenny, pp. 99–102.   [21] PROB 11/444/77.

survey the wills of the PCC were used. It had a wide geographic coverage, and as it included persons of wealth and rank it seemed likely that more individual wives could be traced. This would be important when a qualitative approach was adopted. To compensate for the upper-class bias of PCC it was decided to study the incidence of wives' wills in Oxfordshire also. Oxfordshire records were familiar to the author, so that some wives could be studied qualitatively. The wills formed an all but unbroken series from well before 1558, and they had been calendared.[22] Oxfordshire was a county which occupied a middling to low position so far as the incidence of wives' wills in PCC were concerned,[23] but it had the advantage of having county and diocesan boundaries which more or less coincided, give or take a few peculiars.[24]

Only PCC wills were used to plot changes in the proportion of wives' wills to the total number of wills over the period. PCC wills commence in 1383 and include the whole of our period with a gap between 1653 and 1660. During this period the Commonwealth established central courts under twenty Judges of Probate, so that the distinction between PCC wills and others was lost. Even before this the Civil War and the abolition of bishops in 1646 created problems for PCC. Registration of wills is patchy in the earlier 1640s, whilst, as the local courts collapsed in the latter part of the decade, the number of wills proved in PCC was swollen by wills normally proved locally.[25] The two decades 1640–60 have therefore been omitted.

Calendars have bee published to cover the period 1383–1700.[26]

---

[22] *Probate Records of the Bishop and Archdeacon of Oxford 1516–1732*, ed. D. M. Barratt, British Record Soc. Ltd, Index Library (2 vols., 1981–5), XCIII and XCIV; *An Index of Wills proved in the Court of the Chancellor of the University of Oxford etc.*, ed. J. Griffiths (Oxford, 1862).

[23] About a third of wives' wills proved in PCC were of London and Middlesex women; next came the Home Counties and Somerset, after which came the bulk of Midland counties, among which Oxford occupied a modest position. Last came counties which almost never sent wives' wills to PCC, such as Staffordshire, Lincolnshire, Cornwall, and the Welsh counties. Whether this indicated low levels of will-making in far-flung regions is uncertain, and could only be settled by examining local probate records.

[24] The geographical area covered by the archdeaconry and consistory courts of Oxford is given in *Probate Records of Oxford*, pp. ix–xi.

[25] *Index of Wills proved in the Prerogative Court of Canterbury*, VII, *1653–6*, Index Lib., LIV (1925), pp. xiv–xvii.

[26] *Index of Wills proved in the Prerogative Court of Canterbury, 1383–1558* (2 vols., 1893–5), Index Lib., X, XI. The series continued with varying titles: XVIII

However, women's marital condition did not interest the compilers of the first ones. It is almost never given in the volumes covering 1383–1583, so that it is impossible to plot the changing incidence of wives' wills from the medieval to the early modern period. Some attempt is made to indicate the women's marital condition in the two volumes for the Elizabethan period, but in the first, 1558–83, the marital condition of 32 per cent is not given, and in the second, 1584–1604, it is not given for 43 per cent. Further problems arose from the failure to sort out the marital condition of women described by such ambiguous phrases as 'late wife of'. These problems diminished in later volumes. It was not, however, until the penultimate volume of the calendars (1686–93) that wives were entered in the index of occupations and conditions, and then they were given most grudging recognition: under one-tenth of the 89 wives were listed. The problem of indexing aside, the calendars improved from 1605, and from then until the Civil War the proportion of women whose marital condition was unknown hovered around 10 per cent. It rose slightly at the Restoration, and then fell back, reaching 5.5 per cent in 1694–1700. On reviewing the results, it was decided, reluctantly, that the figures for the two Elizabethan calendars were not reliable enough to be used for statistical purposes.

The question still remained: how many of the women whose marital condition was not known were in fact wives? In such a preliminary survey as this it was not possible to read each doubtful will, and the assumption was made that the proportion of wives in the group whose marital condition was unknown would be the same as it was in the group of women whose marital condition was known, and a second estimated series of figures was accordingly calculated.

Table 1 shows that the proportion of wives' wills to all wills was at all times low, the largest proportion, 8.47–8.97 per thousand wills being still under 1 per cent of the total. Nevertheless during the seventeenth century the proportion pretty well doubled. Two periods show marked increase. The level of wives' wills rose, after the twenty-year gap of Civil War and Interregnum, by nearly two-

(1558–83); XXV (1584–1604); XLIII (1605–19); XLIV (1620–9); LIV (1653–6*); LXI (1657–60*); LXVII (1671–5); LXXI (1676–85); LXXVII (1686–93); LXXX (1694–1700) (*Commonwealth calendars); *Year Books for Probates*, I–IV (1630–52), ed. J. and G. F. Matthews (London, 1902–11); *Wills, Sentences and Probate Acts 1661–70*, ed. J. H. Morrison (London, 1935).

Table 1. *Proportion of wives' wills to every 1,000 wills in PCC in 1558–1700*[a]

Calendars	Known wives' wills	Estimated wives' wills
1558–1583	[2.65]	[3.92]
1584–1604	[2.11]	[3.69]
1605–1619	3.83	4.30
1620–1629	3.35	4.77
1630–1639	4.25	4.69
	Civil War and Interregnum	
1661–1670	6.89	7.84
1671–1675	6.33	6.82
1676–1685	6.85	7.54
1686–1693	6.90	7.35
1694–1700	8.47	8.97

[a] Total wives' wills 1600–1700 = 621, and the total of all wills was estimated at about 105,000. Deductions were made for mariners and persons dying overseas, whose presence distorted the figures, especially in time of war.

thirds. After a slight and temporary fall the same level of wives' wills was maintained until the 1694–1700 period, when there was a rise of over 20 per cent in a much shorter period.

This increase could possibly have been at the expense of business done by local courts, wives having got used to wills being proved centrally. What happened in Oxfordshire? The proportion of wives' wills to all wills seems to have been very low, but Table 2 shows that the number of wills made by wives increased over the period. Before 1640 only four wills were proved in local courts in eighty years, but after the Restoration, twelve in exactly half this time; and this despite the fact that the amount of business done in these courts was dropping off. Some allowance must, of course, be made for increase of population, but even so it is evident that the proportion of wives' wills in Oxfordshire rose during the Civil War, and remained at a higher level thereafter as with PCC wills.

III

Who, then, were these wives who took this extraordinary step and made wills? Can we learn anything from their background to

Table 2. *Oxfordshire wills proved in PCC and other courts*

	Lower courts[a]	PCC	Chancellor's	Totals
1561–1570	1			1
1571–1580				0
1581–1590	1			1
1591–1600	1	1		2
1601–1610				0
1611–1620				0
1621–1630	1			1
1631–1640		1		1
1641–1650	2	2		4
1651–1660	3[b]			3
1661–1670	1	1		2
1671–1680	3			3
1681–1690	4		1	5
1691–1700	3	1		4

Dates are of wills, not probates.
[a] For details of the geographic area covered by these courts, see Barratt, *Probate Records of Oxford*, ix–xi.
[b] Between 1653 and 1660 all wills were proved centrally.

explain why they took such a step? To answer this question we shall make use of samples, taking the first thirty-five wives' wills available, that is those from the 1558–83 calendar, and an equal number from the last years of the seventeenth century – thirty-five at random from the thirty-eight proved in the years 1698–1700. We shall also examine the twenty-seven wills proved for Oxfordshire.

We shall examine social and economic position first. As wives took the rank of their husband on marriage, save where the wife was of noble birth and the husband was not, this normally means that we must start by examining the position of the husband. There is, though, one exception in the earlier PCC sample. Frances Grey, Duchess of Suffolk, mother of Lady Jane Grey and niece to Henry VIII, took as her second husband a commoner, Adrian Stokes, a man half her age, who had been her captain of horse.[27] No other of the higher nobility appears in any sample. This is not surprising, as their number was small. In PCC for both periods the proportion of gentry was high, and disproportionate to their occurrence in the

[27] *DNB*; PROB 11/42B/59.

population.[28] There were two baronets or knights' wives in the earlier period, and four in the later. There were sixteen wills of the wives of gentlemen and esquires in the earlier period, and twelve in the later. The Oxford wills included at least three of gentry wives, but rank or occupation is only given for thirteen of the twenty-seven husbands.

Six of the 1558–83 husbands were MPs (Richard Blackwell, Henry Fanshawe, Sir Thomas Ragland, Adrian Stockes, Sir Thomas Tasburgh, Sir Francis Walsingham),[29] and three in the later group (Sir Francis Compton, William Brownlowe, Sir Charles Kemeys).[30] In the Oxford sample there were two (Roger Taylor, first husband of Elizabeth Bellingham, and George Lowe).[31] At least two eminent MPs had sisters who made wills: Margaret Lane (Sir Francis Knollys)[32] and Dorothy Underhill (Sir Christopher Hatton).[33] Quite a scatter of these, and others associated with the wives, had connections with the Inns of Court. Underhill, for instance, was a member of the Inner Temple, and clerk of the Assizes at Warwick. This and his ownership of New Place in Stratford-upon-Avon, later Shakespeare's house, shows him to be no mere member of the 'parish gentry'. Thomas Lane, husband of Margaret Lane, was connected with Lincoln's Inn, as was Richard Pate, witness to the will of Margerie Stokes. The names of more eminent lawyers occur: Sir Francis Gawdy witnessed Lady Ragland's will (and later married her daughter), Sir Francis Bacon, that of the Duchess of Suffolk; Sir Alan Broderick and Sir John Moore were trustees to Lucy Lewes. Caroletta Nettles was daughter of Sir John Churchill, Master of the Rolls.[34]

---

[28] For Gregory King's estimates see Joan Thirsk and J. P. Cooper (eds.), *Seventeenth-Century Economic Documents* (Oxford, 1972), pp. 780–1.

[29] For Blackwell see S. T. Bindoff (ed.), *History of Parliament: The History of the House of Commons 1509–1603* (3 vols., London, 1982); for the others, P. W. Haslar (ed.), *History of Commons 1558–1603* (3 vols., London, 1981). Entries are alphabetical.

[30] B. D. Hanning (ed.), *History of Commons, 1660–1690* (3 vols., London, 1983).

[31] For Bellingham see Haslar; for Lowe, Hanning, and Andrew Clark (ed.), *The Life and Times of Anthony Wood, Antiquary of Oxford, 1632–1695*, I, Oxford Historical Society, XLIX (1891), pp. 198–9.

[32] T. W. Jones, 'The Knolles or Knollys Family of Rotherfield Greys, Oxfordshire', *The Herald and Genealogist*, ed. J. G. Nichols, VIII (1874), 289–302.

[33] J. H. Morrison, *The Underhills of Warwickshire* (Cambridge, 1932), pp. 150–1; Mark Eccles, *Shakespeare in Warwickshire* (Madison, Wisc., 1963), pp. 88–9.

[34] PROB 11/46/10 (Ragland); PROB 11/42B/59 (Duchess of Suffolk); PROB 11/444/77 (Lewes); PROB 11/448/237 (Nettles).

It might be thought that at this level of society the efforts expended by fathers in conserving estates by the use of life-interests so that their line should continue from generation to generation would mean that they would show no enthusiasm for wives' being granted separate estates devisable by will.[35] Solicitude for the well-being of the individual and of the family were constantly at war wherever there was an estate to be divided or conserved. However, in any of these cases it was not so much a case of division between siblings as how much the husband should be given. Some of the wives were heiresses, many widows. At least 60 per cent of all the wives were widows who had remarried in the early PCC period, and half that number in the later period.

The line between gentry and such patrician merchants as Sir Thomas Lodge or Michael Lok, authors and merchants with an interest in foreign trade, is a fine one.[36] The wives of merchants and other urban tradesmen formed the next largest group, with eight in each PCC sample. This might seem a small proportion considering how widespread and populous this group was, as Gregory King's estimates show. All but one of these were concentrated in London. Probably the wives of the provincial urban elites had their wills proved locally. Three Oxford wives were married to tradesmen or merchants, and there would be more amongst those husbands whose occupation is not given.

As in Elizabeth's reign clerical marriage had still to be recognized by statute,[37] it is not surprising that there are no clergy wives' wills in PCC in 1558–83. There were two in the 1698–1700 sample, and four in the Oxfordshire one; all after mid-century.

Even where no occupation is given for the husband, the wives' wills usually reveal them to be very well off. In the earlier PCC sample there are no wives who were obviously really poor. Valentine Mason had served an apprenticeship to a tailor. Her father's legacy of £40 was still in her old master's hands, and she gave it to her husband. Mary Brackenbury, a haberdasher's wife,

[35] Lawrence Stone and Jeanne C. Fawtier Stone, *An Open Elite? England 1540–1880* (abr. pbk edn, London, 1986), pp. 48–55.

[36] *DNB*.

[37] Mary Prior, 'Reviled and Crucified Marriages: The Position of Tudor Bishops' Wives', in M. Prior (ed.), *Women in English Society 1500–1800* (London, 1985), p. 128.

left four bequests, none over 40s, and the residue to her husband. Elizabeth Smythe left no more than 2s to the poor to pray for her soul, and the residue (in the form of choses in action) to her husband. It is impossible to estimate the value of such residual bequests.[38]

The background of the later PCC wives is often affluent, though three may have been in financial difficulty all the same. Elizabeth Cartaret, widow of Sir Edward and wife of Alexander Waugh, seemed enmeshed in debts contracted in her husband's absence. The gentlewoman Dorothy Fitzsimmons, wife of James Fitzsimmons, was apparently separated. Her will has an undertone of desperation. Adry Freeman suspected her husband would fail to fulfil his contract to allow her to dispose of £50 by will.[39]

The Oxfordshire sample goes further down the social scale than might be expected. The presence of two yeomen's wives is not perhaps surprising, but there are also two labourers' wives, the wife of a husbandman, and three other country wives in quite humble circumstances, whatever their husbands' occupations may have been.

When we turn to the wives and their wills we find that many of them fall into pairs and clusters based on a variety of common factors. The wills of strongly Protestant women whose families had suffered under Mary form one such group. They include two members of the family of Sir William Locke: Elizabeth Worsopp and Jane Lok as well as Frances, the first wife of Sir Francis Walsingham, and Martia or Mary Hales.[40] Within their own families or among their friends they had examples of women acting with confidence and resourcefulness under persecution: such women as Jane Wilkinson, the mother of Jane Lok, one of the financial sustainers of the exile, a constant visitor of the imprisoned Protestant bishops until their deaths; Anne Locke and Rose Hickman, correspondents and friends of John Knox, also exiles; or Joyce Hales, sister-in-law of Martia Hales, active in a cell of Protestant women near Canter-

---

[38] PROB 11/56/46 (Mason); PROB 11/57/4 (Brackenbury); PROB 11/48/5 (Smythe).

[39] PROB 11/454/21 (Cartaret); PROB 11/453/189 (Fitzsimmons); PROB 11/449/40 (Freeman).

[40] PROB 11/46/18 (Worsopp); PROB 11/53/14 (Lok); PROB 11/47/32 (Walsingham); PROB 11/65/20 (Hales).

bury in Mary's reign.[41] As with recusant women later, persecution brought out new strengths. It is not surprising to find among women of this circle wives who took the extraordinary step of making wills.

The world of women revolved strongly around family, and the networks they provided would seem to have been powerful. A wife making a will was an extraordinary event which seems to have reverberated through the family network to the furthest in-law. This was seen more in the 1558–83 sample and the Oxfordshire ones than in the 1698–1700 sample. This may be because wives making wills were commoner and less remarkable by then, but it must be affected by the fact that the time covered is briefer; also less can be known of their influence because adequate calendars to PCC wills after 1700 have still to be compiled.

The influence of family example may be seen in numerous cases. So we find the wills of the successive wives of Oliver St John of Lambeth (1562 and 1566), and the wills of the successive wives of John Hall of Oxford (1685 and 1732). We have Margaret Lane (1562) and her mother Dame Lettice Tresham (1557); Margaret Lane's brother's sister-in-law, Dame Dorothy Packington (1577), and even Dorothy Packington's daughter's successor making a will after remarrying (1614). In the Wright family of Oxford we have the wills of Jane Lowe (1654) and Sarah Wright (1689).

Where a woman of strong character was concerned, the influence on will-making could be transmitted over a lengthy period. Frances, the first wife of John Hall, printer and warehouseman of Oxford, was herself an enterprising businesswoman. The University printed its first almanacks in the 1670s and from 1677 Frances Hall had them printed on handkerchiefs, for which she found a ready sale.[42] When she made her will in 1685 she could claim the aid of an intellectually distinguished circle, for two of her executors and a witness to her will may be found in *DNB*.[43] Her husband remarried, and after his death his widow, Mary, married Tilleman Bobart, a member of a

---

[41] Prior, 'Reviled and Crucified Marriages', p. 128; Patrick Collinson, 'The Role of Women in the English Reformation Illustrated by the Life and Friendship of Anne Locke', *Studies in Church History*, II (1965); Maria Dowling and Joy Shakespeare, 'Religion and Politics in Mid-Tudor England through the Eyes of an English Protestant Woman: the Recollections of Rose Hickman', *Bulletin of the Institute of Historical Research*, LV (1982).

[42] Helen Mary Petter, *The Oxford Almanacks* (Oxford, 1974), pp. 23–4.

[43] Oxford University Archives, Chancellor's Court, Wills, vol. G–HA, Hyp./B/26.

famous family of botanists and gardeners. It was some forty years after the death of her predecessor and exemplar that she made her will in 1726.[44]

Dame Dorothy Packington provides another notable example. Class rather than gender governed her action. As the widow of Sir Thomas Packington, she had become possessed of the manor of the borough of Aylesbury, whose lord nominated two representatives to Parliament, and, in that capacity, she sent up her own nominees in 1572. She remarried, and finally made her will in 1577 as the wife of Thomas Tasburgh.[45] Almost forty years on one finds the second wife of her son-in-law, Sir Walter Long, widowed and remarried, making her will as Catharine Fox, wife of Sir Edward Fox.[46]

When Dame Dorothy made her will, however, she did not lack examples, for her brother-in-law, Benedict Lee, came from a family in which wives made wills. In 1557 Benedict's mother, the thrice-married Dame Lettice, had made her will as the wife of that staunch Catholic gentleman, Sir Thomas Tresham. The will was witnessed by a lady from the highest legal circles. She was Lady Montague, widow of the Chief Justice of King's Bench, and sister of William Roper, biographer of Sir Thomas More, who had married Sir Thomas's favourite daughter, Margaret. She appointed Benedict and his sister Margaret, the wife of Thomas Lane, executors.[47] This experience would give Margaret some knowledge to draw on when she died a few years later, early in 1562.

Her will was interesting in a variety of ways. It embodied a proto-trust. In this it was legally more sophisticated than that of her mother, which had been made with the consent of her husband. Margaret did not need it. Before marrying she had placed money in the hands of the lawyer Richard Cupper, who had married a sister-in-law of Dorothy Packington, and chattels in the hands of her kinsman, Sir Henry Lee of Enslow. To dispose of such choses in action no consent was necessary. She made bequests to her

---

[44] MS Wills Oxon 117/3/12; for the Bobarts see *DNB*.

[45] J. E. Neale, *The Elizabethan House of Commons* (London, 1949), pp. 182–3; PROB 11/59/24.

[46] See Haslar.

[47] J. Burke and J. B. Burke, *Genealogical and Heraldic History of the Extinct and Dormant Baronetage of England and Wales*, 2nd edn (London, 1844), pp. 395–6; Mary Finch, *The Wealth of Five Northamptonshire Families, 1540–1640*, Northamptonshire Record Society, XIX (1956), pp. 67–72, Pedigree III.

daughter Lettice, to her half-brothers, Sir Francis and Henry Knollys, a certain Francis Sparkes, and other friends. To her husband, Master Lane, she left £100. The up-bringing of her daughter was left to her two strongly Protestant half-brothers, the Knollys, men whom her mother had passed over in her will, and she appointed them executors. Her daughter must be ordered in marriage by her father as well as her uncles.[48]

The first will in our sample to be made without explicit consent was made by Alice Wolsaye in 1558[49] on the basis of a contract. But Margaret Lane's is the first which edges towards a trust. By its very nature Margaret's will required nothing from her husband, and yet this experimental will must have interested him, for Thomas Lane was a lawyer and the son of a lawyer. He may even have drawn it up. This will was to influence other wills beyond the members of her family circle, once at least, it would seem, through Thomas Lane himself.

Thomas Lane came from a family which moved very much in legal circles. Both he and his father Thomas Lane, MP for Gloucester, had been admitted to Lincoln's Inn. After his mother's death his father had married a daughter of John Rastell, probably the noted lawyer and printer's elder son, brother of the judge. If this identification is correct, Thomas Lane, the son, had a niece of Sir Thomas More for his step-mother.[50] Once again the evidence suggests a connection between this group of will-makers and early humanism. After Thomas Lane senior's death she married another lawyer of Lincoln's Inn, Richard Pate,[51] and one finds both her new husband and father as witnesses of the will of Margerie Stokes, who was the wife of John Stokes, and executor of the will of William Michell, alderman of Gloucester, her deceased husband.[52] This will was made about six months after that of Margaret Lane. Here, perhaps, we see the members of a legal family giving and receiving professional advice, under the influence of More's innovatory attitude to women. The name Thomas Lane occurs also as that of a witness to one of the most sophisticated and risky wills in the series. As a lawyer, he had probably drawn it up. This is the will of Elizabeth

---

[48] PROB 11/45/9; *Baronetage*, pp. 303–4, 396; Morrison, *The Underhills*, pp. 57–9.
[49] PROB 11/44/34.
[50] Bindoff (Lane and Rastell); *Lincoln's Inn Admissions Register*, 4 August 1515 and 15 November 1545.
[51] Haslar (Pate).   [52] PROB 11/45/30.

Bromehall, the wife of John Bromehall of Stevington, Bedford-shire,[53] and it involved a use on a use, a device often regarded with suspicion by Elizabethan courts.[54] It is as if Lane were testing the limits to which wives' wills could be pushed.

Nor was Thomas Lane the only one to be influenced by the will of Margaret Lane. In the will of Elizabeth Tolwyn we find Francis Sparkes of Wighton, a beneficiary of Margaret Lane's will, acting as a witness. The will is clumsy in its terminology, and would seem to have been drawn up with more zeal than skill.[55]

The wills of many wives whose wills were proved in PCC were drawn up with professional help, as can be shown even further by comparing the names of witnesses with lists of admissions to the Inns of Court, though it would be rash to attempt firm identifi-cations in many cases. But how did wives of husbandmen in obscure rural villages gain the necessary knowhow?

Here again we find ourselves dealing with wills which are linked, but here the link is not family or religion, or the professional interest of lawyers, but land. Of the Oxfordshire sample only seventeen were proved in the consistory or archdeaconry courts, and of these three dealt with land in the ancient demesne manor of Long Hand-borough. They came early and were made in 1587, 1622, and 1650.[56] All followed the same pattern. The wife allowed a life interest to her husband in half-yardland, house, or orchard, as the case might be, then disposed of it to her children as she considered fitting. In the one case which can be fully documented Mary Ives had inherited the property from her mother, and she left it to her elder son, Henry, where according to the custom of the manor her younger son, Thomas, should have inherited.[57] Probably the other wills were con-cerned simply in oversetting the custom of the manor. That the knowledge of how to do this by a wife's will was concentrated in one manor was strange, but it would have seemed less strange if the wills had been concentrated in the neighbouring ancient demesne manor

[53] PROB 11/57/2.

[54] Holdsworth, V, pp. 307–9.   [55] PROB 11/58/1.

[56] MS Wills Oxon 1/1/8 (Alice Androse, 1587); MS Wills Oxon 136/3/20 (Mary Ives, 1622); MS Wills Oxon 13/3/48 (Katherine Coockowe, 1650).

[57] PRO LR 2/224, fol. 116; Blenheim Muniments B/M/208, fols. 7v–8v (I am grate-ful to Dr Janet Cooper and Mr Christopher Day of the *Victoria County History of Oxfordshire* for this material, and for discussing it with me. They should not be held responsible for my conclusions); Oxon RO, Long Handborough Parish Register.

of Long Combe which had been held by Sir Thomas Elyot until 1547. Sir Thomas and his wife had been friends of Sir Thomas More and his daughters, and in his last years Elyot had written *A Defense of Noble Women*.[58] If it is a rather lack-lustre performance, it showed his heart was in the right place. In the court of his manor one might expect women's interests to be given a kindly attention. And so, despite the gap in time, perhaps his influence had somehow affected Long Handborough.

Among the Combe wills of women whose marital condition has escaped the calendar of Oxford wills is that of Elizabeth Jefferey, wife of John Jefferey, made in 1557.[59] In this will the interests of her own two daughters are given priority over her sons' daughters, should the sons have no male issue. This was a departure from the normal rule of succession, more favourable to women. Her father-in-law, Christopher Jefferey, was one of the Combe villagers who witnessed Sir Thomas Elyot's will, made in 1531.[60] Further than this we cannot go.

There are two later wives' wills, of similar sort, that of a labourer's wife of Wootton, another nearby manor of ancient demesne, made in 1663, and a second Combe one, that of a yeoman's wife, in 1687. Only the will of Elizabeth Basley or Beesley, wife of John Basley, of Watlington, labourer, does not conform to this pattern. Her will, of 1672, was made on the basis of an 'agreement'.[61] Whether one sees in the Long Handborough and Combe wills the reflection of some custom peculiar to these manors of ancient demesne, or the lingering influence of the humanist tradition, or the influence of one on the other, we see in Elizabeth Basley's will something new: an example of the wider use of agreements to give wives testamentary powers which, we shall see, became commoner in the seventeenth century.

IV

Superficially the difference between Elizabethan wills and late-seventeenth-century wills is striking. Wills became verbose. Legal

---

[58] Maria Dowling, *Humanism in the Age of Henry VIII* (London, 1986), pp. 239–60.
[59] MS Wills Oxon 185.9v–10 (wrongly calendared as 185.8–9).
[60] MS Wills Oxon 178.151 (Jefferey); PROB 11/31/14 (Elyot).
[61] MS Wills Oxon 6/4/41.

technicalities abound; the furthest stretches of possibility are explored and provided for. The testator's mind is set on alternative earthly contingencies rather than heaven and eternity.

But these are not the only changes. The character of wives' wills changed and showed wives gaining greater independence both economically and psychologically. Thus in the sixteenth-century sample only five out of thirty-five wives made their wills without their husbands' consent in some form. By the end of the seventeenth century thirteen made their wills without consent of any kind.

In the sixteenth-century sample the feeling that husband and wife are one flesh is strong, and though the sixteenth-century wife was doing a much more extraordinary thing in making a will than the late-seventeenth-century wife, she seemed to live more in the shadow of her coverture. Husband and wife were one, but it was the husband whose identity absorbed that of the wife. Only in the will of Jane Lok, made in 1570, does the doctrine of being one flesh have a more equal interpretation, when she speaks of bequeathing, with her husband's consent, 'all my worldly goodes or my husbandes . . . by whose love I have enioyed them'.[62] If what was hers was his, so his was hers. At the other end of the spectrum is the self-abasement of Isabel Catcot, who made her will in 1580. She gave her husband all her goods, for he had married her when she was 'in stiffe con- tention of law' and sickly in body, and she wished that she had been of greater worth that her husband might enjoy it all.[63] Here there is almost something cannibalistic about the sentiment – as if the wife were not merely property, but food.

Again, in the early period only five wives left their husbands nothing. Sometimes this was through ill will, though usually this can only be surmised. In any case, one must be cautious. The fact that a husband is not mentioned in a will may arise from many causes, even from total harmony, the wife's will furthering a shared interest. The relationship between Hannah Smith alias Bowell of Oxford and her husband Cresswell Bowell was loving, but she left him nothing in her will, made in 1644.[64] Oxford was occupied by royalists at the time, and Hannah was dying of 'plague'. Sitting in a chair in her chamber, she said to her husband, 'I am a dead woman and not a woman of the world. I pray, husband, let me make my will, and give my goods which my grandmother gave me.' Her

[62] PROB 11/53/14.   [63] PROB 11/62/46.   [64] PROB 11/196/95.

husband agreed, and she left her property to William and Anne, the children of her husband by a former marriage, telling her husband that she hoped he would perform her will. He promised, thanked her for her kindness and care of his children, and kissed her. 'If I die', she said, 'you maie or will marry again. And I do not intend that any one shall have anything that my grandmother gave me but Will and Nan.' Hannah, being a woman of her period, faced realistically the likelihood of remarriage, but for the present accord was complete.

In the later period the number who left their husband nothing increased more than three-fold, from five to seventeen. Twenty-eight of the wives used trusts or contracts, and five disposed of choses in action.

Favourable pronouncements in Chancery cases in the 1630s had opened the way to a more confident use of trusts. This confidence was increased further by the abolition of feudal dues in 1646, for trusts had been regarded with suspicion by the law, because they could be used to avoid this medieval form of taxation. Nevertheless the sense of the 'agglutination' of husband and wife was breaking down not so much because wives had a greater freedom through trusts to make wills, but because the erosion of medieval constraints on married men which protected widows' rights gave ever more men complete freedom of bequest. Women needed the security trusts could give them. If men had the freedom to leave their property to whom they would, it must put a strain on the doctrine that in marriage husband and wife were one flesh.

A growing independence from the husband is also seen in wives' attitudes to the fate of their children after their own death. According to the law the husband was the child's guardian, and he had the right to appoint any guardian he wished should he die first. His right was, however, extinguished if he were a tenant-in-chief, when the King claimed the right to sell the wardship of the heir. This was a feudal exaction which had been revived by Henry VIII and was abolished along with other feudal dues in 1646.[65] The abolition of the Court of Wards in 1646 strengthened the rights of parents in general, and removed a humiliating display of the weakness of the wife's position in particular.

---

[65] Ivy Pinchbeck and Margaret Hewitt, *Children in English Society*, I (London, 1969), pp. 58–74.

In the sixteenth century the wives submitted to their position, all but entirely. Eleven wills involved young children, and in seven cases there were children of an earlier marriage. Save in the case of Margaret Lane, the husband was accepted as the natural and only guardian. In the late seventeenth century the wives simply assumed they had the right to a voice in the future of their children. Only five wills involved young children, and only in one case was the children's upbringing left entirely to the husband. One set up a trust for her children in her mother's hands; one appointed a brother, and the third a brother-in-law, to act jointly as guardians with the husband; the fourth appointed the wife of a painter guardian of her daughter.

The changes in wives' attitudes which occurred in the seventeenth century were foreshadowed in the sixteenth century by the will of Margaret Lane.[66] This will produced a reaction of outrage from a contemporary which makes clear how extraordinary a will it was.

Margaret Lane made her will without the consent of her husband, disposing freely of money and other goods, and even of the upbringing of her daughter. The clerk who copied the will into the great vellum register in which PCC wills for the year 1562 were entered decorated the margins of the page. The decoration of pages on which the wills of great men occur was no uncommon thing, the wills being embellished with elaborate coats of arms to honour the dead. Here the clerk expressed his feelings about the will of Margaret Lane by defacing the margins with drawings of freaks and abortions. By this juxtaposition he implied that the will went against nature, and perhaps hinted even more.[67]

The increase in the number of wills in the seventeenth century is itself an index to the changing attitudes of wives. The time of greatest increase came in mid-century, and thereafter a higher level was maintained. This parallels almost exactly the pattern of increase in women's published writings for the same period discovered by Patricia Crawford. In her paper 'Women's Published Writings 1600–1700',[68] she shows that the level of women's published writings was low in the early seventeenth century, and that there

---

[66] PROB 11/45/9.

[67] Jean Donnison, *Midwives and Medical Men* (New York, 1977), pp. 4–5.

[68] Patricia Crawford, 'Women's Published Writings 1600–1700', in Prior (ed.), *Women in English Society*, pp. 213–14, 266.

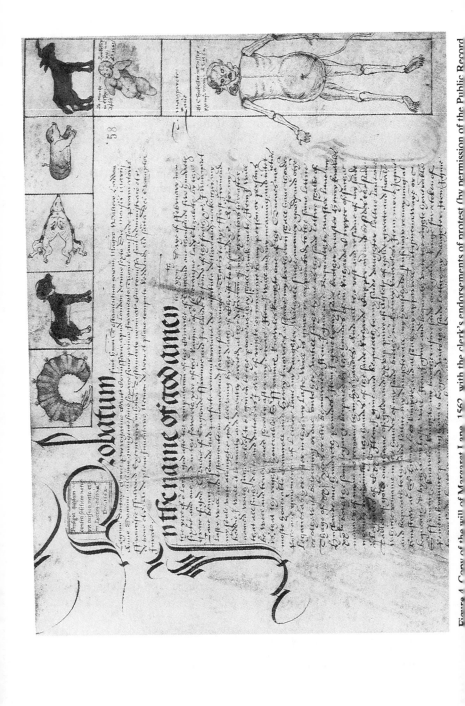

Figure 4. Copy of the will of Margaret Lane, 1562, with the clerk's endorsements of protest (by permission of the Public Record

was the same rise in the decades of the Civil War and Interregnum. There was some fall-off at the Restoration, but nevertheless publication maintained a much higher level after the Civil War and Interregnum than before. Part of the explanation, she held, was that women had been forced into new and unaccustomed roles, and developed a new confidence in their abilities. We have seen that in a situation of stress in the mid sixteenth century, independent and strong-minded women emerged, and from such circles at least four of the will-makers in the 1558–83 sample were drawn. The experience which led some women to publish in the Civil War period must also have led to an increase in wives making wills.

At the same time the revolutionary attack on the vestiges of feudalism had its effect. Women's access of confidence may have given an initial impetus, but the recognition of separate estate had a ratchet effect. Economic freedom gave to some wives the freedom to make wills, to others the confidence and the cash to write and publish their own work in a way never before possible.[69]

We might expect the circles in which wives made wills to overlap to some extent with the world of women who wrote, or in other ways expressed the nascent feminism of the late seventeenth century. The thirty-five wives of the 1698–1700 sample are a minute group, and so is that of the feminists, however broadly defined. To look for evidence here, when our knowledge of most of the wives is very limited anyway, might seem like looking for lost climbers on the Himalayas through a key-hole.

No wives who made wills were writers, yet there is overlap of some sort in the case of two wives, Dame Mary Compton and Dame Mary Kemeys (née Wharton), as we can see from the circles in which they moved. Dame Mary Compton was the daughter of the economist Samuel Fortrey, and granddaughter of Elizabeth Josceline, the author of *The Mother's Legacy to her unborne Childe* (1624).[70] She was related to the Mashams of High Lever, Sir Francis being appointed one of the trustees of a trust she set up for her husband, a notorious spendthrift. She left a bequest of £100 for her

---

[69] *Ibid.*, p. 214.
[70] *DNB* (Fortrey, Jocelyn). The title of Elizabeth Jocelyn's book is interesting: *The Mother's Legacy to her unborne Childe*. In the introduction Dr Goad pointed out that whilst the law disabled married women from disposing of temporal estate by will, there was no embargo on bequeathing moral and spiritual riches. The grand-daughter seems to have taken good care to circumvent common law.

niece Ester Masham. John Locke spent his last years in the Masham household, and his letters to Ester and her more famous step-mother, the philosopher Damaris, Lady Masham, survive. Damaris, Lady Masham was engaged in philosophical controversy with Mary Astell.[71] Both, however, agreed in urging the importance of women's education.

Dame Mary Wharton wrote nothing herself, but her active and independent attitudes and her unpublished correspondence have been described by Philip Jenkins in 'Mary Wharton and the Rise of the "New Woman"'.[72] She was the daughter of Philip, fourth Baron Wharton. She took an active part in running her own estates and those of her husband, and led an active social life. Her will shows her an affectionate mother, and she left to her son and two daughters, amongst other things, her books of divinity. In politics she was a Whig; her husband, until his last years, a royalist. Her sisters-in-law, Mary and Anne Kemeys, high church, where she was low, founded a high-church Anglican sisterhood at Naish Court in Glamorganshire. This was some years before Mary Astell put forward her scheme for a female monastery devoted to piety and learning, in her *Serious Proposal to the Ladies*.[73] It seems likely that it would be known to Mary Astell. Another of Dame Mary's sisters-in-law was the poet Lady Anne Wharton.[74] Her poems appear in a volume entitled *Whartoniana*, published in 1727, containing the work of members of the Wharton family and their friends over two or three generations. It also included poems by Lady Mary Chudleigh, who, at the time of Dame Mary Kemeys's death, was just beginning to appear in print with her anonymous *The Female Advocate* (1700).

The last decade of the seventeenth century was remarkable for the criticism women mounted against marriage. In her *Reflections on Marriage* Mary Astell expressed the feelings of many women

---

[71] *DNB* (Damaris, Lady Masham); *The First English Feminist: Reflections on Marriage and other Writings by Mary Astell*, ed. Bridget Hill (Aldershot, Hants., 1986), pp. 49–50.

[72] Philip Jenkins, 'Mary Wharton and the Rise of the "New Woman"', *Journal of the National Library of Wales*, XX (1981–2), 170–86; *DNB* (Philip Wharton).

[73] *DNB* (Lady Anne Wharton).

[74] Hill, *The First English Feminist*, p. 28; Bridget Hill, 'A Refuge from Men: The Idea of a Protestant Nunnery', *Past and Present*, 117 (1987). I am grateful to Mrs Hill for allowing me to read the typescript; E. H. Plumptre, *The Life of Thomas Ken, D.D.* (2 vols., 1888), II, p. 167.

when she wrote 'If all men are born free, how is it that all women are born slaves?' and so did Lady Mary Chudleigh in her poem 'To the Ladies':

> Wife and servant are the same,
> But only differ in the name.

The improvement in the position of some married women through trusts, which wives' wills so often betoken, resulted, as so often in situations of oppression, in increased criticism.

Making a will was at all times the act of an individual, and for the sixteenth- and seventeenth-century wife, it was an extraordinary one. The conditions under which a wife could make a will were limited. Many of the sixteenth-century wills in particular show evidence of being drawn up with the help and advice of legal relatives, sometimes ingeniously testing their limits. A few of the earliest emanate from circles still tinged with the humanistic tradition, and perhaps reflecting the higher estimation of women to be found there. The wives themselves were often impressive women whose influence can sometimes be traced through women's networks, and their example was followed by other wives.

Wives' wills increased markedly in number in the mid seventeenth century, and late-seventeenth-century wills show an increased independence and assertiveness. Some of the wives moved in circles where the feminists of the late seventeenth century were known, and the wives' wills can themselves be seen as part of the groundswell of feminist sentiment, although here wives claimed for themselves individually rights which other, later, feminists were to claim for all women.

9. The horse trade of Shropshire in the early modern period

PETER EDWARDS

In her seminal work, *Horses in Early Modern England: For Service, for Pleasure, for Power* (1978), Joan Thirsk emphasized the vital role that horses played in the social and economic life of England in the period before the Industrial Revolution.[1] Indeed, in the two hundred years after 1550, horses were required in ever-growing numbers to meet the demands of agriculture and industry, to move people and goods around the country and to service the leisure pursuits of the nobility and gentry. In wartime, demand increased dramatically. The growth in the market for horses was accompanied by a trend towards functional specialization, which further benefited breeders. Naturally, the native stock did not remain unchanged, and over the course of the period considerable modification in some breeds was made, especially through greater selectivity and by the admixture of foreign blood. Initially the impetus was provided by the Crown and the aristocracy and was therefore to be seen earliest in good-quality saddle mounts and coach horses. By the middle of the eighteenth century, however, the effects had percolated down through the social strata and had influenced the quality of the horses possessed by a much wider section of the population.

Small-scale breeding was widespread, but as in other branches of agriculture, production came to be concentrated in those areas where conditions were favourable to the practice. Grass was an essential requirement and thus horse breeding was often pursued in wood-pasture districts. Farmers in mixed farming communities where adequate resources existed were also involved, but in such

[1] J. Thirsk, *Horses in Early Modern England: For Service, for Pleasure, for Power* (Reading, 1978), *passim*.

227

areas horses were increasingly brought in from outside. As a result, a long-distance traffic in horses developed and specialist fairs emerged. These centres often dealt in specific types of horses, acted as nodal points in the trade, and attracted buyers and sellers from considerable distances. At the same time horse trading came under the control of a class of middlemen who in spite of public condemnation of their activities were essential if the market was to be organized on more than a purely local scale.[2]

Shropshire occupied an important position in the trade. The wealth of contemporary material relating to the county allows the developments there to be clearly seen. Of particular value are the toll books which have survived for several Shropshire fairs: similar books from beyond the county can be used to show the activities of local dealers outside Shropshire.[3] These documents, which give details of the horses sold, the prices paid, and the residences of buyers and sellers, were introduced by statute in 1555 and extended in scope in 1589.[4] In 1555 it was stipulated that all transactions had to be entered into a book specially kept for the purpose with 'the names surnames and dwelling places of all the said parties, and the colour, with one special marke at the least of every such Horse Mare Gelding or colte'. After 1589 the buyer had to provide a voucher, a 'sufficient and credible person', who would guarantee his honesty.

[2] P. R. Edwards, 'The Horse Trade in Tudor and Stuart England', in F. M. L. Thompson (ed.), *Horses in European Economic History: A Preliminary Canter* (Reading, 1983), pp. 113–31.

[3] References to toll books of Shropshire fairs: Shrewsbury 1524/5, 1563–74, Shrops. RO, Shrewsbury Corpn Records 2645–68; Bridgnorth 1631, 1644–1720, 1767–78, Shrops. RO, Bridgnorth Corpn Records 4001/Mar/1/268–71; Ludlow 1649–9, 1687–95, Shrops. RO, Ludlow Corpn Records 356/Box 297, 356/32/Box 466; Much Wenlock 1632–8, Much Wenlock Guildhall, Transcript of Toll Books 1632–8.

References to toll books of other fairs: Leominster 1556–7, Herefs. RO, Leominster Borough Records, Bailiffs' Accounts 8; Chester *c.* 1567–79, Chester City RO, Sheriffs' Toll Books SBT/1; Walsall 1628–*c.* 1636, Walsall Town Hall, WTC II/40/1–15; Dudley 1702–10, Dudley Ref. Lib., Dudley Estate Colln Misc. Box; Kidderminster 1694–1711, Kidderminster Ref. Lib. KID 352/no. 1455; Derby 1638–61, 1677, 1697–1700, n.d., Derby Ref. Lib., Derby Horse Fair Books; Nottingham 1634–64, Notts. RO, CA 1504–5; Market Bosworth 1603–32, Folger Shakespeare Lib., Washington, DC, MS V.b.165; Penkridge 1558, 1579, 1640, British Library, MSS Dept, Egerton MS 308 fols. 2v–22v; Stafford 1614–15, Staffs. RO, Matthew Craddock's Commonplace Book D1287/10/2; Banbury 1753–67, Oxford RO, B.B. VII/vii/1 (I am grateful to Dr Wendy Thwaites for this reference); Sutton Coldfield 1750–9, Birmingham Ref. Lib., Ref. 80–2.

[4] 2 & 3 Ph. & M. c. 7; 31 Elizabeth I c. 12.

The first act was passed in the critical years of the mid sixteenth century, a time when similar measures were being taken to regulate agriculture and industry and to deal with the problems of poverty and the supply of labour, and it should be looked at in the context of the government's overall policy of controlling the social and economic life of the country. The statute was specifically designed to curb the incidence of horse stealing but, through the insistence that all horses to be sold should be put on public display in the market place for at least an hour, it was also intended to strengthen those traditional institutions, the markets and fairs.

Other sources that have been used in this chapter include probate inventories, which provide information on the agriculture of the county and which indicate the scale and scope of horse breeding there. Few inventories survive before 1660 for parishes in the diocese of St Asaph's (the north-western corner of Shropshire) or for those in the diocese of Hereford (the southern half of the county), but in the area covered by the diocese of Lichfield documentation begins before the mid sixteenth century. There are also good collections of estate papers which supply additional information on agriculture and give background material on some of the people who worked in the horse trade. More particularly, they illustrate the ways in which the upper classes were involved in horse keeping.

I

Pastoral farming predominated in Shropshire, although good crops were grown on the brown earths and in some favoured districts the economy approximated to the cattle–corn husbandry of neighbouring Herefordshire. On the lighter soils of the heaths and eastern sands, moreover, a sheep–corn system was making some headway in the post-Restoration period.[5] A good deal of enclosure had already taken place by the middle of the sixteenth century and the process was to continue throughout the next two hundred years. Residual commonfield strips were tidied up without much fuss and improvement schemes, often undertaken on a large scale, brought in thousands of acres from the commons and wastes. New farms

---

[5] P. R. Edwards, 'Shropshire Agriculture 1540–1750', in G. C. Baugh (ed.), *Victoria County History of the County of Shropshire*, IV (Oxford, 1990), pp. 119–68.

were created, existing holdings were enlarged, and much land was made available for short-term leasing.[6] There was therefore no shortage of good-quality pasture. In spite of the attack on the wastes, however, the vast tracts of unimproved land that remained offered farmers and smallholders a plentiful supply of rough pasture on which to put their horses and other animals. In the Forest of Hogstow, south-west of Shrewsbury, for instance, tenants could graze their animals on the common, although, according to a document of 1521, horses had to be removed by Martinmas (11 November). Another large upland common, the Forest of Clun, was used by the inhabitants of the whole south-western corner of the county to pasture their beasts. The horses and cattle of the freeholders of Kerry (Montgomeryshire) were regularly to be found there too, having strayed off their own contiguous and unenclosed commons.[7]

Although normally subordinated to other livestock enterprises such as cattle rearing, dairying and sheep husbandry, horse breeding was commonplace. Inventories taken in the 1550s indicate a preponderance of mares and young animals, a feature that was to persist into the post-Restoration period. In the 1740s more male horses were kept on the farm, but this reflected the greater use being made of these animals rather than a declining interest in breeding. By that time horses had largely replaced oxen for all manner of farm work and they, therefore, represented a much greater element in the capital costs of agriculture than they had done in earlier times.[8] Breeding herds were similar in size to those found in the Yorkshire dales and the moors of the South-West, but they tended to be smaller than those kept in fenland areas; they nevertheless provided a valuable source of income for many farmers.[9] Even small husbandmen such as Ralph Wild of Longslowe, Market Drayton, who in 1608 possessed two mares, one

[6] *Ibid.*; P. R. Edwards, 'The Farming Economy of North-East Shropshire in the Seventeenth Century', unpublished D.Phil. thesis, Oxford University, 1976, ch. 4, pp. 225–75.

[7] 'A Roll of a Forest Court of Hogstow Forest 1521', ed. T. E. Pickering, *Transactions of the Shropshire Archaeological Society* (*TSAS*), 4th ser., 4 (1914), 82–6; T. Salt, 'Ancient Documents relating to the Honour, Forest and Borough of Clun', *TSAS*, 11 (1882), 260–2.

[8] Edwards, 'Shropshire Agriculture'.

[9] *Abstracts of Abbotside Wills 1552–1688*, ed. H. Thwaite, Yorkshire Archaeological Society, Record Series, 130 (1967), *passim*; *Devon Inventories of the Sixteenth*

twinter colt and one weaner, would have disposed of one or two animals per year. John Cox, a larger, more prosperous yeoman farmer from the neighbouring parish of Cheswardine, operated on a slightly bigger scale, leaving two mares and a colt worth £3 10s 0d and three twinter colts and three yearlings valued respectively at £5 and £2 10s 0d at his death in 1605.[10] Herd size was related, in general, to the wealth of the individual; the largest and most varied ones naturally belonged to the great landed families.

In the sixteenth century horses known as caples appear regularly in the inventories of farmers living in the northern half of the county. These animals were found in south Shropshire too, for although few inventories survive among the documents of the diocese of Hereford, caples were occasionally mentioned in wills. They were kept throughout the North Shropshire Plain but were particularly numerous in the Wealdmoors, a low-lying area of fen located near the eastern border of the county. In this respect they may have resembled the breed of rough, hardy horses bred and reared in the Lincolnshire fens before enclosure, especially in Wildmore Fen, where they were known as Wildmore Tits.[11] They must also have been closely related to the feral horses that roamed the hills on both sides of the Welsh border. Writing of Montgomeryshire horses in the early eighteenth century, Defoe remarked, 'This county is noted for an excellent breed of Welch horses, which, though not very large, are exceeding valuable and much esteemed all over England.' There, a later commentator observed, farmers rounded up the animals at the age of three, breaking them in before taking them to market: the practice was probably carried on across the border in Shropshire too. These horses increased the size of the herds, so that some large farmers, with extensive rights of common, had a considerable head of wild horses. In June 1740, for instance, Edward Griffiths of the Shropshire–Montgomeryshire parish of Churchstock left sixteen mountain colts (£16), as well as five working horses and three sucking colts (£25), two grey riding mares (£6)

---

and Seventeenth Centuries, ed. M. Cash, Devon & Cornwall Record Society, new series, 11 (1966), *passim*.

[10] Lichfield Joint Record Office, inventory of Ralph Wild of Market Drayton, 30 May 1608; *ibid.*, inventory of John Cox of Cheswardine, 24 May 1605.

[11] W. H. Wheeler, *A History of the Fens of South Lincolnshire* (Boston, 1868), p. 411.

and four yearling colts (£7).[12] Other semi-wild horses grazed the sandy wastes of eastern Shropshire and the heathlands of the adjoining county of Staffordshire. In Hampshire such horses were called 'heath-croppers'; they were extremely small because they had scarcely anything to feed on except ling and heather.[13]

These were the types of horses that Henry VIII sought to eliminate in a statute passed in 1540 which debarred anyone living in twenty-five named counties (including Shropshire) from keeping stallions over the age of two and below fifteen hands on any common or waste ground.[14] In the northern counties the minimum height was set at 14 hands. Henry hoped thereby to increase the number of large horses in the country which he felt threatened 'by reason that little stoned horses and Nags be suffered to pasture in forests etc. and to cover mares feeding there'. In Shropshire, manor court records are full of presentments for the offence – in October 1581, for instance, William Murroll was accused of grazing an undersized colt on the Lower Heath of Prees for two years[15] – but the Act did little to end the practice. Indeed, the measure was counterproductive since these hardy creatures, ideally adapted to a harsh environment, were suitable animals to keep on marginal land. It encouraged small farmers to participate in horse breeding, enabling them to do so at comparatively little expense in spite of the time it normally took horses to be ready for the market. Moreover, these sturdy and sure-footed animals made good pack- and work-horses, furnishing breeders with a very saleable commodity as demand increased with the expansion of trade and industry. Pack-horses provided a particularly effective mode of transport over long distances – wagons were best suited for short and middle-distance hauls – for they were flexible in composition and conveyed goods cheaply and speedily. According to Thomas Blundeville, writing in Elizabeth I's reign, geldings were preferred to stallions as pack-

---

[12] Daniel Defoe, *A Tour through the Whole Island of Great Britain*, ed. P. Rogers (Harmondsworth, 1971), p. 383; 'Montgomeryshire Horses, Cobs and Ponies', *Montgomeryshire Historical Collections*, 22 (1988), 19, 29; Herefs. RO, inventory of Edward Griffiths of Churchstock, 1740.

[13] Edwards, thesis, 119–20; Edwards, 'Shropshire Agriculture'; Staffordshire County Council Education Dept, *Local History Source Book L19*, ed. R. A. Lewis (n.d.), pp. 12–13; J. H. Bettey, *Rural Life in Wessex 1500–1900* (Bradford-on-Avon, 1977), p. 22.

[14] 32 Henry VIII c. 13.

[15] Shrewsbury Borough Library, Local History Dept, MS no. 348 Prees.

horses for they did not eat as much and were more easy to manage on the road.[16]

These horses could be bought at a number of Shropshire fairs, including those held at Bridgnorth, Ludlow, and Shrewsbury. Shrewsbury occupied a prominent position, with droves of horses being taken specifically to the fair, joining others going to the town as part of the general trading activity of an important urban centre. The local textile industry had a considerable impact on the supply of and demand for packhorses. By the early seventeenth century Shrewsbury drapers had wrested control of the North Wales trade from their rivals at Oswestry, and carriers bringing in cloth to be finished would have been a common sight in the town. Other traders needed horses to collect the fine 'March' wool of the county, which after being sorted by local staplers was sent to clothiers in Essex, or to transport consignments of cloth finished in Shrewsbury to Blackwell Hall in London. Clothiers and drapers from the North and the Midlands were regular visitors to Shrewsbury, whilst the records of Bridgnorth and Ludlow seem to establish a connection with the West Country industry in the late seventeenth and early eighteenth centuries. In the late sixteenth century, moreover, dealers from the contiguous parishes of Whitchurch (Shropshire) and Malpas (Cheshire) bought horses at Shrewsbury for resale at Chester, where the purchasers, among others, were men from the textile areas of the North-West.[17] Other industries were supplied with border ponies too. Buyers from the east Shropshire coalfield were well represented at Shrewsbury, Bridgnorth, and Much Wenlock, whilst those from mining communities on the Clee Hills travelled to Ludlow. Outside the county, the Black Country provided the biggest market for Shropshire horses but the fairs, especially those at Bridgnorth and Shrewsbury, had to meet the demands of other industrial districts in the west Midlands (stretching from north Worcestershire, through Birmingham and Coventry,

---

[16] J. A. Chartres, 'Road Carrying in England in the Seventeenth Century: Myth and Reality', *Econ. Hist. Rev.*, 2nd ser., 30 (1977), 82; Thomas Blundeville, *The Foure Chiefest Offices Belongyng to Horsemanship* (1580 edn), fol. 8.

[17] T. C. Mendenhall, *The Shrewsbury Drapers and the Wool Trade in the XVI and XVII Centuries* (London, 1953), pp. 26–47; P. J. Bowden, *The Wool Trade in Tudor and Stuart England* (London, 1971), pp. 81–2; Edwards, thesis, 197; P. R. Edwards, 'The Horse Trade of Chester in the Sixteenth and Seventeenth Centuries', *Journal of the Chester Archaeological Society*, 62 (1979), 94–6.

to the coalfields of north-west Warwickshire). The Rock family of the Stourbridge area were prominent at Shrewsbury at the turn of the sixteenth century, as were the Dabbses of the Atherstone district of Warwickshire in the mid seventeenth century. Although the latter disappear from the records after the Restoration, their place was taken by dealers from nearby Bedworth, of whom the Frizwell and Hanbury families were the most notable.[18] In the industrial areas the dealers could dispose of stock at local fairs. Fragmentary material for the fairs at Much Wenlock in the 1630s shows, for instance, that William Horton of Cressage, a regular visitor to Shrewsbury, sold a nag there in 1639. At Walsall (Staffordshire), where the specialization lay in the manufacture of metal horse tack, several of the men who bought horses at Shrewsbury were in the 1630s selling them in the town. Later records of Dudley and Kidderminster fairs (Worcestershire) indicate other outlets where locally bred stock were sold.

Larger, stronger, and more valuable horses were also bred in Shropshire, especially in the valleys of the Severn and its tributaries, and on the estates of the upper classes. Judging by toll books, these horses often seem to have been bred in the same places as the hill ponies, for many Border parishes were large and included areas of upland moor as well as valley bottom. Such horses can easily be distinguished from hill ponies, however, by the prices paid and, to a certain extent, by their destination. The Severn valley had long been noted for the quality of its horses, a reputation enhanced in this period by the establishment of a royal stud at Caersws (Montgomeryshire) and by the general improvement in breeding standards under the Tudors and Stuarts.[19] In the country as a whole large horses were to be seen in ever-growing numbers as the seventeenth century progressed, initially on the roads and then after the Restoration on the farms. The first to employ them in the countryside were prosperous yeomen, for high prices made it difficult for smaller farmers to afford them; this practice drove another wedge between the two classes.[20] Their introduction on to the farm helped

---

[18] P. R. Edwards, 'The Horse Trade of the Midlands in the Seventeenth Century', *Agric. Hist. Rev.* 27 (1979), 96–8.

[19] 'Montgomeryshire Horses', 28–9.

[20] For road carriage see J. A. Chartres, *Internal Trade in England 1500–1700* (London, 1977), p. 40; J. Crofts, *Packhorse, Waggon and Post* (London, 1967), pp. 7–8. For the farm see J. Goodacre, 'Lutterworth in the Sixteenth and Seven-

to improve the efficiency of agriculture, for by speeding up plough-ing and by pulling the new heavy four-wheeled wagons, they enabled their owners to market crops more effectively. In Shrop-shire these wagons appear only in the eighteenth century, but by the 1740s vehicles drawn by large draught horses were being used by the more substantial farmers.[21]

Breeding herds did not solely consist of home-bred animals; mares and fillies came into the county from outside and brought with them an infusion of fresh blood. Montgomeryshire, with its close links with Shropshire, sent the most, but important sources of supply were to be found in other quarters. Contacts were estab-lished at north Midland fairs such as Derby and Nottingham and through them with the breeding areas of Yorkshire and Lincoln-shire. Shropshire men, living on the eastern border of the county, figure prominently among the buyers at Derby in the mid seven-teenth century, where they obtained large numbers of mares and fillies. They made similar purchases at Market Bosworth (Leicester-shire). Other horses were taken to Shropshire by north Midlands dealers.[22] One group, based at Mickleover, near Derby, bought mares and fillies at Nottingham and Market Bosworth for resale at Derby or for transportation to Bridgnorth and Shrewsbury. A much larger circle of dealers resided in the mixed farming area of east-central Nottinghamshire and used Derby and Nottingham as sources of supply of breeding stock. Although some horses were sold at Derby, many of them were taken to Shropshire, especially to Bridgnorth, where between 1659 and 1677 various members of the group sold a recorded total of 98 horses (of which over four-fifths (83.7 per cent) comprised mares and fillies).

Whereas mares and fillies were imported into Shropshire, colts and horses left the county for rearing districts elsewhere. One important trading connection linked the county with the mixed farming area of south-east Worcestershire, whose dealers often

teenth Centuries: A Market Town and its Area', unpublished Ph.D. thesis, Leicester University, 1977, 196–7; S. Porter, 'Farm Transport in Huntingdon-shire 1610–1749', *J. Trans. Hist.*, 3rd ser., 3 (1982), 34–45, *passim* (I am grateful to Mr Stephen Porter for this reference); M. A. Havinden, 'The Rural Economy of Oxfordshire 1580–1730', unpublished B.Litt. thesis, Oxford University, 1961, 204–7; F. W. Steer (ed.), *Farm and Cottage Inventories of Mid Essex 1635 to 1749* (Chichester, 1969), *passim*.
[21] Edwards, 'Shropshire Agriculture'.   [22] Edwards, 'Horse Trade', 122.

made a number of trips during the course of the year and were among the most prominent purchasers of horses at fairs such as Bridgnorth, Ludlow, and Shrewsbury. They bought large numbers of colts for training on the farms back home, together with some working horses, and nags and geldings for riding. As they paid above average prices for their stock, they presumably purchased large, good-quality horses. Other dealers came from north Oxfordshire, where a similar form of husbandry was practised, and some came occasionally from the east Midlands, the leading rearing district in the whole of England.

Not all of these horses were employed for draught, for as we have seen dealers also bought some riding nags and geldings. Judging by the prices paid, Bridgnorth was the county's most notable centre for saddle horses, a place where gentry families such as the Foresters of Dothill and the Levesons of Lilleshall Hall did business.[23] Valuable mounts could also be bought at Albrighton, Ludlow, Newport, and Shrewsbury.[24] At Shrewsbury some of the best saddle animals on sale in the period after the Civil War can be easily picked out in the toll books by the use of the term 'gelding'. Before the war large numbers of geldings had been sold at prices similar to those paid for mares. At that time 'gelding' was synonymous with 'nag'. By 1646 when the run of books begins again, the term 'gelding' was being reserved for good-quality saddle horses, especially easy-paced pads; the six sold there that year had a mean value of £6 14s 11d, far in excess of £3 8s 2½d, the average price of the 236 nags.

Really top-class saddle horses were taken to Penkridge in Staffordshire, which in the mid seventeenth century was included in the select group of fairs noted by the Duke of Newcastle, one of the foremost judges of horseflesh of the day. Penkridge had few rivals for horses in this category, for as Defoe was to write, 'here were really incredible numbers of the finest and most beautiful horses that can any where be seen'.[25] The fair was supplied with stock from

---

[23] Shrops. RO, Forester Colln (hereafter Forester Colln) 1224/297; Staffs. RO, Sutherland Colln (hereafter Sutherland Colln) D593/F/2/9, 40.

[24] For Ludlow and Shrewsbury see toll books; for Newport see Sutherland Colln D593/F/2/38; for Albrighton see Sutherland Colln D593/F/2/5, and Shrops. RO, Attingham Park Colln (hereafter Attingham Park Colln) 112/20.127.

[25] William Cavendish, *A New Method and Extraordinary Invention to Dress Horses* (London, 1677), p. 60; Defoe, p. 400.

all over the country, but Shropshire men – members of the gentry or their agents, farmers, and dealers – were prominent among them. At the fair held on 23 September 1640, eighty horses are recorded in the toll book and of these, fourteen were sold by Shropshire men at a mean price of £10. Most of the buyers listed in 1640 comprised large-scale London dealers, but according to Defoe, the fair was also patronized by the gentry, who bought racehorses there. One such person was Sir John Chester of Chicheley (Buckinghamshire), whose accounts record expenses incurred at Nottingham and Lutterworth races in 1711. He sent his agents to Penkridge on a number of occasions at the turn of the seventeenth century, and on one visit in September 1697 bought a grey stallion for £37 10s 0d.[26]

Clearly the prices paid for horses varied enormously, and at the top end of the market the upper classes laid out large sums for coach horses, fine saddle mounts, and racers. The price of horses, in general, rose in the period under review too, especially in the hundred years after 1550. At Shrewsbury fair in 1524–5 a mare and a nag were sold for 2s 4d and 2s 8d respectively, hardly a sound statistical base, but perhaps an indication of the sort of prices being paid. No more valuations are available from the toll books until the 1560s, when the mean price for mares was £1 4s 8d and for geldings £1 6s 8d. If this decade, after the revaluation of the coinage in 1560–1, was a period of relative stability, the figures illustrate the tremendous impact that the earlier debasement had had upon prices over the previous twenty years.[27] Seventy years later values had nearly trebled, mares in the 1630s averaging £3 10s 6d and geldings £3 18s 9½d. This rise, confirmed by local inventories for the same period, was greater than that of other livestock or of industrial goods and reflects a real growth in demand for horses and not merely the effect of inflation. Prices peaked during the Civil War, as they did for other commodities, and although toll books for Shropshire fairs have not survived for the war years, the ones made immediately afterwards show values at a consistently higher level than those listed in the 1630s. At Bridgnorth and Shrewsbury prices fell in the 1650s as the market recovered from the shortages caused by the war. Prices did rise in the second half of the seventeenth century, but the ending of the period of rapid population increase

[26] Bucks. RO, Chester of Chicheley Colln D/C/4/11.
[27] D. M. Palliser, *The Age of Elizabeth* (London, 1983), pp. 140–1.

brought greater stability and values did not reach the level of the 1640s until the early eighteenth century. In the following fifty years there was a further appreciation in price, as larger, stronger horses became more widely dispersed around the farms of Shropshire.[28]

It is hardly surprising to find that prices rose during the Civil War as demand increased and as the fighting interrupted the flow of supplies. Shrewsbury was a royalist centre until its capture by parliamentarians on 22 February 1645, but as much of the surrounding countryside was under increasing parliamentary control and skirmishes were often taking place, disruption of trade was inevitable. On 16 May 1643 Lord Capel, the royalist commander in Shropshire, Cheshire, and Wales wrote from Whitchurch in north Shropshire to Sir Francis Ottley, the governor of Shrewsbury, to say that 'a large influx of people to the May fair from the surrounding country bringing horses, sheep, swine, cheese, linen and woollen fabrics afforded a favourite opportunity for treachery or plunder'.[29]

Whilst the war disrupted the trade of markets and fairs, it obviously increased the demand for provisions and livestock of all kinds. Both sides were aware of alienating the local population in areas where they were based, and garrisons spent considerable sums of money in the locality. Carriers were always required, and as long as they could keep possession of their horses and carts, they could make a steady income.[30] Nonetheless, abuses were committed, friend and foe were often treated alike, and many inhabitants viewed the presence of the soldiery in their midst as a mixed blessing which they could well do without. In October 1642 a letter sent from Shrewsbury contained a bitter condemnation of the activities of the royalist army, who terrorized the populace, stole horses, and burgled houses. Horses, because of their strategic and economic value, were prime targets, and garrison commanders received numerous petitions from owners for the restitution of their animals or compensation for their loss. (After the war such claims formed the biggest category of complaints with which the authorities had to deal.)[31] At Ludlow the inhabitants petitioned the county authorities to reform certain abuses, asking among other things for compen-

---

[28] Edwards, 'Shropshire Agriculture'.

[29] Edwards, thesis, 217–18.

[30] D. H. Pennington, 'The War and the Peace', in J. Morrell (ed.), *Reactions to the English Civil War 1642–1645* (London, 1982), pp. 125–7.

[31] Information kindly supplied by Mr Stephen Porter.

sation for the loss of teams, carts, and horses in the town and for prior payment to be made whenever horses or teams were impressed. Among the townspeople affected were men like Samuel France, who claimed to have lost three horses through impressment and in general to have been so heavily pressed that he had been left with nothing to maintain himself and his lame wife.[32] Although one has to be careful in evaluating such stories because of the possibility of exaggeration or special pleading, outrages did take place and the civilian population did suffer at the hands of the soldiery.

Markets and fairs were particularly vulnerable to attack, and whilst attempts were made to keep them open, buyers and sellers were wary of doing business there and trade decreased. In this respect the war hastened the decline of these traditional marketing institutions, already under attack as private and more informal means of trading were developed. At Shrewsbury the toll books became more rudimentary from the mid 1650s with fewer horses and cattle recorded; after 1674 no more lists were made. At the mid-summer fair of 1654 over four-fifths (86 per cent) of the 221 cattle sold were disposed of at three suburban inns, and it is likely that horse sales showed a similar tendency. It was more convenient, and apart from avoiding the crowded town streets, there was no toll to pay.[33] Of course change did not come abruptly, and because the annual cycle of the fairs fitted in with the natural rhythms of live-stock husbandry, the declining role of markets and fairs was least pronounced in the trade in animals. There was a shake-out of marketing outlets, however, as trade was rationalized and a hier-archy of centres developed. At the bottom of the scale a number of fairs served only a small catchment area, and here trade was often moribund or inconsequential.[34] In the mid eighteenth century, for instance, the fair held at Hodnet on 4 May was said by William Owen to have been 'inconsiderable'.[35] Even at leading centres such as Shrewsbury, as the above example suggests, much business was done outside the regulated fair, though people continued to travel

---

[32] Shrops. RO, Ludlow Corpn Records 356/Box 298.
[33] P. R. Edwards, 'The Cattle Trade of Shropshire in the Late Sixteenth and Seven-teenth Centuries', *Midland History*, 6 (1981), 84.
[34] J. A. Chartres, 'The Marketing of Agricultural Produce', in J. Thirsk (ed.), *The Agrarian History of England and Wales*, V, *1640–1750*, pp. 409–14, 438.
[35] William Owen, *An Authentic Account published by the King's Authority of all the Fairs in England and Wales* (London, 1756 edn), Shropshire.

to the town at the times when they were held. They had become fixed points in the calendar and were occasions when business of all kinds could be conducted.[36]

The growth of private marketing was a feature of the period, especially after the Restoration, when the government ceased to intervene so actively in the economy.[37] This did not reflect a change of policy, however, but rather a recognition that conditions had changed with the easing of the pressure upon supplies. In fact the measures remained in the statute book and were enforced from time to time whenever the circumstances warranted it.[38]

II

The main agents of change were the specialist middlemen who came to occupy a vital role in the development of internal trade. For a long time the government sought to curb their activities, fearing that by intruding themselves between the producer and the consumer, the dealers might create artificial shortages and raise prices. In practice, they improved the efficiency of the market and without their intervention the difficulties caused by the inflationary spiral of the late sixteenth and early seventeenth centuries would have been far more severe.[39] Horse dealers were certainly adept at profiting from a situation if market conditions were in their favour, but they were not alone in this, and opportunities came less frequently than they did in the corn and grain trades, for instance. Nonetheless, in day-to-day business horse dealers had a particularly poor reputation, a sign of the importance of the commodity with which they were associated.[40] Just as many people today need a car, so in early modern England they required horses, and not everyone could distinguish between the good and the bad. Horses were prone to injury and disease, the existence of which was not always apparent and which could often be temporarily disguised. Individuals who had made a bad bargain, therefore, would have felt cheated, and this helped to blacken the character of all horse dealers.

In fact, the dealers who appear regularly in the toll books and who

---

[36] *The Journeys of Celia Fiennes*, ed. C. Morris (London, 1947), p. 227.
[37] Chartres, *Internal Trade*, pp. 49–50.
[38] D. C. Coleman, *The Economy of England 1450–1750* (Oxford, 1977), p. 179.
[39] Chartres, *Internal Trade*, pp. 50–2.   [40] Edwards, 'Horse Trade', 114.

moved large numbers of horses around the country emerge as responsible people, well integrated into their local communities and no better or worse than those around them.[41] In the course of their business they quickly became known to the market officials at centres where they carried on their trade, and were treated with consideration and respect. For instance when Henry Bradley of Donnington, Lilleshall, sold a gelding at Bridgnorth on 6 February 1673, he produced only one voucher instead of the two required by law. The toll keeper accepted the one and wrote in the book, 'the seller well known to the toll takers'.

Dealers came from a variety of backgrounds. Some were engaged as middlemen in other commodities and as they needed horses to move their goods, it was natural that many of them should also deal in horses.[42] At Bridgnorth, Ludlow, and Shrewsbury fairs the largest group of dealers from the Black Country consisted of men working in the metalware trades. Innkeepers were another group whose activities allowed them to develop an interest in horses, and butchers, often among the most energetic of local entrepreneurs, were also active participants. In the early seventeenth century a number of Newport butchers operated as wool merchants, collecting the fine March wool for the local staplers and buying and selling horses as part of their business.[43]

Many dealers possessed an agricultural holding which was often similar in scale to those farmed by small yeomen or moderate-sized husbandmen. In pastoral areas dealers could supplement the resources of their farms by grazing their animals on the commons and wastes or by leasing improved pastures. Thus in Shropshire, groups of dealers could be found in parishes on both sides of the Welsh border or in places such as Cardington, Church Pulverbatch, Edgton, and Smethcott in the south Shropshire uplands. They were even more numerous in the east of the county, especially in a string of parishes on or near the north-eastern border, where they could utilize the heaths and fens of the area. The greatest concentration of dealers lived in the parish of Lilleshall, which adjoined the Wealdmoors with its grazing grounds, improved pastures, and meadow lands.[44] Richard Winsor, the most prominent Shropshire dealer in the early seventeenth century, lived in the parish, leasing a small

[41] *Ibid.*, 114.
[43] Edwards, thesis, 192–3.
[42] *Ibid.*, 116.
[44] Shropshire Toll Books, *passim*.

tenement in the township of Donnington from the Leveson family which consisted of a cottage with a yard, a garden and an orchard, and five days' math of meadowing. His father had also rented separately a piece of ground calculated at six beasts' gates, but by the time that Richard had taken over the holding, the pasture had been incorporated into the lease.[45] Half of the dealers in this area lived in houses of two hearths or more.[46]

Dealers needed to live in places which possessed good lines of communication that gave them ready access to supplies and markets.[47] East Shropshire was well served in this respect, and dealers from the area could be found at a number of Midlands fairs, trading in a variety of horses and moving stock from one venue to another. Richard Winsor did business at fairs as diverse as those at Bridgnorth, Penkridge, Shrewsbury, and Stafford, whilst Thomas Galloway of Cherrington, another leading member of the group, was one of those dealers who were responsible for bringing in good-quality breeding stock from the north and east Midlands. Thomas bought two mares, five fillies, and a nag at Market Bosworth in 1626, 1631, and 1632, and had the toll books survived thereafter, he would undoubtedly have been recorded in later years too. He appears in the Derby books when they begin in 1639 and he probably visited both fairs on the same journey. In five trips to Derby between 1639 and 1641 he obtained nine mares, three fillies, and a colt. Like his colleagues he was active at Shrewsbury at the same time, selling a recorded total of twenty-two mares, two fillies, three geldings, and two unknown horses on a number of visits between 1631 and 1638.

Circles of dealers seem to have coordinated their activities, travelling together to various fairs or making their purchases available to other members of the group. At fairs they met their counterparts from elsewhere, did business with them, perhaps privately at an inn, and in general tried to adapt the market to meet their particular needs. Such wayfarers had a long tradition behind them but they only emerged as a recognizable and self-conscious community during the reign of Elizabeth. The mobility which these people

---

[45] Shrops. RO, 38/143–4; Sutherland Colln D593/G/1/1/13.

[46] 'The Shropshire Hearth Tax Roll of 1672', *Shrops. Arch. & Parish Register Society* (1949), *passim*.

[47] Edwards, 'Horse Trade', 116.

enjoyed was, of course, one of the reasons why the government sought to control them, since it was felt that they were a potential disruptive element and threat to settled society.[48]

Horse dealers formed friend and kinship links with others of their class, and this reliance upon personal connection and contacts was characteristic of the way in which internal trade was organized. As commercial activity increased, there were opportunities which dealers could exploit, but because of the inadequacies of the marketing and financial institutions, there was considerable risk. By the use of members of the family, together with friends and neighbours, the chances of deception were reduced.[49]

These links did not last merely for one generation, for families often maintained a connection with a particular occupation. In Shropshire the Dickinses of Ellesmere and Loppington, the Grooms and Tilers of Myddle and Wem, and the Moodeys of Ellesmere acted as cattle drovers, whilst the Bradleys of Lilleshall, the Walkers of Newport, and the Skitts of Lilleshall, Prees and Newport had long-lasting connections with the horse trade. The Walkers, for instance, first appear in the records in the late seventeenth century, trading at Bridgnorth, Derby, Dudley, and Kidderminster, and fifty years later their descendants were to be found at Bridgnorth, Banbury (Oxfordshire) and Sutton Coldfield (Warwickshire) fairs. Three generations are represented in the toll books, beginning with the four brothers, Richard, John, James, and Gabriel. The sons of James and Gabriel, the only ones to have had male heirs, continued the tradition, which was then followed by Thomas, John, and Hewitt, the sons of James's son, Richard, and Richard and Robert, the sons of Gabriel's son, Robert. At first the younger generation accompanied their fathers or uncles to the fair to learn the business and meet other dealers. William Allen of Peplow, Hodnet, took his son, John – a youth, according to the toll book – to Bridgnorth in October 1672 and there used him as one of his vouchers. As they gained in experience, the youngsters would travel to fairs in a family group, and by the time their fathers retired,

---

[48] A. M. Everitt, *Change in the Provinces: The Seventeenth Century*, Leicester University Dept of English Local History Occasional Papers, 2nd ser., 1 (Leicester, 1969), pp. 39–41, 43; *CSPD*, Addenda, 1566–79, p. 458.

[49] A. M. Everitt, 'The Marketing of Agricultural Produce', in J. Thirsk (ed.), *The Agrarian History of England and Wales*, IV, *1500–1640* (Cambridge, 1967), pp. 557–8.

they could take over completely. In 1651 William Skitt junior of Wollerton, Hodnet, then aged sixteen, sold a mare under the supervision of his father, who acted as his guarantor. Shortly afterwards William senior seems to have given up the trade and by the late 1650s his son was dealing on his own account at Bridgnorth, Derby, and Shrewsbury.

III

Much is known about the activities of such dealers because they acted honestly and openly and had some standing in their communities. Unfortunately, since horses were such a vital commodity, the trade attracted a host of lesser men who, because they have left less trace of their existence in the records, remain somewhat shadowy figures. They were not necessarily more dishonest than their superiors, but since they were poorer and less settled, they had added temptation. Significantly, when Charles Moon, a petty chapman, was arrested at Shrewsbury in 1685 upon suspicion of stealing horses, he stated in his examination that he had no habitation but lodged with John Wicketts, who kept the Bell at Deddington (Oxfordshire).[50]

Undoubtedly, the more dubious characters operating on the fringes of the trade were guilty of sharp practice and even overtly criminal behaviour. Horse stealing was widespread in early modern England and thieves would often call themselves dealers to account for the horses in their possession. The problem gave the government great concern and as indicated above, a number of measures were passed which it was hoped would reduce the incidence of the crime. In 1547, in order to increase the deterrent effect, horse stealing was made a felony without benefit of clergy, whilst the two measures of 1555 and 1589 were so constructed as to make it more difficult for stolen horses to be disposed of.[51]

Many cases of horse stealing were of an unpremeditated nature, carried out because the opportunity presented itself. In counties like Shropshire scores of unattended horses grazed on the open commons or in pastoral closes and since it was an easy matter to steal an animal or two, tired travellers or wandering vagrants did at

[50] Shrops. RO, Shrewsbury Corpn Records, 2270.
[51] 1 Edward VI c. 12; 2 & 3 Ph. & M. c. 7; 31 Elizabeth I c. 12.

times succumb to temptation. Some individuals, on the other hand, were clearly on the look-out for horses to steal and came prepared to ride them away. In a deposition heard at the Shrewsbury quarter sessions in 1690 Margaret Hoult of Grinshill recalled that the night one of her neighbours had lost a horse, she saw the suspect carrying a bundle folded in a coat which looked like a saddle. Gangs of thieves were involved too. One group, active in the reign of Charles II, operated in Lancashire and on the Welsh border for six years before being caught. They used Warrington and Shrewsbury as their outlets, selling at one town horses stolen in the area around the other. At the Warrington end, Thomas Fluitt the elder acted as receiver, whilst in Shrewsbury Fluitt's son, Thomas junior, who lived at the Black Dragon, performed a similar task.[52]

By disposing of horses some distance away from the place where the crime was committed, thieves hoped to avoid detection. Thus two Shrewsbury men who stole a couple of horses from Thomas Mackworth, gent., of Sutton in 1606, took them to Smithfield, the great livestock market in London, to sell. The market was a favourite outlet with thieves because of its size and anonymity. Horses stolen in the East and in the South-East were moved the other way. In 1696, for instance, two horses taken from the stable of John Crowfoot, an innkeeper from Blyford (Suffolk) were eventually found at Ludlow in Shropshire.[53]

The preamble to the 1589 Act frankly admitted that the earlier measures had not been entirely successful – 'they have not wrought so good effects for the repressing or avoiding of Horse stealing as was expected'. To a large extent this was due to the casualness with which horses were sometimes bought and sold and to the lack of prudence shown by many purchasers. Horses changed hands repeatedly, often rapidly and in an informal manner, and if transactions between friends and neighbours presented few risks, deals with strangers carried danger. In 1609 George Shepperdson foolishly agreed to exchange horses with Edward Footman, a Shropshire man, without having been present at the making of the bargain. Nicholas Gough, who had been riding the horse at the

---

[52] Shrops. RO, Shrewsbury Corpn Records 2276; PRO, Ches 38/41 part 2.
[53] Shrops. RO, Shrewsbury Corpn Records 2214; West Suffolk RO, P516, transcript made by Mr Peter Christie of PRO, ASSI 16/59. I am grateful to Mr Peter Christie for this reference.

time, had come to an agreement with Footman, whose horse was later proved to have been stolen, and had been told that Shepperdson 'should & might freely & w[i]thout trouble vse & imploy him [his horse] to their best benefitt p[ro]fitt and advantage'.[54] It would be wrong, however, to suggest that the legislation had no effect. Thieves were caught when stolen horses were tolled for at markets and fairs and if they refused either to find vouchers or to have the animals booked, suspicion was aroused and this could lead to arrest. One thief in 1598, having taken a horse out of William Thorley's grounds in Staffordshire, set out for Market Drayton (Shropshire) with it but had second thoughts when told 'he coulde not sell him without some bodie to geve their worde that the horse was trulie come vnto'. He therefore turned round but unable to resist temptation, was caught trying to sell it on the way back.[55]

IV

So far attention has been focussed on the activities of the population at large and little has been said about the involvement of the Shropshire gentry in the business of horse keeping. There was little to distinguish the actions of the bulk of the gentry from those of prosperous yeomen, but the special interests of county families such as the Bridgemans, Foresters, and Levesons and the scale of their expenditure set them apart from the rest of society. The Foresters of Dothill, for instance, bought two hunters at a cost of £60 in 1686 and the Bridgemans of Knockin and the Levesons of Lilleshall Hall were among those families interested in horse racing.[56] Coach horses were another expense and the cost could be considerable. More was also spent on keeping their horses, and outgoings ranged from feeding and stabling charges to the wages of staff and casual payments made to blacksmiths, farriers, horse breakers, and other ancillary workers.

Many of the leading families in Shropshire seem to have been engaged in horse breeding, although perhaps not on the scale practised by the Yorkshire gentry. When Sir Walter Acton of Aldenham

[54] PRO, REQ 2/411/113; see also PRO, STAC 8/225/21 Misc. Jas. I.
[55] *Staffordshire Quarter Sessions' Rolls*, IV, ed. S. A. P. Burne, 1598–1602, Staffs Hist. Collns (1935), p. 148.
[56] Forester Colln 1224/296; Staffs. RO, Bradford Colln, J. Bridgeman's Book of Disbursements, no ref., 22 Jan. 1719; Sutherland Colln D593/P/16/1/3.

died in 1665 he left a herd of twenty-three head valued at £125 3s 4d, comprising three mares and followers (£25), three more old mares (£7 10s 0d), two twinter colts (£6 13s 4d) and three yearlings (£6), as well as four stallions (£60) and five geldings (£20).[57] Sir Walter may have loaned out his stallions to serve the mares of other gentlemen as this was a common practice among members of his class. Thus Edward James, who lived just across the border at Kinvaston in the Staffordshire parish of Penkridge, had his mares covered by the stallions of a number of other gentlemen-breeders living in the two counties.[58] With their greater resources county families could make better provision for their horses, reserving paddocks for their brood mares, allowing their offspring to develop naturally, and giving them generous feeding rations. The Levesons integrated their estates at Lilleshall and at Trentham (Staffordshire), sending their horses into Shropshire for breeding and for summer grazing, and in this way made effective use of their land.[59]

The upper classes did come into contact with a wider section of the population, for as Richard Blome suggests in his book *The Gentleman's Recreation* (1686),

Tis' needless to give directions for Breeding of any other sort of Horses, as for the *Coach*, *Wagon*, *Cart*, *Servants*, and all manner of Drudgery, because there is not that Nicety required; and from the Fairs and Horse-Coursers you may be supplied, and save the trouble.[60]

They were able to keep their distance from the actual business of buying and selling horses, however, by employing their servants and agents to do the work for them. Local estate accounts reveal that they patronized a number of local fairs, though important centres like Bridgnorth were particularly favoured. The Levesons, who bred fine saddle horses, regularly sold animals there, but also took others to even better fairs at Penkridge and Lenton (Nottingham-shire).[61] Because of the money at their disposal such gentry families were well placed to find the right outlets for their stock or to acquire the best horses for their own use. In March 1749 Thomas Bell wrote to his master, Thomas Hill Esquire, to say that he was thinking of

---

[57] Herefs. RO, inventory of Sir Walter Acton of Aldenham 9 Sept. 1665.
[58] Staffs. RO, HM 27/2.
[59] Sutherland Colln D593/F/2/39.
[60] Richard Blome, *The Gentleman's Recreation* (London, 1686), II, i, fol. 2.
[61] Sutherland Colln D593/F/2/6, 8, 37, 38, 40.

buying for him a pair of geldings at Northampton fair, 'where I am told there will be great Choice and as the War is over they are expected to be sold Cheap'. The following year, in February 1750, he contemplated making a similar journey, writing 'I am told there's a fair at Stourbridge on the 17 of March where there usually comes good choice of black horses . . . but if nothing can be done . . . I can't think of any other place where you can be furnished but either Northampton or London.'[62]

The upper classes with their circles of friends and relations were less dependent upon the market place than others and made good use of their contacts to acquire or dispose of horses. By dealing with people they knew, they hoped to avoid being cheated, especially if they were paying out large sums of money for good-quality animals. As Blome commented, 'the surest ways of Buying is to be acquainted with good Breeders'.[63] Transactions were also made with dealers. In spite of the poor reputation of the class as a whole, the gentry or their agents would know and trust the dealers who appear regularly in the toll books, men who may have been tenants on their estates and who occasionally did special jobs for them. In February 1678, for instance, Thomas Wickstead, the Leveson family's steward in Shropshire, took Thomas Rowley of Preston-upon-the-Wealdmoors with him to inspect Mr Benthall's grey horse. Mr Benthall was asking £57 for it, and it paid to have expert advice.[64]

V

The study of the horse trade in Shropshire in the early modern period provides a number of insights into the general conduct of the trade. In the two hundred years after 1550 considerable changes occurred in the organization of the market there which mirrored developments in the country as a whole. As the trade intensified with the increase of long-distance traffic in and out of the county, the traditional institutions – the markets and fairs – found it difficult to cope with increased demand and were increasingly by-passed by people operating in private and more informal ways. The main agents of change, the middlemen, were active in the county; in the

---

[62] Attingham Park Colln 112/20.
[63] Blome, fol. 10.   [64] Sutherland Colln D593/F/2/38.

horse trade they continued to patronize fairs, but the decline in the number of animals entered in the toll books reveals that they made private bargains outside it too. Innumerable sales were also made between friends and relatives or more casually between strangers meeting on the road or in an inn. The upper classes, always somewhat aloof from the hustle and bustle of the market place, developed their own contacts. In short, as a result of these developments, Shropshire, still an important horse-breeding county in 1750, was able to provide horses for a wider market and to do so more efficiently and with less interference from the authorities.

10. 'An essay on manures': changing attitudes to fertilization in England, 1500–1800*

DONALD WOODWARD

This is a subject that deserves particular attention, as it is upon the solid foundation of manuring, that every good system of husbandry must be built.[1]

Throughout the period from 1500 to 1800 many farmers and most agricultural writers were aware that the shortage of manure comprised a major constraint on the improvement of agricultural productivity. This constraint was partially eradicated in the nineteenth century through the development of agricultural science and the increasing availability of commercial fertilizers, which included natural materials such as South American guano and the phosphates and nitrates produced by the developing chemical industries. Before 1800 options were more limited, but many historians, including Joan Thirsk, have demonstrated that new ways of enriching the soil were devised and applied in many parts of the country.[2] The practices adopted to add extra nutrients to the land fall into four main categories. First, there were the internal resources of the farms themselves – yard muck, the sheep-fold,

---

* The quotation is taken from Arthur Young, 'An Essay on Manures', *Annals of Agriculture*, 33 (1799), 577–621. I am grateful to Michael Turner for commenting on an earlier draft of this chapter, and also to the following historians who provided me with valuable references or material: Bruce Campbell, Donald Earl, Barbara English, Alan Harris, Rowy Mitchison, David Postles, Christopher Smout, and Keith Thomas.

[1] Messrs Rennie, Brown, and Shirreff, *General View of the Agriculture of the West Riding of Yorkshire* (London, 1794), p. 26. Spelling in quotations has been modernized.

[2] J. Thirsk (ed.), *The Agrarian History of England and Wales*, IV, *1500–1640* (Cambridge, 1967), pp. 167–8; E. Kerridge, *The Agricultural Revolution* (London, 1967), pp. 240–50; R. E. Prothero, *English Farming Past and Present* (London, 1912), pp. 100–1.

pond mud, marl, ashes derived from the practice of paring and burning, and the addition of any other organic waste, including household refuse.[3] Second, additional natural resources were brought to farms from outside – seaweed, sand, chalk, lime, putrefying fish, and the silt of water-meadows and warp lands. Third, a wide variety of industrial by-products, including crushed bones and woollen rags valued for their water-retaining qualities, were available to strategically placed farmers. Fourth, and this category overlaps with the third, some farmers were able to add urban refuse to their land.

Some years ago B. H. Slicher Van Bath retold the story of Marc Bloch's reproaches to his colleagues for 'skirting so timidly round the dung-heap' despite its crucial significance for human survival. In part this timidity was due to a distaste for the seamier side of life, but there was more to it than that: as Slicher Van Bath suggested, 'it may be that it was less the bad smell than the uncertainties due to the scarcity of data, that kept them at a safe distance'.[4] This is very close to the heart of the matter. The spreading of muck was so routine and ordinary a process, taking place everywhere, every year, that documentary evidence is difficult to find.[5] Much more material is available in the tracts of agricultural writers and as a result, this chapter, along with earlier discussions of the subject, is forced to rely in large measure on this rich source of nourishment. Unfortunately, it can be a highly misleading source since, throughout the period, authors tended to notice the remarkable and pass lightly over the ordinary. Such concentration is understandable since they often wished to publicize and encourage best practice, but the historian who follows can easily give the impression that such practice was common practice.[6] Nevertheless, it is possible to make some suggestions, albeit of a tentative nature, about changing attitudes to

[3] Also of vital importance were the practices of fallowing, and up-and-down husbandry: these subjects will not be treated here since this chapter concentrates on fertilizers added to the soil.
[4] B. H. Slicher Van Bath, *The Agrarian History of Western Europe, AD 500–1850* (London, 1966 edn), p. 259.
[5] Originally I had hoped to write an essay about manuring practices on individual farms, but the scarcity of data has precluded such an approach.
[6] Eric Kerridge accepted too readily what contemporary authors had to tell him. For a critique of Arthur Young's 'best practice' approach see J. Thirsk, *English Peasant Farming: The Agrarian History of Lincolnshire from Tudor to Recent Times* (London, 1957), p. 261.

fertilization during the three centuries which Joan Thirsk has made her own. But, as students of agrarian history will be fully aware, much of what follows is not new. Wherever we turn, whether we are looking at the introduction of new crops, new techniques, new employment opportunities, new explanations of old problems – and the list seems endless – we find that Joan Thirsk has been there before us. She has been a great inspiration and mentor to so many of us for so many years.

The discussion which follows is in five sections. Section I deals with the sixteenth and seventeenth centuries, while section II covers the eighteenth century. A detailed discussion of manuring practices in Cambridgeshire and Essex at the end of the eighteenth century follows in section III, and the fourth section deals with problems relating to the acceptability, availability, and transport of off-farm manures. Section V concludes the chapter and looks briefly at the employment implications of off-farm manures.

I

The two earliest English agricultural writers, Fitzherbert and Tusser, were aware of the value of manuring but had relatively little to say on the subject. Fitzherbert discussed the time to dung and the depth of the subsequent ploughing, advised that dung should be 'meddled with earth' since 'it will last the longer', declared that of all dung he preferred that of doves although 'it must be laid upon the ground very thin', and discussed how to organize a sheep-fold.[7] Tusser pointed out that the produce of 'foul privies . . . buried in garden . . . shall make very many things better to grow', and advised the careful management of dung, but he had little else to say about manuring:[8] indeed, he did not mention 'the value of marl, lime, chalk, soot, or town refuse, all of which were used in the Middle Ages'.[9] Other writers of the later sixteenth century were not so reti-

---

[7] W. W. Skeat (ed.), *The Book of Husbandry by Master Fitzherbert, 1534* (English Dialect Society, 1882), p. 27. G. E. Fussell's two books on early agricultural authors were an invaluable guide to the literature: G. E. Fussell, *The Old English Farming Books from Fitzherbert to Tull* (London, 1947), and *more Old English Farming Books from Tull to the Board of Agriculture* (London, 1950).

[8] T. Tusser, *Five Hundred Pointes of Good Husbandrie* (1580), ed. W. Payne and S. J. Herrtage (London, English Dialect Society, 1878), pp. 58–9, 62, 77, 87, 90, 106.

[9] Prothero, pp. 94–5.

cent. They, like their successors in the following century, 'absorbed a long tradition' of books on agriculture, and borrowed freely from classical authority, from continental writers (themselves often heavily indebted to the classics), and from each other.[10] The first English writer to be deeply influenced by classical authority was Thomas Hill, who published a number of books on gardening from 1563. In an edition of 1568 he added:

> such profitable and pleasant matter, as I found written in the Italian or Latin tongue, that intreated of this art, whose names (or the most of them) do after appear, digested into the form of a table.[11]

He listed twenty authorities besides 'sundry others, whose names be here for brevity omitted', and in *The Gardeners Labyrinth* of 1577 he included many more. After Hill, reference to classical authority became the normal practice, to which was added a number of continental works.

The first German agricultural writer, Conrad Heresbach, was presented to English readers by Barnaby Googe in 1577;[12] nearly a century later John Evelyn was still quoting from 'honest Barnaby Googes noble Heresbachius'.[13] By using Heresbach, and not forgetting Fitzherbert and Tusser, Googe attempted to marry together:

> the rules and practices of the old ancient husbands, as well Greeks as Latins, whose very orders (for the most part) at this day we observe, and from whom (if we will confess the truth) we have borrowed the best knowledge and skill that the skilfulest husband have; but also have joined herewithal, the experience and husbandry of our husbands of England, as far as mine own observations, or the experience of sundry my friends would suffer me.[14]

---

[10] J. Thirsk, 'Plough and Pen: Agricultural Writers in the Seventeenth Century', in T. H. Aston *et al.*, *Social Relations and Ideas: Essays in Honour of R. H. Hilton* (Cambridge, 1983), p. 297.

[11] T. Hill, *The proffitable Arte of Gardening, now the third tyme set fourth* (London, 1568), p. Aiii v. For a discussion of the influence of the classical tradition see G. E. Fussell, *The Classical Tradition in West European Farming* (Newton Abbot, 1972), which, strangely, does not mention Hill.

[12] C. Heresbach, *Foure Bookes of Husbandry, Newely Englished and increased by Barnabe Googe* (London, 1577).

[13] J. Evelyn, *Pomona* (London, 1664), p. 10. For a similar comment see Thirsk, 'Plough and Pen', p. 299.

[14] C. Heresbach, *The Whole Art and Trade of Husbandry, contained in Foure Bookes, enlarged by Barnaby Googe* (London, 1614), epistle to the reader.

The ideas of the influential French writer and original thinker Bernard Palissy were publicized by Sir Hugh Platt in 1594. 'Master Barnard' [*sic*] was the first to propose a theory of the mineral nutrition of plants in his *Discours Admirable* of 1580. As Platt put it:

> it is not the dung itself which causeth fruitfulness, but the salt which the seed hath sucked out of the ground. And hereupon it commeth to pass that all excrements as well of man as beast, serve to fatten and inrich the earth . . . I speak not here of common salt, but of the vegetative salt.[15]

Under the influence of classical and continental authorities, and by borrowing freely from each other and observing the practices of farmers around them, a growing body of agricultural and horti-cultural writers poured out their advice on the subject of manuring. By the middle of the seventeenth century, assiduous readers were left in no doubt about the value of intermixing lands, of applying marl, chalk, sand and lime, and of dunging their land: indeed, dung-ing, folding, liming, and marling were regarded as 'the usual husbandries'.[16] Farmers were also frequently exhorted to apply other dressings to the land, including ashes, 'the filth of sinks and privies', pilchards, metropolitan refuse, and countless other sub-stances well summarized by Walter Blith in 1649:

> And in thy tillage are these special opportunities to improve it, either by liming, marling, sanding, earthing, mudding, snail-codding, mucking, chalking, pigeons-dung, hens-dung, hogs-dung, or by any other means, as some by rags, some by coarse wool, by pitch marks, and tarry stuff, any oily stuff, and many things more, yea indeed anything almost that hath any liquidness, foulness, or good moisture in it, is very natural enrichment to almost any sort of land.[17]

To this list he added many other substances including fish, bones,

[15] H. Platt, *The Jewel House of Art and Nature* (London, 1594), pp. 15–16; A. La Rocque (ed.), *The Admirable Discourses of Bernard Palissy* (Urbana, Illinois, 1957). Platt returned to Palissy's ideas in *Floraes Paradise* (London, 1608).

[16] *A Direction to the Husbandman in a New, Cheape, and Easie way of Fertiling [sic], and Inriching Areable Grounds* (London, 1634) (STC no. 6902), p. B2r.

[17] W. Blith, *The English Improver, or a New Survey of Husbandry* (London, 1649), p. 100. See also: Hill, *The proffitable Arte of Gardening*, p. 13r; Heresbach, *Foure Bookes of Husbandry*, pp. 19v–20v; Platt, *The Jewel House*, pp. 20–60; Platt, *Floraes Paradise*, pp. 17–24, 45, 56; J. Norden, *The Surveyors Dialogue* (London, 1607), pp. 226–30.

the shavings of horns, 'man's urine', which 'will fatten land more than you are aware of', soot, and salt.[18]

Others followed, adding to the list items which were both practical and less so. Hartlib was impressed by the Dutch fondness for cows' urine and told the tale of a Kentish woman's exertions:

> I know a woman who liveth five miles south of Canterbury, who saveth in a pail, all the droppings of the houses, I mean the urine, and when the pail is full, sprinkleth it on her meadows, which causeth the grass at first to look yellow, but after a little time it grows wonderfully, that many of her neighbours wondered at it, and were like to accuse her of witchcraft.[19]

After praising the usual dungs, Ralph Austen suggested that 'dead dogs, carrion, or the like, laid or put to the roots of trees . . . is found very profitable unto fruit bearing',[20] but did not pause to calculate the likely correlation between dead dogs and fruit trees in the average orchard. But most writers were rather more prosaic in their suggestions.

Attitudes in the later seventeenth century are well summarized by the work of John Evelyn, who set out in *A Philosophical Discourse of Earth* of 1676 to combine the wisdom of the classical tradition with a scientific examination of the properties of different manures and their appropriateness for different soils. Echoing Bernard Palissy he declared that the most important ingredient was salt, 'which gives ligature, weight and constitution to things, and is the most manifest substance in all artificial composts'.[21]

The discovery that Greek and Roman authors waxed lyrical on the subject of manure did much to encourage English writers to do likewise. Much ancient advice was valuable – classical and early English authorities were agreed that pigeon dung was highly effective[22] – but some of the suggestions made were of little help in an

---

[18] For similar long lists of fertilizers, see: S. Hartlib, *His Legacie: or an Enlargement of the Discourse of Husbandry used in Brabant and Flanders* (2nd edn, London, 1652), pp. 32–7; J. Worlidge, *Systema Agriculturae* (London, 1669), pp. 58–71.

[19] Hartlib, *His Legacie*, p. 36. The story was repeated by Blith, *The English Improver Improved* (London, 1653), p. 151, and by Worlidge, *Systema Agriculturae*, p. 69.

[20] R. Austen, *A Treatise of Fruit-Trees* (Oxford, 1653), p. 66.

[21] J. Evelyn, *A Philosophical Discourse of Earth* (London, 1676), pp. 100–1; this work was presented to the Royal Society in 1675.

[22] H. B. Ash (ed.), *Columella, On Agriculture*, vol. 1, Loeb Classical Library (London & Cambridge, Mass., 1948), p. 195; H. B. Ash (ed.), *Cato and Varro:*

English context. Thomas Hill advocated the use of asses' dung 'because it bringeth up least weeds'.[23] In this he was following the advice of the Roman author Columella, who was especially keen on asses' dung:

> because that animal chews very slowly and for that reason digests his food more easily, and he gives in return a manure that is well prepared and ready for the field immediately.[24]

This advice was repeated by Hill and Heresbach, and, a century later, by John Evelyn, who explained that its value was because of 'its being better digested by the long mastication and chewing of that dull animal'. However, he did have the wit to add that 'since we have no quantity of it [i.e. asses' dung] in this country, it does the less concern us'.[25] Columella, Cato, and other classical authorities also recommended ploughing in lupins to enrich the soil, and the advice was passed on to a more modern audience by Heresbach and Hartlib.[26] In seventeenth-century Staffordshire, Robert Plot saw vetches being ploughed in, which he regarded as 'the oddest sort of manure that ever I met with'; but, back home in his library he soon found reassurance when:

> upon consultation found it to be no new thing; Varro and Palladius both acquainting us of old, that they did not only plough in vetches to fertilize their land . . . but also lupins, and sometimes beans, for the same purpose.[27]

Both Hill and Googe followed classical authority in recommending farmers to dung when the wind blew out of the west, and the moon was decreasing. This advice was based on ancient beliefs that the waning moon freed the crops from weeds, and that the blowing of the west wind in February was the harbinger of spring – a rather dubious suggestion in normal English conditions.[28]

On Agriculture, Loeb Classical Library (London & Cambridge, Mass., 1936), pp. 53, 263–5; Fitzherbert, *The Book of Husbandry*, p. 27; Hill, *The proffitable Arte of Gardening*, pp. 13r, 13v; T. Hill, *The Gardeners Labyrinth* (London, 1577), p. 18; Heresbach, *Foure Bookes of Husbandry*, p. 19v.

23 Hill, *The proffitable Arte of Gardening*, p. 12v.
24 Ash, *Columella*, p. 197.
25 Hill, *The Gardeners Labyrinth*, p. 18; Heresbach, *Foure Bookes of Husbandry*, p. 19v; Evelyn, *Philosophical Discourse of Earth*, p. 122.
26 Ash, *Cato and Varro*, p. 53; Ash, *Columella*, p. 193; Heresbach, *Foure Bookes of Husbandry*, p. 19v; Hartlib, *His Legacie*, p. 37.
27 R. Plot, *The Natural History of Stafford-Shire* (Oxford, 1686), p. 346.
28 Hill, *The proffitable Arte of Gardening*, p. 13v; Hill, *The Gardeners Labyrinth*, p. 20; Heresbach, *The Whole Art and Trade of Husbandry*, p. 19b; Ash, *Cato and*

Not all authors followed every suggestion made by the ancient authorities – many remained silent, for example, on the question of asses' dung – but only a few were prepared to disagree openly with the classical tradition. Having accepted that attention to moon and wind conditions was necessary when dunging, Googe proceeded to recommend the application of dry dung, for 'though Columella do bid the contrary, our own experience wills us not to follow him'. Similarly, John Evelyn refused to recommend human excrement, although 'mentioned by Columella', since it would taint vegetation. But, despite such minor reservations, the classical tradition held most agricultural writers in thrall to the end of the seventeenth century: in 1657 John Beale was hoping that someone 'would publish a well-corrected copy of the four Roman husbandmen'.[29]

The impact of the torrent of advice which flowed from the printing presses of the sixteenth and seventeenth centuries is difficult to determine. When we turn to that trio of well-known seventeenth-century farmers who left their records for posterity – Henry Best, Robert Loder, and Nicholas Toke – we find that they rarely went beyond the 'usual husbandries' of dunging, folding, liming, and manuring: Henry Best folded his sheep on the fallows and carted yard muck out to the field; Robert Loder did likewise, but sometimes dressed his fields with pigeon dung, 'black ashes' which he bought in, and malt dust partly produced by his own malt house; Nicholas Toke used dung, lime, and marl on his land.[30] If, as seems highly likely, those three men were more market-aware than most of their contemporaries, their experience would suggest that few farmers of the sixteenth and seventeenth centuries were able to benefit from the acquisition of off-farm fertilizers, especially those of the more exotic varieties.

Varro, p. 67; Ash, *Columella*, p. 137; *Pliny: Natural History*, ed. H. Rackham, vol. 5, Loeb Classical Library (London & Cambridge, Mass., 1950), p. 41.

[29] Heresbach, *The Whole Art and Trade of Husbandry*, p. 19b; Evelyn, *Philosophical Discourse of Earth*, p. 118; J. Beale, *Herefordshire Orchards, A Pattern for All England* (London, 1657), p. 61.

[30] *The Farming and Memorandum Books of Henry Best of Elmswell, 1642*, ed. D. Woodward, The British Academy Records of Social and Economic History, new series, VIII (London, 1984), pp. 16–19, 122 – Joan Thirsk was appointed overseer of this project by the British Academy and I owe her a great debt for her help and encouragement. *Robert Loder's Farm Accounts, 1610–1620*, ed. G. E. Fussell, Camden Society, 3rd ser., vol. LIII (London, 1936), p. xviii; E. C. Lodge, *The Account Book of a Kentish Estate, 1616–1704*, The British Academy, Records of Social and Economic History, VI (London, 1927), pp. 35, 59, 81, passim.

II

In the early eighteenth century the tradition of listing all materials which could be used for fertilizing the land was continued by that great manuring enthusiast, William Ellis of Little Gaddesden.[31] He barely missed a substance adumbrated in previous centuries and added a few new suggestions of his own, such as dogs' dung or old thatch. His whole approach was practical, reporting on what he did himself, and on what he saw around him, or on his travels. He was aware of the work of some of his predecessors and made an occasional reference to Houghton and Worlidge, but only once in the long disquisition on manure is there an oblique reference to classical tradition: he knew a man who sowed his seed 'in the promiscuous, old, Virgilian way'.[32] As with the work of the two previous centuries it is impossible to obtain any clear impression from his work about the frequency with which a particular practice was used. At first sight it would seem that the problem might be solved for the later part of the century by reference to the *General Views of Agriculture* for each county, published between 1793 and 1817. They fall into two groups – pilot surveys ordered by the Board of Agriculture, published mostly in 1794, and the more thorough second series, written to a standard format laid down by the Board, and based in part on information submitted by readers of the first series.[33]

The almost complete absence from the *General Views* of reference to classical authority marks them off sharply from the literature of previous centuries. John Duncomb, writing in 1805 on the agriculture of Herefordshire, referred to Virgil's discussion of paring and burning and to Columella's advocacy of intermixing soils,[34] but nowhere else in the discussions of manuring is there a reference to classical literature. Arthur Young felt the need to parade his knowledge of his English and classical predecessors in his

---

[31] W. Ellis, *Husbandry, Abridged and Methodized* (London, 1772 edn), vol. I, pp. 28–128. His books were published between 1732 and 1756.

[32] *Ibid.*, pp. 91, 107.

[33] All of the *General Views* for England have been consulted, but references will be given only for those referred to for a specific purpose.

[34] J. Duncomb, *General View of the Agriculture of the County of Hereford* (London, 1805), pp. 100, 106. Hereafter reference to the *General Views* will be as follows: J. Duncomb, *Herefordshire* (London, 1805).

'Essay on Manures', but it is evident that the literature of the late eighteenth century was of a different order from that of previous centuries, relying less on inherited lore and more on practical experience and observation.

Both sets of *General Views* demonstrate that certain practices were widespread: yard muck is mentioned in most volumes; lime is referred to, generally with approbation, in three-quarters of the 1794 reports and nearly all of the later ones; marl, not available in all regions, appears in just over half of the reports, although, as with liming, comments suggesting limited application appear quite frequently.[35] In addition, a vast array of alternative manures was sniffed out by the diligent reporters and they enthused about the use of town muck, woollen rags, malt dust, peat ash, rabbit dung, salt, seaweed, soapers' ashes, bones, sticklebacks, and the like. But, once again, in most cases it is impossible to tell what proportion of farmers, or even what proportion of parishes, adopted a particular practice, and the problem is exacerbated because some writers – Arthur Young is a notorious example here – concentrated on best practice and frequently failed to make general comments.[36] No doubt there were many progressive farmers, like the Nottingham gentleman who declared, 'I raise heaven and earth, to make manure',[37] but there are enough comments scattered throughout the *General Views* to make it plain that many farmers had a great deal to learn. In Leicestershire, few farm yards were 'well adapted to the economy of the dung-hill; on the contrary, they are mostly paved with a dip for the drainage to run away' so that much of the benefit of the dung was lost. Similarly in north Yorkshire, 'no branch of rural economy is managed with less attention or judgement, than that of making and preserving the manure produced upon the farms'. Hill farmers in the Cheviots had at their doors 'immense dunghills, the accumulations of unnumbered years, probably centuries', but some – wiser than their besieged neighbours – '*ingeniously contrived* to build their houses near a "*Burn side*" for the *convenience* of having it *taken away by every flood*' (italics in the

---

[35] For the distribution of references to liming and marling in the *General Views* see the excellent map in H. C. Prince, 'England *circa* 1800', in H. C. Darby (ed.), *A New Historical Geography of England* (Cambridge, 1973), p. 416.

[36] For a comparison of the reports on Lincolnshire by Thomas Stone and Arthur Young, see: Thirsk, *English Peasant Farming*, pp. 260–2.

[37] R. Lowe, *Nottinghamshire* (London, 1794), p. 101.

original). In Devon, Charles Vancouver thought it strange that relatively little yard dung was made despite the large numbers of stock, while in Huntingdonshire very few farmers purchased off-farm manures and 'the miserable practice' of inadequate sheep-folding was noted.[38] Writing on Cornwall, G. B. Worgan declared yard dung to be 'the principal manure on every farm in every county', but worried about its mismanagement, whereby it was left 'promiscuously' in heaps over the winter. Indeed, he added:

> On the whole it must be admitted, that this essential branch of rural economy is hardly anywhere sufficiently attended to, and yet how many pithy proverbial incentives have we to impress our minds with its importance? Such as, 'Manure is the life and soul of husbandry'; 'Muck is the mother of the mealchest', with many other appropriate mottoes to excite a sedulous and anxious attention to the collection, preservation, and application of this very necessary article.[39]

Even in Hertfordshire, long noted for its dependence on London muck, the business was 'indifferently executed on very small farms'.[40]

Two major debates emerged from the *General Views* – the issue of paring and burning, and what might be called 'the pigeon question'. Paring and burning, that is, skimming off the top layer of earth and vegetation, heaping it up to dry and then firing it, was an old process. It was mentioned in over 40 per cent of the 1794 reports and received a mixed reception: it was very much approved of in Gloucestershire,[41] but disapproved of in six counties, while reporters in ten counties sat firmly on the fence. In the later reports the practice was commented on for most counties, and most authors recognized that paring and burning had a valuable part to play in preparing some land for cultivation. However, it was stressed repeatedly that the process was not suitable for all soils, and that it needed to be controlled carefully. It was regarded as particularly

---

[38] J. Monk, *Leicestershire* (London, 1794), p. 17; J. Tuke, *N. R. Yorkshire* (London, 1794), p. 51; J. Tuke, *N. R. Yorkshire* (London, 1800), p. 232; J. Bailey and G. Culley, *Northumberland* (Newcastle upon Tyne, 1797), pp. 113–14; C. Vancouver, *Devon* (London, 1808), pp. 311–12; R. Parkinson, *Huntingdonshire* (London, 1811), p. 119.

[39] G. B. Worgan, *Cornwall* (London, 1815), pp. 120–1, 123.

[40] A. Young, *Hertfordshire* (London, 1804), p. 26.

[41] G. Turner, *Gloucestershire* (London, 1794), p. 21.

suitable for land overgrown with coarse and intractable vegetation; as one gentleman in the Fens of Cambridgeshire remarked, 'burning beats the mucking cart'. Similarly in Berkshire, where paring and burning was 'an ancient practice', it was considered indispensable for 'all sour, tenacious soils, and where brakes, furze, and coarse grass cover the surface'; moreover, it was given the approval of the royal bailiff and practised in Windsor Great Park. In Gloucestershire, paring and burning was regarded as 'almost essential to the very existence of the agriculture of this county'.[42]

The pigeon question aroused stronger passions at the end of the eighteenth century. Pigeon dung, a favourite of classical authors, was praised in England from the time of Fitzherbert, and regarded as the hottest of all dungs by Ellis, and was 'certainly very much coveted by all husbandmen'. Perhaps pigeon dung was more available in Ellis's day than previously: interest in pigeon keeping had been renewed after the Restoration.[43] In the first series of *General Views* pigeons made very few appearances, but they were complimented for the quality of their dung, and Arthur Young continued a long tradition in his 'Essay' of 1799 when he declared:

> I have not the least doubt of the dung only of a well-stocked pigeon-house paying more than the necessary interest for building the house; an object greatly deserving a gentleman's or rich farmer's attention.[44]

Here we get a glimpse of Young in his role as friend and cultivator of the influential of rural society. But in his support for the pigeon he was out of sympathy with other agricultural writers, many of whom in the second series of reports commented on the excellent quality of pigeon dung, but condemned the birds for the damage they did to crops. Much of the profit going to the owners of dovecotes was held to be 'a kind of public plunder, being derived from the corn-stacks and fields of the neighbouring farmers'. Thus, 'no one who wishes to be upon good terms with his neighbours ought to keep them', and, since they were 'entirely granivorous, and withal

---

[42] W. Gooch, *Cambridgeshire* (London, 1811), p. 249; W. Mavor, *Berkshire* (London, 1809), pp. 349–54; T. Rudge, *Gloucestershire* (London, 1807), p. 264. See also Thirsk, *English Peasant Farming*, p. 223.

[43] Ellis, *Husbandry*, pp. 101–4; J. Thirsk, *The Agrarian History of England and Wales*, V, *1640–1750* (2 vols., Cambridge, 1984–5), II, pp. 575–6.

[44] Young, 'An Essay on Manures', 599; Lowe, *Nottinghamshire*, pp. 16, 26, 30, 36, 39; I. Leatham, *E. R. Yorkshire* (London, 1794), p. 53.

extremely voracious', those 'insatiate vermin' were estimated to consume nearly five million bushels of grain a year, valued at nearly one-and-a-half million pounds.[45] To offset against such devastating plunder, some authors stressed the value of pigeons in picking up the seed of weeds, but only in a few Midland counties was this characteristic felt to outweigh the damage to crops.[46]

In his *General View of Essex* published in 1807 Arthur Young joined the popular platform by declaring that pigeons were 'universal depredators . . . far beyond any compensation finally made, I believe, by their value to anybody'. But he did not maintain this line consistently, and in the other four reports he published between 1799 and 1809 he did not discuss the pigeon issue. Similarly, his son, reporting on Sussex, failed to say anything detrimental about the 'winged vermin'.[47]

III

Although it will never be possible to analyse agricultural practices for a whole county at the level of the individual farm, insights at a parish level can be gained from the very detailed *General Views* compiled for two East Anglian counties – Cambridgeshire and Essex – by Charles Vancouver.[48] Authors of the first series of reports toured their allotted counties, observing and collecting information from interested parties, but only Vancouver gave a detailed description of the soils and, to a lesser extent, of the agricultural practices of each parish for which he could get information. Vancouver's approach to the two counties differed somewhat: he divided 398 Essex parishes into 14 districts, whereas he did not group the 142 Cambridgeshire parishes, although his discussion of individual parishes was much fuller for Cambridgeshire than for Essex. Charles Vancouver had little to say about dunging and folding in the parishes of Cambridgeshire and Essex, although he

---

[45] T. Batchelor, *Bedfordshire* (London, 1808), p. 577; St J. Priest, *Buckinghamshire* (London, 1810), p. 332; C. Vancouver, *Devon* (London, 1808), pp. 357–8.

[46] R. Parkinson, *Huntingdonshire* (London, 1811), p. 264; R. Parkinson, *Rutland* (1808) (annexed to W. Pitt, *Leicestershire* (London, 1809)), pp. 144–5; Lowe, *Notinghamshire* (London, 1798), pp. 108, 132.

[47] A. Young, *Essex* (London, 1807), II, p. 362; *Lincolnshire* (London, 1799); *Hertfordshire* (London, 1804); *Norfolk* (London, 1804); *Oxfordshire* (London, 1809); *Suffolk* (London, 1813); Rev. A. Young, *Sussex* (London, 1808).

[48] C. Vancouver, *Cambridgeshire* (London, 1794); *Essex* (London, 1795).

recorded large flocks of sheep in many places, and it is evident that he failed to discuss such basic issues simply because they were so widespread. From the manuring viewpoint, Essex was divided into two zones – a maritime zone running along the coast and penetrating inland along the rivers, and a much more extensive inland zone. In the last-named area farmers were heavily dependent on their own local resources. At Boreham, near Chelmsford, Vancouver was told that:

> in general the farmers depend chiefly on that which arises from their own lands: the dung from the farm yard therefore is carted out in the spring, which is carefully turned over and mixed with soil, wherever it can be spared from the sides of lanes or roads, or from the skirts of the enclosures; and sometimes a portion of lime, chalk or rubbish, is added, where it can easily be obtained.[49]

Mixing together soils of different qualities was an important way of improving the land in inland Essex: in district one – a group of eighty-four parishes running down from the north of the county through the central areas – the mixing of soils was reported for sixteen parishes. As Vancouver remarked about a group of four parishes in east central Essex:

> Great benefits have resulted in this neighbourhood from claying the light lands, and correcting the natural defects of the several soils, by mixing the opposites of each other together.[50]

In district twelve, immediately to the west of district one, the practice of 'claying the land' was also common (mentioned in thirteen out of forty-six parishes), and in this land-locked area the 'small portion of manure afforded' was 'very industriously collected and applied upon the fallows for wheat and barley, and sometimes (though but rarely) for beans'.[51] Similarly, in district thirteen, which lay in the north-west of the county, he remarked:

> Very little is to be noticed in this district on the article of manure, if we except only the light top dressings, which are used . . . in the open field country, bordering upon Hertford and Cambridgeshire.[52]

The only places in the inland zone to receive substantial quantities of off-farm fertilizers lay in the south-west corner of the county. However, Vancouver warned that, since those parishes

---

[49] Vancouver, *Essex*, p. 202. For similar comments see pp. 195, 199.
[50] *Ibid.*, p. 31.   [51] *Ibid.*, p. 102.   [52] *Ibid.*, p. 107.

were:

> so very near to the metropolis, and so completely within the reach of the London muck, no conclusion applicable to the general improvement of the country is to be drawn from their husbandry or other management.[53]

Away from London's orbit, few top dressings were available: Vancouver referred to soot only once, and was told by a correspondent about the occasional application of tanners' and fellmongers' waste.[54]

By contrast, the maritime zone was characterized by the widespread application of 'foreign manures'. Starting in the north, in parishes along the river Stour, farmers mixed fresh soil with 'London muck' available 'at the wharf' for 15s a waggon load, and it was used in the Colchester area, along the Colne, 'where the distance from the wharf, or landing-place, does not absolutely forbid it'. London muck, together with chalk, was also widely used along the coast between the Colne and Stour estuaries, although such 'foreign composts' did not penetrate very far inland: Vancouver based his costings on the assumption that the wharf was:

> within distance of making three turns in a day, with a waggon and five horses; where the team makes but two turns in the day, and where indeed one load is a complete day's work, the above expense must be proportionably augmented.[55]

Further south along the coast and penetrating up the rivers, 'chalk rubbish brought in vessels from the Kentish cliffs' was applied 'with very good effect', and on wet, heavy lands it was believed that, after chalking, 'the land will require little or no dung, or other manure, for a period of twenty years'.[56] But as with London muck, the cost of carrying the chalk inland meant that the maritime zone was extremely narrow, a thin ribbon of land a few miles wide along the coast and river banks. As Vancouver remarked on the mainland area just north of Canvey Island:

> The length of carriage through the northern parts of this district [nowhere more than about four miles from the Thames estuary],

---

[53] *Ibid.*, p. 112. They were the parishes of Barking, Great and Little Ilford, East and West Ham, and Wanstead.

[54] *Ibid.*, pp. 12, 208.

[55] *Ibid.*, pp. 38, 41, 45.

[56] *Ibid.*, pp. 47, 49, 53, 55–7, 65–7, 71, 80, 190–1. On the use of Kentish chalk in Essex see also: J. Boys, *Kent* (London, 1805), p. 159; Young, *Essex*, pp. 203–4, 206, 215.

has in a great measure precluded the use of chalk, and lime has there been substituted in its place, mixed with earth, and farm yard dung.[57]

For Cambridgeshire, Vancouver obtained information for 105 of his 142 parishes, and he discussed manuring practices in 82 of them. Cambridgeshire, an inland county, was forced back on its own local resources rather more than Essex, but the impression given by Vancouver is that the practices of mixing soils and of claying, together with chalking and liming, were little used. However, the application of other 'foreign manures' was rather more widespread than in inland Essex. Vancouver referred to artificial manures for forty-eight parishes, although for eighteen of them he added the qualification 'occasional', and for fourteen parishes he specifically mentioned that such manures were not in use. The artificial manures included malt dust, oil-cake dust, old woollen rags, and cinder ashes, but often they were not named, but simply referred to as 'hand dressings', 'top dressings', 'foreign composts', or the like. Such fertilizers were in use especially around Cambridge, where the annual influx of undergraduates helped to swell the volume of 'town muck'. At Barnwell, less than four miles from the town, farmers were 'assisted by a considerable quantity of dung, procured in return for straw used in Cambridge, with great quantities of brick, and old house rubbish obtained from thence', while at Grantchester 'as much manure as can possibly be procured from Cambridge' was applied to the land.[58]

Cambridgeshire was divided into two major zones from the manuring point of view – the Fens, and other areas. Outside the Fens, yard muck, the sheep-fold, and 'foreign composts' were commonly applied, although despite the great detail of Vancouver's survey it is impossible to say what proportion of farmers used such dressings. But in the Fens, such off-farm manures were not required. For a group of five fenland parishes he noted that:

> The large herds of cattle, which depasture on these commons, and the fodder, straw, and litter, which is produced and gathered from the fens, accumulate such prodigious quantities of manure, as to preserve the arable land in good heart, and condition, with-

---

[57] Vancouver, *Essex*, p. 84.
[58] Vancouver, *Cambridgeshire*, pp. 50, 102; see also pp. 52, 101, 104, 119, 122.

out the dung from the dove-cotes, which is generally sold to the farmers in the higher country.[59]

However, Vancouver was able to gather detailed information from less than half of the fenland parishes: at Doddington he got 'No information upon twice calling', while at March nothing could be procured 'without paying for it'. Part of the trouble was that he was collecting his material 'before the objects of it were generally known' so that 'I became here a suspected person, and could obtain no information whatever.' Elsewhere, 'being unfortunately suspected to be in the interests of the rector, I was not only received coolly, but treated with great jealousy and distrust'.[60] This problem pin-points one of the difficulties of evaluating the information presented in the *General Views*. Sometimes Vancouver was forced to rely on 'a short conversation I had with one of the principal farmers', or on the vicar, who 'obligingly favoured me by letter with this account'.[61] But given the inevitable biases which appear in all contemporary accounts of farming, Vancouver's descriptions provide a uniquely detailed insight into farming methods in two adjacent counties. The chief impression left with the reader is that the majority of farmers were heavily dependent, like their fore-fathers, on the internal resources of their own farms; but also that buying in dressings was important, especially in Cambridgeshire which, outside the Fens, was more heavily arable than much of Essex,[62] and that bulky additives – such as Kentish chalk – were applied in large quantities when the costs of transport did not out-weigh the benefit gained.

IV

Despite the many thousands of words written about manure, most English farmers probably had little access to off-farm dressings before the nineteenth century, and there were three major constraints on the more widespread application of such 'foreign manures'. First, such materials were not available in all areas; thus, only farmers close to the shore were likely to apply sand to their holdings in significant quantities. Second, only a minority of

---

[59] *Ibid.*, pp. 125–6. Compare this with Thirsk, *English Peasant Farming*, p. 30.
[60] Vancouver, *Cambridgeshire*, pp. 125, 153–4, 186.
[61] *Ibid.*, pp. 24, 39.   [62] Prince, 'England *circa* 1800', p. 405.

farmers had easy access to water transport, which allowed the movement of bulky manures over longer distances, although the transport revolution of the eighteenth and early nineteenth centuries undoubtedly allowed more farmers to acquire town muck or other additives at realistic prices. Third, there were difficulties which precluded the efficient use of night-soil as a fertilizer: some farmers were prejudiced against its use since it was believed to 'taint' the vegetation it assisted, and there were also logistical problems connected with the collection and distribution of that noisome material.

Before 1800 farmers might read about the myriad manures recommended for use, but as the Scottish author James Donaldson suggested in 1697:

> Though some curious persons recommend horn and hoof, blood and guts of cattle, and shells of fishes, and salt-petre *etc.* as very strong and durable nourishment for the ground; yet seeing these things cannot be had by everyone, I shall speak of those which may be had everywhere, viz. dung of cattle, ashes, lime, marl, and sea-ware.[63]

Even this modest list was too long, since lime, marl, and 'sea-ware' could not be obtained in all places at prices which facilitated use. Similarly, town muck 'can only be used in large quantity by those who are conveniently situated for conveying it'; in Suffolk, farmers living near the towns had been 'very assiduous in purchasing all sorts of manures', although, for those living five miles away, transport costs created 'an expense so enormous, as to leave it a question whether it answers'.[64] Many dressings were obtainable only in a few places: blubber was used around Whitby and Liverpool; bones, mostly refuse from the city's cutlers, were applied for twenty miles around Sheffield, but they were 'so scarce an article' in Cheshire 'that few farmers have it in their power to procure it'; slam, a waste-product from the alum works, was used around Marske in north Yorkshire; the Nottinghamshire gentleman who raised heaven and earth to make manure sang the praise of sticklebacks – 'but alas! I have not been able to get any for these last ten years'; finally, around Sheffield a substance was used 'which can never be more

---

[63] J. Donaldson, *Husbandry Anatomised, Or, An Enquiry into the Present Manner of Tilling and Manuring the Ground in Scotland* (Edinburgh, 1697), p. 20.

[64] W. Pitt, *Staffordshire* (London, 1796), p. 26; Young, *Suffolk* (London, 1813), p. 194.

than a local one, viz. the refuse of hogs' bristles from the brush manufactories'.[65]

The list of such localized manures could be extended easily, but the mere availability of a substance did not always guarantee that it would be used. During the early seventeenth century the burgesses of Newcastle upon Tyne 'cast their ashes and dung on a heap adjoining the castle walls in the middle of the town, which was carted away once a year by country farmers'.[66] Unfortunately, the farmers, 'having found so great quantities of dung near hand their dwelling, viz. at the outside of the said town', had not collected the muck for six or seven years. As a result:

> the said dunghill did grow so great, that the mayor and aldermen were inforced to build a wall about the said dunghill to keep the people from casting any more dung thereon, as also to keep the same dung from falling into the high street or paved causey thereby to stop the passage of the people.[67]

Further south, along the Cleveland coast, farmers ignored a valuable manure, there for the taking: sea-sand was an excellent dressing for the 'wet adhesive clays', but it was 'probably not generally used, because it may at all times be had, and always for nothing, and is therefore too plentiful to be valued'.[68]

In addition, not all of the potential fertilizers produced on the farm were put on the land. As in many Third World societies today, dung was used for fuel when other combustibles were in short supply: Arthur Standish complained that 'the want of wood in many places of this kingdom, constraineth the soil of cattle to be burned, which should be imployed to the strengthening of land', and later in the century Celia Fiennes observed its use near Leicester.[69] The practice was still common in the eighteenth century. In Cambridgeshire:

> cow-dung dried is used as firing for dairy purposes and by the poor; it is spread on grass (common or waste-land) about one inch

---

[65] Tuke, *N. R. Yorkshire* (1800), p. 238; J. Holt, *Lancashire* (London, 1795), p. 127; R. Brown, *W. R. Yorkshire* (Edinburgh, 1799), pp. 153–4; H. Holland, *Cheshire* (London, 1808), p. 235; Tuke, *N. R. Yorkshire* (1794), pp. 52–3; Lowe, *Nottinghamshire* (London, 1794), p. 101.

[66] Thirsk, *Agrarian History*, IV, p. 167.

[67] PRO, E134, 20 Jas. I, Easter 18.

[68] J. Tuke, *N. R. Yorkshire* (1800), pp. 238–9.

[69] A. Standish, *The Commons Complaint* (London, 1611), p. 2; *The Journeys of Celia Fiennes*, ed. C. Morris (London, 1949), p. 162.

and a half thick, and cut into pieces about eight to ten inches square, and lies till dry.[70]

Similarly, in Huntingdonshire and Lincolnshire dung was one of the fuels of the poor, while on the Isle of Portland the inhabitants were said to use cow dung for fuel and pig dung for soap:

whence the following, rather coarse, couplet, has become proverbial –
In the Isle of Portland, in fam'd Dorsetshire,
The pigs sh— soap, and the cows sh— fire.[71]

The widespread use of straw for thatching also reduced the amount of manure available, although the loss could be offset if the old thatch was ploughed in, as Ellis suggested. Farmers were warned against selling off their hay and straw, unless it was for town use and a return load of manure obtained, since 'profit is the great object, and we must never carry any rules so far as to lessen it'.[72]

Water transport was usually required if manures were to be carried more than a few miles. London muck had long been sent by river boat into Hertfordshire and neighbouring counties, and no doubt other rivers were used for similar purposes from time to time. The richest information relating to the carriage of manure comes from the *General Views*. As we have seen, large quantities of Kentish chalk were shipped to Essex, and there were similar trades all around the coast: colliers returning to the North-East sometimes carried, as ballast, chalk for the lime kilns; chalk was carried along the Hampshire coast, sometimes from as far away as Kent; while along the Sussex coast 'the chalk is shipped in sloops' to the lime kilns.[73]

During the eighteenth century river and canal development created new opportunities for moving manure around. The

[70] Gooch, *Cambridgeshire* (1811), p. 290.
[71] Parkinson, *Huntingdonshire* (1811), p. 270; F. M. Eden, *The State of the Poor* (1797), II, pp. 394–5. For a similar piece of doggerel relating to late-seventeenth-century Lincolnshire, see R. W. Malcolmson, *Life and Labour in England 1700–1780* (London, 1981), p. 147.
[72] I. Leatham, *E. R. Yorkshire* (London, 1794), p. 27; Ellis, *Husbandry*, pp. 117–18; Young, 'An Essay on Manures', pp. 579–80.
[73] Thirsk, *Agrarian History*, IV, p. 52; P. Foot, *Middlesex* (London, 1794), pp. 26–7; W. Stevenson, *Surrey* (London, 1809), pp. 494, 509–11; J. Bailey, *Co. Durham* (London, 1810), p. 204; C. Vancouver, *Hampshire* (London, 1810), p. 340; A. Young, *Sussex* (London, 1793), p. 31.

improvement of the River Kennet facilitated a wide distribution of ashes from the turf and peat pits between Reading and Newbury, while the improved River Rother in Sussex allowed a much greater application of chalk.[74] The opening of the Grand Junction Canal led to an increased use of lime in Bedfordshire, and of London ashes in Buckinghamshire and Hertfordshire. However, road carriage from the metropolis into Hertfordshire continued for some time, this 'apparent absurdity' being due to the inadequacy of wharfage and storage facilities in London. The Basingstoke Canal allowed London rags to be carried into Hampshire.[75] In Worcestershire lime was carried 'by the canals, or by land carriage', while the building of the Cromford Canal brought 'great expectations', since it facilitated the carriage of lime derived from the 'immense rocks of the stone about Cromford and Crich in Derbyshire' through the county and into Nottinghamshire.[76] The great value of canals was recognized by the author of the *General View* for Middlesex, although he realized that roads still had a significant role to play:

> The extension of canals may become the most powerful means of promoting general cultivation. Good roads are certainly very essential, and I think canals are at least equally so, in an agricultural view. On the best roads, produce and manure can seldom be carried more than ten miles with profit, at the present price of horse-keep: but if canals were as numerous as roads, corn, hay, manure, etc. could be sent to every part of Britain without using more road than the towing paths, and ten times the former distance without increasing the expense.[77]

The growing use of 'foreign manures' owed something not only to the improvement of the transport network, but also to the policies adopted by the transport authorities. Most turnpike Acts specified that manure was to be toll-free,[78] and many river and canal Acts laid

---

[74] J. Priestley, *Historical Account of the Navigable Rivers, Canals and Railways Throughout Great Britain* (1831; 2nd edn 1967), p. 391; Ellis, *Husbandry*, pp. 65–6; Young, *Sussex* (1808), pp. 201–2.

[75] Batchelor, *Bedfordshire* (1808), p. 497; Priest, *Buckinghamshire* (1810), p. 272; Young, *Hertfordshire* (1804), pp. 17, 166; Vancouver, *Hampshire* (1810), p. 348.

[76] W. Pitt, *Worcestershire* (London, 1813), p. 198); J. Farey, *Derbyshire*, II (London, 1813), pp. 408–9; Lowe, *Nottinghamshire* (1794), p. 128; Lowe, *Nottinghamshire* (1798), pp. 106–7.

[77] J. Middleton, *Middlesex* (London, 1798), p. 406.

[78] W. Albert, *The Turnpike Road System in England, 1663–1840* (Cambridge, 1972), p. 82.

down either that manure was to be carried at a low toll, or toll-free. For a total of ninety English canals listed by Joseph Priestley there were sixty-eight specific references to manure, and in twenty-eight instances it was to be toll-free. However, exemption from toll was qualified in most cases: only on three canals, including the Bridge-water, was manure to be carried toll-free without restriction. Else-where manure often travelled free only when it was either destined for lands close to the canal (ten cases), or when it belonged to or was for the land of a riparian owner (eleven cases). In many instances it was also laid down that manure should be free only when there was an adequate supply of water in the canal (fourteen cases), while on two canals manure only travelled free if it did not pass through a lock. However, only on the Gloucester and Berkeley Canal was lime carried toll-free; goods exempted from toll there included 'all dung, soil, marl, ashes of coal and turf, and lime for manure, for the improvement of lands only within three miles of the canal'.[79] For the rivers, far less information is available since often Priestley was not able to give the tolls, and, where he could, manure was not always mentioned. However, manure travelled toll-free on six rivers, and it seems highly likely that other river authorities adopted similar policies. Certainly, one improvement scheme must have delighted all agriculturalists as it passed through Parliament: the Tamar Manure Navigation received the royal assent on 26 April 1796, and as Priestley wrote:

> This canal was designed principally for the supply of coal, sea-sand and lime as manure, and affords an opening for the export of the agricultural products of the country through which it passes.[80]

Some years ago it was suggested that 'contemporary objections to the use of human ordure as manure' made it doubtful if it were ever spread anywhere but on waste land, and, more recently, that before the eighteenth century 'human waste was usually eschewed and buried deep and well out of the way'.[81] Such attitudes can be found echoed in contemporary literature: in the sixteenth century, Thomas Hill felt that 'that which men make, although it be thought most excellent, yet is it not so needful to be desired', unless it was for

[79] Priestley, p. 317.   [80] *Ibid.*, p. 650.
[81] G. E. Fussell, *Village Life in the Eighteenth Century* (Worcester, 1947), pp. 33–4; Kerridge, *The Agricultural Revolution*, p. 241.

exceedingly poor land, and he later added that its hotness made it 'greatly disliked'. His distaste was mirrored by Reynolde Scot's remark that some men refused to dung their corn land 'because they would not *beraye* it with so uncleanly a thing'.[82] One of the strongest condemnations of the use of human excrement came from the pen of John Evelyn in the seventeenth century, who feared that plants 'contract the smell and relish of the ferments, applied to accelerate their growth'. Hence:

> we omit to enumerate amongst our soils, *stercus humanum*, which
> . . . with that of fowl and cattle, does, unless exceedingly venti-
> lated and aired, perniciously contaminate the odour of flowers,
> and is so evident in the vine, as nothing can reconcile it.[83]

In the following century, Ellis described the proper manner of composting night-soil, since 'want of knowing how to manage this hot dressing . . . has discouraged many from using it',[84] but the prejudice continued in some circles throughout the century. In his *General View* of agriculture in Gloucestershire, Thomas Rudge pointed out that:

> Night-soil, or human excrement, though from a variety of
> experiments proved to be a highly fertilizing manure, is seldom,
> if ever, used in this county. Prejudice is in a great measure the
> cause of this neglect; so that the whole which is supplied by the
> city of Gloucester is thrown into the Severn.[85]

Despite such hostile opinions, night-soil, and town muck in general, had been used by English cultivators since at least medieval times, and such usage was reinforced by the study of classical authority which enthusiastically recommended the 'residue of human banquets as one of the best manures'.[86] Heresbach, Platt, Blith,

---

[82] Hill, *The proffitable Arte of Gardening*, p. 13r; Hill, *The Gardeners Labyrinth*, p. 19; R. Scot, *A Perfite Platforme of a Hoppe Garden* (London, 1574), p. 36.

[83] Evelyn, *A Philosophical Discourse of the Earth*, pp. 117–18; for a further discussion of tainting see J. Evelyn, *Acetaria: A Discourse of Sallets* (London, 1699), pp. 31–4.

[84] Ellis, *Husbandry*, pp. 107–8; on composting of night-soil see also H. Platt, *Sundrie New and Artificial Remedies Against Famine* (London, 1596), unpaginated.

[85] Rudge, *Gloucestershire* (1807), p. 272.

[86] B. M. S. Campbell, 'Agricultural Progress in Medieval England: Some Evidence from Eastern Norfolk', *Econ. Hist. Rev.*, 2nd ser., XXXVI (1983), 34. Bruce Campbell has supplied me by letter with more material relating to the use of urban waste in medieval Norfolk, and David Postles has done likewise for Oxford and Southampton: I am most grateful to them both. See also E. L. Sabine, 'City

Hanmer, Ellis, and others endorsed the practice, and a number of authors of the *General Views* confirmed its use around London and other towns.[87] After reviewing the use of night-soil in various parts of the world, Arthur Young declared that 'it is a vulgar error to imagine that manuring a field with this substance will give a bad taste to plants'.[88] Nevertheless, feelings of distaste do seem to have limited the application of human faecal matter to English fields.

For information on Mediterranean attitudes to night-soil, Young relied on the witty observations of Tobias Smollett, who took a close interest in the habits of the natives of Nice. Smollett introduced an important consideration when he pointed out that the quality of night-soil – as with the dung of four-footed beasts – depended on the quality, and quantity, of the food consumed:

> The jakes of a protestant family, who eat *gras* every day, bears a much higher price than the privy of a good catholic who lives *maigre* one half of the year. The vaults belonging to the convent of Minims are not worth emptying.

This was because the Minims kept a continual lent, and thus ate poorly.[89]

The use of night-soil in agriculture was also limited by problems of collection and distribution. The total volume of human ordure increased substantially over three centuries since the population of England and Wales, which stood at over nine million in 1801, was more than three times the size it had been in 1500. Arthur Young suggested that:

> If the farmer manages his necessary-house in such a manner as to suffer nothing to run off from it, and frequently throws malt-dust, saw dust, fine mould, or sand, into it, he may from a moderate family, every year manure from one to two acres of land.

Cleaning in Mediaeval London', *Speculum*, XII (1937), 23–5; E. L. Sabine, 'Latrines and Cesspools of Mediaeval London', *Speculum*, IX (1934), 21. Rackham, *Pliny*, p. 37; Ash, *Columella*, p. 195; Ash, *Cato and Varro*, p. 265.

[87] Heresbach, *Foure Bookes of Husbandry*, p. 19v; Platt, *Sundrie New and Artificial Remedies*; Blith, *The English Improver*, p. 120; E. S. Rohde (ed.), *The Garden Book of Sir Thomas Hanmer Bart* (London, 1933), p. 7; Ellis, *Husbandry*, pp. 107–8; Duncomb, *Herefordshire* (1805), p. 107; Middleton, *Middlesex* (1798), p. 301.

[88] Young, 'An Essay on Manures', p. 605.

[89] T. Smollett, *Travels Through France and Italy* (1766), ed. F. Felsenstein (Oxford, 1979), pp. 185, 425. For comments on the relationship between animal feed and the quality of dung, see: Holland, *Cheshire* (1808), p. 229; Middleton, *Middlesex* (1798), p. 305.

Thus, if nothing were allowed to seep away, the two million or so families of 1801 should have been able to fertilize between two and four million acres of land a year. But much was lost since many were guilty of 'letting their chamber-pots be emptied anywhere but where they ought'.[90] This was especially true of the towns, where ditches, streams, and rivers frequently had all the characteristics and charms of open sewers. Privies were frequently sited on bridges and, as in London, passing under them by boat could be a daunting prospect.[91] Where privies were sited away from water-courses the filth, periodically dug out of the pits or removed from latrine barrels, was tipped into the nearest stream or river.[92] Certainly, in England things were not as well organized as in Nice, where:

> Every peasant opens, at one corner of his wall, a public house of office for the reception of passengers; and in the town of Nice, every tenement is provided with one of these receptacles, the contents of which are carefully preserved for sale. The peasant comes with his asses and casks to carry it off before day, and pays for it according to its quality, which he examines and investigates, by the taste and flavour.[93]

Although the refuse of urban stables and the sweepings of town streets and chimneys may well have added substantially to the productiveness of nearby farms, it seems likely that no more than a small proportion of the large quantities of human excrement produced annually was similarly employed in England. Certainly, this was the view taken by John Middleton at the end of the eighteenth century:

> Unfortunately, ninety-nine parts in a hundred of the soil of privies is carried, by the common sewers, into the Thames; which is a very great loss to agriculture, as night-soil is not only more

---

[90] Young, 'An Essay on Manures', p. 603.

[91] L. Wright, *Clean and Decent* (London, 1963), pp. 50–2.

[92] Fussell, *Village Life*, p. 33; Sabine, 'City Cleaning', 20, 33–5; Sabine, 'Latrines and Cesspools', 307–12; V. Parker, *The Making of Kings Lynn* (London & Chichester, 1971), pp. 27, 159–62; D. Portman, *Exeter Houses, 1400–1700* (Exeter, 1966), p. 15; A. Redford, *The History of Local Government in Manchester* (3 vols., 1939–40), I, pp. 109–15; D. M. Palliser, 'Civic Mentality and the Environment in Tudor York', *Northern History*, XVIII (1982), 95; A. D. Dyer, *The City of Worcester in the Sixteenth Century* (Leicester, 1973), pp. 206–7; G. Jackson, *Hull in the Eighteenth Century* (Oxford, 1972), p. 312.

[93] Smollett, *Travels*, pp. 184–5.

quick in its operation than any other dressing, but is by far the richest manure that ever was laid on land.[94]

V

The impressionistic evidence on which this chapter is based suggests that by the eighteenth century, and especially with the improving transport network of that era, the desire and ability to tap reserves of off-farm fertilizers had increased and probably played its part in improving agricultural productivity, which, while being impossible to quantify with any degree of certainty, undoubtedly did rise over the three centuries under consideration. Through the increasing use of 'foreign manures' a number of problems pressing on society could be resolved at a single blow: the collection and application of various natural products, of industrial refuse, and of urban waste produced a cleaner environment, raised agricultural yields, and provided substantial employment in an age of chronic under-employment.[95]

The possibility of creating new employment was not lost on contemporary writers: John Norden reported that Cornish sand was carried up to six miles inland, 'and poor men live by fetching it and selling it to the more wealthy', while Walter Blith told a similar tale about the exploitation of river sludge – 'Many men get gallant livings only by taking it up . . . and selling it again by the load.' The cleansing of London's streets in the early seventeenth century employed 'innumerable carts' to carry 'the filth of the city' out into the surrounding countryside, and, a century later, Kalm saw custom-built carts, specially designed for carrying away street sweepings.[96] Keeping institutions clean also created employment: at Hull during the seventeenth century a labourer was employed at the rate of 6d a week for emptying the 'tubs of office' at the Town Hall, and at Trinity House, the home of a substantial number of pensioners, the task of digging out the privy pits created employ-

---

[94] Middleton, *Middlesex* (1798), p. 301.

[95] On schemes to cope with unemployment and under-employment, see J. Thirsk, *Economic Policy and Projects: The Development of a Consumer Society in Early Modern England* (Oxford, 1978).

[96] Norden, *The Surveyors Dialogue*, p. 227; Blith, *English Improver*, p. 112; *Cal. S. P. Venetian, 1617–19*, p. 318; J. Lucas (ed.), *Kalm's Account of his Visit to England on his Way to America in 1748* (London, 1892), p. 143.

ment more than once a year. At King's Lynn in 1630 'the great muckhill at the East Gate' was carried away and spread by men and women at the rate of 6d and 4d a day respectively.[97] Later in the century, John Worlidge suggested that two birds might be killed easily with the same stone:

> Great quantities of this dung [i.e. of sheep] might be obtained, if poor women and children were imployed to pick up the same on the roadways, and burning tops of hills, where it seldom doth any good, but would prove much more advantageous than the cost or trouble, by far.[98]

Similarly, in the *General Views* there are comments about the potential for employment creation offered by the increased traffic in manure: in Hertfordshire, 'many poor persons employ themselves in picking up dung on the turnpike-roads, which they sell to farmers at 2d. a bushel'; in the Lincolnshire Fens sticklebacks were so numerous 'that a man has made 4s. a day by selling them at a halfpenny a bushel'; London rags and leather shreds were 'gathered by women' and sent to the farmers around Guildford.[99] Likewise, the carting of muck from Cambridge, of bones from Sheffield, of slam from the Yorkshire alum works, and the manning of river and coasting vessels which carried dung, chalk, lime, and urban refuse all created employment.

Further progress in delineating the changing sources of manure in England during the three centuries before 1800 will come only through further investigation of agricultural practices at the level of individual farms, or through further studies of the disposal of industrial or urban waste. A wide range of manures was available to English farmers, but problems connected with the collection and distribution of many such materials often precluded their wide-spread adoption. Overland carriage soon rendered the movement of manure uneconomic, and, no doubt, inertia and conservatism often exacerbated the problem. Before the nineteenth century, it seems likely that most farmers – like Joan Thirsk's peasants in

---

[97] Hull City Archives Office, BRF/3/53, 54, 55; Trinity House, Hull, Account Books 1544–96, 1597–1638, passim; Parker, *King's Lynn*, p. 160.

[98] J. Worlidge, *Systema Agriculturae; The Mystery of Husbandry Discovered* (London, 1687), p. 70.

[99] Young, *Hertfordshire* (1804), p. 173; Young, *Lincolnshire* (1799), p. 259; Stevenson, *Surrey* (1809), p. 511.

seventeenth-century Lincolnshire – 'knew only four ways of fertilising their land, to leave it fallow, or to apply animal manure, vegetable waste, or other substances drawn from the soil such as clay and marl'.[100]

[100] Thirsk, *English Peasant Farming*, p. 165. I regret that I shall not be able to have the benefit of Joan Thirsk's observations on this essay until after publication.

11. *Root crops and the feeding of London's poor in the late sixteenth and early seventeenth centuries*

MALCOLM THICK

The theories that commercial gardening was introduced by Protestant refugees from the Low Countries in the second half of the sixteenth century and that they were instrumental in the big increase in gardening around London at the end of that century are not new. Samuel Hartlib and Thomas Fuller wrote as much in the mid seventeenth century, and many later historians have reproduced their comments. Professor Fisher quoted both men in his important article on the London food market in 1937 in which, amid a wide-ranging analysis of sources of supply to feed Londoners in the late sixteenth and early seventeenth centuries, he drew attention to the rise of market gardening around the capital in the early seventeenth century. This chapter will examine the role of Protestant refugees in introducing edible root production in England as a source of food for the poor in the sixteenth century, their links with the rise of root growing around London in the early seventeenth century, and the opinions of some contemporary observers as to the potential value of roots as food for the poor in times of famine.[1]

I

Protestant refugees began to arrive in England in some numbers towards the end of the reign of Edward VI. Persecution drove French, Dutch, and Flemings to England throughout the remainder of the sixteenth century and they settled in and around many major English towns. The largest and most economically successful com-

---

[1] F. J. Fisher, 'The Development of the London Food Market, 1540–1640', *Econ. Hist. Rev.*, VII (1937).

munities of refugees at this time were generally called 'Dutch' and came from the Low Countries.

The settlement of the foreigners was carefully regulated by central and local government. A royal patent allowed a total of 406 strangers to settle in Sandwich in 1561 and a similar licence was obtained by the Norwich council allowing 30 masters with their families and servants to stay there in 1565. Behind the sympathy expressed for persecuted Protestants in the Patents was a desire to acquire skilled men, particularly makers of the 'New Draperies', to strengthen the English economy. Norwich and Sandwich hoped to reverse economic decline by taking in foreigners and other towns, such as Colchester, hoped similarly to benefit.[2]

Local authorities produced detailed sets of regulations to reduce the economic and social impact of foreigners on often xenophobic native communities. The original numbers allowed to settle were closely controlled, but subsequent arrivals and natural increases led the most successful communities to expand fast: Norwich was granted permission to receive 300 'Douchemen' in 1565; by 1568 it contained 1,471 strangers, 3,995 in 1571, and 4,679 in 1583. Strangers made up about one-third of the population of Norwich in 1571.[3]

Colchester's Dutch community developed largely as an overflow from Sandwich: sixty-one aliens are recorded on the Subsidy Roll for 1563; eleven Dutch households arrived in 1565, a second party came in 1570, and by 1584 1,184 Dutch people lived there.[4]

Occupational censuses of the sixteenth-century Dutch settlers show that most of them were concerned with textiles. Some gardeners, however, are found in many of the communities. According to the General Muster for Colchester seven gardeners lived in All Saints Ward in 1590, and the list of strangers mustered in the North Ward was headed 'Dewchmen in the North Ward,

---

[2] William Boys, *Collections for an History of Sandwich* (1792), pp. 740–3; D. L. Rickwood, 'The Norwich Accounts for the Customs on Strangers' Goods and Merchandise, 1580–1610', *Norwich Record Society*, XXXIX (1970), 81, 82; W. J. C. Moens, 'The Walloon Church of Norwich', *Huguenot Society of London*, vol. I, pt 1 (1887–8), 18–20.

[3] Rickwood, 82.

[4] L. F. Roker, 'The Flemish and Dutch Community in Colchester in the Sixteenth and Seventeenth Centuries', unpublished MA thesis, London University, 1963, 84.

Generally Baymakers and Gardeners'.[5] A return of strangers in Norwich in 1568 lists two gardeners and in 1622 eight were named.[6] These are small numbers in view of the prominence the argument below gives to immigrant gardeners, but the Dutchmen combined gardening with other trades: in the early seventeenth century a Maidstone alien was gardening and threadmaking, a Hythe Fleming worked at 'Practize in Phisick, plantinge and gardening', and later in the century a Sandwich Dutchman divided his time between say weaving and gardening. Moreover, many officials compiling census or tax returns would not have recognized commercial gardening as a distinct occupation.[7] Gardeners from the Low Countries were also to be found in small numbers in the city of London before 1600.[8]

Protestant settlers came from the area of Europe with the most technically advanced agriculture. The Low Countries had a high population density and a high degree of urbanization. The towns had to be supplied regularly with food, and industry demanded raw materials: flax, hemp, madder, weld, woad, and teasels for the textile industry, as well as hops to use in brewing, for which the Low Countries were then famous. The response to these demands was intensive agriculture. Market gardening developed near towns, with root crops in particular being grown for both human and animal consumption. The industrial crops were often labour-intensive and some, such as hops, hemp, and flax, were produced largely by horticultural methods. Animals were stall-fed on root crops.[9]

It is no surprise that the Dutch imported their agriculture as well as their textile expertise into areas of England where they settled: several hop growers are recorded in the early lists of aliens' occupations: Dutch descendants of original settlers at Sandwich continued to grow quantities of flax in the late seventeenth century, and one of the benefits the Dutch bestowed on Norwich was said, in

---

[5] R. E. G. Kirk and E. F. Kirk, 'Returns of Aliens Dwelling in the City and Suburbs of London', *Hug. Soc. Ldn*, vol. X, pt II (1902), 90.

[6] Moens, iv, 207.

[7] W. D. Cooper (ed.), 'Lists of Foreign Protestants and Aliens Resident in England, 1618–1688', *Camden Society* (1862), 13–14; Kent Archives Office, PRC 10/67 no. 265.

[8] Kirk and Kirk, 'Returns of Aliens', *Hug. Soc. Ldn*, vol. X, pt II (1902), 5, 7, 61, 90.

[9] B. H. Slicher van Bath, *The Agrarian History of Western Europe, A.D. 1500 to 1850*, tr. O. Ordish (1965), pp. 239–43.

1575, to be 'they digge and delve a number of acres of grounde and so sowe flaxe, and do make it out in lynen clothe which set many on worke'.[10]

Dutch gardeners made a significant impact on food supplies to the markets of Norwich, Colchester, and Sandwich before 1600. Sandwich, as well as having an early foreign settlement, was an entry port for Protestant refugees who, after the short sea crossing from the Continent, dispersed to other French, Flemish or Dutch congregations. By 1582, 13 of a total of 351 Dutchmen at Sandwich were described as gardeners, almost certainly an understatement of those who wholly or partially lived by horticulture. Four Dutchmen were described as cowkeepers. In 1615 the tithes of the vicar of St Clements in Sandwich included 'tythe of Dutchmens gardens of all manner of hearbes, roots, cabbages, and such like', and had been taken at least since 1570. William Folkingham, in 1610, wrote of the excellence of the 'Sandwich carrot'.[11]

A number of inventories of Dutch gardeners, who died in the 1620s and 1630s at Sandwich, survive. They show that some small gardeners were cultivating kitchen gardens, growing vegetables, and occasionally keeping cows. Other, more substantial men were farmer-gardeners who worked farms of thirty acres or so, using a small acreage for garden crops, growing also grain, pulses, canary seed (a local speciality introduced by the Dutch), and keeping a few cows. Inventories from later in the century show increasing specialization in canary seed, vegetable seeds, and industrial crops.[12]

Little is known of the horticulture and agriculture of the Protestant refugees at Colchester, although the town was noted in 1607 for its carrots and, as we shall discuss below, qualtities of roots were shipped from the port to London in the 1590s. In the second half of the seventeenth century the town was a centre of garden seed production and regular shipments of seeds went to London.[13]

Although only small numbers of foreign gardeners are found in

---

[10] State Papers Domestic, Elizabeth vol. 20, no. 49.

[11] P. Morant, *History of Colchester* (1768), p. 80; Boyes, pp. 230, 747; William Folkingham, *Feudigraphia* (1610), p. 42.

[12] Kent Archives Office, PRC 10/68 no. 142; PRC 10/71 no. 251; PRC 10/67 no. 265; PRC 10/67 no. 25.

[13] John Norden, *The Surveyor's Dialogue* (London, 1607), p. 207; K. H. Burley, 'The Economic Development of Essex in the Later Seventeenth and Early Eighteenth Centuries', unpublished Ph.D. thesis, London University, 1957, table XXXI, p. 278; PRO E.190.1250/4; E.190.1253/14; E.190.1251/15.

lists of Norwich strangers before 1600, the foreigners had a noticeable impact on that city's food supplies. One of the benefits said, in 1575, to have accrued from the strangers was that 'they digge and delve a grete quantitie of grounde for rootes which is a grete succor and sustenaunce for the pore bothe for themselves as for all others of citie and countrie'.[14] This statement, part of an anonymous list of the economic benefits of strangers to Norwich preserved in the State Papers, implies the production of roots by digging, for human consumption, on a scale large enough to make a noticeable impact on food supplies for the poor of Norwich and its hinterland. One Dutch gardener had a close sown with roots outside the city walls near St Stephen's Gates in 1596. The probate inventories of two other Dutch gardeners provide some details of the horticultural activities of the Norwich strangers at the turn of the sixteenth century.[15]

Adrian Coesse's inventory was taken on 2 December 1595 and that of Francis van Dycke on 28 May 1597. They both grew garden vegetables; Coesse was a kitchen gardener, whereas van Dycke was a farmer-gardener.[16] Coesse's growing crops were 'turneppes and roots', leeks, parsnips, 'hearbes' (i.e. vegetables), and 'sallets'. He had small quantities of leeks, peas, and barley; probably for household use, in store, along with £2 worth of onions. Unspecified seeds worth 17s were on hand together with a measure containing 'roote seedes' worth 5s, presumably for next season's sowing. Coesse kept five cows and a neat; maybe these animals were fed partly on garden refuse and roots, for the Dutch were well known as cowkeepers. His crops were grown in a garden of plots and beds and, apart from a plough, he possessed a rake, a hoe, spades, and other implements. In short, Coesse was a kitchen gardener and cowkeeper.[17]

Van Dycke kept four cows and his implements included a spade as well as a plough. His crops in the ground (two acres of roots, four acres of barley, and two acres of wheat and rye) are a mixture of field crops and vegetables typical of other farmer-gardeners to be found in the seventeenth century at Sandwich, Fulham, and Sandy.

[14] SPD. Eliz., vol. 20, no. 49.
[15] William Hudson and J. C. Tingey (eds.), *The Records of the City of Norwich* (1910), 2, p. 196; Norwich Records Office, INV/14 no. 42; INV/12 no. 232.
[16] *Ibid.*; Malcolm Thick, 'Market Gardening in England and Wales', in *The Agrarian History of England and Wales*, V, *1640–1750* (1985), p. 504.
[17] NRO INV/14 no. 42; INV/12 no. 232; Sir Thomas Overbury, *The Overburian Charactery*, ed. W. J. Tayler (Oxford, 1936), pp. 59–60.

His ground would have been dug for roots and ploughed for cereals, the roots forming part of a rotation.[18]

In both inventories the most valuable crops were roots; Coesse's 'platte of ground with turneppes and roots' was appraised at £13 10s while the two acres of growing roots owned by van Dycke were worth £10. Of more significance is the relative value of these crops. Five pounds an acre was the valuation of van Dycke's roots; his barley was worth £1 5s per acre and the wheat and rye £2 5s. Clearly roots were important to the business activities of Dutch gardeners at Norwich, who were like the 'Drunken Dutchman' described by Sir Thomas Overbury in about 1610 who 'Of all places of pleasure . . . loves a common garden, and with the swine of the parish had need be ringed for rooting.'[19]

Yarmouth, outport for Norwich and a large town in its own right, had a community of Dutch settlers, which included gardeners producing roots for the market, by the third quarter of the sixteenth century. Roots were grown, probably by immigrants, at Orford in the Suffolk Sandling country in the 1590s, and, by the first decade of the seventeenth century, carrots were also produced at Ipswich, Bury, Framlingham, 'many sea townes in Suffolke', and 'many places in Norfolke'.[20] In the 1620s carrots and parsnips grew in the open fields of Bradwell, a village just outside Yarmouth. They were probably destined for the Yarmouth food market, but we may discern here the beginnings of field cultivation of roots in East Anglia which was to make such a significant impact on the feeding of livestock in this area by the middle of the seventeenth century.[21]

II

Immigrant gardeners, therefore, were making a definite contribution to the food supply of East Anglia at the end of the sixteenth

---

[18] NRO, INV/14 no. 42; INV/12 no. 232; KAO, PRC 11/76/85; PRO E.134, 2 & 3 Anne, Hill 1; F. Beavington, 'Early Market Gardening in Bedfordshire', *Transactions and Papers, Institute of British Geographers*, no. 37 (1965).

[19] NRO INV/14 no. 42; INV/12 no. 232; Overbury, pp. 59–60.

[20] A. R. Michell, 'The Port and Town of Great Yarmouth and its Economic and Social Relationships with its Neighbours on Both Sides of the Seas, 1550–1714: An Essay in the History of the North Sea Economy', Ph.D. thesis, Cambridge University (1978), 261, 302; Norden, p. 207.

[21] E. Kerridge, 'Turnip Husbandry in High Suffolk', *Econ. Hist. Rev.*, 2nd ser., VII (1956).

Table 1. *Shipments of roots from East Anglian ports, 1590–1601*

	October	November	December	January	February	March
From						
Colchester, 1590–1	12 tons 6 load	—.	30 tons	30 tons	—	—
Yarmouth, 1593–4	10 tons 300 bush	57 tons 300 bush	65 tons	84 tons	78 tons	9 tons
Yarmouth, 1597–8	136 tons	210 tons	232 tons	22 tons	—	
Yarmouth, 1598–9	78 tons	120 tons	78 tons 1 last	307 tons	59 tons	20 tons
Yarmouth, 1600–1	—	—	40 tons 50 bush 8 cwt	72 tons		
Aldeburgh 1600–1	20 load	—	42 load	—	—	—

Table 2. *Destinations of shipments of roots from East Anglian ports, 1590–1601*

To:	Boston	Berwick	Hull	London	Newcastle
Colchester, 1590–1	—	—	—	72 tons 6 load	—
Yarmouth, 1593–4	5 tons	10 tons	—	281 tons 600 bush	7 tons
Yarmouth, 1597–8	—	—	4 tons	596 tons	—
Yarmouth, 1598–9	—	—	23 tons	639 tons 1 last	—
Yarmouth, 1600–1	—	—	—	112 tons 8 cwt	50 bush
Aldeburgh, 1600–1	—	—	—	62 load	

century. Bad grain harvests in the 1590s allowed them to extend their markets to London and some other east-coast ports because roots, especially carrots, can, unlike much garden produce, withstand a long journey with some manhandling and still be fit to eat.

Grain harvests were bad in 1594 and 1595, disastrous in 1596 and 1597, and again poor in 1600. The resultant price fluctuations can be judged from Table 3. London, with by far the largest concentration

Table 3. *Prices, 1585 to 1605*

Harvest year	Barley	All grains	All arable crops
1585	547	556	460
1586	697	684	552
1587	361	365	333
1588	399	407	350
1589	568	531	421
1590	720	624	550
1591	451	443	394
1592	287	296	319
1593	379	350	369
1594	520	621	518
1595	740	681	569
1596	971	1,039	819
1597	779	778	631
1598	545	518	430
1599	617	557	472
1600	816	768	645
1601	583	555	499
1602	617	480	424
1603	338	420	411
1604	487	501	453
1605	639	543	499

Source: The Agrarian History of England and Wales, IV, 1500–1640, (1967), statistical appendix, pp. 819–20.

of landless people in the country, was faced with the difficult task of obtaining food from a countryside already feeling the effects of dearth. The Privy Council was concerned with the provision of food for the capital, and turned its attention to securing grain and white-meats to feed the poor. Even when provisions had been purchased by London merchants, the Council had to exhort provincial authorities to allow the food to be sent to the capital rather than be stored for use at home.[22]

Table 2 shows the contribution made towards the feeding of London at this time by the export of roots from East Anglian ports. No roots were exported from the ports listed before 1590 and none were sent in the years immediately after 1601, indicating that the

---

[22] PRO E.190.594/9; E.190.474/17; E.190.480/5; E.190.477/8; E.190.481/11; E.190.418/10; W. G. Hoskins, 'Harvest Fluctuations and English Economic History, 1480–1619', *Ag. Hist. Rev.*, XVI, 1 (1968); *Acts of the Privy Council*, 1595, pp. 11–12, 16–17, 37–8; 1596, pp. 370, 451–2; 1596/7, pp. 124–5, 148.

shipments were an exceptional response to the bad grain harvests. The lack of exports in the worst year of dearth, 1596, shows that prices were high enough at home to forestall any demand from London. Similarly, the reason for the lack of shipments from Norwich in 1595 is indicated by the expenditure of £200 by the authorities there on rye from Denmark to sell at 4s a bushel to the poor.[23]

One shipment of roots only (80 bushels in October 1598) from Sandwich to London has been recorded in the period 1590 to 1601, although Sandwich was nationally known as a carrot-growing area in the first decade of the seventeenth century; here too local demand may have absorbed all production.[24]

The bulk of the roots were shipped from Yarmouth. Most went to London, with only occasional exports to Boston, Berwick, Hull, and Newcastle. In 1593/4 the first shipment departed from Yarmouth on 1 October; in 1597/8 on 26 October; in 1598/9 on 13 October. Shipments continued through November, but the largest tonnages left Yarmouth and the other East Anglian ports for London in December and January. No shipments occurred between April and September in any year. Individual cargoes of roots were usually large, 30 tons being the most common size leaving Yarmouth in 1597/8. Often roots were the sole cargo of the ships carrying them.[25]

Carrots formed the bulk of all shipments. Of thirty-six shipments from Yarmouth in 1597/8, thirty-one were described as carrot roots, two simply as roots, two as carrots, turnips, and cabbages, and one as carrots and cabbages. Other years show a similar pattern. It appears that the shipments were predominantly of maincrop carrots which are usually drawn from the middle of October. Carrots deteriorate in the ground if heavily frosted and so those shipped early in the new year had probably been harvested and clamped.[26]

Most of the shipments of roots from Yarmouth did not originate in the port; of thirty-six shipments in 1597/8, thirty were in transit. Yarmouth was the outport for Norwich, and it is reasonable to suppose that the cargoes came from that city and its immediate hinterland both because of the importance of root production

---

[23] Michell, 153, 302; J. C. Drummond and A. Wilbraham, *The Englishman's Food* (1939), p. 63.
[24] PRO E.190.646/9.
[25] PRO E.190.479/16; E.190.480/5.   [26] *Ibid.*

around Norwich and because several shippers are known to have lived there.[27]

A striking feature of the trade in roots from East Anglia at this time is the predominance of Dutch and Flemish shippers. Thirty of the thirty-six cargoes of roots that cleared Yarmouth in 1597/8 were consigned by aliens, and port officials struggled to record such names as Jan van Speagle, Peter Heibond, and Cornelius van Monterock. Several made more than one shipment: Markus Firmis made seven; William Vertigance and John Vitverangle made four each; and five others made two or three shipments each. William Rottengoose, who sent fifteen tons of carrots to London in December 1593, may be the gardener with the same name who died in St Stephen's parish, Norwich, in 1622 and who, under his alias of Vertngose, had a close of roots growing in Norwich in 1596. He may also be the same person as the William Vertigance referred to above. Francis van Dycke, whose inventory has already been mentioned, shipped twelve tons of carrots to London through Yarmouth in November 1593. Van Dycke, and other enterprising foreigners like him, not only pioneered the large-scale production of roots to feed the poor of Norwich but also saw the opportunity to supply London in times of dearth.[28]

Roots grown at this time were for human consumption. The note of the benefits to Norwich of roots in 1575 quoted above mentions only human beneficiaries, and other English references to the use of carrots, turnips, and parsnips, as well as cabbages, printed before the 1630s are concerned with human consumption. Roots are not mentioned as fodder in the various books published at this time on the care of horses or cattle, although some poultry were fed carrots.[29]

Thomas Cogan in a book on diet published in 1596 summed up the demand for carrots and parsnips thus: 'they are comon meate among the common people, all the time of Autumne, and chiefly uppon fish daies'. In December 1596 five men, one a cobbler,

[27] PRO E.190.479/16.
[28] PRO E.190.481/10; E.190.594/9; E.190.474/17; E.190.480/5; E.190.477/8; E.190.481/11; E.190.418/10.
[29] John Gerard, *The herbal, or general historie or plants* (1597), pp. 178, 873; John Parkinson, *Paradisi in sole* (1629), pp. 504, 506, 508; R. Trow-Smith, *A History of British Livestock Husbandry to 1700* (1957), pp. 234–58. *The Agrarian History of England and Wales*, IV, *1500–1640*, p. 194.

another a mason, were granted bail on a charge of illegally entering a close sown with roots by 'one Vertngose' in Norwich. Since it was midwinter and a time of rocketing grain prices, it is reasonable to suppose that these were poor men intent on stealing roots to eat. At around the same time a Shrewsbury gardener also was plagued with thefts from his garden; he despaired of the thieves who took his cabbages, 'those catterpillers doe never repent, untill they come to tyburne or the gallowes'.[30]

The immediate impact of roots sent to London in the years of dearth was not large: the 639 tons shipped in 1598/9 from East Anglia, assuming 2 lb for a meal for one adult, would have provided about four meals per head for each Londoner. In times of dearth, however, marginal sources of food assume some importance. The dearth years did demonstrate to gardeners a potential long-term market for roots in London and produced a quantitative and qualitative change in market gardening around the capital.

III

Market gardeners, both native and foreign-born, traded in and around London before the 1590s. A market for surplus produce from private gardens had existed near St Paul's in the fourteenth century and Stow recalled that a gardener named Cawsway worked land at Houndsditch towards the end of Henry VIII's reign and 'served the markets with herbs and roots'.[31]

Censuses and tax returns contain names of French and Dutch gardeners in the City of London and in various Southwark parishes from the 1570s. Foreign gardeners in the parishes on the Surrey bank of the Thames are found within the Returns of Aliens taken in 1618, although in none of the various returns in the sixteenth or early seventeenth centuries are more than a handful of French and Dutch Protestant refugees or their descendants listed as gardeners.[32]

[30] Richard Gardiner, *Profitable instructions for the manuring, sowing and planting of kitchen gardens* (1599), no pagination; Thomas Cogan, *The haven of health* (1596), pp. 61, 63, 74; Hudson and Tingey, 2, p. 196.

[31] H. T. Riley, *Memorials of London and London life* (1868), pp. 228–9; John Stow, *A survey of London* [1598], ed. Henry Morley (n.d.), p. 151.

[32] Cooper, 'Lists of Foreign Protestants and Aliens'; Kirk and Kirk, 'Returns of Aliens', *Hug. Soc. Ldn*, vol. X, pt I (1900); vol. X, pt II (1902); vol. X, pt III (1907).

Market gardening significantly increased around London soon after the years of high prices, and this was thought by writers in the middle of the seventeenth century to be due initially to the arrival of gardeners from the Low Countries. Samuel Hartlib in 1651 wrote:

> About 50 years ago, about which time Ingenuities first began to flourish in England; this Art of Gardening, began to creep into England, into Sandwich, Fulham, and other places.
>
> Some old men in Surrey, where it flourisheth very much at present; report that they knew the first Gardiners that came into those parts, to plant Cabages, Colleflowers, and to sowe Turneps, Carrets, and Parsnips, to sowe Raith [or early ripe] Rape, Pease, all which at that time were great rarities, we having few or none in England.[33]

Thomas Fuller echoes Hartlib; in 1662, writing of Surrey, he commented that commercial gardening was first introduced to England 'some seventy years since'. 'Since gardening hath crept out of Holland to Sandwich in Kent and thence into this county, where though they have given six pounds an Aker and upward, they have made their Rent, lived comfortably and set many people on work.'[34]

The role of both foreigners and roots in helping to avert hunger in the 1590s was seen clearly by Richard Gardiner in 1603:

> It is not unknowne to the Citty of London, and many other townes and cities on the sea coast, what great abundance of carrets are brought by forraine nations to this la[n]d, whereby they have received yeerly great summes of mony and commodities out of this land, and all by carelesnes of the people of this realme of England, which do not endevor themselves for their owne profits therein, but that this last dearth and scarcitie hath somewhat urged people to prove many waies for their better reliefe whereby I hope the benefit of Carret rootes are profitable.

The complaint that garden produce was unnecessarily imported was made also in the 1570s, and a mid-seventeenth-century writer thought that much of the garden produce consumed in the sixteenth century had been imported. Such evidence as survives of foreign shipments to London in Elizabeth's reign does not indicate large imports. In 1559/60 imported cabbages and turnips were valued at £157 16s 8d at 1588 Book of Rates values (for comparison ginger-

---

[33] Samuel Hartlib, *His legacie* (1651), pp. 8, 9.
[34] Thomas Fuller, *Worthies of England* (1662), p. 77.

bread valued at £165 was imported in the same year), while in 1599/
1600 cabbages worth £24 3s 4d and carrots worth £42 10s 0d were
imported to London from abroad. Gardiner may have confused
imports from abroad with coastal shipments by foreign refugees.[35]

John Norden detected, and sought to encourage, an increase in
carrot growing: 'And it begines to increase in all places of this
Realme, where discretion and industrie sway the mindes of the
inhabitantes: and I doe not a little marvaile, that husbandmen and
Farmers doe not imitate this, for their owne families, and to sell to
their poore neighbours, as in some places they begin, to their great
profit.'[36]

The terrible prospect of starvation amongst the poor brought an
immediate response in a hastily produced pamphlet by Sir Hugh
Platt, 'Sundrie new and Artificiall remedies against Famine' (1596).
Platt was a Londoner, and a lifelong student of agriculture and
gardening as well as a renowned inventor knighted for his work in
1605. His 'remedies' are a mixture of the practical and the out-
landish. Whilst giving no particular prominence to roots he included
a recipe for parsnip cakes which he thought might also be tried with
carrots or turnips. He also commented of turnips, 'there are both
good store and the price of them likewise very reasonable'.

IV

Three years after Platt's pamphlet, Richard Gardiner produced a
practical book on famine relief which advocated garden vegetables,
particularly carrots, as food for the poor. He was a wealthy dyer of
Shrewsbury who for many years was also a market gardener. He
wrote *Profitable instructions for the manuring sowing and planting
of kitchen gardens* when in his seventies. A pious and philanthropic
man, Gardiner was deeply conscious of the distress caused by harvest failures and believed that 'Amongst all the practises, knowl-
edges and experiences which ever I received from Gods mercies
intemporal blessings, I doe undoubtedly perswade myself, that my
practise and experience in Garden stuffe, or the good benefits

---

[35] Gardiner, *Profitable instructions*; Fuller, p. 77; Dietz, 'Port and Trade of
Elizabethan London', *London Record Society* (1972), appendix III; PRO, SP
12/8/31; E.190.11/1 & 3; William Harrison, *The Description of England*, ed.
George Edelen (New York, 1968), pp. 2763–4.
[36] Norden, p. 207.

therein, dooth best benefite, helpe and pleasure the generall number of people.' The book is a detailed, clear, and practical guide to the most common vegetables, for 'I rather desire to provide sufficient victuals for the poore and greatest number of people, to relieve their hungrie stomackes, then to pick dainty sallets, to provoke appetite to those that doe live in excesse.'[37]

Gardiner gives advice on growing vegetables, growing and saving seeds, and storing vegetables for some time before sale. He was concerned about the poor quality of much garden seed sold in England and advertised his own seeds at both retail and wholesale prices.[38]

He knew by recent experience the benefits of gardening to the poor and was earnest in his desire to convince his readers:

Beloved in Christ Jesus, I desire you to accept of this my good enterprise, in respect I desire the benefit of the commonwealth heerein, and is a speciall meane to helpe and relieve the poore, as by experience was manifest in the great dearth and scarcitie last past in the Countie of Salop and else where, for with lesse garden ground than foure ackers planted with Carrets, and above seaven hundreth close cabbages, there were many hundreds of people well refreshed thereby, for the space of twenty daies, when bread was wanting amongst the poore in the pinch or fewe daies before harvest. And many of the poore said to me, they had nothing to eate but onely carets and Cabedges, which they had of me for many daies, and but onelie water to drinke. They had commonly sixe ware poundes of small close Cabedges for a penny to the poore. And in this manner I did serve them, and they were wonderfull glad to have them, most humbly praising God for them.[39]

As to how the poor used carrots:

Carrets in necessitie and dearth, are eaten of the poore people, after they be well boyled, instead of bread and meate. Many people will eate Carrets raw, and doe digest well in hungry stomackes: they give good nourishment to all people, and not hurtfull to any, whatsoever infirmities they be diseased of, as by experience doth proove by many to be true . . . Therefore sow Carrets in your Gardens and humbly praise God for The[m], as for a singular and great blessing.[40]

---

[37] Gardiner, *Profitable instructions*.
[38] *Ibid.*   [39] *Ibid.*   [40] *Ibid.*

Although he wrote about recent events in Shrewsbury, it is easy to imagine London's poor consuming carrots in similar ways in the years of 'necessitie and dearth'.

V

Gardiner's analysis of the need for vegetables, particularly roots, to feed the poor and the commercial viability of supplying that need was shrewd and accurate, especially as far as London was concerned. The London poor were accustomed to supplementing their diet with vegetables. The cheap turnips recommended by Sir Hugh Platt in 1596 probably came from Hackney, where, according to Gerarde in 1597, the 'small turnip' grew 'in a sandie ground, and [was] brought to the Crosse in Cheapside by the women of that village to be solde'. The Hackney turnip was known to William Folkingham in 1610, but by that date the parish of Fulham appears to have been the major area of root production and probably accounted for much of the significant increase in the supply of roots to London markets.[41]

Norden included Fulham in his list of carrot-producing areas in 1607, and by 1610 the 'Fulham Parsnip' was well known. In 1616 the husbandmen and gardeners of Fulham were in dispute with the Gardeners Company of London over their unregulated growing and selling of 'Carretts Parsonipps and Turnupps' within the Company's jurisdiction.[42] The dispute was referred to a committee of Aldermen but was not finally resolved until 1633. By that time root growing had expanded into the neighbouring parishes of Chelsea and Kensington. It was carried on largely in the open fields of those parishes, where the husbandmen 'sowe seeds for parsnipps turnopps and carroitts and the like in their Comon fieldes whereof most of them they plough upp and others they digge up with the spade according to the nature and richness of their grounds And ye same fields some tymes sowe with Corne whereby their grounds are the more fruitful'. This is a concise description of farmer-gardening,

---

[41] Corporation of London, *City Reportories*, 33, f. 74, recto; Gerard, p. 178; Cogan, pp. 63, 74; Harrison, pp. 763–4; Stow, p. 15; Folkingham, p. 42.

[42] Norden, p. 207; Folkingham, p. 42; Corporation of London, *City Reportories*, 33, f. 74, recto.

and such rotations were employed by the Dutch settlers in Sandwich at this time.[43]

The Gardeners Company sought to restrict the output of these suburban husbandmen, and the committee found them to be within the six-mile radius of the City, where the Company's regulations held force. The husbandmen, however, won their case. They were not considered gardeners by the Aldermen because they worked the open fields with both spade and plough. 'And they use not to make knotts arbors walks or other such like workes which properly belong unto Gardiners.' Such doubtful reasoning would have excluded *all* kitchen gardeners within the Gardeners Company's jurisdiction. A more telling reason for the committee's decision was the importance of the contribution made by these parishes to London's food supply:

And we finde that by this manner of husbandry and ymployment of their grounds the Cittys of London Westminster and places adjacent are furnished with above fower and twenty Thousand loads yearly of Rootes as is credibly affirmed unto us and as wee believe whereby as well the poore as the ritch have plenty of that victuall at reasonable prices and wee are of the opinion that if the petitioners should bee brought into the Compasse of ye Gardiners patent and submitt to the orders and Charges of that Company much inconvenience would thereby ensue . . . whereby these Commodities could not bee brought to the Marketts in such abundance and plentifull a manner as now they are.

By the 1630s, therefore, the mass production of cheap roots west of London was of greater importance than the maintenance of the Gardeners Company's monopoly there.[44]

VI

Without too much conjecture, threads of innovation can be followed through the events so far described. The bulk production of roots by spade cultivation, either in gardens or as part of small mixed farms, was introduced to England by Protestant refugees from the Low Countries in the 1550s, 1560s, and 1570s. The market for these vegetables was initially other refugees in the large towns where they settled, but quickly the native poor learned to

[43] Corporation of London, *City Reportories*, 49, ff. 261–3.
[44] *Ibid.*

appreciate them. English husbandmen and gardeners copied the foreigners so that, by the early seventeenth century, many places in East Anglia grew roots. This innovation may have helped to lay the foundation for turnip growing as cattle fodder a few years after.

The dearth years of the 1590s gave an opportunity to enterprising East Anglian carrot growers, mostly still the foreign settlers, to seek a market amongst the poor of London. The high prices did not last, but the potential market for roots in London caused an influx of foreign gardeners into the suburbs. Their methods of production and crops were copied by the husbandmen of Fulham, who in turn were emulated by their neighbours in Chelsea and Kensington. Intensive vegetable growing was inserted into the open-field system of Fulham with no apparent bother and continued there until Victorian London extinguished cultivation with rows of villas.

Astute observers of agricultural change such as Norden and Gardiner noticed the process of innovation, saw its potential, and sought to encourage it. Gardening, the ability to produce a large amount of food from a small area of land, was recognized as one way of supplying large towns with minimal transport problems and wastage. High-yielding carrots and other roots might, they thought, solve the problem of what to feed the poor in years when grain harvests failed. Later in the century the potato replaced the carrot as the vegetable to end hunger; John Foster's 'Englands happiness increased, or a sure and easie remedy against all suceeding dear years; by a plantation of the roots called potatoes' is reminiscent of Gardiner's book with its directions for cultivation, recipes, and suggestions for cooking potatoes, and the enthusiastic advocacy of this vegetable 'for the good of the poorer sort'.

Gardiner claimed that many hundreds of the poor of Shrewsbury lived for many days on nothing but his carrots and cabbages. We have indirect evidence that some of the poor of London were reduced to similar fare. A prolonged diet of roots and cabbages as a soup or weak stew produces hunger-oedema; the limbs swell as tissue becomes waterlogged and eventually death results. John Parkinson, a London apothecary, wrote in 1629 that turnips, much eaten by the poor, 'engender moist and loose flesh'. This could be hunger-oedema, and could confirm that some people in London depended on roots for prolonged periods.

By the mid seventeenth century the success of gardening in supplying food in bulk for the poor of London was recognized and the task was then to encourage it elsewhere. Samuel Hartlib in 1651 wrote:

Briefly, for the advancement of this ingenuous calling, I only desire, that Industrious Gentlemen would be pleased to encourage some expert workmen into the places where they live, and to let them land at reasonable rate, and if they be poor and honest, to lend a little stock; they will soon see the benefit will rebound, not onely to themselves, but also to all their neighbours, especially the poor, who are not a little sustained by the Gardiners labours and Ingenuities.[45]

[45] Hartlib, p. 10; Gardiner, pp. [22], [23]; Drummond and Wilbraham, *The Englishman's Food*, pp. 106–9; Parkinson, p. 508.

12. 'Thirty years on': progress towards integration amongst the immigrant population of Elizabethan London

ANDREW PETTEGREE

During the course of the sixteenth century England experienced foreign immigration on a very significant scale. Between 1540 and 1600 something over fifty thousand men, women, and children crossed the Channel to settle in this country, mostly in London or in smaller towns and villages in Kent and East Anglia. Immigration of this sort was not an entirely new phenomenon; London, in particular, had played host to an established foreign community for several centuries, and foreign merchants and craftsmen were a familiar sight in the metropolis. But the sixteenth-century influx was different, and not just in its scale: for the first time the newcomers included a substantial proportion forced to leave their homelands as a result of religious persecution. These religious refugees gave the immigration a special character, and focussed contemporary attention on the issue in a new way. By the middle years of Elizabeth's reign the refugees, mostly Flemings and Walloons from the Spanish Low Countries though with a fair smattering of French Huguenots, were a substantial and permanent presence in the capital; in some provincial towns like Norwich and Canterbury they made up a third of the total population.[1]

The immigration provoked very different reactions from different sections of the native population. To the English authorities the refugee craftsmen were on the whole very welcome. The Privy Council saw in the exploitation of their skills the opportunity to restore faltering sections of the domestic economy, and the same

---

[1] The literature on the immigration is reviewed in my *Foreign Protestant Communities in Sixteenth Century London* (Oxford, 1986), pp. 4–7. See also W. J. C. Moens, *The Walloons and their Church at Norwich*, Huguenot Society Publications, 1 (London, 1887–8), I, pp. 44–5.

motive is evident in a series of initiatives undertaken by enlightened municipal authorities. Planned settlements of foreign workmen were negotiated by Sandwich in 1561 and Norwich in 1565, and by the end of the decade Stamford, Southampton, Maidstone, and Colchester also had colonies of privileged foreign workmen.[2] English craftsmen, however, regarded these developments with altogether less equanimity. The skills the newcomers brought with them were widely feared and their privileges deeply resented, and if the municipal authorities would not act to curb their competition the native craftsmen were occasionally prepared to take matters into their own hands. Serious riots against the immigrants were only narrowly averted in London in 1563 and in Norwich in 1570, and English artisan groups kept up a steady battery of complaints and petitions for much of Elizabeth's reign.[3]

How did the foreigners themselves react to such profoundly felt and occasionally violent antipathies? Initially at least, they tended to huddle together for mutual protection. Most of the refugees settled in areas with established concentrations of foreign residents, and in all the towns where they were sufficiently numerous they gathered together to form their own foreign churches. These churches quickly became the central institutions of the foreign communities, providing their members with a degree of practical help that went far beyond their ostensible religious purpose.[4] But it would be wrong, in any case, to exaggerate the degree of tension between native and foreign workers. Most of the refugees seem to have lived harmoniously enough amongst their English neighbours; or so at least they claimed in letters to their friends and relatives at home.[5] And in the course of time many of the foreigners gradually abandoned the protective network of their own kind and began to assimilate themselves into the host community. It is this process of

---

[2] Moens, pp. 17–19; Joan Thirsk, *Economic Policy and Projects: The Development of a Consumer Society in Early Modern England* (Oxford, 1978), pp. 43, 47; *Tudor Economic Documents*, ed. R. H. Tawney and E. Power (London, 1924), I, pp. 297–8; V. Morant, 'The Settlement of Protestant Refugees in Maidstone during the Sixteenth Century', *Econ. Hist. Rev.*, 2nd ser., IV (1951), 210–14.

[3] Moens, 27; *Foreign Protestant Communities*, pp. 282–95.

[4] *Foreign Protestant Communities*, ch. 7.

[5] *Tudor Economic Documents*, I, pp. 299–301, translated from H. Q. Janssen, 'De Hervormde vluchtelingen van Yperen in Engeland, geschetst naar hunne brieven', *Bijdragen tot de Oudheidkunde en Geschiedenis, inzonderheid van Zeeuwsch-Vlaanderen*, 2 (1857), 211–304.

assimilation which I wish briefly to examine here, though with the frank recognition that because of the nature of sixteenth-century documentation no very precise scientific investigation is possible. That immigrants eventually made their way into English society is clear enough: one has only to think of the great business and banking dynasties who trace their ancestry back to the foreign immigrants of the sixteenth and seventeenth centuries.[6] But examples of this sort are not very illuminating about the experience of the generality of foreign immigrants in the sixteenth century. How successfully had they negotiated the tensions and jealousies experienced by the first wave of refugees? More specifically, what progress had been made towards assimilation by the end of the century, a generation after the arrival of the first Elizabethan immigrants?

I

In attempting a tentative answer to this question I will be steering clear of expressions by contemporary English commentators. Although plays and petitions can furnish important evidence of how some sections of English society regarded their new neighbours, it is by no means easy to establish how typical were the fears and attitudes expressed in these contexts.[7] To see how the immigrants saw their own situation, it is necessary to seek out some form of personal expression on the part of the foreigners themselves. One possible source of such information is provided by their wills. Testamentary records have been much used of late by social and economic historians, sometimes for purposes for which they are not well suited. Wills can be disappointingly uninformative and routine, or occasionally misleading. But it remains the case that for an ordinary law-abiding member of the community the making of a will is often the only occasion on which he might review his life and circumstances, and record the names of those closest to him. By examining a number of these wills, taken from the two ends of Elizabeth's reign, a generation apart (together with what other information about the testators and their friends may be extracted

[6] W. Marston Acres, 'Huguenot Directors of the Bank of England', *Proceedings of the Huguenot Society of London*, XV (1933–7), 238–48.

[7] A. B. Feldman, 'Dutch Exiles and Elizabethan Playwrights', *Notes and Queries*, 196 (1951), 530–3.

from subsidy or other records), we may be able to gain some insight into the circumstances of the foreigners living in London, and how they had changed in the intervening thirty years. In particular, how far they were by the end of the century making their way into London society on their own merits, rather than merely enjoying the sufferance afforded to privileged outsiders.

With this in mind I have examined something over one hundred foreign wills, divided equally between the first and last decades of Elizabeth's reign.[8] The wills made by foreigners dying in London in the 1560s need not detain us long. For the most part they are short and relatively uninformative, often simply consigning the testator's soul to God and the unspecified remains of his worldly goods to wife and family. Where sums of money are mentioned they are mostly small, a legacy of ten or fifteen pounds being very much the exception. This is, perhaps, much as one would expect. The large proportion of the foreigners whose wills have survived from the first decade of Elizabeth's reign died in the two years 1563–4, victims of the plague epidemic which swept the capital during these years. The epidemic carried off 20 per cent of the city's inhabitants, and the immigrant community, crowded into the poorer quarters of the town, was particularly hard hit.[9] Amongst the victims were many who had arrived in London with the first wave of Elizabethan refugees, and had therefore been in England no more than a couple of years. These new arrivals had hardly had time to build up much in the way of wealth or property, and their wills reflect this. Even those testators who went to some trouble over the disposal of their goods often had little more to leave than clothing and household stuff; their relatives had to be content with the gift of a favourite cloak, a bed or a pair of sheets, occasionally a cup or ring.[10]

---

[8] Foreigners dying in London had their wills proved in a variety of jurisdictions. For the purposes of this comparison I have made use of wills proved in two London courts, the Commissary and Archdeaconry Courts (hereafter Comm. and Archd.) and the Prerogative Court of Canterbury (PCC) over two periods of five years (1563–7, 1593–7). Other foreign wills are to be found in the Archdeaconry Court of Surrey (which covered Southwark) and the peculiars of the Dean and Chapter of Westminster (which included part of the Liberty of St Martin-le-Grand, where large numbers of foreigners were settled).

[9] Paul Slack, *The Impact of Plague in Tudor and Stuart England* (London, 1985), pp. 147–64.

[10] See, for instance, the wills of Stephen Mulicum (Comm. 1563), Redulle Decarry, Rembalde Henedux (Comm. 1564), Jacobi Pittes, John Mongoyen, Leonard Nicholas (Archd. 1563).

Nevertheless these early wills, short and sparse though many of them are, are not wholly uninformative about the circumstances in which London's foreign residents lived at the beginning of the reign. In the first place, if we look beyond the main body of the will to the instructions at the end, it is striking how often those named as witnesses or executors include representatives of the foreigners' own churches. The churches' ministers frequently appear, presumably as a consequence of their attendance on the sick on their death beds, but so too do the elders and deacons, who are frequently charged with the responsibility of disposing of a man's goods, or supervising the upbringing of his children. This high level of involvement was partly a reflection of the special circumstances of the plague years. Both French and Dutch churches took emergency measures to cope with the sudden mortality crisis, appointing visitors of the sick and special officers to cope with the sudden rush of wills.[11] But the fact that so many of those who succumbed were new arrivals is also relevant. Arriving in a new and unfamiliar land, many of the newcomers had no friends and family to whom they could turn for help. They looked instead to the churches. These surviving wills provide eloquent testimony of how conscientiously the churches responded to their needs.

Interesting, too, is the considerable number of these early wills which mention goods or property left abroad. This was because many of those who had come to England at the beginning of Elizabeth's reign did not necessarily envisage remaining on a permanent basis. They did not therefore take the trouble to sell up their continental goods before coming to England, and many had still not done so when the plague carried them off. This applied not only to merchants (who had an occupational reason for leaving property and stock abroad) but men like the shoemaker Francis Derickson from Delft and the Brabant tailor James Isacke.[12] Others left their small stock of possessions in England to be disposed of amongst their friends back home, a reminder that emigration often involved considerable family dislocation and personal hardship. For exiles separated from normal kinship ties the churches had an important function, recreating a sense of community in a strange environment.

There were, of course, even in the 1560s, exceptions to this

---

[11] *Foreign Protestant Communities*, pp. 198, 206–9.
[12] Francis Derickson, Comm. 1564; James Isacke, Archd. 1564.

general pattern. The plague of 1563 also carried off a number of foreigners who had been in England a considerable time, some of them survivors of a foreign community which predated even the first wave of religious immigration of the 1540s. Several of these longer-term residents had built up substantial property by the time of their deaths, and their wills form a marked contrast to those of their recently arrived compatriots. These wills tend to be longer and more detailed, revealing not only greater prosperity but also the first indications of a move away from exclusive dependence on their own kind. Some mention an English friend or neighbour, or a gift to their local parish church, or leave instructions for the future bestowal of a lease.

Thus Garrett Williamson, who settled in one of the strangers' favourite haunts, the liberty of St Martin-le-Grand, some time before 1537, had acquired considerable property there by the time of his death. This he left to his wife, together with that due to him from his family back in Antwerp. The friends who witnessed his will were mostly English citizens, presumably neighbours, together with the local rector.[13] Other of these longer-term residents similarly made careful provision for the disposal of real property. The brewer Arnold Lothbury left his son two tenements within the precinct of St Katherine by the Tower, Henry Leke, a Southwark brewer, also left his property to his son, but Leke had prospered sufficiently to allow him to diversify his business interests: in his will he described himself as 'citizen and clothworker of London'.[14] Perhaps the most interesting will in this group was that left by Anthony Anthony, another brewer settled outside the city in the parish of St Botolph Without Aldgate. Anthony left a substantial estate, and his will made provision for gifts to his Livery Company and the poor of the parish as well as several English friends and business associates. Like Leke, Anthony had gone on from his brewhouse to greater things: according to his will he was now 'Surveyor General of the Ordinance of our Sovereign Lady the Queen's Majesty'. Anthony provides an almost perfect model of an integrated alien. By the time of his death he was playing an active role in his local community; his

---

[13] PCC 1563. See also *Returns of Aliens dwelling in the City and Suburbs of London*, ed. R. E. G. and E. F. Kirk, Huguenot Society Publications, 10 (London, 1900–8), I, p. 17.

[14] Henry Leke, PCC 1563; Arnold Lothbury, PCC 1565.

will differs very little from that of any other successful London craftsman dying about this time. His overseers and witnesses are all local English citizens and he even has a 'fowling handgun' and cross-bow (which he left to his servant).[15] Such affluence is, as has been demonstrated, in marked contrast to the circumstances of most foreigners dying in London in this decade.

II

These occasional examples of foreigners whose circle of acquaintance had moved beyond their own immigrant community we will find repeated many times over when we turn to consider the foreign wills which survive from the 1590s. By this time many more foreigners had been in England for a generation or more. The survivors of the plague epidemic of 1563 were reinforced by a further substantial influx in the late 1560s and 1570s, and by the last decade of the reign many of these newcomers had also married, settled, and prospered. Nevertheless, it is worth emphasizing before we go any further the large measure of continuity between these two groups of wills, for many of those from the last decade were remarkably similar to those we have already described. Many foreigners still died leaving only the simplest testamentary instructions for the disposal of their goods. And a considerable number continued not to look beyond the narrow circle of their immigrant friends in their dispositions: when we look at the names of those appointed executors or summoned to act as witnesses we see how firmly anchored in their own communities these men remained.

The foreign churches still figured largely, through their ministers and elders, amongst those required to witness wills, but for executors and overseers (a crucial function, for overseers undertook to protect the portion of under-age children) testators now more usually looked to their own friends or workmates. Where it has proved possible to identify those named in this capacity they usually fall into one of these two categories: neighbours would usually witness a will, but business associates were sometimes better placed to assist a man's widow in winding up his affairs. Just occasionally friends named seem to fall into neither category, and it seems that some of these may have been acquaintances from the

[15] PCC 1563.

time when both they and the testator still lived on the Continent.[16] None of this should surprise us very much. Uprooted from their village or town communities abroad, these refugees were not unnaturally eager to recreate a secure environment in their new homes. For most this meant building a protective circle of friends, relatives, and business partners among those who shared their experience of dispossession and exile. Many, too, seem to have been able to re-establish contact with familiar faces from their former home communities: one happy consequence of the sheer scale of the exodus brought about by the religious persecution.

Nevertheless, alongside this impressive evidence of a continuing sense of community, these wills from the 1590s also provide plentiful indications that many of the foreigners had by this time found the confidence to look beyond their own communities in their personal and professional relationships. Such confidence often went hand in hand with worldly success, so it is significant that by the 1590s many of London's foreign residents had begun to enjoy a level of prosperity inconceivable to the vast majority of their compatriots in the 1560s. An indication of this is provided by the sums left to the foreign churches as gifts for the poor-chest in the two periods. Most foreign testators left something to be distributed among the immigrant poor by the churches' deacons, but in the 1560s this might be as little as 5s or a purely nominal shilling. Many, no doubt, could not afford more: certainly at this time £10 represented an exceptional windfall for the church. In the 1590s, in contrast, gifts of this order were commonplace. Most gave between £5 and £15, and 40s was really the meanest sum that could decently be given.

III

This change did not necessarily represent any greater generosity on the part of these testators; indeed, the smaller sums donated in the 1560s may have represented a larger proportion of the total estate. For by the 1590s some foreigners had amassed very considerable fortunes. The merchant Gilles Hueriblock left the poor of the Dutch

---

[16] Perrett Berger (Comm. 1594), John Angele (Archd. 1596), Giles de Coster (Archd. 1597) for examples of neighbours appearing as executors or witnesses; Engelbrecht Kempen (Comm. 1594), Cornelius Peterson, William van Hees (Archd. 1597) all appointed men from their own trades as overseers or executors.

church £15, but his other testamentary arrangements reveal that he was worth well in excess of £1,000 at the time of his death.[17] Sebastian Bonfoye left ten marks to the French church, but he too was able to pass on more than £1,000 in cash and goods to his wife and children. It is worth noting too that Bonfoye was a craftsman (a 'featherdresser') rather than a merchant: by the end of the century it was not just the big international merchants who could accumulate wealth on a substantial scale.[18] Brewers, of course, had always been among the foreign elite, and the Dutch church stood to gain £125 from the will of Peter Frances, a Southwark brewer, if his daughter predeceased him. Unfortunately if the girl survived the church would get only 50s.[19] Such contingency arrangements were not uncommon, but even without having to rely on eventualities of this sort the foreign churches were beginning to benefit from some bequests of a very substantial nature. The death of the Dutch merchant Jan van der Beke in 1597 brought the foreign churches a total of almost £300 in gifts to the poor, the ministers, and their educational institutions. Van der Beke had been a stalwart member of the Dutch church for thirty years and the churches' educational efforts were particularly dear to him: his largest gift, £100, was given to allow poor students sponsored by the consistory to complete their studies at the university.[20]

The substantial sums mentioned in these wills provide impressive evidence of the foreign community's growing economic power. Most wills, however, gave little impression of the total value of the estate, as the bulk of the property would be divided between a widow and surviving children without any indication of how much they would receive. It is fair to assume that the smaller legacies to friends and relatives listed in detail would usually have represented only a small proportion of the testator's total worth. Nevertheless, these other incidental bequests can also be quite revealing, for even where testators confine themselves to gifts of household goods or

---

[17] PCC 1594.
[18] PCC 1593. A featherdresser was a dealer in feathers and plumes.
[19] PCC 1594.
[20] Comm. 1597. The students went either to Cambridge or Leiden. The previous year the French church had received an equally large bequest from the will of the Spanish-born confectioner Balthazar Sanchez. Sanchez specified that his legacy should be used to establish a regular income of £30 per annum for the French poor-house. PCC 1596, cited in W. K. Jordan, *The Charities of London, 1480–1660* (London, 1960), p. 145.

small keepsakes there is a perceptible change in the quality of these gifts since the first Elizabethan decade. Then friends and relatives had usually to be content with gifts of clothing or humble household furniture. By the 1590s some foreigners were able to distribute some very handsome artefacts.

Thus the widowed Sarah Bien left her kinsfolk silver plate and cutlery along with her rings and clothing (which included two of the newly fashionable ruffs).[21] Another widow, Susanna Johnson, also carefully distributed her clothes among her friends, reserving for her brother her most prized possessions, her silver beads and pearl ring. Mistress Johnson was evidently a keen seamstress; one friend, perhaps a companionable neighbour with whom she had whiled away some happy evening hours, was left her sewing cushion and silver 'tuckehook'.[22] These homely widows were particularly careful over the distribution of their household goods, but male testators also on occasions took pains to ensure that their most treasured possessions went to an appreciative home. Sebastian Bonfoye, for instance, gave each of his daughters a cup, one of mother of pearl set in silver, the other a magnificent vessel, 'being a Nut with the story of Job fooled and garnished with silver and gilt and having a cover . . . to my daughter Elizabeth Lothard wife of Owen Lothard'.[23]

The merchant John Wiet distributed among his friends silver, plate, and his gold ring. One merchant friend was to receive a silver goblet and a Turkey carpet; the daughter of another a pair of virginals.[24] Since the foreign immigrants had made such an important contribution to the development of a consumer society in England it was entirely appropriate that they should also have shared in its fruits. Wills like that of Wiet demonstrate that the more prosperous of them enjoyed a standard of living available to few Englishmen by the end of the century.

We may remember that Sebastian Bonfoye's cherished coconut cup was to go to his daughter Elizabeth, the wife of Owen Lothard. He, clearly, was not a member of the immigrant community. Such an alliance between a prosperous immigrant family and a local citizen was increasingly common by the 1590s: the fifty wills examined here yield at least a dozen examples. Bonfoye's case is not untypical; given that he was a £25 subsidy man and worth in total well over

---

[21] Comm. 1593. [22] Comm. 1594. [23] PCC 1593. [24] Comm. 1597.

£1,000, his daughter was a very desirable match. Elizabeth would certainly have nothing to fear from parental prejudice as her father had himself married an Englishwoman.[25] A number of other testators in this sample had also taken English wives or husbands, among them Arnold Taunt and Elizabeth van Brechte. Taunt attended the parish church, and had established a circle of mainly English friends. Van Brechte, who had married two Englishmen in turn, had also drifted away from her foreign roots, though her will reveals that she had brought into her new family considerable property which she owned in her own right in Antwerp.[26]

In the case of other foreign immigrants it was the marriage of a daughter or niece which enabled them to breach the citadel of English society. Lewis Sohier, a religious exile of the first Elizabethan generation, was proud thirty years later to remember in his will his niece Judith, married to an English haberdasher: she was to receive a silver beaker and six silver spoons. Perrett Berger the widow of a Norman coppersmith, left £6 to her nephew Christopher Dunn.[27] The French merchant John Verie, another religious refugee, had seen his daughter married to one Thomas White. To this respectable son-in-law and his English grandson he left the most potent symbols of his new allegiance, his picture of the Queen and copy of the Queen's arms.[28] For London citizens such eminently respectable immigrant families must have represented a good match, particularly if they brought with them, like the daughter of Nicholas Remy, a sizeable marriage portion. Remy, a silkweaver of thirty years' residence in England who employed at least five men in his business in Colman Street, left his daughter two silver beakers as a memento 'over and above that which she hath been by me already sufficiently advanced with'.[29]

---

[25] *Returns*, II, p. 252. *Returns of Strangers in the Metropolis, 1593, 1627, 1635, 1639*, ed. I. Scouloudi, Huguenot Society Publications, 57 (London, 1985), p. 152.

[26] Both PCC 1595. See also *Returns*, II, pp. 50, 284.

[27] Sohier, Comm. 1597, *Returns*, I, p. 304, III, p. 355; *Letters of Denization and Acts of Naturalization for Aliens in England, 1509–1603*, ed. W. Page, Huguenot Society Publications, 8 (London, 1893), p. 223. Berger, Comm. 1594, *Returns*, II, p. 2.

[28] Comm. 1594, *Returns*, I, pp. 289, 454, II, p. 257.

[29] Comm. 1596. *Returns*, I, p. 397, II, pp. 81, 191. *Returns of Strangers, 1593 etc.*, p. 203.

IV

Such marriage alliances represented the most obvious means by which the more prosperous members of the foreign community integrated themselves into the host community. But not all foreign residents could rely on a marriageable daughter to secure them their entrée into English society. Others, instead, built up their network of contacts more slowly through their business and social dealings. At this level integration was a much more subtle process, but some examples may still be culled from this sample of foreign wills. The brewer Peter Frances, for instance, has already been mentioned in connection with his gift to the Dutch church. But his will was witnessed by two English neighbours, and the overseers of his daughter's inheritance were also two English friends, the drapers Clement and Robert Bucke. Frances also left a small gift for his partner, again an Englishman.[30] Two others who appointed English overseers were Lewis Sohier and Gilles Hueriblock, in the case of Hueriblock his son-in-law John West, in Sohier's case the London Grocer Nicholas Warren.[31] To name an Englishman in such a position of trust suggests a bond of affection which went beyond a casual business acquaintance. If many of London's residents still looked to friends amongst their fellow countrymen to perform these tasks, others had already been able to forge other significant relationships outside the immigrant community.

The basis of these relationships was undoubtedly, again, the foreigners' economic success. Several of their wills make provision for the future bestowal of leases of houses or business premises, one of the best indicators of successful integration into the local economic structure. Among those who mention such leases were Sebastian Bonfoye and Peter Francis, who were certainly two of the best-integrated members of the foreign elite. So too was Marie de Helencourt, a widow who at her death in 1595 was able to pass on to her daughter property built up by her husband over a long career in England. Together with a house and lease her will recalled a debt due to her by one Nicholas Darcy, presumably an English business acquaintance of her deceased husband.[32] That the foreigners prospered by trading with their *English* neighbours deserves

---

[30] PCC 1594.   [31] PCC 1594, Comm. 1597.
[32] Archd. 1595. *Returns of Strangers, 1593 etc.*, p. 182.

emphasis, for this was not universally recognized at the time. In the 1570s it had been frequently objected against the foreigners by native craftsmen that they deliberately excluded Englishmen from their business dealings; that they would buy and sell only with other foreigners and jealously guarded the secrets of their superior techniques. By the last decade of the reign this was clearly not the case (if indeed it ever had been). Here we do not need to rely exclusively on evidence from wills: a survey of the London foreign population in 1593 confirmed that 1,500 foreign householders employed between them more than 1,600 English workmen, a convincing rebuttal of the charge of business exclusivity.[33]

V

By the end of the century, then, London's foreign community had an increasingly settled and prosperous air about it. A high proportion of its more affluent members had developed fruitful contacts with their English neighbours, and even among the less well-off the growing number of children born in England suggested that the process of peaceful assimilation would quicken as time went on. That is not to say that the immigrant community had by the end of the century lost all the characteristics of the first generation. On the contrary, the foreigners' own churches still played a prominent role in their community life, and their wills are not without other reminders that many of the immigrants first arrived in England as penniless refugees. Prosperity and the passing of years seem not to have diminished their religious ardour. Thus Rene Tardiffe left £30 to be given to the town of Geneva, to be employed there 'towards the aid and entertainment of poor scholars studying in Divinity'.[34] Few wills mention a testator's books, but the widow Anthoatt Lowdell left her Great Bible and book of Martyrs to her son, and Francis de Brulle wished her daughter to have 'one book of Theodore Beza sur la resurrection'.[35] These wills also contain the occasional reminder of the pain and dislocation that exile might entail. The Lady Margaret van Lithewelde died in sadly reduced circumstances, very conscious that she was unable to reward those dear to her in an appropriate manner. Nevertheless, she left clear

---

[33] *Returns of Strangers, 1593 etc.*, p. 90.
[34] PCC 1594.   [35] Comm. 1594 (De Brulle), 1597 (Lowdell).

instructions that her dispossessed children should still 'be brought up and instructed in the true religion and for nothing in the world to send them into the Low Countries by their kinsfolk for to be instructed in papistry, for it were better to suffer them to go begging their bread than to have such a bringing up'.[36]

Grief and hardship of this nature are, though, perceptibly less evident in these wills than in those of twenty years before. By the 1590s some of the wounds of the religious wars and persecution had begun to heal. With the fall of Antwerp in 1585 and the accession of Henry IV in France those who wished to return home had either done so or, in the case of Protestants from the Southern Netherlands, reconciled themselves to the impossibility of doing so. The London community, in consequence, had taken on a much more settled air. But this was still, as these wills have served to illustrate, a community very much in a state of transition. Whereas some foreign residents, particularly the more prosperous, had begun to put down roots in the English community, others still spent most of their time among those who shared their background and experiences, that is other immigrants. Sometimes this transitional quality is evident in a single will. Thus Engelbrecht Kempen, a survivor of the first wave of Elizabethan refugees, continued until his death in 1594 to attend the Dutch church, of which he was an elder. The overseers of his will were two Dutch friends, both tailors like himself. But Kempen had married an Englishwoman, and his five children were all English-born. They would have the chance to complete the transition into the English community that their father had only partially effected.[37]

It would be interesting to pursue the fate of Kempen's children and that of other second-generation immigrants by examining a further sample of foreign wills a generation later, say from the 1620s. That task unfortunately lies outside the scope of a short piece of this sort, but it is worth, finally, making one further observation about the foreign community at the end of Elizabeth's reign. And that is this: that although the process of assimilation was already well underway, a remarkable proportion of the immigrant community retained some connection with the foreign churches. This continuing sense of identification was not inconsistent with the

---

[36] Archd. 1594.
[37] Comm. 1594. *Returns*, II, p. 89; *Returns of Strangers, 1593 etc.*, p. 187.

integratory process described above. Many of those who had made considerable progress towards assimilation into the host community still remembered the foreign churches when they came to make their wills, and these included some, like Arnold Taunt and Lewis Sohier, who had not been to the French or Dutch church for many years. These two veteran members of the immigrant community had both attended local parish churches for at least twenty years before they came to write their wills, but they still remembered the foreign poor along with the native poor of their respective parishes.[38]

Examples of this sort make the point that a continuing sense of identification with the institutions of the foreign community did not prevent foreigners making a real contribution to English society as a whole. I have argued elsewhere against seeing the foreign churches as a factor inhibiting peaceful integration.[39] On the contrary, the churches played an important role in helping the immigrant newcomers adapt to their new environment, and in defusing possible points of tension with the local population. This was not always well understood at the time, least of all by Archbishop Laud, who in the 1630s made a determined effort to break the power of the foreign churches. The churches, deprived of friends at Court, resorted to passive resistance, and in the event were able to outlast their formidable adversary. With the fall of Laud their privileges were once again guaranteed, and the further political upheavals of the mid seventeenth century left the foreign communities comparatively unscathed.[40]

This is not a bad note on which to end. By the last decade of Elizabeth's reign London's foreign community had come a long way since the first religious refugees flooded into England in the 1540s and 1560s. Many of those who settled in the capital had prospered beyond all expectation, and although by the end of the century the process was far from complete, had begun also to put down roots in the local community. The foreign community as a whole had acquired an impressive stability and resilience. The immigration of the second half of the sixteenth century made a considerable con-

---

[38] PCC 1595, *Returns*, II, p. 50 (Taunt); Comm. 1597, *Returns*, III, p. 355 (Sohier).
[39] *Foreign Protestant Communities*, pp. 299–305.
[40] *Ibid.*, pp. 298–9. H. R. Trevor-Roper, *Archbishop Laud* (London, 1940), pp. 197–204.

tribution to the transformation of the English domestic economy, particularly through the introduction of new skills and manufacturing techniques. There can be no doubt that English towns, and ultimately the whole of society, were the principal beneficiaries of this process. But it is heartening to think that the immigrants themselves, at least on the evidence of their wills, were also able to share in the new prosperity generated as a result of their industry and endurance.

13. No English Calvados? English distillers and the cider industry in the seventeenth and eighteenth centuries

JOHN CHARTRES

Several themes have recurred in Joan Thirsk's many studies of the process of improvement and innovation in the early modern economy. Her work has stressed the possibility of rapid and dramatic developments in both industry and agriculture from relatively small and perhaps unpromising beginnings. Small farmers and artisans in both town and village showed a surprising capacity to adopt new crops or products during the sixteenth and seventeenth centuries. If at first many were inferior goods, their supply nonetheless created employment and served also to both broaden and deepen the market for consumer goods. When, as with the new draperies or metallurgy, imported human capital was added to the process, or, as in the paper or linen industries after 1650, protective tariffs were provided in support, large-scale import substitution became possible, and the basis for long-term industrial growth was established. Joan Thirsk's analysis of the developing industrial 'projects' and of the agrarian improvement of seventeenth-century England is thus linked directly with the process of economic expansion well beyond 1700, and to the functions of the home market and of domestic production in the growth ultimately underpinning industrialization.[1]

One such industry is considered here, appropriately one that processed a variety of agricultural products into a premium consumer good. The new English distilling industry of the seventeenth century thus unified the agrarian and the industrial elements of this Thirsk model. It was an industry serving a new taste, for spirits consumed as beverages; at first a foreign, probably Dutch, good, it was

[1] Joan Thirsk, *Economic Policy and Projects: The Development of a Consumer Society in Early Modern England* (Oxford, 1978), passim.

gradually subjected to import substitution from the beginning of the seventeenth century, and then dosed liberally with protection at its end; from the late 1680s it was promoted as one of many props for the oppressed English cereal farmer; and, in the case of cider, it offered a means to improvement for an unconsidered farm product.[2] The following study attempts to link all of these elements in answering the question posed in the title: why, in a land with an apparently plenty of apple trees, a cider spirit, an English Calvados, was not a major element of the reign of Queen Gin.[3]

I

The consumption of distilled liquors as beverages in England dates only from the later sixteenth century. Before then, alcohol in this form was a feature of the apothecary's shop, but its use for purposes other than as an input to medicines and tinctures can only be documented after 1580. Even in Scotland, where the tradition of drinking uisge beatha was older, it was only from the middle of the sixteenth century, with the introduction of the worm still, that output began to expand significantly.[4] In this chronology of the shift of strong waters from the apothecary's shop to the public house Britain's experience was not unusual. Braudel's survey of the use of spirits showed a similar timing of the change over much of western Europe. It was only in the last years of the sixteenth century and the early part of the seventeenth that the taste for this luxury good spread, primarily through the promotional commerce of the Dutch.[5]

As Joan Thirsk herself has noted, there is evidence for England of the spread of the trade after 1580. In 1593, significantly a plague year, the first major monopoly patent for the production of spirits was granted to Richard Drake. Through the monopoly, it was

---

[2] *Ibid.*, pp. 93, 95, 97; J. Thirsk (ed.), *The Agrarian History of England and Wales*, V (Cambridge, 1985), II, pp. 334–8.

[3] From the play by Jack Juniper, *The Deposing and Death of Queen Gin, with the Ruin of the Duke of Rum, Marquee de Nantz, and the Lord Sugarcane etc., An Heroic Comi-Tragical Farce* (London, 1736). The obituary was premature. I am indebted to Negley Harte for posing the question.

[4] Michael S. Moss and John R. Hume, *The Making of Scotch Whisky* (Edinburgh, 1981), pp. 31–2.

[5] F. Braudel, *Capitalism and Material Life, 1400–1800* (Glasgow, 1974), pp. 170–2.

hoped to eliminate the manufacture of unwholesome spirits and vinegars, and the temptation to produce prophylactic 'plague waters' from 'hogwash and dregs and the washings of coolbacks' would be overcome.[6] As with so many of the projects of the 'scandalous phase' of monopoly, the grant soon proved more an indirect tax than a true patent, and it was challenged in 1596 and in the Commons debate of 1601. The latter debate produced the clearest evidence for the consumption of aqua vitae as a beverage. The burgess for Warwick, Mr Spicer, complained of the restrictions on the sale of spirits in his town through the abuses of the patentees and their agents. In a memorable statement prefacing the proclamation setting aside this and the other monopolies Cecil provided proof of the transition of spirits into a beverage:

> I say therefore, there shall be a Proclamation general through the Realm, to notify Her Majesties Resolution in this behalf. And because you may eat your Meats more Savoury than you have done, every Man shall have Salt as cheap as he can buy it, or make it, freely without danger of that Patent, which shall be persesently Revoked. The same Benefit shall they have which have cold Stomacks, both for Aqua-Vitae, and the like: And they which have weak Stomacks shall have Vinegar and Aleagar set at Liberty . . . [7]

Though confined by supply and price to a limited market, foreign and domestic spirits were well established as consumer goods in England by the beginning of the seventeenth century.

Substantial growth seems to have taken place in home production between this first restriction of monopoly and the second in the 1620s. Joan Thirsk's study of the trade indicated that by 1621 home output had grown to the extent that 200 distillers with 5,000 employees were operating in London alone. Both figures appear exaggerated, stemming as they do from the early skirmishing that led in 1629 to the grant of a charter to the Distillers Company of London. Exports did indicate the continued progress of the domestic industry: by 1662/3 these reached between 34,000 and

---

[6] J. Strype, *A Survey of London* (London, 1720), book V, pp. 236–7; Thirsk, *Policy and Projects*, pp. 93–6.

[7] *Tudor Economic Documents*, ed. R. H. Tawney and E. Power (London, 1924), II, pp. 271, 290.

60,000 gallons.[8] While there was clearly some growth in home production before 1660, imports rose still more quickly, and to London alone had reached 77,000 gallons by 1637.[9] However, the home market for spirits both imported and home-produced remained small until the last quarter of the seventeenth century. The limited returns of the first year of the Excise in 1654/5 indicated that up to 80,000 gallons of spirits were legitimately consumed in that year.[10] Even if this figure approximates to the truth, it is nonetheless minute by comparison with the average of spirits excised annually for sale after the take-off in consumption in the 1670s and 1680s. The average quantity of spirits excised for sale in England and Wales, 1684–8, exceeded 533,000 gallons.[11] Spirits consumption, as indicated by these very fragmentary data, did begin to grow from the second quarter of the seventeenth century, but was only reaching levels indicative of a more generalized demand in its last two decades.

While Thirsk was correct to stress that some part of this market was supplied from home production, before 1689 the bulk came from abroad, and consisted primarily of French brandies. This pattern changed dramatically after 1688. The combination of war with France and the consequent liberation of spirits production from the restrictions of the Distillers Company monopoly permitted the rapid development of home substitutes for these imports.[12] By the end of the century the taste for spirits as beverages had become sufficiently established to generate a wartime industry in *ersatz* products, much as indicated by Stout's autobiography under the year 1689: 'Also abundance of stills were set up for extracting good

---

[8] Thirsk, *Policy and Projects*, p. 97. The discrepancy arises from one figure, cited by Thirsk, for exports to Africa, '204 tuns £8,160'. This values these spirits at half that of all the others listed, and suggests that 'tuns' should in fact be pipes, and on this basis the figure should be just under 34,000 gallons.

[9] A. M. Millard, 'The Import Trade of London, 1600–1640', University of London Ph.D. thesis, 1956, table 13, based upon PRO E 190/41/5 and E 190/42/1. I am indebted to Dr W. B. Stephens for this reference.

[10] Brit. Lib., Lansdowne MS 1215, fol. 7. The returns included large sums for 'strong waters' under the heading 'London' and under 'spirits' for the rest of England and Wales. Quantities have been estimated from the totals of duty received.

[11] Custom House MS, 'Excise Revenue Accounts, 1662–1827', 255–6.

[12] Thirsk (ed.), *Agrarian History*, V, II, p. 335. Liberty for all to distil, irrespective of existing charters or letters patent, was granted by the Act 2 William & Mary, session 2, c. IX, 'for encouraging the distilling of brandy and spirits from corn'.

and strong spirrits from mault, melosses, fruit and other materials, instead of French brandy.'[13] Although the consumption of distilled liquors had been growing since the late sixteenth century, its diffusion to a broad domestic market seems to have been confined to the last decades of the seventeenth, and until the war with France, the bulk of supplies had come from abroad. The initial impetus to the great development of the industry after 1688 was therefore substitutive.

II

If in 1688 the history of distilling in England had been relatively short, its future was to be very remarkable indeed. From the 1680s to the 1750s spirits were the principal dynamic element in the home market for drink. Almost alone among the alcoholic beverages available in the years before 1750, spirits exhibited significant increases in per capita consumption. It is possible that the available data to support this view are defective, derived as they are from the records of the Excise and from the Inspector General's ledgers (for retained imports of wine), and that they seriously understate the levels of consumption of other drinks. This seems unlikely: historians are generally agreed as to the efficiency of the Excise in England, and any under-assessment may be assumed to apply in equal proportions to all home-produced goods. Wine imports naturally understate the extent of home consumption, the smuggler supplementing legitimate supplies by an unknown amount. As will be clear from the following analysis, it was unlikely that even the most active contrabander could have altered the main trends in drink consumption very radically. All beverages, both alcoholic and non-alcoholic, were equally liable to adulteration, and for this no allowance can presently be provided. With these reservations, the trends in drink supplies are provided in Table 1 as decadal averages, 1684–9 to 1760–9.

These absolute quantities employ radically different units of measurement, and do not reveal the changing patterns of consumption with sufficient clarity. It is hard to determine the degree to which the gallon of beer, the gallon of proof spirits, and the gallon

---

[13] *The Autobiography of William Stout of Lancaster, 1665–1752*, ed. J. D. Marshall (Manchester, 1967), p. 94.

Table 1. *Quantities of principal categories of drink excised for sale or imported, averages by decades, 1684–1769 (000 gallons)*

Years	British spirits	Foreign spirits	Strong beer	Small beer	Wines imported	Cider
1684–9	539.2	1,363.0	173,920	83,866	n.d.	4,878.3
1690–9	843.3	79.2	129,406	82,591	n.d.	4,678.9
1700–9	1,464.0	107.6	128,390	79,128	3,943.5	3,876.5
1710–19	2,262.4	115.4	123,347	73,350	4,803.6	3,683.1
1720–9	3,796.1	442.8	132,991	79,319	5,943.9	4,249.0
1730–9	5,139.4	870.9	129,874	75,964	5,513.8	4,580.5
1740–9	7,200.4	776.5	126,511	73,181	3,877.8	4,580.5
1750–9	4,477.9	1,215.8	134,532	70,211	3,841.2	4,205.8
1760–9	2,374.9	1,718.6	137,178	65,891	4,328.1	4,377.4

Sources: Custom House, 'Excise Revenue Accounts', pp. 255–6, 232; 'Quantities, Rates & Amounts of Excise Duties, 1684–1798', pp. 2–9; and 'An Account of the Quantities of the Several Articles which have been charged with Excise Duties in each year', pp. 38–9. Wine imports have been calculated from the figures in E. B. Schumpeter, *English Overseas Trade Statistics, 1697–1808* (Oxford, 1960). All figures are in wine gallons, except for the beers, which are in the ale measure. Barrels of both strong and small beer have been converted according to the London beer barrel of 36 gallons, and may overstate gallonage slightly because nationally barrels of 32 and 34 gallons were in common use.

of cider were equivalents. For this reason an alternative approach to the description of trends has been adopted, employing a crude adaptation to eighteenth-century circumstances of the modern 'units of alcohol' approach. Here, therefore, these Excise and Customs data have been transformed by assuming an equivalence between the standard units in which all these alcoholic beverages were retailed in this period: unlike the modern 'unit of alcohol' approach the method in no way attempts to assess alcohol equivalence or risk factors. Thus, the five principal beverages have been transformed into their standard retail units: wine in wine pints; strong and small beer in quarts; spirits in quarterns; and cider in wine pints. The results are presented at five-year intervals, 1685–1770, in Table 2, and plotted on an annual basis for 1685–1785 in Figure 5. Although not an issue for direct consideration here, the community level of alcohol consumption indicated by the final column of Table 2, total units deflated by reference to Wrigley and Schofield's population estimates, was sufficiently high to lend real substance to impressionistic assessments of the extent of drink-

Table 2. *Estimated percentage share of the market by principal beverages (units of alcohol)*

Year	Wine	Strong beer	Small beer	Spirits	Cider	Units per capita
1685	n.a.	61.8	27.3	5.6	5.3	209.6
1690	n.a.	60.3	34.0	2.5	3.1	227.7
1695	n.a.	53.8	35.6	3.7	6.9	180.8
1700	5.3	52.6	32.9	5.0	4.2	171.7
1705	n.a.	56.3	34.5	5.3	3.8	188.3
1710	3.5	53.2	33.1	8.0	2.2	175.4
1715	4.4	52.7	31.0	7.8	4.1	189.1
1720	3.9	59.4	25.5	8.5	2.7	181.1
1725	4.3	50.1	29.1	12.3	4.3	212.9
1730	3.7	50.4	30.0	14.0	1.8	201.5
1735	4.2	45.3	27.4	19.3	3.7	217.2
1740	2.7	46.0	28.0	21.0	2.4	205.2
1745	2.7	45.3	25.9	21.9	4.1	207.7
1750	2.7	47.5	26.9	20.6	2.4	203.5
1755	3.0	49.9	26.0	16.7	4.4	189.5
1760	2.9	53.9	28.4	11.3	3.5	176.0
1765	3.5	54.2	25.7	12.5	4.1	167.4
1770	3.2	55.3	25.0	13.6	2.9	164.0

Sources: as for Table 1. Units of alcohol have been defined as follows: wine – pints; strong and small beer – quarts; spirits – quarterns; and cider – pints. They have been aggregated as direct equivalents and the percentages calculated accordingly, no allowance being made for the four years in which data for wine imports are not available. Units consumed per capita are expressed in terms of the figures for England from E. A. Wrigley and R. S. Schofield, *The Population History of England 1541–1871: A Reconstruction* (London, 1981), pp. 533–4.

related problems in early Georgian England.[14] In addition, these data suggest that the late seventeenth and early eighteenth centuries represented a plateau of per capita consumption from which the later eighteenth century saw a steady decline.[15]

[14] Sources as for Table 1. The units employed are derived from numerous literary sources, and from P. Mathias, *The Brewing Industry in England, 1700–1830* (Cambridge, 1959), pp. 11f.; population figures from E. A. Wrigley and R. S. Schofield, *The Population History of England, 1541–1871: a Reconstruction* (London, 1981), Table A3.1, pp. 528–9. For a recent comment on the level of alcohol-related problems in eighteenth-century England, see Roy Porter, 'The Drinking Man's Disease: The "Pre-History" of Alcoholism in Georgian Britain', *British Journal of Addiction*, 80 (1985).

[15] Changes in age structure of the population during the period could be regarded as countervailing influences, but even if one expresses these figures in terms of the population aged fifteen and over, the differences are marked in the levels, but

Figure 5   Estimated consumption of units of alcohol in England, 1685–1785

The patterns of consumption of these units emerge more clearly in Figure 5, from which the very small figures for cider consumption have been eliminated for clarity. Some very general conclusions should be drawn from these curves. For all three series running through the origin of the graph, the onset of war and additional Excise duties that accompanied it led to a marked reduction in estimated levels of consumption, from which the beers never recovered. Thereafter, there was a long-term trend in favour of the strong beers against the small, but within a diminished total market; throughout the period, wine consumption seems to have been stagnant or falling; and, as indicated in Table 2, cider followed an erratic path around a fairly steady but very small market share. The sole dynamic element in the domestic drink market before the 1750s was thus spirits. So far as per capita consumption rose from the trough of the late 1690s to the mid century plateau, then spirits were the principal contributor, and wine may perhaps be regarded

the turning points and the trends remain unaltered (age structures from Wrigley and Schofield, *Population History of England*, Table A3.1).

as the principal sufferer from the additional substitutive effects also involved. The pattern of spirits consumption reversed dramatically after the effective fiscal controls in 1752, and for the rest of the period the growth of the stronger beers was the dominant influence on the market.

It is hard to judge to what extent this picture may be distorted by the variations of the Excise and its operation, but it is broadly consistent with what more detailed studies of individual parts of the drink industry have suggested. The pattern derived from the beer data fits exactly with the analysis by Mathias of the eighteenth-century industry, in which, from the 1720s in particular, the larger London breweries making the strong beers and porter came to play an increasingly dominant role. Wine in contrast is almost certainly understated by these data. Not only were smugglers active in adding to the supply, but, on the evidence of much of the contemporary literature, adulteration was rife: the waters of the Thames and other rivers; spirits themselves; sugars; and the juices of the indigenous berries were all summoned to the extension of the effective supply of wine. Even so, the data in Tables 1 and 2 and the points of Figure 5 can be taken as reasonable reflections of real trends. Excise control was strong enough to make it clear that these data adequately indicate trends in the patterns of consumption, if not exact absolute values. From the letter books of the Excise, to the Customs cutters, and the memoirs of the officer on the ground riding out to assess duty, the Excise system appears a modern and effective bureaucracy even in the early eighteenth century, and one whose statistical evidence is not too enfeebled by leakiness.[16]

This case may not hold as strongly for cider. As discussed below, both total output and the quality of the product varied greatly from year to year. In many years, up to three-quarters of total output may have been of insufficient quality to enter the formal market place, and this pattern continued throughout the eighteenth century. While one can assume that cider was a major consumption good in certain areas of England and Wales, it is much harder to prove on the basis of the Excise statistics. Formal statistical attempts to

---

[16] Adulteration would be a study in itself, but is at present impossible to measure. That the Excise was efficient is evinced by a wide range of authorities, and displayed by the plentiful evidence of close control in the Excise letters, PRO, CUST 47 and CUST 48, and by the memoirs of a West Country schoolmaster and Excise Officer, John Cannon, 1684–1742, Somerset RO, DD/SA 5 C/1193.

follow Mathias in employing observed regional variations in beer output as a proxy for direct evidence on cider consumption proved contradictory and inconclusive.[17] As yet no direct evidence on the regional make of cider or the other beverages equivalent to the data on beer for the years 1754–61 employed to this end by Mathias has been located.[18] Regional variations in the excised output of small or strong beer do not prove sufficient indicators of what Mathias termed the 'cider counties'.[19]

Despite the problems of plotting the geography and level of cider consumption, it seems clear that it was modest, and that the share of total units of alcoholic drink indicated in Table 2 was not an order of magnitude out. The random evidence from fires and similar disasters destroying stocks confirms this impression. In the fire of Wellingborough (Northamptonshire) in June 1739, cider comprised less than 0.25 per cent by volume of all the bulk liquors destroyed, and in the cider country, the fire of Crediton (Devon) in August 1743 destroyed only 13½ hogsheads of cider, as against 110 barrels of beer, the equivalent by volume of 23 per cent. More interesting still, in the latter case, was the fact that cider appeared in only eleven of the forty-one victualling houses making claims for the refund of Excise duty.[20] Set alongside the recurrent contemporary

---

[17] Following a suggestion in Mathias, *Brewing Industry*, an attempt was made to make estimates of the per capita consumption of beers and thus to identify the cider districts from deviations from the mean. This involved combining the Excise districts and the county population estimates generated by Rickman, assuming the two geographical units to be conterminous, and that demand for small beer in provincial England was relatively income inelastic. The results of this exercise were sufficiently unconvincing to raise real doubts about the geographical assumption, and perhaps to suggest a wider dispersion of income levels in provincial England than generally assumed.

[18] Brit. Lib. Add. MS 38382, fols. 5–6, 'An Account of the Number of Barrels of Strong Beer and Ale and of the Barrels of Small Beer brewed in the Several Collections of England . . . Midsummer 1754 to Midsummer 1761'.

[19] Small beer county means showed immense variation (Coefficient of Variation of over 58 per cent), but only Cornwall, Northumberland, and Gloucestershire emerged one standard deviation or more below the mean. Strong beer was less variable county/Excise District by district, and identified more known cider counties among those more than one standard deviation below the mean: these were Hereford, Sussex, Cornwall, Hampshire, and Wales. The other five in this group in no way fitted this description: Essex, Suffolk, Warwickshire, Lancashire, and Cumberland, and a known cider county, Kent, appeared in both exercises more than one standard deviation above the mean for beer 'consumption'.

[20] PRO, CUST 48/13, p. 267, 21 June 1739; CUST 48/13, p. 450, 27 Oct. 1743.

Table 3. *Value of drink consumption at retail prices, total consumers'
expenditure, and expenditure per capita, 1685–1770 (£ million)*

Year	Wine	Strong beer	Small beer	Spirits	Cider	Total expenditure	Expenditure per capita
1685	n.a.	8.38	3.15	0.40	0.23	12.16	2.50
1690	n.a.	8.44	3.96	0.18	0.15	12.73	2.59
1695	n.a.	6.02	3.31	0.21	0.26	9.80	1.98
1700	2.29	5.67	2.95	0.27	0.15	11.33	2.25
1705	n.a.	6.85	3.49	0.33	0.15	10.82	2.09
1710	1.63	6.11	3.17	0.46	0.08	11.45	2.19
1715	2.19	6.54	3.20	0.49	0.17	12.59	2.40
1720	1.91	7.20	3.62	0.52	0.11	13.36	2.49
1725	2.46	7.21	3.49	0.89	0.21	14.26	2.64
1730	1.97	6.69	3.32	0.94	0.08	13.00	2.47
1735	2.46	6.66	3.35	1.43	0.18	14.08	2.60
1740	1.53	6.57	3.32	1.51	0.11	13.04	2.34
1745	1.60	6.60	3.14	1.60	0.20	13.14	2.35
1750	1.55	6.93	3.26	1.52	0.12	13.38	2.33
1755	1.67	7.02	3.05	1.19	0.21	13.14	2.21
1760	1.56	7.23	3.17	0.77	0.16	12.89	2.11
1765	1.83	7.08	2.80	0.82	0.18	12.71	2.03
1770	1.69	7.27	2.73	0.90	0.13	12.72	1.99

Sources: as for Tables 1 and 2. Valuations of the retail price of the beverages above
are at constant 1720–1740 prices, and are as follows: wine, 1s per pint; strong beer,
3d per quart; small beer, 2½d per quart; spirits, 1½d per quartern; and cider, 1d per
pint. They make no allowances for the effects of Excise tax or for the probable
adulteration of wine and perhaps beer or the cutting of the spirits from proof with
water, and thus deliberately understate the total value of the market and estimated
per capita consumption.

demands for the improvement of cider growing so as to expand its
market share, this evidence confirms that the figures of Table 2
approximate to reality in terms of goods sold on the open market.
Within the limitations of the data available, and the problems of
testing them except for internal consistency, spirits are left
unchallenged as the main dynamic element of the English drink
market before 1760.

It is not proposed to investigate the reasons for this here, but
rather to point to some general implications before considering the
production of spirits in greater depth. Conventional measures of
trends in real income are particularly defective for the eighteenth
century, and variations in consumers' expenditure on drink may
represent a valuable additional guide to movements in welfare.
Table 3 restates the volumes of spirits excised in terms of valuations

at approximate retail prices for five-year intervals, 1685–1770. This confirms that in terms of pure alcohol purchased, for the bulk of the period spirits represented the 'best buy'. In a society that seems to have prized drinking, and in which effective social controls such as religion had become weak, this clearly opened the way to the very rapid growth of the distilling industry.[21] It also suggests that, despite the growth of exotic new goods in English shop windows, that range was not such as to divert a great deal of consumer spending from the alcoholic beverages: as in modern experience, alcohol was revealed as a sensitive indicator of rising real incomes.[22] While the consumption of spirits may thus have had real adverse social effects, and the distilling industry achieved a very remarkable peak in fifty years of growth sustained from the beginnings of effective protection in the late 1680s, it is also important to note that valued as above, in terms of consumer spending on its products, it was always small, even within its own sector of the economy. At its peak, it did no more than achieve equality with the wine trade, or generate sales equivalent to 16 per cent of those of beer at the same time. But it was the most dynamic element in the process of import substitution in drink that occurred in the later seventeenth century. By the 1720s and 1730s, the great bulk of the market for drink in England was being supplied by domestic products, no small matter when, on the estimates of Table 3, consumers' spending on drink exceeded the value at prime cost of the whole of English overseas trade.[23] In the almost total substitution of brandy, British spirits were also a major element in that change.

III

As we have seen, until the 1750s, spirits showed the most rapid and consistent growth among all alcoholic beverages sold in England. Within this category, for the bulk of this period, 'British spirits' were the principal component. Before 1690, the bulk of these spirits had come from overseas, and the English market had been dominated by foreign brandies. In 1689, over three-quarters of the spirits

---

[21] Porter, 'Drinking Man's Disease', pp. 385–7.

[22] S. Toland, 'Changes in Living Standards since the 1950s', *Social Trends*, 10 (1980), 25–6.

[23] Compare P. Deane and W. A. Cole, *British Economic Growth, 1688–1959* (2nd edn, Cambridge, 1967), pp. 42–8.

excised for sale in England were from overseas, and it is clear that the initial impulse in the rapid extension of the industry was to provide a substitute for these. There is even evidence to suggest that brandies remained superior goods throughout our period, and that in the absence of war and protection, there may have been no 'age of gin'. Despite continuing low prices for grain, at least compared with those of the 1720s, the years 1731–3 saw a great resurgence of brandy imports, aided by buoyant export earnings and the diplomatic entente between Walpole and Fleury after the treaties of Seville (1729) and Vienna (1731).[24] When the output of British spirits again fell, after the early 1750s, under the pressures of severe increases in taxation, the share of brandy in the home market again increased, as did the absolute level of imports. As the smuggler's trade showed, under conditions of free trade the superior and preferred good, French brandy, would have enjoyed a much greater share of the English market.

There were two other main components of the market for spirits: the products of the Scottish and Irish distillers; and the rum imported from the West Indies. Before 1752, when, with the onset of bad harvests, distillation from grain was banned, and punitive sumptuary taxation introduced, none of these had enjoyed a great share of the English market. The output of Scottish distilleries is extremely hard to assess, partly because of the privilege of exemption from the Excise granted to Duncan Forbes at Ferintosh, and partly because of the strength of illicit trading.[25] Similar considerations apply to Ireland. These reservations accepted, it remains unlikely that market shares, as described in Table 4 below, were significantly different so far as England and Wales were concerned. All the series indicate a distinct discontinuity in the 1750s, the point at which sumptuary legislation effectively ended the age of English gin.

These figures also point to the principal beneficiaries from the restriction of English distilling: the sugar interest. As will be seen below, sugar was a major raw material source for distilling throughout the period, but West Indian rum had been a relatively small part of the total trade until the middle years of the eighteenth century.

---

[24] On the short-term influences, see T. S. Ashton, *Economic Fluctuations in England, 1700–1800* (Oxford, 1959), pp. 59, 145; D. Ogg, *Europe of the Ancien Regime, 1715–1783* (London, 1965), p. 134.

[25] Moss and Hume, *Scotch Whisky*, pp. 33–4.

Table 4. *Estimated percentage shares of the principal spirits in the United Kingdom legitimate market, 1684–9 to 1760–9*

Years	British spirits	Brandy	Rum	Scotch	Irish	UK total (m gallons)
1684–9	28.3	71.7				1.9
1690–9	91.4	8.6				0.9
1700–9	87.6	6.4		6.0		1.7
1710–19	82.5	4.2		7.6	5.6	2.7
1720–9	83.3	9.7		3.7	3.2	4.6
1730–9	78.5	10.3	3.0	4.9	3.3	6.5
1740–9	81.2	3.5	5.3	5.3	4.7	8.9
1750–9	67.2	4.9	13.3	7.8	6.7	6.7
1760–9	49.5	14.2	21.6	1.3	13.5	4.8

Sources: Custom House, 'Excise Revenue Accounts'; and for the Scottish and Irish output, *Parliamentary Papers*, 1870, XX, pp. 4–9. The Scottish figures for the years 1707–23 have been estimated from total duty paid.

Once it was clearly distinguished in the Excise records from brandy, in 1734, it was revealed as an import growing rapidly as the distillation in the West Indies came to replace the use of the unrefinable tail of molasses for distillation in England. Throughout the twenty-year debate on the social destructiveness of spirits, the London sugar interest issued propaganda to stress the great intrinsic qualities of sugar-based spirits: they contained the essence of 'the genial heat of the sun', and thus produced healthier liquors than the grains and fruits of cold northern climates.[26] Despite their arguments, for the core of the period of spirits consumption, the 1690s to the 1750s, as the figures of Table 4 indicate, the principal component of the market was 'British spirits'.

IV

What then were these 'British spirits' that so dominated the drink market in the first half of the eighteenth century? It was suggested above that the initial impulse behind the expansion of the industry in the 1690s was the drive to produce a substitute for imported brandies. Such *ersatz* brandy was made and sold throughout the

---

[26] Adam Holden, *A Vindication of a Pamphlet lately published Intituled The Tryal of the Spirits* (London, 1736), pp. 16–17.

period, and clearly produced satisfactory financial returns. It was produced from any satisfactory source of proof spirit, with flavourings and other chemicals added in the process of rectification in order to 'dulcify' the spirit, and to add both colour and vinosity when the rectified spirit was subsequently cut with water for retail. A recipe for English brandy 'as good as French' from 1718 indicates the process and the nature of the product. Fine Malaga fruit (raisins), two balls of bean flour, and a quarter of a pound of saltpetre were to be added to each cask of wash for distillation, and vinosity provided by the subsequent addition of an infusion of prunes in water at the rate of 20 gallons per hogshead of proof spirit.[27] Two goals were met by such methods: an import substitute was produced, albeit one that would probably not pass a discerning modern palate; and, at the same time, a means to sell immature spirit distilled from corn, malt, wine lees, spent molasses, or cider was conceived. Buoyant sales of such goods aimed at the 'quality' end of the market thus promised the high levels of profit required to sustain the first phase of expansion.

The evidence of contemporary tracts on the business suggests that these high levels of profit were indeed obtainable. George Smith of Kendal, one of the most respected and least tendentious authors of tracts on the subject, suggested that 'English brandy like French' in 1725 could sell at 8s or 9s a gallon. On his own figures this represented a yield of over 80 per cent on raw material costs, and a rate of profit of 46 per cent per gallon on the wholesale price. Even higher returns were possible on a good that represented a link between the apothecary and the distiller, 'plague water': this could sell at three times the costs of the raw materials, and yield around 70 per cent profit on a gallon sold at 8s.[28] Smith's figures point to the easy market for any possible prophylactic in time of plague, and thus suggest some validity to the monopoly patent of 1593.[29]

Yet early-eighteenth-century England is known not for brandy, ratafia, usquebaugh, or plague water, but for geneva, the prime 'British spirit'. The various grades of geneva – contracted to 'gin' – were little different in their inputs. The cheapest grades had the

---

[27] *The Practical Distiller, or a Brief Treatise of Practical Distillation* (London, 1718), pp. 40–3.

[28] George Smith, *A Compleat Body of Distilling* (London, 1725), p. 6.

[29] *Ibid.*, pp. 24–5; Thirsk, *Policy and Projects*, p. 95.

greatest inputs of juniper berries and of water, even then always referred to as 'liquor' in the trade. Unit rates of return were also very much lower on the cheapest genevas than on other grades of British spirits. Smith suggested that the basic geneva returned 55 per cent on raw material costs, or 30 per cent plus on a gallon wholesaling at 1s 8d. In this lay the key to the apparent paradox: while unit rates of profit were lower, gin used the cheapest spirits and raw materials.[30] It at once committed less capital and offered the probability of a more rapid return by selling to a mass market. What may thus have started as a home substitute for a high-quality imported good soon proved capable of more generalized sale at low price to the mass market. Gin represented a very dramatic example of the potential of Joan Thirsk's seventeenth-century 'projects'.

The key to this transition to the mass market was clearly the price of raw materials, principally that of the proof spirits which were sold on to the secondary rectifiers, who redistilled the final product. Direct evidence on all the raw materials employed by the primary distillers does not survive. However, for 'British spirits' alone, Excise figures exist on the major sources of 'Low Wines', the once-distilled intermediate product which was subjected to a separate duty. As the discussion of the early history indicated, a wide range of raw materials could be employed to make the wash from which Low Wines and thus proof spirits could be produced. As we have seen, in the sixteenth century, wine lees, brewers' wash, and other waste products were being employed for the production of both vinegar and aqua vitae, and these were both used in our period. As William Stout indicated, the English distillers were promiscuous in their search for raw materials at the beginnings of the great expansion, in the 1690s. Within a decade, however, malted corn, molasses, and cider had come to form the main sources of all the proof spirits produced in England. This is clearly indicated in the figures of Table 5 above, the principal sources of Low Wines describes as decennial averages. As these figures indicated, malted corn was dominant as the source of distillates, and they probably understate the extent to which corn spirits were the base of the industry: over time, partly under the pressure of taxation, increasing use was made of mashes made at least in part of unmalted corn. Second place in the raw material base for spirits was always held by the Excise

[30] Smith, *Compleat Body*, pp. 48–9.

Table 5. *Principal sources of Low Wines in England, decennial averages, 1691–1769 (% of total)*

Years	Imported materials	Malt	Cider	Brewer's wash
1691–9	13.7	82.4	3.7	0.3
1700–9	22.7	71.7	5.6	0.1
1710–19	22.1	75.7	2.1	—
1720–9	16.7	81.8	1.5	—
1730–9	15.4	83.4	1.1	—
1740–9	6.3	93.3	0.4	—
1750–9	12.1	87.4	0.5	—
1760–9	15.7	83.9	0.4	—

Source: Custom House, 'An Account of the Quantities', pp. 38–47.

category of 'imported materials', which included wine, fruits, and cider, but consisting overwhelmingly of molasses. This source declined in the long term, partially as the result of growing colonial production of rum, but throughout the first half of the eighteenth century had been the consistent 'second best' raw material for the distiller's washes. It also provided an important adjunct to the sugar trade, allowing the fermentation for spirits of the tail of sugar boiling, thus producing a marketable product from residues unable to yield further sugar at an economic rate.[31]

The cider base of spirits production was therefore always small, although it did rise significantly in certain years. The peak years for distillation from cider appear in Table 6. They do not conform to a common pattern, although particular demand factors operated in each. The year 1695 was the third successive year of severe disruption of the import trade by the war, and the use of cider probably expanded to fill the gap left by molasses; 1705 came at the end of a

---

[31] *A Collection of Letters Published in the Daily Papers Relating to the British Distillery* (London, 1736), letter III, pp. 14–23: 'Your Constant Reader, A.B.' put the consumption of molasses by distillers at 14,000 hogsheads per year, all of which had exhausted their economic life as sources of refined sugar: 'They will not answer the charge of boiling up for coarse sugars' (p. 18). This source indicated that 11 per cent of the volume of imported sugars and 5½ per cent of their value were directly attributable to distilling. *The Case of the Merchants and Others, of the City of Bristol, Trading to the British Colonies in America* (London, 1736) confirmed this opinion.

Table 6. *Peak years for the use of cider as a source of Low Wines (% of total)*

Year[a]	Imported materials	Malt	Cider
1695	5.5	85.0	9.4
1705	24.5	67.4	8.0
1707	18.2	74.0	7.8
1715	22.9	71.4	5.7
1725	16.0	78.8	5.2
1735	13.3	84.4	2.3
1759	89.3	0.0	10.7

[a] The Excise Year runs Midsummer to Midsummer for these goods, and thus overlaps two harvest years.
Source: as for Table 5.

period in which malting had been restricted, and here cider was secondary to molasses as a substitute for malt; the years 1707, 1715, 1725 and 1735 were all characterized by considerable expansion in total output of spirits, and here cider may have been summoned to relieve raw material shortages; and 1759 shared the abnormal features of 1705, in that malting was prohibited, and thus molasses and cider had to provide the entire domestic raw material supply for distillation.[32] Cider was clearly a source of 'British spirits', but no better than the third-best choice as a raw material. Why then was its position not larger?

V

The explanations for cider's position in the hierarchy of raw materials for the distiller lie on both supply and demand sides. While the analysis so far has indicated that for the distiller cider seemed to be an inferior good, and one to be adopted after grain or molasses, the cider grower's capacity and willingness to supply also affected the choice. While no single factor determined that cider was not more fully used for spirit production, together the wide range of adverse features of cider as a raw material for the distiller

[32] Custom House MS, 'An account of the Quantities of the Several Articles', pp. 38–47.

made it almost as surprising that it was used at all as that there seemed to have been no English Calvados.

First, as was implicit in the figures of Table 5, the long-term trend away from the use of cider for distillation after the early decades of observations was a comment upon the nature of the final good for which these Low Wines were intended. The English distillers had abandoned the *ersatz* brandies they had first sought to produce within a relatively short time from the beginnings of expansion, and adopted the cheap mass consumption good, geneva, which permitted rapid returns on capital, albeit at lower unit rates of profit. Even England's first major propagandist for the distillation of cider, Richard Haines in 1684, had advocated the practice to strengthen and improve cider itself into 'cider royal' by the addition of the distillate to standard cider. Haines's 'cider royal' was a proposal for fortification designed to increase sales and quality of the base product: the apple spirits were clearly not regarded as an end product.[33]

So far from being an end product in itself, the spirit distilled from cider was widely held to be disadvantaged in both quality and taste. The technical literature of the period did not commend cider spirit, and there seems to have been no market in it *per se*: Haines saw these spirits only as the improvers and stabilizers of cider; and none of the many recipes in the best technical treatise of the period, George Smith's *A Compleat Body of Distilling* (1725) required or mentioned them.[34] Peter Shaw's *Essays in Artificial Philosophy* of 1731 ranked cider spirit low, well behind malt spirit and the sugar spirits of London and Nantes, because of its intrusive taste: 'its particular flavour is not so desirable' but it could 'by care, be rendered very pure, and almost insipid, upon rectification'.[35] The oils and esters which would produce distinctive character in a long-matured spirit, the essence of Normandy's Calvados, were undesirable in a market dominated by the demand for a bland 'white' spirit for rectification into geneva for immediate sale.

This in part accounted for its third place in the hierarchy of

---

[33] R. Haines, *Aphorisms upon the New Way of Improving Cyder of Making Cyder Royal* (London, 1684). I am indebted for this reference to Mr P. G. M. Gregory.

[34] Smith, *Compleat Body*, passim.

[35] Peter Shaw, *Three Essays in Artificial Philosophy or Universal Chemistry* (London, 1731), p. 130.

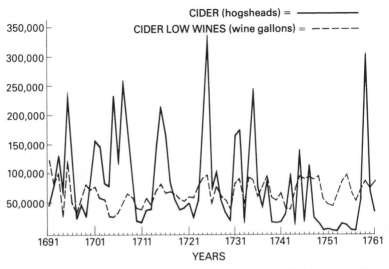

Figure 6 Excised output of cider and cider low wines, 1691–1761 (source: as for Tables 1 and 5)

preference of raw materials for the gin distiller, but it was not a complete explanation. Though used on average on but a small scale, cider was a continuing source of spirits and, after all, the preferred base, malt, also gave unwanted character to the distillate.[36] Cider may therefore be expected to have performed some substitutive role in the supply of raw materials for the distiller, rising in use when malt was scarce and expensive. This hypothesis is borne out by the evidence of the Excise statistics, although the formal statistical testing of expected relationships produced somewhat inconclusive results. There was an inverse correlation, as one would expect, between the volume of Low Wines drawn from cider and from malt, expressed most clearly because of the great disparity of quantities involved, in the logarithmic transformation of the equation.[37] Perhaps surprisingly, further examination of these data failed to generate statistically significant relationships with either the total

---

[36] Holden, *A Vindication*, pp. 11–12.

[37] The strongest expression of the relationship occurred in the logarithmic form:
LOG CIDER LOW WINES = 4.7843 − 0.8777 (LOG MALT LOW WINES)
$$t = 5.446 \quad t = -2.730$$
F = 7.452, r^2 = 0.1230, N = 75.

volume of malt excised each year, or any of four series for the price of malt. Cider Low Wines varied inversely with the total output of malt, and with the better of the malt price series, drawn from the Navy Victualling Office and from Combrune, but while the signs in the low equations calculated were thus as expected, the results were of low statistical significance.[38] Transfers at the margin were therefore occurring between raw materials, as determined by the harvests and the movements of relative prices, but the relative weakness of calculated statistical relationships indicates that other factors may have been more significant.

Rather better explanations may be found on the supply side. Cider yields from English orchards, even under modern cultivation, are extremely variable, and were still more so in the eighteenth century. According to Turner's moderately well-informed *General View of the Agriculture of the County of Gloucester* (1794), apple crops yielded a 'hit' no more than one year in four, and this view seems to be sustained in the curve of cider excised for sale in Figure 6.[39] Assessed by the evidence of the quantities excised, cider was a much more variable commodity than malt: it displayed a far greater

---

[38] The best equation was also in the logarithmic form:

LOG CIDER LOW WINES = 8.0405 − 1.9933 (LOG TOTAL MALT)

$$t = 1.875 \quad t = -1.319$$

F = 1.739, r^2 = 0.0158, N = 63.

Four separate price series for malt were tested against cider Low Wines: T. S. Ashton's series, in *Economic Fluctuations*, p. 182, drawn from J. Marshall, *Digest of all the Accounts* (London, 1834), which proved upon close examination to be almost valueless; malt and barley series from Bowden's statistical appendix to Thirsk (ed.), *Agrarian History*, V, II, pp. 829–31; The Navy Victualling Office series from W. Beveridge, *Prices and Wages in England from the Twelfth to the Nineteenth Century*, I (London, 1939), pp. 574–5; and M. Combrune, *An Enquiry into the Prices of Wheat, Malt and Occasionally other Provisions; of Land and Cattle etc.; as Sold in England from the Year 1000 to the Year 1765* (London, 1768), pp. 64–98. The strongest relationships were:

  (a) CIDER LOW WINES = 185868.84 − 4296.49 (NAVY VICTUALLING PRICE)

$$t = 3.698 \quad t = -2.043$$

F = 4.175, r^2 = 0.0646, N = 72;

  (b) CIDER LOW WINES = 227184.06 − 474.63 (COMBRUNE PRICE)

$$t = 2.682 \quad t = -1.688$$

F = 2.850, r^2 = 0.0387, N = 74.

The Combrune series differed from the other Michaelmas quotations in being the average of Lady Day and Michaelmas.

[39] George Turner, *General View of the Agriculture of the County of Gloucester* (London, 1794), p. 52.

coefficient of variation (34.4% as against 21.3% for malt).[40] If a 'hit' is defined as a yield of excised cider more than one standard deviation from the mean of the series, thirteen years of the seventy-six between 1691 and 1765 were 'hits', just under one in six, as against one in sixteen for malt. More significant, perhaps, in determining the choice of an industrial raw material was the risk of what Turner might appropriately have termed a 'miss': this occurred on ten occasions of the seventy-six in the cider series, as against only twice in sixty-four years in the malt data.[41] If we assume, for reasons discussed below, that it was the better qualities of cider that entered the formal market place and fell foul of the scrutiny of the Exciseman, then it is clear that it was inferior to malt as a source of supply on account of this extreme variability.

This view is strongly reinforced by the formal statistical analysis of the relationship between the Low Wines distilled from cider, and the size of the cider crop as defined above. The regression of Low Wines drawn from cider against the total cider excised by relative first differences, a very severe test, produced the following equation:

FIRST DIFFERENCE OF CIDER LOW WINES =
$-89.1227 + 2.1176$ (FIRST DIFF. CIDER)
$t = 0.008$ $t = 3.929$
$F = 15.435$; $r^2 = 0.2513$; $N = 75$

This relationship, significant at above 95 per cent level, clearly indicated that it was the supply of cider that probably dominated the capacity of the distillers to employ it as a raw material.[42] The intense variability of the English cider crop thus helped, on the supply side, to mitigate against its wider employment for distillation. An industry such as distilling in this period enjoying an almost uninterrupted half-century of expansion, achieving rates of growth dramatic by the standards of the period, but seeking constantly to economize on the costs of raw material inputs, simply could not afford a base as unreliable as cider.

[40] Custom House MS, 'Excise Revenue Accounts', pp. 232, 234.
[41] Defined here as an Excised quantity more than one standard deviation below the mean of the series.
[42] Calculated as above from Custom House MS, 'Excise Revenue Accounts', p. 232, and 'An Account of the Quantities of the Several Articles', pp. 38–9. I am indebted to Jane Binner for her assistance in computing these results.

Not only were the annual crops of apples and the yields of cider variable in quantity, but cider was also defective in other qualities sought by the distillers. Above all it seems to have been a good produced mainly on a small scale, even in such important regions as Herefordshire and Worcestershire, the primary commercial producers. No really large-scale cider makers have been identified to date in these researches, and none were discussed by the contributors to the *Agrarian History of England and Wales*.[43] Cider seems to have been the product of small to medium mixed-farm enterprises and producers such as the Rev. Daniel Renaud, of Whitchurch, Herefordshire selling on average five to six hogsheads a year, 1730–66, may have been typical. In support of the variability of the cider supply, discussed above, Renaud significantly failed to market any cider in eight of these thirty-seven years.[44] Concentrated sources of supply were therefore probably few, and given the costly bulk of cider, this made it additionally unattractive to the distillers who were concentrated in England's great towns, principally London and Bristol.[45] The only significant concentration of distillers employing cider as a major raw material identifiable from the Excise records was Bristol, where transport via the Severn and the Avon could help overcome these otherwise prohibitive transport barriers.

Despite this, cider was used in distilling in London as well as Bristol, but more commonly for the production of vinegars from 'spent' ciders. It could only make sense in transport terms to employ cider for distillation in the capital if it was available, a means of recovering some value from a waste product analogous to the employment of molasses to the same end. To put the transport barrier more graphically, for the same distance of journey a single trow or hoy of 40 tons burden could supply enough malt to manu-

[43] Thirsk (ed.), *Agrarian History*, V, pp. 157, 166, 186, 192–3, 298, 352, 383–4, 410.

[44] Hereford RO, Account Book of the Rev. Daniel Renaud of Whitchurch, Herefordshire, 1730–66, A98/1. Mean output per non-compounding cidermaker in the Excise year 1764–5 was 8.4 hogsheads, but rose to over 547 in the Hereford collection, and 316 in Exeter, PRO, CUST 48/17, pp. 204–5.

[45] No parallel figures for spirits to those for beer in Brit. Lib. Add. MS 38382 have been found, and this comment is therefore an impression, supported by the shaky evidence of *The Life of Mother Gin*, by an Impartial hand (London, 1736). This noted that Mother Gin, 'a woman of exceeding high spirit', was of Anglo-Dutch parentage, and for a time had the 'voice of the People . . . intirely under her Influence and direction . . . particularly in the two Cities of London and Bristol', p. 28.

facture 5,600 gallons of proof spirits; the same vessel could carry at best 136 hogsheads of cider, barely enough to distil 110 gallons of spirits.[46] In this light it is hardly surprising that in the long term distillation of cider became confined to being the vice of Devon farmers' wives, according to Marshall, the source via their lead vessels of the notorious Devon colic.[47] The transport logic of the distilling industry was that the primary distillers should concentrate in the mass urban markets, near to the secondary rectifying retailers. In transport terms it was not surprising to find so little cider being distilled, but rather to find it done at all.

Even ignoring the highly unstable quantity of cider supply, discussed above, the English weather added a further disincentive to the employment of cider for distillation: our relatively poor endowment with sunshine affected the quality of ciders that could be produced. Sunshine is the sole determinant of the sugar content of apples, the source of the alcoholic strength that was really the only bait for the distiller. English apples thus tended to be relatively low in sugar content, and cider was in consequence widely regarded as a poor source of distillates. Although a source coming from the end of the period under present consideration, *The Case of the County of Devon* of 1763 makes the point clearly, in identifying four qualities of cider, of which only one was suitable raw material for the distiller. According to this source, half of all output was 'farm cider', in strength inferior to small beer, and capable only of local sale. At the top of the hierarchy was the cider made from choice fruit, no more than 1 per cent of the total, destined to compete with wine for the gentleman's table; and at the bottom was windfall cider, only fit for domestic consumption.[48] Thus only a part of total output was potential raw material for the distiller, and even then this required refermentation before it could make an economic wash for the distiller. A technical tract of 1692 had made this issue clear: 'Cyders yield but little quantity of Spirit, let them never be so

---

[46] Based upon extraction rates of the daily make of Cooke & Co., Brit. Lib., Add. MS 39683, and the official assessment of the yields of various raw materials for spirit, 13 April 1732, PRO, CUST 48/12, pp. 374–5.

[47] William Marshall, *The Rural Economy of the West of England including Devonshire and parts of Somersetshire and Cornwall* (London, 1796), I, pp. 236–7.

[48] *The Case of the County of Devon with Respect to the Consequences of the New Excise on Cyder and Perry* (London, 1763), pp. 5–7. As with all the pamphlet material for this subject, it is clearly tendentious and a high discount factor needs to be applied to its evidence.

fine by age.'[49] This was confirmed by other experts, as well as by the more formal appraisal of the Excise. Peter Shaw rated cider as wine and wine lees as a source, yielding between one-eighth and one-sixteenth of proof alcohol by volume, as against one-fifth for malt wash.[50] The Excise explanation of the charging of duty in 1732 treated Low Wines derived from cider as yielding half as proof spirit, implying around one-eighth by volume from the original wash; imported wines at the same; foreign materials, a synonym for molasses, at two-thirds; and malt at three-fifths.[51] Other things being equal, then, molasses and malt were the rational choices as raw materials for the distiller.

Other things, however, were far from equal. To all the other disadvantages under which cider laboured were added the inequalities of the Excise. Taxation compounded this hierarchy of preference for raw materials and, at times, induced dramatic switching. Duties fell on the manufacturing of spirits at several stages: on many of the raw materials; on the intermediate product, the Low Wine; and on the proof spirit.[52] Malt paid $6^{16}/_{21}$d Excise per bushel, 1697–1759, and this was a cost to be borne by the distillers.[53] However, the position of cider before 1729 was much less clear. Cider had been subjected to a duty of 4s per hogshead from 1692, but there was widespread dispute as to whether cider destined for distillation was liable.[54] In some areas, certainly, it seems to have been assumed that it was not, and no real effort was made by the Excise officers to collect, though this may have indicated the small scale of the usage. However, in the Bristol area, from 1701 to 1708, officers made a consistent effort to collect the duty from the distillers, under explicit instruction from London. A series of prosecutions for non-payment ensued, and the uncertainty in past interpretations of the law was resolved to the distillers' disadvantage. The Excise report noted that the Bristol cider distillers had not been paying this duty, but

---

[49] W. Y-Worth, *Introitus Apertus ad Artem Distillationis; or The Whole Art of Distillation Practically Stated* (London, 1692), p. 18.

[50] Shaw, *Three Essays*, pp. 127–30.

[51] PRO, CUST 48/12, p. 374.

[52] 'Proof', a term still causing immense confusion, seems to have meant about 50 per cent alcohol by volume until 1806, according to John Owens, *Plain Papers relating to the Excise Branch of the Inland Revenue Department from 1621 to 1878 or a History of the Excise* (Linlithgow, 1879), pp. 465–6.

[53] 8 & 9 Will. III c. 22.   [54] 4 Will. & M. c. 3.

only because they 'constantly disputed the charge'.[55] Thereafter, until the duty was apparently lifted, this was an additional cost to the cider distiller.[56] Although the leader of the Bristol cider distillers in the case before the Exchequer, John Pickering, put a brave face upon the decree, 'that if he should be obliged to pay he should be no loser thereby', it is hard to see how a spirit could be distilled from cider and bear the costs of duty unless it commanded a premium price.[57] Unless the consumers of Bristol were untypical of the rest of the country, or perverse in preferring to pay higher prices for what seem to have been inferior goods, then Pickering was probably crying in the wind.

That it is hard to believe Pickering's boast is exemplified by a simple model of the comparative costs of producing basic proof spirits from a range of raw materials. Thus Table 7 attempts to specify the raw material and duty costs of producing 10 gallons of proof spirit from a variety of washes. They incorporate the official yields according to the Excise, which were probably 10 per cent pessimistic and compounded later in the eighteenth century in a complex of formal and informal allowances.[58] The model therefore tends to overstate the prime costs of raw materials, and to assume full payment of the duty at each appropriate stage. Each row of Table 7, therefore, tends to overstate the total costs involved. The quantities of inputs required for mashes of grain, malt, and molasses are of a higher presumptive reliability, being derived from the business records of Cooke & Co., distillers of London in the 1760s, and can be taken as best practice for the period. Cider, by contrast, is evaluated only on the basis of the official Excise figures, and certainly suffers by the comparison. Pricing of both molasses and cider is also fairly arbitrary in the figures of Table 7: the former is given the lowest valuation for the period, from the 1660 Book of Rates, but inevitably valued as whole, not spent molasses; and the latter is

---

[55] Orders within Excise records for the charging of the duty can be observed from early in 1701, after the Treasury had taken legal opinion, PRO, CUST 47/21, p. 1. Zepha[niah] Lumby's fine for non-payment was reduced in consideration of his ignorance of the law, *ibid.*, p. 11, and the case was ultimately resolved in the Exchequer, PRO, E 126/19, fol. 49, 3 July 1708 and E 134 5 and 6 Anne no. 24, Crown v. Pickering and others.

[56] By the Act 3 George II c. 7 (1730), the relevant clauses of which are not printed in the standard editions of the statutes, e.g. *Statutes at Large*.

[57] PRO, CUST 48/10, fols. 211–14, 21 February 1708, 10 March 1708.

[58] Owens, *Plain Papers*, p. 468.

Table 7. *A simple model of the comparative raw material and Excise costs of producing 10 gallons of British spirits*

Raw materials			Excise duties			
Source	Quantity	Price	Raw material	Low Wine	Spirit	Total
Malt	4.13 bu	9.59s	2.24s	1.39s	2.50s	15.72s
Malt/Barley	1.38 bu (m) 2.54 bu (b)	3.19s 5.90s } 9.09s	0.78s	1.39s	2.50s	13.76s
Malt/Barley/ Wheat	1.77 bu (m) 1.63 bu (b) 0.41 bu (w)	4.11s 3.79s } 9.53s 1.63s	1.00s	1.39s	2.50s	14.42s
Molasses	120 lb	10.00s		7.50s	5.00s	22.50s
Cider	80 gallons	19.05s	[5.08s]	2.50s	2.50s	29.13s

Sources: Grain prices from *Agrarian History*, V, II, pp. 864f.; quantities and yields of Low Wines, PRO CUST 48/12, pp. 374–5; mixtures of unmalted corn from records of Cooke & Co., 1760s, B.L. Add. MSS 39683; cider prices, *Case of the County of Devon*, and accounts of Daniel Renaud, 1730–66, Herefs. RO, A98/1; and molasses, Schumpeter, *English Overseas Trade*, p. 72. No suitable valuations for spent molasses have yet been found, and this row clearly overstates the raw material costs, but even at fifth prime cost, fiscal differences still advantage grain mashes. If the real comparison for cider is the post-1730 tax cost, 24.05s, ignoring any sugar added in refermentation, it remains hard to see how the prime cost of the hogshead, assumed here to be 15s, could fall sufficiently to bear any costs of transport.

valued at 15s the hogshead, the lowest credible price for the second grade of cider, the equivalent of common ale.[59]

The figures of Table 7 thus tend to make unfavourable comparisons between cider and the alternative sources of spirits, but even substantial error terms would not compensate for the revealed disadvantages. In an industry in which it has been assumed the governing factor was the price of the most effective raw material source for proof spirits for selling on to the rectifiers, it is hard to see how cider could compete in any but exceptional years. When, throughout the 1730s, the going rate for such proof spirits 12½ per cent below proof was around 1s 8d the gallon, cider would therefore only be adopted as the source of these characterless white spirits in

---

[59] See notes to Table 7.

particular circumstances, principally perhaps a cider 'hit' and constraints in the supply of malt.[60]

VI

The English cider orchard remained a favoured subject for the authors of tracts for the improvement of agriculture from Haines and Worlidge in the seventeenth century to William Marshall in the eighteenth and the Royal Agricultural Society in the nineteenth. It remained a constant source of irritation to these improvers that their advice was so little heeded: the cider orchard was widely left to its 'natural' state, and constantly appeared as a major element of the unfulfilled potential of the rural economy. Valued locally and regionally as an economic resource, cider was fiercely prized by farmers and gentry in many counties, but cider growing seems to have been unresponsive to their blandishments.[61]

This is perhaps particularly surprising during the first great phase of agricultural improvement from the later seventeenth century when the rising interest in the commercial exploitation of rural resources coincided with unusually favourable circumstances for the suppliers of the beverage trades. A very substantial growth in real incomes took place between the middle of the seventeenth century and the middle of the eighteenth, and the evidence of this study points strongly to this being translated into a surge in demand for beverages, alcoholic and otherwise. It may well have been that the first half of the eighteenth century was the great age of tea, coffee, chocolate, and 'Mother Gin' in part because of the still limited range of alternative new goods for consumption. Whatever the causes, the period was one of great opportunity for the beverage trades, and protectionism ensured that these opportunities accrued largely to the home-produced alcohols. Throughout the period, more than 80 per cent of expenditure upon drink seems to have gone on domestic products.[62]

---

[60] The wholesale price for rectified malt spirits was 1s 8d in Smith, *Compleat Body* (1725) and 1s 9d in *The Farmer Restored: or the Landed Interest Preserved* (London, 1736).

[61] See the comments in J. Williams-Davies, *Cider Making in Wales* (Cardiff, 1982), pp. 13–14.

[62] From Table 3. In the absence of comparative data on previous or subsequent periods, this is hard to judge, but it appears likely that this represented a gain for

Within this age of opportunity for the brewer and the distiller, conditions also superficially favoured the cider maker and cider distiller. The most dynamic element in this expansion after 1690 was the distilling industry, and one would have expected, following Stout's comments, distillers questing raw material sources to sustain very rapid growth to turn to cider on a large scale. Equally, the opportunities created the possibility of a substantial upgrading of the cider industry on to a more commercial footing, and its development into a specialized segment of agriculture supplying the distiller and the market direct.[63]

Closer examination of the nature of the distilling business in this period has made it clear that the lowly position of cider spirits in its great expansion was unsurprising. The cider-growing industry exhibited structural weaknesses which mitigated against its attainment of greater markets for its produce in any form: small farm units of production could never be linked effectively to mass urban consumption given the prohibitive costs of transporting bulk liquid. Even if these problems could have been circumvented, cider's lack of saccharine content, the high variance in the volume of its production from year to year, and the intrinsic undesirability of the spirit it yielded, ensured that it attained but a small place in the period of expansion. When, for the most part, malt was cheap by long-term historical standards, mashes of up to two-thirds unmalted corns were developed, and spent molasses were easily and cheaply available at the principal centres of consumption; cider simply could not compete.

As this chapter has made clear, in large part the rapid and dramatic growth of the distilling industry was the unforeseen result of protection. Much of the initial stimulus was to produce an *ersatz* brandy, and without trade discrimination against the French, the industry would not have existed on the same scale. The growth of this industry supplying the mass market was in part the fortuitous

---

home producers by comparison with the early seventeenth century, when wine was rather more significant.

[63] Very crude calculations indicate that the cider industry of this period was considerable. If we assume that total cider output, including that too poor in quality to leave the farm, was double that Excised for sale; that peak output was 120,000 Excised hogsheads before 1770; and that an acre of orchard could yield 6–8 hogsheads, then cider growing occupied 30,000–40,000 acres in the period. To set this in context, in the 1870s the five principal cider counties had 80,000 acres under apples, not all for cider (information from Mr F. A. Roach).

consequence of the development of gin in this period of substitution, a development which then determined the nature of demand facing the primary distiller. To this was added a further adverse factor for the cider-grower, the unplanned but real additional discrimination by the Excise. For the cider-grower, then, the action of government at once created an opportunity and took it away, thus helping to make the improvement of English apple-growing a long-run unfulfilled 'project'. Joan Thirsk's analysis of projects in this period has stressed the great benefits that could accrue to employment-creating import substitution. Some, such as the growing of tobacco, were stamped out as facets of colonial policy; others, like stocking-knitting, exhibited rapid and unrestrained growth; and the English distilling industry exhibited mushroom growth before contracting rapidly in the face of sumptuary taxation. Paradoxically, the gains for the distilling industry as a whole were probably the source of the arrested development of cider distillation: a more restricted market, with higher average unit prices for spirits, might have offered a market niche in which apple spirits were valued for their intrinsic qualities. A most promising project, then, liberally dosed with protection, foundered on the quirks of the Excise and the dramatic success of the industry as a whole.

14. The origins and early growth of the Hallamshire cutlery and allied trades

DAVID HEY

Joan Thirsk's investigations into the many ways that industries grew both in the towns and in the countryside during the early-modern period have been amongst her most stimulating and fruitful lines of enquiry. Her essay 'Industries in the Countryside', published in 1961, is still the essential starting point for other ventures in this field and her Ford Lectures, published in 1978 as *Economic Policy and Projects: The Development of a Consumer Society in Early Modern England*, provided an explanatory framework that seemed at a stroke to make clear so many matters that had hitherto been vague and unconnected. It is therefore appropriate that the final chapter in a volume published in her honour should be devoted to an exploration of the beginnings of a distinctive group of local trades that achieved international renown, in the hope that along the way light will be cast on the origins of other industries. It will attempt, in the Thirsk manner, to gain insights by a patient and detailed investigation of the scattered and fragmentary evidence. She will well understand that the records will frustrate the historian who hopes to provide clear answers to all the questions that are posed. The excitement is less in the conclusion than in the chase.

In her Ford Lectures Dr Thirsk showed that from the 1540s a group of Commonwealth men advocated the setting up of new industries to provide employment and to reduce the country's dangerous dependency on foreign imports. The government sponsored or inspired projects, including some which were introduced by foreign workmen. The best-known example is the Sussex iron industry; by 1544 at least forty French ironworkers were employed in the Weald. Under Elizabeth such projects were 'launched on a new and much more expansive phase'. In the 1560s religious persecution drove large numbers of Protestant artisans and their families from France and Holland. They were encouraged to settle in such places as Sandwich (1561), Norwich (1566), Stamford, Maidstone, and Southampton (1567), Colchester (1568), and Canterbury (1574). Smaller groups set up home in many of the market towns of the eastern and southern counties and also in the South-West. Their craft skills often transformed ancient local industries: for instance, many of the New Draperies were introduced by them into Norwich and subsequently into numerous parts of the East Anglian countryside. In Joan Thirsk's words, 'a new expansive phase marked an abrupt change of fortune'.[1]

I

It is clear from her work that government projects and the influx of skilled foreign workers could produce qualitative changes in English industry. Here we have an explanation of how certain locations became the acknowledged centres of particular trades. The cutlery industry seems at first sight to fall readily into this pattern. The craft was an ancient one, but until the early-modern period knives were crude in design. In *A Discourse of the Common Weal of this Realm* (1549), Sir Thomas Smith lamented that iron and steel, knives and daggers, were imported from abroad and that foreign knives were displayed prominently in London shops; even country folk preferred foreign cutlery. By the early eighteenth century, however, all that had changed; in 1719 Monsieur Misson, a French traveller, observed that 'the best knives in the world' were made in England.[2] During the intervening 170 years the English cutlery industry had been transformed. How had this happened? An oft-quoted story from the early nineteenth century maintains that the success of the Hallamshire cutlery industry and the precise location of specialist crafts within the area were the result of French, indeed Huguenot, immigration, comparable with that in the eastern and southern counties, but as we shall see there is no evidence for foreign settlers taking up the cutlery and allied trades in Hallamshire. The beneficial transfer of human capital that helps to explain

---

[1] J. Thirsk, *Economic Policy and Projects: The Development of a Consumer Society in Early Modern England* (Oxford, 1978), pp. 24, 43–4.

[2] Sir Thomas Smith, *A Discourse of the Common Weal of this Realm*, ed. E. Lamond (Cambridge, 1954), p. 10; M. Misson, *Memoirs and Observations in his Travels over England* (London, 1719), p. 171.

the success of the New Draperies in Norwich is absent from the Sheffield neighbourhood. The story is much more complicated than that. Any stimulus from foreign craftsmen came only indirectly through London.

The earliest documentary reference to the staple trade of the Sheffield district occurs in the lay subsidy return of 1297,[3] when Robertus le Cotelar was one of the local men who were taxed, but no doubt the making of knives and other metal goods was already an ancient activity by the time that the first records begin. The Tankersley seam of ironstone outcropped within the parish of Sheffield, and other necessary resources such as coal for the smithy fires and suitable stones and water power for grinding were at hand. The occupation of cutler gave rise to a local surname. John Cutler of Attercliffe was named in a deed of 1329; twenty years later Adam Cotelor was a witness to another deed.[4] Amongst those who paid the poll tax in 1379 were Johannes Coteler of Sheffield and his Handsworth namesake, a baker who was presumably descended from a metalworker. Few cutlers paid more than the basic rate of 4d in 1379. The returns recorded occupations when the higher rate of 6d was paid, but they named only three cutlers in Handsworth, one in Ecclesfield, and one in Tinsley. South-west Yorkshire had forty-four smiths and four arrowsmiths who were taxed at the sixpenny rate, however.[5]

At this time Hallamshire (which anciently consisted of the large parishes of Sheffield and Ecclesfield and the chapelry of Bradfield) was not pre-eminent in the manufacture of cutlery. High-class wares were made in the capital, where by the thirteenth century the London cutlers had organized themselves into a guild. A medieval guild was also established at Thaxted, where the place-name Cutlers Green still commemorates the trade. Many another provincial town had a group of cutlers amongst its craftsmen. Cutlery is known to have been made in medieval Ashbourne and Doncaster, for instance, and a Chesterfield street still bears the name of Knife-smithgate. A Sheffield knife was amongst the King's possessions at

[3] W. Brown (ed.), *Yorkshire Lay Subsidy 25 Edward 1*, Yorkshire Archaeological Society Record Series, XVI (1894).
[4] T. W. Hall, *A Catalogue of the Ancient Charters belonging to the Twelve Capital Burgesses and Commonalty* (Sheffield, 1913), pp. 7–8, 16.
[5] *The Returns of the Poll Tax for the West Riding of Yorkshire, 1379*, Yorkshire Archaeological and Topographical Society, V (1882).

the Tower of London *c*. 1340, however, and about fifty years later Geoffrey Chaucer referred to a Sheffield whittle (a multi-purpose knife) in *The Reeve's Tale*. His description of the miller of Trumpington includes the line: 'A Sheffield thwytel bare he in his hose.'[6] Such a knife, recovered from excavations at Sheffield Castle and attributed to the fourteenth century, is on display at the City Museum as the earliest local knife in existence. It consists simply of a wooden handle hafted on to a pointed blade. The unpretentious design of such knives hardly changed before the Elizabethan period.[7]

Evidence for the growth of the cutlery trades in the Middle Ages is scrappy, but late in the reign of Henry VIII John Leland observed, 'Ther be many good smithes and cuttelars in Halamshire' and 'very good smithes for all cutting tooles' in Rotherham.[8] One of the most difficult problems for the historian of early-modern industry is to assess the limited evidence for the extent and the quality of local crafts in the late-medieval period. In the Sheffield region the quality of the medieval product may have been low, but Leland's remarks suggest that numerous craftsmen were already employed before the Commonwealth men turned their attention to the need to encourage native industries.

The evidence becomes richer in the mid sixteenth century. At this time the manufacture of cutlery within Hallamshire was supervised by the manorial courts of the mighty Earls of Shrewsbury. Individual marks were assigned to cutlers by the court. The earliest record of such a mark is that granted to William Ellis in 1554. Does this record indicate a fresh interest in local industry by a manorial lord who was well acquainted with the new thinking amongst the Court circle, or is it merely the first surviving documentation of an

---

[6] G. I. H. Lloyd, *The Cutlery Trades* (London, 1968), pp. 87–92; R. E. Leader, *History of the Company of Cutlers in Hallamshire in the County of York* (Sheffield, 1905), I, pp. 4–5 (all quotations from the company's bye-laws are taken from this source); J. Hunter, *Hallamshire* (London, 1819), p. 59n.; F. N. Robinson, *The Complete Works of Geoffrey Chaucer* (Oxford, 1961), p. xx notes that as a boy Chaucer served Elizabeth, Countess of Ulster, as a page while she was living at Hatfield in south Yorkshire. The possibility therefore arises that Chaucer heard of Sheffield knives when he was in the vicinity. However, *The Canterbury Tales* were not written until thirty or forty years later, so it is more likely that Sheffield was known in London.

[7] H. R. Singleton, *A Chronology of Cutlery* (Sheffield, 1970), p. 1.

[8] L. T. Smith (ed.), *Leland's Itinerary in England and Wales* (London, 1964), IV, p. 14.

old practice? The 'constitutiones, ordaines and devises' drawn up by the Sheffield manor court in 1565 by 'the whole consent of the Cutlers, makers of knyffes and the cutler occupacion wythin the Lordeshyppe of Halomeshire' were said to conform to 'the aunncyants customes and ordainces . . . made and heretofore used'. They included an insistence upon a seven-year apprenticeship, the forbidding of work during a fortnight's holiday in August and a month at Christmas, and the refusal to supply outsiders with partly finished articles or to complete wares that had been fashioned by outsiders. How ancient were the 'aunncyants customes' of 1565? The records show that by 1578 some sixty marks had been registered by the manor court; thirty-nine of them had been granted to the makers of knives, two to shearsmiths, one each to a sickle-maker and an arrowhead smith and seventeen to craftsmen in unspecified trades.[9]

The forty-five wills which survive for Sheffield parish during the period 1539–1600 frequently refer to cutlers' smithies, grinding wheels, and the tools of the trade. The terminology is similar to that used in later centuries, right through to modern times. Thus, in 1547 Richard King bequeathed to his daughter Alice 'the best stithie, bellowes, hammers and tonges, with all things belonging to the same harthe', his servant Otwell Cutler received 'the little stithie, the bellowes, a pair of tonges, a stovente [chimney?], a harth staffe', his wife was given the grinding wheel and other property, and his son Geoffrey inherited 'an axiltre of yron' which was kept at Thomas Hobson's at Wadsley Bridge. Likewise, in 1550 Richard Hobson of Steel Bank[10] left his apprentice, William Hall, 'a pare of gret tonges, a pare of litle tonges', together with a 'borne axe' for burnishing and a heavy hammer known as a 'fore hammer'. It is apparent that little capital was required to set up in business once an apprenticeship had been served. Smithies were humble buildings erected in back yards; the basic equipment comprised a hearth, a pair of bellows, a stithy and stock (an anvil set on a stone base), a coultrough for hardening, a few tongs, hammers, and other simple tools, a supply of iron and steel obtained on credit, and the opportunity to rent part of a grinding wheel from time to time. When

---

[9] *Extracts from the Records of the Cutlers' Company* (Sheffield, 1972), pp. x–xii.
[10] 'Steel' is a corruption of 'stile'.

demand for metalware was high the trade could expand enormously by the multiplication of such establishments.[11]

Favourable literary references leave no doubt that by the reign of Elizabeth the Hallamshire cutlers enjoyed a national reputation. In 1590 Peter Bates, author of the *Writing Schoolmaster*, advised, 'First, therefore, be the choice of your penknife, a right Sheffield knife is best.' On the other hand, a passage in *The Cobbler of Canterbury* (1590) reads: 'Women's wittes are like Sheffield knives, for they are sometimes so keene as they will cutte a haire, and sometimes so blunt that they must goe to the grindstone.' When George, sixth Earl of Shrewsbury, sent a present of knives to Lord Burghley he described them as 'such things as his poor country affordeth with fame throughout the realm'.[12] By the 1580s chapmen were hawking Sheffield wares far afield. 'Hallamshire knives' were being exported to Ireland via Liverpool and Chester, including pocket knives, paring knives, and carving knives; most were referred to simply as 'Hallamshire cutts'.[13] When Robert Secker alias Clarke of Attercliffe died at Worcester during the winter of 1580–1 he had with him three packhorses and a stock of knives which he was apparently selling wholesale in Birmingham, Worcestershire, and Herefordshire.[14] Rarely do we obtain such insights into the extent of the inland trade of Elizabethan England. It seems clear, however, that by then Sheffield had become the leading provincial centre for the manufacture of cheap, all-purpose knives which ordinary families could afford. Surviving examples show that the blades of such knives had become longer and narrower, but they were still hafted mainly with wood or bone and less commonly with horn and brass. Until well into the seventeenth century knives of a more elegant style were made only by London craftsmen.

II

How was it that the Hallamshire cutlers were able to triumph over their provincial rivals by the Elizabethan era and eventually even to

[11] T. W. Hall, *Sheffield and Rotherham from the Twelfth to the Eighteenth Centuries* (Sheffield, 1916), contains abstracts of these wills, which are housed at the Borthwick Institute of Historical Research, York.

[12] Lloyd, pp. 95–6.

[13] D. M. Woodward, *The Trade of Elizabethan Chester* (Oxford, 1970), p. 18.

[14] A. Dyer, *The City of Worcester in the Sixteenth Century* (Leicester, 1973), p. 91.

surpass the skilled craftsmen of London? Before we attempt to answer this question we must first of all dismiss the old story that the expansion of the cutlery trades and the marked specialization of various villages in particular crafts can be accounted for by large numbers of Huguenot refugees who were invited to settle in and around Sheffield by the Earl of Shrewsbury. This suggestion was first advanced in the Sheffield *Iris* of 15 September 1803 by a writer who signed himself 'A Descendant of a Refugee', and it was subsequently embroidered in another newspaper, the *Mercury* of 3 October 1818 and of 19 and 26 May 1821. This story (which was written well over 200 years after the events it purports to describe) has been critically demolished on several occasions. In particular, Dr J. E. Oxley has effectively dismissed claims that certain words in local industrial terminology have French origins.[15] Nor do the surnames recorded in the Sheffield parish register support the idea of a significant influx of foreigners. But a simple, spectacular explanation such as this has an appeal that is apparently indestructible. The study of innovation in early-modern industry is more complicated than such stories allow.

The half-forgotten folk memory behind this tale can now be identified. Mr B. J. Awty has recently shown[16] that a small group of metalworkers of French, though not Huguenot, extraction were indeed brought into the Sheffield area during Elizabeth's reign by George, the sixth Earl of Shrewsbury. These men were not innovators in the cutlery trades but were instrumental in erecting the first charcoal blast furnaces in this locality. When the Earl put his new ironworks in blast during the winter of 1573–4 he employed workmen of French nationality or descent who had previously worked at similar ironworks in the Sussex Weald. Mr Awty suggests that up to twenty or thirty workers would have been needed to establish the blast furnaces at Attercliffe, Kimberworth, and Wadsley. He has used parish and manorial records to identify five names of French origin and Wealden connections, i.e. Lawrence Dippray (1573), Giles Maryon (1576), John Valliance (1576), Jordan Russell (1577), and James Tyler (1578). Dippray and

---

[15] J. E. Oxley, 'Notes on the History of the Sheffield Cutlery Industry', *Transactions of the Hunter Archaeological Society*, VII, I (1951), 1–10.
[16] B. J. Awty, 'French Immigrants and the Iron Industry in Sheffield', *Yorkshire Archaeological Journal*, LIII (1981), 57–62.

Maryon stayed for only a few years, but the others founded local dynasties that continued to work the neighbouring furnaces and forges. John Valliance moved to the Monk Bretton smithies and the Russells went to Norton forge, but the Tylers continued at Wadsley forge well into the eighteenth century. The importance of this group of foreign immigrants in establishing new methods of smelting iron cannot be doubted.

The Vintins and Perigoes whose names appear in local parish registers during the seventeenth century were also descended from French families which had previously worked in Sussex. The Gelleys of Wadsley forge and the Gillams of Attercliffe and Stone forges likewise have surnames that point to French origins. Mr Awty suggests that other names that may lead in the same direction include Almond (with Alman as a variant), Bartholomew, Binny, Gillot, Grout, Jordan, Lambert, and Longley. However, other origins for these names can be postulated and Binny, Gillot, and Longley (the name of a hamlet on Sheffield's northern boundary) are well evidenced locally well before the sixteenth century. Even if we allow them all, the long-term significance of this immigrant group is debatable. Only a handful of surnames that came from French stock were recorded in the local returns of the Hearth Tax for 1670 and 1672, i.e. William Russell at Norton (two hearths), Richard Jelley in the Southey quarter of Ecclesfield parish (two hearths), Humphrey Almond of Attercliffe township (one hearth), and John Bartholomew and Gyles Gillam of Brightside township, who were both exempted from paying the tax on their single hearths on the grounds of their poverty. They were hardly a prosperous group. The French immigrants who were responsible for establishing the charcoal blast furnaces a hundred years earlier played little part in the subsequent growth of the metal trades.

Mr Awty accepts that the lay subsidy rolls of 1568 and 1598 for Strafforth and Tickhill wapentake (which included Hallamshire) do not contain a single entry for foreigners who were subject to a tax on aliens, whereas in south-eastern England considerable numbers of immigrants were taxed. Nevertheless, he has revived the idea that the Hallamshire cutlery trades were boosted by foreign immigrants, though he agrees that they were not Huguenots and that they did not arrive in great numbers. His case rests on the fact that some descendants of the Elizabethan ironworkers were apprenticed to local cutlers, though this penetration occurred gradually and rather late. So late in fact that it is rare to find any names from this group in the records of the Cutlers' Company before the 1670s; indeed, the Gillams and Lamberts do not appear in the apprenticeship records until the eighteenth century. Mr Awty's trump card is that George Valliance, the son of John Valliance the ironworker, became Master Cutler in 1633. But in 1627 this same George Valliance, along with several other cutlers, challenged the Company's ordinance which prohibited the gilding of knives that were worth less than 5s a dozen, on the grounds that they were 'poore men and not of ability to make gilded knives and wares of that value'. They claimed that the new ordinance meant they were thereby 'wholly disabled in the practice and use of their trade'. In 1658 George Valliance received charitable aid from the company. It cannot be seriously argued that he was the leader of a group of immigrants who had greatly improved the quality of the local cutlery products. As we have already seen, the design of Hallamshire knives did not improve significantly until well into the seventeenth century, long after the settlement of this particular group of French furnacemen.

How, then, did the Hallamshire cutlers and edge-tool makers triumph over their competitors? The availability of iron ore was obviously a factor in the growth of the metal trades, but it was not a crucial one. Few places are as land-locked as Hallamshire, yet by the sixteenth century metal of sufficient quality to provide a cutting edge for knives and tools had to be imported from overseas. As early as 1537 – before the days of the Commonwealth men – Henry Renshaw, a Chesterfield metalworker, had £9 worth of 'Speynyshe yron unwroight' which had presumably come from Spain via the Trent and the Idle to the inland port of Bawtry. The steel recorded in the probate inventories of Lawrence Boller (1568) and Philip Yates (1582), two scythesmiths from Chesterfield parish, must also have come this way, for none was made locally at this period.[17] The bailiff of the manor of Sheffield imported Spanish iron through Bawtry in 1574, presumably for the local cutlers.[18] Obviously, the region had already acquired other advantages and a strong tradition of craftsmanship in order to overcome this handicap. During the

[17] J. M. Bestall and D. V. Fowkes (eds.), *Chesterfield Wills and Inventories, 1521–1603*, Derbyshire Record Society, 1 (1977), p. xxv.
[18] Sheffield Record Office, MD 192.

seventeenth century German and then Swedish ores were favoured. Even the moorland township of Dore, which never supported more than a handful of cutlers, obtained high-quality metal this way; in 1617, for instance, Christopher Hodgkinson of Dore was using iron that had been imported from Lübeck.[19]

III

What, then, was the advantage that Sheffield possessed over its provincial rivals? Undoubtedly, it lay in the superior facilities that were available for grinding fine cutting edges. The importance of water power in Sheffield's industrial development can hardly be over-emphasized. The rivers Don, Sheaf, Loxley, and Rivelin, the Porter Brook and neighbouring streams such as the Moss Beck and the Blackburn Brook are only small, but they fall rapidly from the western hills before levelling out beyond Hallamshire. Goits channelled the water into dams at frequent intervals in order that overshot wheels could power numerous grinding wheels and other mills, tilts, and forges. Thomas Jeffreys's map of Yorkshire of 1767–72 shows that Sheffield had a greater concentration of water-powered sites than anywhere else in contemporary Britain. The first steam grinding works was not built until 1786 and long remained a rarity. In 1819 Joseph Hunter, the eminent antiquary, described the local rivers and streams as the very life of Sheffield's manufactures.[20] Even after the disastrous Sheffield Flood of 1864 all the industrial sites along the Loxley valley were rebuilt as water-powered units. When steam-powered cutlery factories were eventually built at Sheffield they were known at first as 'steam wheels'. However, Sheffield's good fortune in this respect lay not just in the availability of water power; it was also blest with abundant quarries of sandstone of an ideal quality for grinding knives and edge tools. One of the most notable resources of the manor of Sheffield, according to John Harrison's survey of 1637, was its 'course grinding stones for knives and scithes'. By that time 400–500 master workmen were said to use the lord's grinding wheels on a regular basis.[21]

References to local grinding wheels in the Middle Ages are few and far between. One on the Moss Beck near Ford was recorded in

[19] Lichfield Joint Record Office, wills and inventories.
[20] Hunter, p. 6.   [21] Sheffield Record Office, ACM S75.

1350, so it is likely that several others were then in existence nearer the town on the larger rivers.[22] In 1497 Richard Lee of Norton and Richard Bawer of Ecclesall, cutlers, leased from William Brasse of Millhouses 'a water wheel and its watercourse, a pair of trendylls, and a naxyltree' on the river Sheaf.[23] From the mid sixteenth century onwards the evidence becomes fuller and bequests in wills show that grinding wheels were being worked on most of the local rivers and streams. A 1581 rental of the manor of Sheffield named fifteen grinding wheels shared by twenty-three tenants.[24] A few other wheels had already been established in neighbouring manors. Most were in secluded rural situations. At this period they were timber-framed structures, as of course were most of the local houses and farm buildings. The construction of the Ashingar wheel on the river Loxley, on land belonging to the lord of the manor at Owlerton, illustrates this point. In 1549 two cutlers, William Shooter of Wadsley and Thomas Creswick of Owlerton, employed John Lawe, a Beauchief labourer, to build 'III honest bey off trwyfing II watter whells II Cogge wheel troghes and trondyll' and to make a substantial dam with goit and shuttle; the terms of the leases allowed the felling of a dozen trees from the waste.[25]

Several mid-sixteenth-century wills mention leases of wheels or shares in them. The whole building was commonly known as a wheel and separate compartments were referred to as ends. Thus, in 1558 Jeffrey Hobson of Scraith left his three sons his 'ende of the whele'. An end often contained about six or eight positions for grinders to sit astride a wooden seat or 'horse' behind a small grinding wheel. The terminology gets confused when these individual grinding wheels – each of them geared to the water wheel which powered the whole building – were also referred to as 'wheels'. Thus, in 1554, when James Tailor of Heeley divided his property between his sons, James and Robert, James inherited two 'wheels', i.e. 'the whele on the Farrside and the whele in the Nooke that Robert my sonne shall have one day gryndynge every weeke and

[22] R. Hawkins, *The Distribution of Water-powered Sites in Sheffield*, Sheffield City Museum Information Sheet, 4 (1975), p. 1. See D. Crossley (ed.), *Water Power on the Sheffield Rivers* (Sheffield, 1989), for a survey of all the water-powered wheels, forges, and mills.
[23] Sheffield Record Office, Oakes deeds, 887 and 892.
[24] Sheffield Record Office, ACM S114.
[25] Sheffield Record Office, Beauchief muniments, 365.

that the said Robert do gyve the said James warnynge on the Sonday what day he will have yt'. James was to find 'for the said two wheles horse and harness', in other words seats and belting to connect the grinding wheels to the source of power. A third son, Thomas, was given 'the whele before the doore'.[26] Joan Thirsk has drawn attention to the way in which partible inheritance was often a feature of areas where industry flourished. Hallamshire practice – though it was never formalized – was to provide for all the male members of the family.

The Hallamshire cutlers remained under manorial supervision while the Earls of Shrewsbury were the local lords, but with the death of Gilbert, the seventh earl, in 1616 the male line failed and henceforth Sheffield's lords were non-resident. The cutlers had anticipated the event two years earlier when they purchased a book to enter the marks of the 182 cutlers then working within Hallamshire. With the consent of Earl Gilbert a jury of sixteen cutlers assumed responsibility for issuing marks and for 'receipts and disbursements', though the lord continued to enjoy the manorial perquisite of receiving the fines. The names of the jurors indicate that the leading men of the company came from long-established families. They were William Wilkinson, Nicholas Turton, Thomas Webster, Robert Sorsby, William Webster, John Parkin of Southey, Godfrey Birley, George Hobson, John Parkin, William Wylde, Robert Pearson, Anthony Webster, John Creswick, Lawrence Sheppard, Francis Carr, and John Oxspring. These surnames betray no trace of immigrant influence and can often be traced back locally to the Middle Ages.

Two months after the first entry in the book, seventeen cutlers who lived just beyond Hallamshire in Derbyshire were accepted within the new company even though they lived within different lordships. The following year a second jury was elected and the annual accounts were passed; the company had clearly been established on a formal footing. It was not until 1621, however, that a bill was presented to Parliament 'for the good order and government of the cutlers of Hallamshire'. Somehow this bill was delayed, but in 1624 an Act was passed whereby:

[26] Hall, *Sheffield and Rotherham from the Twelfth to the Eighteenth Centuries*, pp. 87, 105–6, 109, 112, 120.

all persons using to make Knives, Blades, Scissers, Sheeres, Sickles, Cutlery wares, and all other wares and manufactures made or wrought of yren and steele, dwelling or inhabiting within the said Lordship and Liberty of Hallamshire, or within six miles compasse of the same, be from henceforth, and hereafter may be in deed and in name one body politique, perpetuall, and incorporate of one Master, two Wardens, sixe Searchers, and foure and twenty Assistants a comminalty of the said Company of Cutlers, of the Lordship of Hallamshiere, in the County of Yorke.

The main functions of the new company were to enrol apprentices, admit freemen, make orders, and act on behalf of the membership, both on an individual and collective basis. Robert Sorsby was chosen as the first Master Cutler, with Godfrey Birley and John Rawson as Wardens.

The preamble to the Act claimed that:

Whereas the greatest part of the Inhabitants of the Lordship and Liberty of Hallamshire in the said County of Yorke, doe consist of Cutlers, and of those that make Knives, and other Cutlery Wares, and other Wares made and wrought of Iron and Steele, as Sickles, Scissors and Sheeres, and by their industrie and labour in the same Artes and Trades, have not onely gained the reputation of great skill and dexterity in the said faculty, but have relieved and maintained their families, and have been enabled to set on worke many poore men inhabiting thereabouts, who have very small meanes or maintenance of living other then by their hands, and dayly labour as workemen to the sayd Cutlers, and have made knives of the best edge, wherewith they served the most partes of this Kingdome, and other foreine countreys.

In other words the cutlers were claiming to constitute the major part of the local workforce and to make goods for a wide market. Their specific mention of knives 'of the best edge' supports the idea that it was the grinding process that gave Sheffield an advantage over its competitors.

London excelled in the manufacture of high-quality knives, while Sheffield catered for a mass market. Thomas Fuller wrote in 1662 that most of the common knives of country people were made in Yorkshire and that Sheffield, 'a remarkable market', was 'the staple town for this commodity . . . One may justly wonder how a knife may be sold for one penny.'[27] A variety of materials were used for the handles. In 1595 a servant of the Earl of Shrewsbury sent 'two cases of knives, one hefted in dudgeon and the other in Hart horns' to London; dudgeon was wood of a type used by turners for handles.[28] In 1616 Roger Barber, an Eckington cutler, had a quantity of 'Olivant', i.e. elephant or ivory, in his smithy[29] and early knives on display in Sheffield City Museum include one made in 1632 by William Creswicke of Sheffield with a brass handle and one made about 1658 by Thomas Tucker of Sheffield with a bone handle.

The best London cutlers were remarkably skilled. Joan Thirsk has noted that in 1571 Richard Mathew received a patent for making knives and knife handles of a Turkish design. Edmund Howe, who revised John Stow's *Annals of London* in 1615, wrote that Mathew was the first Englishman to attain perfection in the art of making knives and handles, having learned his art abroad. He went on to say that in earlier times 'there were made in diverse parts of this kingdom many coarse and uncomely knives' but that 'at this day the best and finest knives in the world are made in London'. Foreign immigrants had helped to establish London's reputation. By 1622 a number of foreign cutlers who lived in St Martin le Grand were famous for the quality of their wares.[30] It has been said that knives of the first half of the seventeenth century were the most distinctive and attractive type ever produced in this country. Handles were often made with 'small panels or fillets or amber, ivory, agate or bone, separated from the blade by a long slender shoulder finely decorated with chiselled silver work' and the terminal cap often bore 'a delicate finial of silver filigree'.[31]

London was the leading centre of cutlery manufacture, but by the first quarter of the seventeenth century some of these high-quality wares were being made in Sheffield. The bye-laws of the Cutlers' Company, passed in 1625, stated that no gold or silver was to be put on blades, bolsters, or hafts of knives that cost less than 5s a dozen and that no cutler was to 'damaske, inlay or studd any knives or wares, or intermix the same with any pewter, tin, lead, brass, or other counterfeit stuff, whereby any ignorant man may be induced

[27] T. Fuller, *The Worthies of England* (1662), (London, Folio Society, 1987), p. 423.
[28] Sheffield Record Office, ACM Talbot Letters, 2/133.
[29] Lichfield Joint Record Office, probate inventories.
[30] Thirsk, p. 128.   [31] Singleton, pp. 1–2.

to take the same to be silver or gold'; only real silver or gold was to be used. Sheffield craftsmen recorded during the middle years of the seventeenth century include Richard Creswicke, goldsmith (1637), Edward Fisher, silversmith (1641), Martin Webster, goldbeater (1645), William Kirkham, goldbeater (1655), George and Thomas Steven, silversmiths (1655), and Godfrey Nodder of Handsworth, goldbeater (1669).[32] Again, we may note the absence of foreign names. Somehow local craftsmen had acquired sufficient skill to work with precious metals. We have no evidence at all to suggest how this came about, but it is reasonable to assume that Sheffield craftsmen copied the cutlery that was being produced in the capital. Hallamshire wares were sold in London by local factors; indeed some traders set up residence there. Sheffield was connected to the capital by a weekly carrier service by the reign of Charles I, if not before, and Hallamshire cutlers were often in trouble for stamping their knives with London marks. In 1663, for instance, London searchers destroyed seventy-five dozen and four knives stored at Leadenhall that had been made in Sheffield with the London mark of a dagger. Further raids took place in succeeding years, but this did not stop the Cutlers' Company of Hallamshire from issuing the dagger mark, or from stamping goods: LONDON.[33] The likely explanation for the improved quality of Sheffield knives seems to be that indigenous local craftsmen were well able to imitate the work of the London cutlers and that it paid them handsomely to make high-quality knives as well as common wares if they were able enough.

IV

Nearly all the skilled cutlers of Hallamshire lived in the town of Sheffield rather than in the countryside. We shall see, however, that some specialist skilled crafts were entirely rural-based. Hardly any probate inventories from the parish of Sheffield survive before 1689, but sixteenth-century wills contain sufficient evidence to show that local cutlers, even some of those who lived in the town rather than the surrounding countryside, commonly farmed a smallholding. For example, in 1542 John Archdale bequeathed horses,

---

[32] West Yorkshire Archive Service, quarter sessions records; Cutlers' Company apprenticeship lists; Sheffield parish register; Hall, *Sheffield and Rotherham*, p. 188.
[33] Leader, 1, pp. 158–9.

mares, and sheep as well as a smithy. In the same year Richard Boyer left his son John two wains and two ploughs 'with all things appertaining to husbandry', his two daughters each a heifer and his son Richard a share with John Hobson of all his 'smythe gere and the coltroughe'; Agnes Firth received a cow and three others each received a lamb. In 1545 John Birley, an Attercliffe yeoman, bequeathed to Hugh Swan the lease of his farm, together with his bellows, stithies, hammers and tongs and 'all things belonging to the smythe', for despite his occupational description he was a cutler as well as a farmer. And in 1546 Edward Hawke's bequests included smithy gear and two cows. Deeds provide similar evidence. In 1539, for instance, Thomas Creswicke, an Owlerton cutler, bought 5 acres of meadow and 2½ acres of arable land.[34] In having such a dual occupation the local metalworkers pursued a similar way of life to those contemporary craftsmen whom Joan Thirsk has described as forming perhaps half the farming population of early-modern England.[35] Even many of the townsmen still had a small investment in agriculture during the sixteenth and seventeenth centuries and urban cutlers with no land were often able to keep a pig. In 1566, for example, Hugh Storey paid 3s rent for 'a smythye and a swyne hoowle'.

'A Survey of Lands belonging to the Mannor of Sheffield' dated 1611[36] included some rural farms that had smithies amongst the out-buildings. Thomas Slatter's property was described as 'One house 3 baies 1 parler 1 Chamber one barne 3 baies one ould barne 3 baies one oven house 2 baies one Smethey 1 bay'. He farmed forty-three acres of pasture and eleven-and-a-half acres of meadow and he leased part of the nearby Hall Wood. His neighbour, Thomas Greene, rented 'One Dwelling house 3 baies 2 parlers 1 chamber one Kitchen with an oven 1 bay one new Barne 3 baies one other Barne 2 baies 1 Stable 1 bay one wainehouse 2 bay one Smythey 1 bay, one Kilne house', and he farmed fifty-five acres of pasture,

[34] T. W. Hall, *Sheffield Wills Proved at York Prior to 1554* (Sheffield, 1913), pp. 71, 73–4, 76; T. W. Hall, *A Descriptive Catalogue of the Wheat Collection* (Sheffield, 1920), p. 40; J. D. Leader, *Records of the Burgery of Sheffield* (London, 1897), p. 15.

[35] J. Thirsk, 'Seventeenth-Century Agriculture and Social Change', in J. Thirsk (ed.), *Land, Church and People: Essays Presented to Professor H. P. R. Finberg*, *A.H.R.*, Supplement (1978), p. 172. See also D. Hey, *The Rural Metalworkers of the Sheffield Region* (Leicester, 1972).

[36] Sheffield Record Office, Ronksley Collection, 158.

twenty-six acres of meadow, and three acres of wood. They were typical of many of the local craftsmen-farmers in combining a pastoral form of husbandry with the manufacture of cutlery, edge tools, or nails. Some of the metalworkers in the region grew a considerable quantity of cereals, however. The Norton scythesmiths in particular were often substantial farmers as well as craftsmen.

It is worth examining the origins and early growth of the Norton scythemaking trade in some detail for the light which it sheds on the other metal trades and indeed much of rural industry in general. The manufacture of scythes was an ancient local industry which was well established by the late-medieval period but which expanded considerably during the sixteenth and seventeenth centuries. When John Meysham was accused of sedition against Richard II in 1378 his occupation was recorded as 'Sithemaker'. He is the first Derbyshire man of whom we have knowledge who worked at that particular craft, but during the following two centuries several other scythemakers can be located in Derby and Chesterfield and in parts of the adjacent countryside. The north Derbyshire parish of Norton, which lay on the county boundary immediately south of Sheffield, eventually became the recognized centre of the trade. Scythes were made in the parish by the mid fifteenth century, for in 1459 John Parker of Little Norton was described as a scythesmith. During the early sixteenth century a few scythesmiths can be identified in the neighbouring parishes of Dronfield, Eckington, Chesterfield, and Barlow, and Dr I. S. W. Blanchard has identified another cluster north of Derby and east of the river Derwent at Belper, Horsley, Kilburn, Makeney, and Swanwick, on the coal-measure sandstones where iron was mined and within easy reach of the water-powered grinding wheels that were established from at least the mid fifteenth century onwards.[37]

By the reign of Elizabeth scythes and edge-tools were being made in small quantities in widely scattered parts of England, but two areas had become pre-eminent. Both of these specialist districts lay at the edges of the country's major metalworking regions. The north Worcestershire parishes of Belbroughton, Chaddesley Corbett, and

---

[37] I. S. W. Blanchard, 'Economic Change in Derbyshire in the Late Middle Ages, 1272–1540', unpublished London Ph.D. thesis, 1967, 356–7 (I am grateful to Dr Blanchard for permission to quote from this thesis); R. A. Mott, 'The Water-Mills of Beauchief Abbey', *Transactions of the Hunter Archaeological Society*, IX, IV (1969), 203–20.

Clent and the south-west Staffordshire parishes of Himley and Womborne were the centres of the West Midlands trade, near to the grinding mills on the small, but fast-flowing streams.[38] In the Hallamshire metal-working region Norton parish flourished as the scythe-making district while the trade withered in neighbouring communities. Probate records name three scythesmiths in Chesterfield parish between 1559 and 1582 and one at Coal Aston in Dronfield parish in 1592, but none later, and although a branch of the Parkers, the Norton scythemaking family, had set up a business at Whitley in Ecclesfield parish by 1510, the records of this enterprise cease after 1552.[39] Few scythesmiths even crossed the river Sheaf, the boundary between Norton and Sheffield; Joseph Barnes, scythe-grinder of Wadsley,[40] and William Bullock, scythe-grinder of Stannington,[41] were unusual in plying their trade in Sheffield's northern rivers in the early eighteenth century. Both these men were members of Norton families. Norton parish had acquired a near monopoly of the trade. It is not easy to see why this should have happened.

As we have seen, water power was of fundamental importance to the industrial development of the Sheffield region, and it undoubtedly played a large part in the localization of the scythe trade in the parish of Norton. The first recorded scythe mill in north Derbyshire was situated on the river Rother at Holbrook, near Staveley, in 1489,[42] but the Sheaf, which formed Norton's northwestern border, soon became the river where most of the scythemakers went to grind their blades.[43] In 1686 Robert Plot noted a similar factor in the West Midlands, that other great scythemaking area, when he wrote that grinding wheels were situated on the fast-flowing streams and 'all the little waters hereabouts'.[44]

The wrought iron that formed the outer parts of the scythe – as distinct from the steel cutting edge – was produced locally. Both in Norton and in the West Midlands proximity to a flourishing metal-

---

[38] P. Large, 'Urban Growth and Agricultural Change in the West Midlands during the Seventeenth and Eighteenth Centuries', in P. Clark (ed.), *The Transformation of English Provincial Towns, 1600–1800* (London, 1984), pp. 169–89.

[39] W. T. Miller, *The Water-Mills of Sheffield* (Sheffield, 1949), p. 94.

[40] Sheffield Record Office, ACM S375.

[41] Lichfield Joint Record Office, probate inventories.

[42] Lloyd, p. 88.

[43] See Mott; Miller, pp. 29–42.

[44] R. Plot, *The Natural History of Staffordshire* (Oxford, 1686), p. 374.

working centre offered gains in reducing the cost of transporting ores. There was no marketing advantage in lying so close to Sheffield, for the scythesmiths distributed their wares to the western market towns and country fairs independently of the Sheffield cutlery factors, but the shared need for abundant supplies of iron may have been one of the reasons why the Derbyshire scythemaking trade moved north. On the other hand, Norton parish had a significant number of scythesmiths even before French ironworkers erected the first charcoal blast furnaces in the Sheffield region. The trade was well established in the parish before detailed records begin.

The Elizabethan baptism register for Norton parish[45] names eleven scythesmiths, two scythe-strikers, and a scythe-seller during a twenty-year period between October 1559 and September 1579. Some of these craftsmen were already producing considerable quantities of scythes for sale. When Richard Urton, alias Steven, a Norton scythesmith, died in 1574 he had '12 hundrethe scythes every hundrethe £8', worth together £96, with '12 packs of sycklles' valued at £26 12s 0d and 'all the smethe geyre' appraised at £7. His scythes therefore cost about 1s 7d each at his smithy, which compares closely with the 1s 6d value that was placed on each of the 650 scythes belonging to John Waldern of Belbroughton in 1541 and the valuations of 1s 8d for each of forty dozen scythes made by Richard Brookehouse of Oldswinford, north Worcestershire, in 1594.[46] Transport costs and the middleman's profit inflated these prices by the time they reached the buyer. Thus, the mowers employed by Henry Best of Elmswell on the Yorkshire Wolds 'usually buy theire sythes att some faires here-aboutes; the price of a sythe is usually 2s.2d. or 2s.4d.; sometimes they may bee bought for 22d. and sometimes againe they cannot bee bought under 2s.6d.'.[47]

The probate inventories of seventeenth-century Norton scythesmiths show that considerable quantities of finished and unfinished scythes were stocked in their smithies or at the grinding wheels. For example, Edward Hudson of Sickhouse (1622) had sixteen dozen scythes valued at sixteen guineas, Henry Brownell of Jordanthorpe (1634) had 'Two Hundreth 4 dozen and 5 Sythes' worth £17 5s 4d

[45] L. L. Simpson, *Norton Parish Registers* (Derby, 1908).
[46] J. S. Roper, *Early North Worcestershire Scythesmiths* (Dudley, 1967).
[47] H. Best, *Rural Economy in Yorkshire,* Surtees Society, XXXIII (1861), p. 32.

and Thomas Bower of Norton Lees (1640) had '9 dossen sythes at John Gillots wheele' appraised at nine guineas. The north Worcestershire scythesmiths were manufacturing on a similar scale. In 1541, for instance, John Waldern of Belbroughton had 650 scythes worth £52 listed in his inventory. Peter Large has shown how the Worcestershire scythesmiths made their scythes in the early months of the year, when the rivers were fast-flowing and work on the farm was less demanding, but the Norton scythesmiths often had stocks of scythes recorded at home through the summer and into autumn. The Belbroughton scythesmiths sold most of their wares in the south Midlands; the Norton scythesmiths sold their goods in the market towns and principal fairs of north-eastern England and even Scotland. When William Blythe of Norton Lees, yeoman, died in 1632 his finished stock consisted of 650 long scythes, 450 scythes of a second sort, 450 of a third sort, and 350 Scottish scythes. His son and namesake carried on the business in the same style, selling scythes in Wakefield, Beverley, York, Boroughbridge, Morpeth, and Newcastle upon Tyne. He may even have been making scythes to suit regional requirements, for packs of Scottish scythes and Holderness scythes were identified by the appraisers of his inventory upon his death in 1666. It is clear from a study of these and other inventories that by the Elizabethan and early Stuart period the parish of Norton had become a leading specialist centre in the production of agricultural edge tools.

V

Immediately to the east of the Norton parish boundary, the manufacture of hand-made sickles became the speciality of the various hamlets of Troway quarter of Eckington parish, where in the space of two miles eight or nine grinding wheels were once at work in the Moss Valley. A wheel on the Moss Beck had been recorded as far back as 1350, though at that time it was probably used for grinding cutlery. Sickle-making in this part of the parish of Eckington was a later development. It appears to be one of those rural industries which migrated from a nearby town some time during the sixteenth century. Its history casts a different light on the origins and localization of the secondary metal trades.

The local origins of the trade are to be found in central Sheffield and its easterly township of Attercliffe. Even there, however, no direct reference to the craft has been found earlier than Elizabeth's reign. John Staniforth was awarded a mark as a sicklemaker by the Sheffield manorial court in 1565, but he was exceptional. At this period the making of sickles was normally regarded as a task for the shearsmith. A by-law issued by the Cutlers' Company in 1662 stated that the making of knives had time out of mind been accounted one distinct trade, the making of scissors was another, and the making of shears and sickles was a third; a £10 penalty was imposed on anyone found manufacturing the wares of another craft. When the Cutlers' Company was incorporated in 1624 it included within its jurisdiction not only cutlers but the makers of scissors, shears, and sickles. In contrast to the urban shearsmith-sicklemakers the rural scythesmiths did not join the Company until 1682, when thirty-three of them were admitted into membership.

The number of urban shearsmiths remained small throughout the seventeenth century and few specialist sicklesmiths emerged there. Nicholas Staniforth of Attercliffe was described as a sicklesmith in 1630, but Sheffield parish had only one sicklemaker and six shear-smiths amongst the 1,140 men whose occupations were recorded in the baptism and burial register between 1 October 1698 and 30 September 1703. The trade had gradually migrated southwards into the countryside, where it had been established in a modest way since the late sixteenth century. We have already seen that in 1574 Richard Urton, a Norton scythesmith, had twelve packs of sickles worth £26 12s 0d, but the other probate inventories from the parish suggest that Norton scythesmiths rarely made sickles. The scythe-making trade became established a little further to the east, in the Moss Valley.

The Staniforth family played a leading role in this part of Eckington parish during the seventeenth and eighteenth centuries and they may well have been the earliest sicklemakers to move from Attercliffe or Sheffield across the boundary into Derbyshire. Their surname is one of those which can be shown to have had a peculiar local origin. It can be identified with a lost place-name near Winco-bank on the boundary between the parishes of Sheffield and Eccles-field, a 'stony ford' across the river Don or perhaps the Blackburn Brook. In 1434, for example, John de Stannyford appeared at the Sheffield manorial court to surrender land in Stannyford to the use

of Richard de Stannyford, his son and heir.[48] When John Staniforth
of the parish of Eckington died in 1597 he had a medium-sized farm
and 'Syckles ready made xxix dozen, £2.2s.8d., Sheres ready made
ix dozen and vii, £2, knyves ready made xix dozen, £1.4s.0d., yron
unwrought, £1.13s.0d., Steele unwrought, 2s.8d.'; the trades of
shearsmith and sicklesmith were not yet distinct. William
Staniforth, who died at Litfield, near Sload Lane, in 1630, was
making sickles as well as running a farm and an alehouse. His son,
Robert, was apprenticed to William Cowley of Little Norton, shearsmith, the following year. Other Staniforths combined their farming
with other trades in the Moss Valley. In 1639 Robert Staniforth of
Ford was a tanner and in 1651 George Staniforth of Geer Lane was
described as a yeoman. George's son, John, however, was apprenticed to a Ridgeway Lane shearsmith. Later in the century, William
Staniforth was a sicklesmith-farmer at Hackenthorpe, just across
the parish boundary in Beighton.[49] Gales and Martin's *Directory of
Sheffield* shows that in 1787 members of the Staniforth family were
still making sickles at Ford, Hackenthorpe, Moorhole, and
Ridgeway.

The Cowleys were another Eckington family who were active in
the early years of the sickle trade. Their name, too, was derived
from a local place-name. When Robert Cowley of Renishaw made
his will in 1612 he thought of himself as a shearsmith. On his farm he
had six oxen, six kine, five bullocks and one heifer, five young
beasts, three mares, four swine, seventy-five old sheep and fifteen
lambs, 9 acres sown with wheat, rye and barley, 10 acres of peas,
and oats and grain stored from the previous harvest in his chambers.
Both the Norton scythesmiths and the Eckington sicklesmiths had
sizeable farms devoted to mixed husbandry. In this they were unlike
so many contemporary craftsmen whose smallholding was geared to
pastoral farming, but they were similar to the prosperous
scythesmith-farmers of north Worcestershire and south Staffordshire. In his smithy Cowley possessed: 'three Stythies two payre of
bellowes with other smythie tooles with the wheele gayre and
grindle stones, £8, in wares siccles and sheares viz xx in siccles forty

[48] Sir A. S. Scott-Gatty, 'Records of the Court Baron of the Manor of Sheffield',
Transactions of the Hunter Archaeological Society, I, 3–4, pp. 257–329.
[49] The genealogical records of the Eckington sicklesmiths are taken from parish and
probate records, some of which were published in 'W. F.', *Ridgeway Village*
(Sheffield, 1950).

hundreth eight grosse of sheares, £50, in Iron and steele, £3'. He was also owed £209 by various persons, mostly on 'specialtyes'. He bequeathed 'all my Smythie gayre and Ymplements thereunto belonging as bellowes stythies tonges hammers toyles wheeles stones' to his sons, William and Henry. Perhaps William was the Little Norton shearsmith of that name who had taken Robert Staniforth as his apprentice in 1631?

Other sickle-making families included the Turners and the Booths. When Thomas Turner of Troway died in 1598 he had seven old sickles valued at 1d each. Edward Turner, the apprentice of Stephen Beardsall of Ridgeway Lane, became a freeman of the Cutlers' Company in 1628. Anthony Turner of Troway, who died in 1641, was a scythesmith, and William Turner of Mosborough, who had died seven years previously, was an axe-smith with a medium-sized farm. Within two or three generations branches of the family were established at Ridgeway, Troway, Ford, Lightwood, Norton, Bramley, Mosborough Moorside, and Sload Lane. Three Turners were making sickles in 1787. The Booths were sicklemakers from at least the middle years of the seventeenth century in and around Ridgeway; they were still there in 1787.

Both families were included amongst those metalworkers who refused to pay tax on their smithy hearths in 1672.[50] Together with a cutler and three blacksmiths, seventeen men with thirty-four smithy hearths were listed in Eckington parish. They included five Staniforths, three Turners and a Booth, but no Huttons, the family who were eventually to become the best-known firm in the trade. They came to the valley in 1678 when Richard, the son of Henry Hutton, a farmer of Swinton, a few miles north-east, was apprenticed in the sickle trade to Thomas Staniforth of Sload Lane. In turn, his eldest son, Joseph (1699–1775) was apprenticed to Jonathan Booth of Ridgeway. The local sickle-making families were intimately connected in this way. Joseph Hutton II (1728–80), who was apprenticed to his father, developed the family business during the third quarter of the eighteenth century, selling his sickles in London, Deptford, and the east Midlands. By 1830 William

---

[50] PRO, E 179/94/394. The others named were Thomas Andrew, Stephen Beardsall, Nathaniel Creswicke, John Hadfield, Henry Hancock, George Kirkby, William Leake, and William Taylor.

Cobbett could report that 'a prodigious quantity' of sickles and scythes were exported to America.[51]

Although sickle-making was practised most evidently in the Troway quarter of Eckington parish, it eventually spread a little further afield. The Norton parish register mentions sicklesmiths at Backmoor, Herdings, Hurlfield, Norton, and Woodseats between 1734 and 1749, though none had been recorded in the Elizabethan period when the register had previously noted occupations. Likewise, scythes were occasionally made in Eckington parish; Samuel Staniforth of the parish of Eckington was named as scythesmith in 1718, but seven years later he was described as a sicklesmith. The 1787 directory makes it clear, however, that the manufacture of sickles was centred in the parish of Eckington, for at that time twenty-five of the thirty-one sicklemakers lived there and the other six worked just across the parish boundary.

The ability to dam the Moss Beck at various points in its descent towards the river Rother was the crucial factor in the industrial development of the area. To take but one example, the Birley Hay Wheel was in use in 1626 when George Savage, a Sheffield yeoman, leased to Ralph Leake of Ford, yeoman, and Robert Staniforth of Ford, yeoman, a farm with 'a Cutlers milne or wheel'. In 1641 John Savage of Birley Hay, sicklesmith, married Elizabeth Staniforth of Geer Lane and leased his wheel, smithy, and farm to George Savage of Eckington, yeoman, and John Newbould of Hackenthorpe, yeoman. A 1757 mortgage of the Birley Hay Forge and Wheel referred to freehold sickle shops and grinding wheels. In 1787 it belonged to Staniforth and Booth and in 1836 it was converted by Thomas Hutton into a scythe forge, though with continued facilities for sickle-grinding.[52] The story is a typical one of enterprise and willingness to adapt to changing circumstances, characteristics that Joan Thirsk has frequently commented upon in her studies of agricultural and industrial innovation in the early-modern period. Sickle-making was not a trade established by outsiders, least of all by foreign immigrants, but an ancient local craft that in the seventeenth century became a specialist occupation developed by a small group of closely connected families in a restricted area where it was

---

[51] W. Cobbett, *Rural Rides*, Everyman edition (London, 1930), II, p. 609.

[52] See 'W. F.'; Sheffield Record Office, MD 4013.

possible to combine metalworking with farming close to water-powered grinding wheels.

VI

The Hallamshire metalworkers could readily turn their hands to the making of other metal goods if economic opportunities arose to make it worth their while. They worked in a culture that admired ingenuity and invention. Indeed, the Cutlers' Company encouraged innovation by allowing the patenting of new ideas for a three-year period. Joan Thirsk has written of the ways in which stocking-knitters responded to 'The Fantastical Folly of Fashion'. Hallamshire cutlers were just as ready to meet changes in demand. Thus, in the late seventeenth and early eighteenth centuries some of them made buttons from brass, from alcomy (a base alloy that resembled gold), and from horn, for they were already using horn to haft their knives. So successful were they in this new enterprise that button making soon became a separate craft. The trade lay outside the jurisdiction of the Cutlers' Company and so its growth was unhampered by apprenticeship regulations. It provided welcome employment opportunities at a time when Sheffield's population was beginning to grow dramatically and it was no doubt adopted thankfully by many of the young immigrants who came into the town from the surrounding countryside. When Thomas Boulsover founded the Old Sheffield Plate industry in 1743 by discovering how to plate copper with silver he used his new invention to start a button-making business. He too had a local surname. The Hallamshire cutlers and allied workers were well able to create new industries from the old without the stimulus of foreign immigrants. They participated eagerly in the innovatory spirit of the age to establish Sheffield as the leading provincial centre of cutlery manufacture, and they were none too scrupulous in passing off their high-quality wares as the products of the finest foreign cutlers in London.

15. *Joan Thirsk: a bibliography*[1]

MARGERY TRANTER

ABBREVIATIONS

Ag. H.	*Agricultural History*
AH	*Amateur Historian*
AHR	*Agricultural History Review*
Ant. Jnl.	*Antiquaries Journal*
Arch.	*Archives*
Ec. H. R.	*Economic History Review*
EHR	*English Historical Review*
Geog. Mag.	*Geographical Magazine*
H	*History*
HT	*History Today*
J. Hist. Geog.	*Journal of Historical Geography*
J. Interdisc. Hist.	*Journal of Interdisciplinary History*
J. Mod. Hist.	*Journal of Modern History*
LH	*Local Historian*
Lincs. H.	*Lincolnshire Historian*
Lit. Hist.	*Literature and History*
MH	*Midland History*
NSJFS	*North Staffordshire Journal of Field Studies*
P & P	*Past and Present*
TH	*Textile History*
THES	*Times Higher Education Supplement*
TLS	*Times Literary Supplement*
UHNL	*Urban History News Letter*

[1] The bibliography includes Dr Thirsk's major academic writings: shorter notes and book reviews of less than a half page have therefore been omitted. An exhaustive search of indexes, academic books, and journals has been made, but the range of books and periodicals in which her work has been published is such that some items in foreign publications may inevitably have been omitted: not all are readily available in England.

1950
  'The Sale of Delinquents' Estates during the Interregnum and the Land Settlement at the Restoration – A Study of Land Sales in South-eastern England', University of London Ph.D. thesis
1952
  'The Sales of Royalist Land during the Interregnum', *Ec. H. R.*, 2nd ser., V, 188–207. Reprinted in *Rural Economy* (1984)
1953
  Fenland Farming in the Sixteenth Century, University College of Leicester, Department of English Local History, Occasional Paper 3, 45pp.
  'The Isle of Axholme before Vermuyden', *AHR*, I, 16–28, reprinted in *Rural Economy* (1984)
Reviews
  A. R. B. Haldane, *The Drove Roads of Scotland*, in *AHR*, I, 55–8
  M. E. Seebohm, *The Evolution of the English Farm*, in *AHR*, I, 60–1
1954
  'The Restoration Land Settlement', *J. Mod. Hist.*, XXVI, 315–28, reprinted in *Rural Economy* (1984)
  'The Agrarian History of Leicestershire, 1540–1950', *Victoria History of the County of Leicester*, ed. W. G. Hoskins and R. A. McKinley, II (Clarendon Press), 199–264
Reviews
  C. Hole, *The English Housewife in the Seventeenth Century*, in *AHR*, II, 61–2
  E. Kerridge, *Surveys of the Manors of Philip, First Earl of Pembroke and Montgomery, 1631–2*, in *Ec. H. R.*, 2nd ser., VI, 331
  F.-K. Riemann, *Ackerbau und Viehhaltung im vorindustriellen Deutschland*, in *AHR*, II, 66
1955
  'Die agrargeschtliche Forschung in England seit 1945: ein Überblick über das agrarhistorische Schrifttum', *Zeitschrift für Agrargeschichte*, III, 1, 54–65
  'Corn Laws down to 1791', *Encyclopaedia Britannica*, VI, 458–60 (revised for 1967 edition)
  'Farming in Kesteven, 1540–1640', *Lincolnshire Architectural and Archaeological Society Reports and Papers*, n.s., VI, 37–53, reprinted in *Rural Economy* (1984)
  'The Content and Sources of English Agrarian History after 1500, with Special Reference to Lincolnshire', *Lincs. H.*, II, 31–44
  'The Content and Sources of English Agrarian History after 1500', *AHR*, III, 66–79, reprinted in *Rural Economy* (1984)
  'List of Books and Articles on Agrarian History issued since September 1953', *AHR*, III, 41–7
Reviews
  M. W. Beresford, *The Lost Villages of England*, in *AHR*, III, 52–4
  A. E. Kirkby, *Humberstone: The Story of a Village*, *AHR*, III, 57

Lord Leconfield, *Petworth Manor in the Seventeenth Century*, in *Ec. H. R.*, 2nd ser., VII, 392

1956

'List of Books and Articles on Agrarian History issued since September 1954', *AHR*, IV, 52–7

1957

English Peasant Farming: The Agrarian History of Lincolnshire from Tudor to Recent Times (Routledge & Kegan Paul), 350pp., reprinted 1981

'List of Books and Articles on Agrarian History issued since September 1955', *AHR*, V, 52–7

Reviews

M. G. Davies, *The Enforcement of English Apprenticeship, 1563–1642*, in *Kyklos*, fasc. 2, 207–8

J. W. F. Hill, *Tudor and Stuart Lincoln*, in *EHR*, LXXII, 536–7

Lord Leconfield, *Sutton and Duncton Manors*, in *Ec. H. R.*, 2nd ser., X, 297

R. C. Russell, *The 'Revolt of the Field' in Lincolnshire*, in *AHR*, V, 116–17

1958

With J. Imray, *Suffolk Farming in the Nineteenth Century*, Suffolk Records Society, I, 178pp.

'List of Books and Articles on Agrarian History issued since September 1956', *AHR*, VII, 42–51

'Work in Progress', *AHR*, VII, 101–10

Reviews

J. D. Chambers, *The Vale of Trent, 1670–1800*, in *EHR*, LXXIII, 723–4

R. Trow-Smith, *A History of British Livestock Husbandry to 1700*, in *AHR*, VI, 54–5

1959

'Tudor Enclosures', Historical Association, General Series, 22pp., reprinted in *Rural Economy* (1984)

'Sources of Information on Population', *AH*, IV, 129–32, 182–4

'List of Books and Articles on Agrarian History issued since September 1957', *AHR*, VII, 38–47

'Work in Progress', *AHR*, VII, 110–20

Reviews

W. G. Hoskins, *The Midland Peasant: An Economic and Social History of a Leicestershire Village*, in *EHR*, LXXIV, 682–4

F. W. Jessup, *A History of Kent*, in *EHR*, LXXIV, 146

R. C. Shaw, *The Royal Forest of Lancaster*, in *AHR*, VII, 123–4

1960

'List of Books and Articles on Agrarian History issued since September 1958', *AHR*, VIII, 38–44

With G. E. Mingay, 'List of Publications on the Economic History of Great Britain and Ireland', *Ec. H. R.*, 2nd ser., XII, 519–52

'Tudor Enclosures', *Tochiseidoshigaku* (Tokyo), II, 2, 35–43

Reviews

K. Cameron, *The Place-names of Derbyshire*, in *AHR*, VIII, 120–1

The Victoria History of the County of Wiltshire, IV, ed. E. Crittall, in *Ec. H. R.*, 2nd ser., XIII, 299–300

D. R. Denman, *et al.*, *Bibliography of Rural Land Economy and Land Ownership, 1900–1957*, in *EHR*, LXXV, 552

J. G. O'Leary, *Dagenham Place-names*, in *EHR*, LXXV, 146

The Victoria History of the County of Stafford, V, ed. L. M. Midgley, in *Ec. H. R.*, 2nd ser., XIII, 133–4

H. H. Wächter, *Ostpreussische Domänenvorwerke im 16. und 17. Jahrhundert*, *AHR*, 54–5

1961

'Industries in the Countryside', *Essays in the Economic and Social History of Tudor and Stuart England in Honour of Professor R. H. Tawney*, ed. F. J. Fisher (Cambridge University Press), 70–88, reprinted in *Rural Economy* (1984)

'List of Books and Articles on Agrarian History issued since September 1959', *AHR*, IX, 55–63

'Work in Progress', in *AHR*, IX, 112–19

Reviews

Court Rolls of the Manor of Tottenham, 1510–1531, and *Court Rolls of the Manor of Tottenham, 1547–1558*, ed. F. H. Fenton, in *AHR*, IX, 126–7

G. H. Green, *Historical Account of the Ancient King's Mills (Castle Donington, Leics.)* in *AHR*, IX, 127

H. Grieve, *The Great Tide: The Story of the 1953 Flood Disaster in Essex*, in *EHR*, LXXVI, 186–7

J. M. Lambert *et al.*, *The Making of the Broads: A Reconstruction of their Origin*, in *EHR*, LXXVI, 704–5

M. Kirkus, *The Records of the Commissioners of Sewers in the Parts of Holland, 1547–1603*, in *EHR*, LXXVI, 142–3

1962

'List of Books and Articles on Agrarian History issued since September 1960', *AHR*, X, 46–55

'List of Publications on the Economic History of Great Britain and Ireland 1960', *Ec. H. R.*, 2nd ser., XIV, 524–51

Reviews

The Sibton Abbey Estates, 1325–1509, ed. A. H. Denney, in *EHR*, LXXVII, 140

E. Juillard, *et al.*, *Structures agraires et paysages ruraux* (1957) and *Géographie et histoire agraires* (1959), in *AHR*, X, 57

Victoria History of the County of Middlesex, III, and *Index* to II and III, ed. S. Reynolds, in *Ec. H. R.*, 2nd ser., XV, 535

1963

Introduction, A. H. Johnson, *The Disappearance of the Small Landowner* (Merlin Press), v–xii

'Unexplored Sources in Local Records', *Arch.*, VI, 29, 8–12

'List of Books and Articles on Agrarian History issued since September 1961', *AHR*, XI, 8–12
'List of Publications on the Economic History of Great Britain and Ireland 1961', *Ec. H. R.*, 2nd ser., XV, 610–34
Reviews
H. W. Brace, *A History of Seed Crushing*, in *AHR*, XI, 53–4
C. S. Davies, *The Agrarian History of Cheshire, 1750–1850*, in *AHR*, XI, 50
The Domesday Geography of Eastern England, ed. H. C. Darby and E. M. J. Campbell; *The Domesday Geography of Northern England*, ed. H. C. Darby and I. S. Maxwell, in *H*, XLVIII, 355–7
Lord Ernle, *English Farming Past and Present*, in *EHR*, LXXVIII, 590
Hatfield WEA, *Hatfield and its People*, book 9, *Farming Yesterday and Today*, in *AHR*, XI, 60–1
The Morphogenesis of the Agrarian Cultural Landscape, ed. S. Helmfrid, in *AHR*, XI, 62–3
S. Helmfrid, *Östergötland – 'Västanstang' – Studien über die ältere Agrarlandschaft und ihre Genses*, in *AHR*, XI, 58–9
Thaxted in the Fourteenth Century, ed. K. C. Newton, in *EHR*, LXXVII, 367–8
J. West, *Village Records*, in *Ec. H. R.*, 2nd ser., XVI, 161
1964
'The Beginning of the Village', *AH*, VI, 166–8
'The Common Fields', *P & P*, XXIX, 3–25, reprinted in *Rural Economy* (1984)
'The Family', *P & P*, XXVII, 116–22, reprinted in *Rural Economy* (1984)
'List of Books and Articles on Agrarian History issued since September 1962', *AHR*, XII, 47–56
'List of Publications on the Economic History of Great Britain and Ireland 1962', *Ec. H. R.*, 2nd ser., XVI, 539–59
Reviews
Court Rolls of the Manor of Tottenham, 1377–1399; *Court Rolls of the Manor of Tottenham, 1558–1582*, ed. F. H. Fenton, in *AHR*, XII, 61–2
H. M. Heybroek, *Diseases and Lopping for Fodder as Possible Causes of a Prehistoric Decline of Ulmus*, in *AHR*, XII, 58–9
W. G. Hoskins, *Provincial England*, in *Ec. H. R.*, 2nd ser., XVII, 401
1965
Sources of Information on Population, 1500–1760, and *Unexplored Sources in Local Records* (Phillimore, 1965), 24pp., reprinted in *Rural Economy* (1984)
'List of Books and Articles on Agrarian History Issued since September 1963', *AHR*, XIII, 50–60
'List of Publications on the Economic History of Great Britain and Ireland 1963', *Ec. H. R.*, 2nd ser., XVII, 648–69
'Stamford in the Sixteenth and Seventeenth Centuries', *The Making of Stamford*, ed. A. Rogers (Leicester University Press), 58–76, reprinted in *Rural Economy* (1984)

Reviews

Deutsche Agrargeschichte, II, III, IV, ed. Prof. Dr G. Franz, in *AHR*, XIII, 69–72

R. C. Russell, *The Enclosures of East Halton, 1801–1804, and North Kelsey, 1813–1840*; R. C. Russell, *The Enclosures of Bottesford and Yaddlethorpe, 1794–97, Messingham, 1798–1804, and Ashby 1801–1809*; V. H. T. Skipp and R. P. Hastings, *Discovering Bickenhill*, in *AHR*, XIII, 64–5

M. Devèze, *La Vie de la forêt française au XVIe siècle*, in *AHR*, XIII, 68–9

1966

'The Origin of the Common Fields', *P & P*, XXXIII, 142–7, reprinted in *Rural Economy* (1984)

Reviews

J. D. Chambers, *Laxton: The Last English Open Field Village*, in *AHR*, XIV, 135–6

L. W. Hanson, *Contemporary Printed Sources for British and Irish Economic History, 1701–1750*, in *AHR*, XIV, 136

Sir Francis Hill, *Georgian Lincoln*, in *UHNL*, 6, 10–11

1967

Ed., *The Agrarian History of England and Wales*, IV, *1500–1640* (Cambridge University Press), xl + 919pp.

'The Farming Regions of England', *ibid.*, 1–112

'Farming Techniques', *ibid.*, 161–99

'Enclosing and Engrossing', *ibid.*, 200–55

'Enclosure', *The Encyclopaedia Britannica*, VIII, 361–3

Foreword, G. C. Cowling, *The History of Easingwold and the Forest of Galtres* (Huddersfield Advertiser Press), 13–14

Reviews

Devon Inventories of the Sixteenth and Seventeenth Centuries, ed. M. Cash, in *Arch.*, VIII, 98–9

1968

Reviews

W. Abel, *Agrarkrisen und Agrarkonjunktur*, in *AHR*, XVI, 77

N. Sanchez-Albornoz, *Las crisis de subsistencias de España en el siglo XIX*, *AHR*, XVI, 172

D. Cromarty, *The Fields of Saffron Walden in 1400*, in *EHR*, LXXXIII, 161

R. J. Forbes, *Notes on the History of Ancient Roads and their Construction*, in *AHR*, XVI, 75–6

F.-W. Henning, *Herrschaft und Bauernunvertänigkeit: Beiträge zur Geschichte der Herrschaftsverhältnisse in den ländlichen Bereichen Ostpreussens und des Fürstentums Paderborn vor 1800*, in *AHR*, XVI, 78

Warwick County Records IX: Quarter Sessions Records, Easter 1690 to Michaelmas 1696, ed. H. C. Johnson and N. J. Williams, in *Ec. H. R.*, 2nd ser., XXI, 171

1969
'Horn and Thorn in Staffordshire: The Economy of a Pastoral County', *NSJFS*, IX, 1–16, reprinted in *Rural Economy* (1984)
'Younger Sons in the Seventeenth Century', *H*, LIV, 358–77, reprinted in *Rural Economy* (1984)
Reviews
W. Abel, *Geschichte der Deutschen Landwirtschaft vom frühen Mittelalter bis zum 19 Jahrhundert*; F. Lütge, *Geschichte der Deutschen Agrarverfassung vom frühen Mittelalter bis zum 19 Jahrhundert*, in *Zeitschrift für Agrargeschichte und Agrarsoziologie, Jahrgang 56, Heft 4*
A. E. Chibnall, *Sherington: Fiefs and Fields of a Buckinghamshire Village*, in *H*, LIV, 158
G. Schröder-Lembke, *Martin Grosser: Anleitung zu der Landwirtschaft*; *Abraham von Thumbschirn, Oeconomia*, in *AHR*, XVII, 154–5
P. and M. Spufford, *Eccleshall: The Story of a Staffordshire Market Town and its Dependent Villages*, in *AHR*, XVII, 82
L. Symons, *Agricultural Geography*, in *AHR*, XVII, 148–50
W. E. Tate, *The English Village Community and the Enclosure Movement*, in *H*, LIV, 159
1970
Ed., *Land, Church and People: Essays Presented to Professor H. P. R. Finberg*, *AHR*, XVIII, Supplement, 204pp.
'Seventeenth-century Agriculture and Social Change', *AHR*, XVIII, 148–77
'Roots of Industrial England', *Geog. Mag.* (August), 816–26
Reviews
H.-J. Schmitz, *Faktoren der Preisbildung für Getreide und Wein in der Zeit von 800 bis 1350*, in *AHR*, XVIII, 78–80
G. von Below, *Geschichte der deutschen Landwirtschaft des Mittelalters*, in *AHR*, XVIII, 79.
H. Wiese and J. Bölts, *Rinderhaltung im Nordwesteneuropäischen Küstengebiet vom 15 bis zum 19 Jahrhundert*, in *AHR*, XVIII, 83–5
1971
Reviews
Agrarian Change and Economic Development: The Historical Problems, ed. E. L. Jones and S. J. Woolf, in *EHR*, LXXXVI, 894–5
R. E. F. Smith, *The Enserfment of the Russian Peasantry*, in *AHR*, XIX, 102–3
E. Le Roy Ladurie, *Les Paysans de Languedoc*, in *AHR*, XIX, 178–80
P. A. J. Pettit, *The Royal Forests of Northamptonshire: A Study in their Economy, 1558–1714*, in *EHR*, LXXXVI, 407–8
Stability and Change: Some Aspects of North and South Rauceby in the Nineteenth Century, ed. A. Rogers, in *Ec. H. R.*, 2nd ser., XXIV, 147–8
The Victoria History of the Counties of England: General Introduction, ed. R. B. Pugh, in *Ec. H. R.*, 2nd ser., XXIV, 483

1972

Seventeenth-Century Economic Documents, ed. with J. P. Cooper (Clarendon Press), 849pp.

Reviews

American Agricultural History: Eighteenth-Century Agriculture: A Symposium, in *EHR*, LXXXVII, 191–2

Household and Family in Past Time, ed. P. Laslett, in *The Tablet*, 16 Dec., 1201

The Victoria County History of the County of Oxford, IX, ed. M. D. Lobel and A. Crossley, in *Ec. H. R.*, 2nd ser., XXV, 357–8

H. Mendras, *La Fin des paysans: changement et innovations dans les sociétés rurales françaises*, in *AHR*, XX, 89–90

1973

'Field Systems of the East Midlands', *Studies of Field Systems in the British Isles*, ed. A. R. H. Baker and R. A. Butlin (Cambridge University Press), 232–80

'The Fantastical Folly of Fashion: The English Stocking Knitting Industry, 1500–1700', *Textile History and Economic History: Essays in Honour of Miss Julia de Lacy Mann*, ed. N. B. Harte and K. G. Ponting (Manchester University Press), 50–73, reprinted in *Rural Economy* (1984)

'The Peasant Economy of England in the Seventeenth Century', *International Colloquium on Peasant Economy before and during the Early Period of the Industrial Revolution* (Biatowieza), 47–59

'Roots of Industrial England', *Man Made the Land*, ed. A. R. H. Baker and J. B. Harley (David and Charles), 93–108

Reviews

D. M. Barratt, *Ecclesiastical Terriers of Warwickshire Parishes*, II, in *Ec. H. R.*, 2nd ser., XXVII, 342

The Victoria History of the County of Oxford, X, ed. A. Crossley, in *Ec. H. R.*, 2nd ser., XXVII, 683–4

The Victoria History of the County of Gloucester, X, ed. C. M. Elrington and N. M. Herbert, in *Ec. H. R.*, 2nd ser., XXVII, 472

J. Z. Titow, *Winchester Yields: A Study in Medieval Agricultural Productivity*, in *Ant. Jnl.*, LIII, 128–9

E. Wiest, *Die Entwicklung des Nürnberger Gewerbes zwischen 1648 und 1806*, in *AHR*, XXI, 68–9

1974

'New Crops and their Diffusion: Tobacco-growing in Seventeenth-century England', *Rural Change and Urban Growth, 1500–1800: Essays in English Regional History in Honour of W. G. Hoskins*, ed. C. W. Chalklin and M. A. Havinden (Longman), 76–108, reprinted in *Rural Economy* (1984)

Reviews

Konrad Heresbach: Vier Bücher über Landwirtschaft: Band I. vom Landbau, ed. W. Abel and H. Dreitzel, in *AHR*, XXII, 186–7

Rufford Charters, I, ed. C. J. Holdsworth, in *MH*, II, 197–200

M. Morineau, *Les faux-semblants d'un démarrage economique: Agriculture et démographie en France à XVIIIe siècle*, in *AHR*, XXII, 82–3

Abstracts of Wiltshire Inclosure Awards and Agreements, ed. R. E. Sandell, in *EHR*, LXXXIX, 905–6

1975

'Professor H. P. R. Finberg', *AHR*, XXIII, 96

'Professor H. P. R. Finberg: a Tribute', *LH*, XI, 306–7

'The Peasant Economy of England in the Seventeenth Century', *Studia Historiae Oeconomicae*, X, 5–16

Reviews

Early Records of the Bankes Family at Winstanley, ed. J. Bankes and E. Kerridge, in *EHR*, LXXXX, 644–5

J. R. Gillies, *Youth and History: Tradition and Change in European Age Relations, 1770 to the Present*, in *New Society*, XXXIII, 17 July, 150

Rufford Charters, II, ed. C. J. Holdsworth, in *MH*, III, 149

Village Life and Labour, ed. R. Samuel, in *New Society*, XXXII, 22 May, 489–90

J. Wake and D. C. Webster, *The Letters of Daniel Eaton to the Third Earl of Cardigan, 1725–1732*, *EHR*, LXXXX, 653–4

1976

The Restoration (Longman), 205pp.

Ed. with J. Goody and E. P. Thompson, *Family and Inheritance: Rural Society in Western Europe, 1200–1800* (Cambridge University Press), 337pp.

'The European Debate on Customs of Inheritance, 1500–1700', *ibid.*, reprinted in *Rural Economy* (1984)

'Projects for Gentlemen, Jobs for the Poor: Mutual Aid in the Vale of Tewkesbury, 1600–1630', *Essays in Bristol and Gloucestershire History: The Centenary Volume of the Bristol and Gloucestershire Archaeological Society*, ed. P. McGrath and J. Cannon, Bristol and Gloucestershire Archaeological Society, 147–69, reprinted in *Rural Economy* (1984)

'Seventeenth-century Agriculture and Social Change', *Seventeenth-century England: Society in an Age of Revolution*, ed. Paul S. Seaver (New Viewpoints), 71–110

Reviews

G. Ahrens, *Caspar Voght und sein mustergut flottbek englische Landwirtschaft im Deutschland am Ende des 18 Jahrhunderts*, in *AHR*, XXIV, 80–2

G. E. Fussell, *Jethro Tull: His Influence on Mechanized Agriculture*, in *AHR*, XXIV, 161–2

G. E. Mingay, *The Gentry: The Rise and Fall of a Ruling Class*, in *New Society*, XXXVIII, 21 Oct., 155–6

1977

'The Present State of Local History Studies in England', *Chihoshi Kenkyu* (Local History Studies), 149, 2–8

'Economic and Social Development on a European-world Scale', *American Journal of Sociology*, LXXXII, 5, 1097–1102

Reviews

M. L. Bush, *The Government Policy of Protector Somerset*, in *Lit. Hist.*, VI, 256–8

Trade, Government, and Economy in Pre-Industrial England, ed. D. C. Coleman and A. H. John, in *The Magazine of the London School of Economics and Political Science*, 53, June, 14–15

E. Le Roy Ladurie, *Times of Feast, Times of Famine: A History of Climate since the year 1000*, in *H*, LXII, 77–8

L. Stone, *The Family, Sex and Marriage in England, 1500–1800*, in *THES*, 28 Oct.

1978

Economic Policy and Projects: The Development of a Consumer Society in Early Modern England (Clarendon Press), 199pp. (The James Ford Lectures for 1975). Japanese translation by Yoko Miyoshi (Tokyo 1984)

'Horses in Early Modern England: For Service, for Pleasure, for Power', University of Reading, Department of History, the Stenton Lecture Series, 11, 28pp., reprinted in *Rural Economy* (1984)

General Preface to *The Agrarian History of England and Wales*, VIII, 1914–1939, v

'Albrecht Daniel Thaers: Stellung unter der zeitgenöschischen Agrar-schriftstellern Europas', *Albrecht-Daniel-Thaer-Tagung*, Bd 5: *Land-wirtschaftliche Produktion und Agrarwissenschaften im 19 Jahrhundert* (DDR, Akademie der Landwirtschaftswissenschaften), 35–9

Reviews

J. Blum, *The End of an Old Order in Rural Europe*, in *THES*, 27 Oct.

B. Henrey, *British Botanical and Horticultural Literature before 1800*, in *AHR*, XXVI, 59–61

Paysannerie française, paysannerie hongroise, XVIe–XXe siècles, ed. B. Köpeczi and E. H. Balàzs, in *AHR*, XXVI, 58–9

E. Le Roy Ladurie, *Montaillou, village occitan de 1294 à 1324*, in *J. Hist. Geog.*, IV, 301–2

R. Mandrou, *Introduction to Modern France, 1500–1640*, in *Lit. Hist.*, VII, 113–15

Medieval Settlement, ed. P. Sawyer, in *LH*, XIII, 50–2

The Victoria County History of Wiltshire, X, ed. E. Crittall, in *EHR*, XCIII, 150–1

1980

'Saving the Medieval Farms of Laxton Village', *Popular Archaeology*, Feb., 21

Foreword and Bibliography in W. Abel, *Agricultural Fluctuations in Europe from the Thirteenth to Nineteenth Centuries*, ix–x, 351–6

'Policies for Retrenchment in Seventeenth-century Europe', review article in *Comparative Studies in Society and History*, XXII, 4, 626–38

Reviews

'Crisis in Cumbria', review of A. E. Appleby, *Famine in Tudor and Stuart England*, in *TLS*, 11 Jan., 35

J. O. Appleby, *Economic Thought and Ideology in Seventeenth-century England*, in *Lit. Hist.*, VI, 260–1

R. Ashton, *The English Civil War: Conservatism and Revolution, 1603–49*, in *Ec. H. R.*, XXXIII, 276–7

I. Bog, G. Franz *et al.*, *Wortschaftliche und soziale strukturen in saekularen Wandel: Festschrift für Wilhelm Abel zum 70 Geburtstag*, in *AHR*, XXVIII, 140–1

The Court Rolls of the Manor of Wakefield from October 1639–September 1640, I, ed. C. M. Fraser and K. Emsley, in *EHR*, XCV, 213–14

J. Patten, *English Towns, 1500–1700*, in *AHR*, XXVIII, 129–30

G. Schröder-Lembke, *Studien zur Agrargeschichte, Quellen und Forschungen zur Agrargeschichte*, 31, *AHR*, XXVIII, 130–3

K. P. Witney, *The Jutish Forest: A Study of the Weald of Kent from 450–1380 A.D.*, in *EHR*, XCV, 399–400

1981

Reviews

A Selection from the Records of Philip Foley's Stour Valley Ironworks, 1668–74, 1, in *EHR*, XCVI, 912

Change in the Countryside, ed. H. S. A. Fox and R. A. Butlin, in *J. Hist. Geog.*, VII, 311–12

E. E. Rich and C. H. Wilson, *The Cambridge Economic History of Europe*, V, *The Economic Organization of Early Modern Europe*, *AHR*, XXIX, 58–60

J. A. Yelling, *Common Fields and Enclosure in England, 1450–1850*, in *EHR*, XCVI, 208–9

1982

'The Rural Economy', in *Our Forgotten Past: Seven Centuries of Life on the Land*, ed. J. Blum (Thames & Hudson), 81–108

'Large Estates and Small Holdings in England', P. Gunst and T. Hoffman (eds.), *Large Estates and Small Holdings in Europe in the Middle Ages and Modern Times* (Budapest, 1982)

'Ausländische Wahrnehmungen des englischen landlebens im 16 und 17 Jahrhundert', *Wolfenbütteler Forschungen*, Band 21, *Reiseberichte als Quellen europäischer Kulturgeschichte*, ed. Antoni Mączak and Hans Jürgen Teuteberg, 115–29

Reviews

J. Bowle, *John Evelyn and his World: A Biography*, in *Ec. H. R.*, XXXV, 307

I. J. Gentles and W. J. Sheils, *Confiscation and Restoration: The Archbishopric Estates and the Civil War*, in *AHR*, XXX, 85–6

1983

Social Relations and Ideas: Essays in Honour of R. H. Hilton, ed. with T. H. Aston, P. R. Coss, C. Dyer, 337pp.

'Plough and Pen: Agricultural Writers in the Seventeenth Century', *ibid.*, 295–318

'The Horticultural Revolution: A Cautionary Note on Prices', *J. Interdisc. H.*, XIV, 299–302. Reprinted in *Hunger and History*, eds. R. I. Rotberg and T. K. Rabb (Cambridge University Press, 1985)

Reviews

The Lisle Letters, ed. M. St Clare Byrne, in *Lit. Hist.*, IX, 262–5

M. Turner, *English Parliamentary Enclosure: Its Historical Geography and Economic History*, in *EHR*, XCVIII, 199–200

1984

Ed., *The Agrarian History of England and Wales*, V, *1640–1750*, 1, *Regional Farming Systems* (Cambridge University Press), 480pp.

Preface, *ibid.*, xv–xvi

Introduction, *ibid.*, xix–xxxi

'The South-West Midlands: Warwickshire, Worcestershire, Gloucestershire, Herefordshire', *ibid.*, 159–83

The Rural Economy of England: Collected Essays (Hambledon Press), iv + 420pp.

'Patterns of Agriculture in Seventeenth-century England', *Seventeenth-Century New England: A Conference held by the Colonial Society of Massachusetts*, The Colonial Society of Massachusetts, 39–54

Reviews

J. G. L. Burnaby and A. E. Robinson, *'Now Turned into Fair Garden Plots' (Stow)*, in *AHR*, XXXII, 101–2

Clifton and Westbury Probate Inventories, 1609–1761, ed. J. S. Moore, in *MH*, IX, 131–2

Francesca Bray, 'Agriculture', in J. Needham, *Science and Civilization in China*, VI, 2 (Cambridge University Press), in *THES*, 2 Nov.

The Origins of Open Field Agriculture, ed. T. Rowley, in *EHR*, XCIX, 407

G. D. Ramsay, *The English Woollen Industry, 1500–1750*, in *Ec. H. R.*, XXXVII, 276–7

1985

Ed., *The Agrarian History of England and Wales*, V, *1640–1750*, 2, *Agrarian Change* (Cambridge University Press), 952pp.

Preface, *ibid.*, xxvii–xxviii

'Agricultural Policy: Public Debate and Legislation', *ibid.*, 298–388

English Agrarian History before 1700: Some Current Themes of Research (St Paul's University, Tokyo), translated into Japanese by Prof. Kaoru Ugawa, 115pp.

'The Agricultural Landscape: Fads and Fashions', *The English Landscape, Past Present and Future*, Wolfson College lectures, 1983, ed. S. R. J. Woodell (Oxford University Press), 129–47

'The Englishman's Food in the Seventeenth Century', *Rikkyo Keizaigaku Kenkyu (St Paul's Economic Review)*, XXXIX, 2, 1–18, translated into Japanese by Prof. Kaoru Ugawa

Foreword, *Women in English Society, 1500–1800*, ed. Mary Prior (Methuen), 1–21

'Forest, Field and Garden', *William Shakespeare: His World, his Work, his Influence*, ed. J. F. Andrews (Charles Scribner's Sons), vol. I, 257–67

Hadlow Castle: A Short History (Hadlow Historical Society), 20pp.

Reviews

Medieval Industry, ed. D. Crossley, C.B.A. Research report, 40, in *EHR*, C, 879

D. B. Grigg, *Population Growth and Agrarian Change: An Historical Perspective*, in *EHR*, C, 652–3

E. Le Roy Ladurie and J. Gay, *Tithe and Agrarian History from the Fourteenth to the Nineteenth Centuries: An Essay in Comparative History*, translated by S. Burke, in *EHR*, C, 661–2

1986

'Agricultural Conditions in England, *c.* 1680', *The World of William Penn*, ed. R. S. Dunn and M. M. Dunn (University of Pennsylvania Press), 87–97

'L'Inghilterra dalla Restaurazione alla Gloriosa Rivoluzione', *La Storia: I grandi problemi dal Medioevo all'Età Contemporanea*, ed. Nicola Tranfaglia and Massimo Firbo, vol. V, *L'Età Moderna*, 3, *Stati e società* (Utet), 481–500

Reviews

H. C. Darby, *The Changing Fenland*, in *EHR*, CI, 500–1

N. Evans, *The East Anglian Linen Industry: Rural Industry and Local Economy*, in *TH*, XVII, 103

N. Landau, *The Justices of the Peace, 1679–1760*, in *Ec. H. R.*, XXXIX, 298

M. M. Rodriguez, *Pensamiento econòmic español sobre la Población*, in *Ec. H. R.*, XXXIX, 151–2

D. W. Sabean, *Power in the Blood: Popular Culture and Village Discourse in Early Modern Germany*, in *AHR*, XXXIV, 213

1987

Agricultural Regions and Agrarian History in England, 1500–1750, Studies in Economic and Social History, ed. for the Economic History Society (Macmillan Education), 77pp.

'Raleigh's England', *Raleigh and Quinn: The Explorer and his Boswell*, paper presented at the International Sir Walter Raleigh Conference (North Carolina Society, inc.), 35–49

Review

Land, Kinship and Life Cycle, ed. R. Smith, in *AHR*, XXXV, 108–9

1988

General editor, *The Agrarian History of England and Wales*, II, *1042–1350* (Cambridge University Press), 1086pp.

'Zur mittelalterlichen Siedlungsgeschichte in England', *Genetische Siedlungsforschung in Mitteleuropa und sienen Nachbarräumen*, ed. Klaus Fehn *et al.* (Verlag Siedlungsforschung, Bonn), pp. 257–69

Review

> *The Victoria County History of Wiltshire*, XIII, *South-west Wiltshire. Chalke and Dunworth Hundreds*, ed. D. A. Crowley, in *EHR*, CIV, 207

1989

> *Tudor Enclosures*, second revised edition, Historical Association, general series, 41, 24pp.
>
> General editor, *The Agrarian History of England and Wales*, VI, *1750–1850* (Cambridge University Press), 1214pp.
>
> Ann Bermingham, *The English Rustic Tradition, 1740–1860*, *Journal of Forest History*, XXXII, 222–3

Review

> 'The Hand Knitting Industry', *Four Centuries of Machine Knitting, commemorating William Lee's Invention of the Stocking Frame in 1589*, ed. John T. Millington and Stanley Chapman (Knitting International)
>
> R. Lachmann, *From Manor to Market: Structural Change in England, 1536–1640*, *Ec. H. R.*, 2nd ser., XLII, 406–7
>
> Max Schultz, *Paradise Preserved: Recreations of Eden in Eighteenth- and Nineteenth-Century England*, *Journal of Forest History*, XXXII, 222–3

Index

Past and Present Publications

General Editor: PAUL SLACK, *Exeter College, Oxford*

The English Rising of 1381, edited by R. H. Hilton and T. H. Aston*
Praise and Paradox: Merchants and Craftsmen in Elizabethan Popular Literature, Laura Caroline Stevenson
The Brenner Debate: Agrarian Class Structure and Economic Development in Pre-Industrial Europe, edited by T. H. Aston and C. H. E. Philpin*
Eternal Victory: Triumphal Rulership in Late Antiquity, Byzantium, and the Early Medieval West, Michael McCormick*†
East-Central Europe in Transition: From the Fourteenth to the Seventeenth Century, edited by Antoni Mączak, Henry Samsonowicz and Peter Burke†
Small Books and Pleasant Histories: Popular Fiction and its Readership in Seventeenth-Century England, Margaret Spufford**
Society, Politics and Culture: Studies in Early Modern England, Mervyn James*
Horses, Oxen and Technological Innovation: The Use of Draught Animals in English Farming 1066–1600, John Langdon
Nationalism and Popular Protest in Ireland, edited by C. H. E. Philpin
Rituals of Royalty: Power and Ceremonial in Traditional Societies, edited by David Cannadine and Simon Price
The Margins of Society in Late Medieval Paris, Bronisław Geremek†
Landlords, Peasants and Politics in Medieval England, edited by T. H. Aston
Geography, Technology, and War: Studies in the Maritime History of the Mediterranean, 649–1572, John H. Pryor
Church Courts, Sex and Marriage in England, 1570–1640, Martin Ingram*
Searches for an Imaginary Kingdom: The Legend of the Kingdom of Prester John, L. N. Gumilev
Crowds and History: Mass Phenomena in English Towns, 1780–1835, Mark Harrison
Concepts of Cleanliness: Changing Attitudes in France since the Middle Ages, Georges Vigarello†
The First Modern Society: Essays in English History in Honour of Lawrence Stone, edited by A. L. Beier, David Cannadine and James M. Rosenheim
The Europe of the Devout: The Catholic Reformation and the Formation of a New Society, Louis Châtellier†
English Rural Society, 1500–1800: Essays in Honour of Joan Thirsk, edited by John Chartres and David Hey

*Published also as a paperback
**Published only as a paperback
†Co-published with the Maison des Sciences de l'Homme, Paris